WITH MY HEAD IN THE CLOUDS

Part 1

by Gwyn Mullett

Typeset in Gentium Book Basic and Philosopher

Editing, design and publishing by UK Book Publishing

www.ukbookpublishing.com

ISBN: 978-0-9926433-2-4

In Memory

Captain Koos Vermaak, a South African, was born in 1943 and
spent his complete life in the world of aviation beginning in the
military and then onto civilian flying with South African Airways,
Asiana in Korea, Cargolux in Luxembourg and finally with a new
South African airline called Mango where he finished his career
in his late 60s. He died in March 2013 after a long illness.
I met up with him in Korea in 2001 and we hit it off straight away.
We enjoyed each other's company and many an evening was
spent together in the company of other pilots with his unique
South African humour shining through. He married Rina at
about that time and together they were a fantastic team.
He will be sorely missed.

Dedication

The year is 2013 and I have been retired from British Airways for twelve years now. I now live in Berlin and I am at the tender age of 67.

Both of my kids are now grown up with Jenny, now 30 years of age, living in Aylesbury, England and she has a son Jamie who is 6 years of age and has just started full-time school. I am a proud granddad. Paul is 33 years of age and doing his own thing. My ex-wife Moya works for a company based at Heathrow. I wish all four the very best for the future.

My marriage to Jo went through some rocky times but we are now as one. It is Jo that I dedicate this book to since it is Jo and Jo alone who will look after me as I get older and who knows what that may bring.

I rest my case.

Acknowledgements

Below is a list of people, organisations or web sites that helped me writing my book.

The picture is the work of the artist Chris French as distributed by Hansen Fine Art and is a superb creation of the VC-10 bedecked in the colours of BOAC flying just above the clouds

The pictures of the various aircraft were copied from the following web sites:

- *www.airliners.net*
- *www.britishairways.com/travel/museum-collection/public/en_gb*
- *www.vc10.net/index2.html*
- *www.hansenfineart.co.uk*

ACKNOWLEDGEMENTS

Individual pictures were kindly approved by the following people or organisations:

- British Airways Heritage (B.377 Stratocruiser, Bristol Britannia and D.H. Comet 4)
- Aris Pappas (B. 747-100 in the original British Airways colours)
- Paul Goddard (B. 747-100 in the BOAC colours)
- Simon Thomas (Auster J-1/N G-APIK)
- Geoff Hall (Picture of me in the VC-10 Flight Deck)
- Dave Cook (Standard VC-10 'VM' in the original British Airways colours)
- Steve Fitzgerald (Standard and Super VC-10 in the BOAC colours)
- Paul Kipping (Super VC-10 in the original British Airways colours)
- The VC-10 web site '*www.vc10.net*' as constructed by Jelle Hieminga
- Hansen Fine Art and, in particular, the 'VC-10 Elegance' print by the artist Chris French
- The Wikipedia, the free encyclopaedia web site

ACKNOWLEDGEMENTS

Various news items and quotations were courtesy of:

- Wikipedia, the free encyclopaedia web site

Various family members and friends contributed towards jogging my brain cells into action.

I would also like to give a huge thanks to my sponsors who had absolute faith in me allowing the book to be published. They are my very good friends:

- Captain Bob Young: Ex-BCAL and BA who flew the DC-10 and 747-400
- Captain Ian Davis: Ex-BEA and BA who flew the Trident and 747-400
- Captain Tony Partridge: Ex-BEA and BA who flew the Trident and 747-400
- Captain Ernie Sailor: Ex-BEA and BA who flew the Trident and 757/767
- Captain Martijn Kolthof: Ex-TNT who flew the A330, 747-400 and A320

Without them my story would still be a dream.

Preface

It was at a very early age that I developed the passion for all things flying. My father, at the time, flew with BOAC and I often saw him all dressed up in his uniform ready to leave the house to go flying to some exotic place that I had never heard of. But it was when I lived in Bristol at the age of about six that I saw my first aircraft flying low over my house in the shape of the infamous Bristol Brabazon. Something stirred in me that day. In my teenage years I endured the fun and games of learning to fly. This was followed by two years of college life where my flying skills would hopefully be honed to the point that I could follow my passion and earn my passage in my working life as a pilot. I made it and joined BOAC and ended up flying my dream aircraft in the shape of the VC-10.

My name is Gwyn Mullett and I was born on 27th January 1946 in Montreal, Canada. We moved to Bristol, England in 1949. In 1953 we then moved again to the town of Wokingham which was about 30 miles to the west of the new London airport named Heathrow. It was here that I grew up until I completed my education and, in 1964, had qualified to go to the College of Air Training on the south coast at Hamble, near to Southampton.

I graduated in the summer of 1966 and joined BOAC in the August. I started my airline life flying the superb Vickers VC-10. On May 5th 1967 my lovely mother died and left a big void in my life. In 1968 I qualified as a Flight Navigator and ended up both flying and navigating up to 1971 when I converted onto the new 747 that had just been delivered from Mr Boeing. In late 1971 BOAC and BEA combined their talents to form British Airways – or BA for short. In 1976 I went back to the VC-10 and completed a command course that year and became the youngest Captain in the airline since 1949. In 1981 I converted to the 737 and discovered Europe, and in particular Berlin. I stayed until 1992 when I then converted onto the newer 747 model and remained there until my retirement on 27th January 2001.

My private life is pretty colourful as you will find out.

Part 1 is the story of my life to the end of 1979 when I left the VC-10 as a Captain.

There were times when I was sad and there were times when I was happy. There were times when I could not believe what I had done. I was stupid on some occasions but the funny thing is that if I was asked to do it all over again I would do exactly the same.

My story starts here.

Enjoy Part 1

Chapter 1

– MY EARLY YEARS

Let me introduce myself to you. My name is Gwyn, son of George and Mauvis Mullett. I was born in the Queen Elizabeth Hospital, Montreal, Province of Quebec, Canada on the 27th January 1946. My first few years were spent living in Neptune Boulevard, Dorval, Montreal, a suburb very close to the airport of Dorval, so even at that very early age the aviation world was not far away. I was baptized Lawrence Gwyn since it was planned we would live in Canada. The Lawrence was named after the nearby St Lawrence Seaway and the Gwyn after the Welsh connection. I was apparently nicknamed 'Butch'. I can't think why!

I can recall nothing of my Montreal life and have only picked up various happenings from my parents. One of which is, for my own security, I was always tied up to a tree by my reins in the front garden. I think that even at that early age I was already becoming a challenge for my mother since Dad was away a lot flying from Dorval to the UK. Well, one day when both of them were at home, assuming me to be tied to the tree, a neighbour rushed round and announced that I had broken free and was off at a gallop down the road.

You might ask what's the drama in this situation. Well, let me explain.

I was known to have a fascination for a deep lake at the end of the road to the point of obsession. The unfortunate thing was that a six-lane highway stood between our road and the lake. My dad described doing a rugby tackle to arrest my travels just short of this highway. Not a good start to my life you might say.

The other incident that I was told about occurred when we were living for a short while in an apartment on an upper level. My dad was wondering where I was when suddenly my friend and I appeared outside the window, on the fire escape. I think I inherited my dad's sense of adventure. My poor mum!

At a very tender young age the family moved to England. My dad was, at the time, a Radio Officer with British Overseas Airways Corporation (BOAC). Montreal, Dorval, was the base just after the Second World War. BOAC then moved to the UK base at Bristol. Hence the family upped and moved. My first recollections of Bristol were of wintertime. There was this wonderful hill at the end of the road and all of us kids would meet for sledging. In those days sledges were not available in the shops so the constructional skills of the parents were employed. Dad was pretty good with his hands and made a really good mean machine.

This is a good point to introduce my sister, Cynthia, who was five years older than me. As this story unfolds I will refer to her many times. All I can say is that at that age we had the standard 'love-hate' relationship. On the sledge, however, we would hurtle down this hill as one, clearing a path vocally as we went and woe betide anyone in our way. We were champions! If I really analysed the success we had I could put it down to the superior craft plus plenty of body weight since, even at that early age, I was a big lad.

What was good in those days, I think, was that the seasons of the year were very definitive. There was winter, spring, summer and autumn. You could set the season by the date on the calendar. I remember the spring well because my mum would embark on a cleaning spree around the house and look out to anyone getting in her way. The summer was long and sultry and was, together with spring, my favourite season. The autumn was boring with lots of rainy days but then came the winter which was unique in its own right. We lived in a semi-detached council house that had an open fire in the lounge as the only heating source and many a day I would wake up with ice on the inside of the windows and my breath steaming outside the covers. I would force myself up knowing that breakfast was ready. I did love my food!

I can remember my dad bought me a tricycle once and I felt it would further my yearning for travel. All very well you might say. So off I would go on my bike maybe for a couple of miles. But to me it was a huge distance and when I finally stopped I thought the best idea was to leave the bike and walk home since it was lunchtime and I was hungry and the bike would slow me down.

"Where's your bike?" my dad would ask with trepidation.

"Just up the road, Dad," I would meekly reply.

There would then follow a routine repeated many times (to the despair of my dad). In the family Austin 12 car we would go and I would try to recall where the bike was residing.

"Up this road I think, Dad," I would splutter out, fearing the worst.

"It better be!" was the reply.

I would sink further into the seat. Suddenly out of the corner of my eye there was my bike, standing proud on some street corner. I would shout: "There it is, Dad!" at the top of my voice, causing my dad to startle at this screeching boy in the back seat, braking, turning and cursing me all at the same time. Poor old car! Poor old Dad! Got my lunch though!

My dad was based at the nearby Whitchurch airfield and would disappear off flying for days on end leaving my mum to bring up Cynthia and me. When he returned from his travels he would get a list of things that had happened while he was away. I can remember many a time pleading with Mum not to tell Dad my latest crime, with my sister taunting me that if Mum didn't tell Dad then she would. Sisterly 'love-hate' would rear its ugly head again.

I went to the local church school just down the road and there my formal education started. I can't recall too much about the school except that it was a very religious establishment with an enormous church in the grounds that required my attendance occasionally. That must have been an endurance test for me having to keep still for an hour or so. Life as a kid in those days was totally different from today. There were no security problems, mobile phones, McDonald's, heavy traffic, drugs or major crime. We were free to roam and only governed by the words:

"Lunch will be on the table at 12 o'clock – don't be late!"

Stupid statement for one who loved his food!

Holidays were taken in St Ives, Cornwall and the journey was an epic. Consider the fact that there were no motorways, but roads about the same size as your average country lane nowadays. As mentioned before the car was the famous Austin 12. Dad driving, Mum trying to navigate with me and my sister crammed into the back together with all the kit for a fortnight piled up around us. It made the call "Are we there yet?" ever so relevant.

I would have thought about 10 hours was a good journey time. The poor car would overheat many times so we would all bundle out on the middle of Dartmoor while the car cooled down. Dad would consult the map, overriding Mum's opinion as to which was the right road. Let me expand a little on my dad. Great provider for the family he was; we never went short. He was the boss though! When I look back over my childhood there were times when I hated him but only like a kid not getting his way. I loved him really and he loved me but we both had funny ways of showing it. My mum was my confidante in those days and I owe everything to her in later life whenever things went wrong. Equally, in later life my dad became my hero for what he had achieved in aviation.

Anyway, one thing my dad had was a short temper which, in the middle of Dartmoor on the wrong road, car boiling over, kids moaning, was at its best. The rest of the journey was usually carried out in complete silence, which made the journey endless. We stayed in a guesthouse a short distance from the beach. In those days St Ives was never really crowded so you could park right in town. I think that the car was the most thankful one amongst us to get there. I can recall that these holidays were classic English ones with a fierce landlady who commanded meal times to the minute. Suited me though! I would play on the beach all day. I can remember the mid-morning steam train arriving every day right on time. The beach was never crowded and the main feature was the lifeboat station that sat there on the hard standing with a tractor ready to drag it into the sea when needed. The station was open to wander around. There were these lifeboat models on the side and I kept pestering dad for one. He finally gave in and said that when we would come next year he would buy one for me. He must have known that we were never to come back again. I never I got my model. And I never forgave him!

The other place on the travelling trail was Cardiff in South Wales where my Auntie Betty lived with her two children. The journey was somewhat simpler whereby we travelled to the coast just west of Bristol and went on the ferry over to the Welsh coast and then on to Cardiff. In mileage terms it was much shorter than going to Cornwall. In summer it was not too bad since the ferry journey was very welcome to get those limbs working again but in winter it was a nightmare. The poor old car had no heating and the journey was long, so, apart from lack of blood in the limbs, I was bloody frozen. By the time we got to Cardiff, in silence as usual, my sister and I were extracted from the car and thawed out.

My Auntie Betty was, like my mum, a lovely lady and her two children were Gillian and John. John and I hated each other and would spend our early days competing against one other. On some occasions in the summer when we were in Cardiff we would all go to Rest Bay, a beach at Porthcawl, which was about one hour's driving to the west along the coast. I remember that in those days beaches were not fully exploited or populated and we spent many wonderful days there. In winter we would sometimes go to Cardiff for Christmas.

In those days my dad smoked along with my auntie. So what, you might say, but consider further: in the evenings my dad and his sister had a calling for a nip of whiskey. Well, this nip became a gulp and the cigarette consumption went up accordingly. The lounge where this ritual took place was small, so very quickly if you could see the end of your arm you were lucky. Why ever did I start smoking! I know my mum did not approve of these smoky evenings but that was the routine. I can never remember my dad showing any signs of drink effect but in the morning his temper was a bit shorter than usual.

My first introduction to aviation was when my dad took me one day to Filton airfield in Bristol. This was where the aviation company Bristol resided. We parked the car and I was taken to a huge hangar and allowed to peep in through a side door. The sight that greeted me was awesome: There was this monstrous creation all shining under the hangar lights. The thing that struck me the most was the sheer amount of shiny metal that was wrapped around a frame. It was uncovered in certain areas revealing a labyrinth of circular steel frames and stringers. The wings seemed to stretch forever and the propellers – well there were so many of them. The sight has stayed in my mind forever.

I was actually looking at the infamous Bristol Brabazon. This machine was built to show the ultimate in aircraft design for its day. She was huge and somewhat graceful when she flew, only to be struck down by metal fatigue and the lack of suitable power plants at a very early part of her development. The Bristol test pilot Bill Peggs who commanded the 'beast' on its short development span must have been overcome by the size and grace of this airliner. A few months later, whilst we kids were playing in the street I can remember this thundering noise coming from the sky somewhere above the houses. Suddenly there she was – The Bristol Brabazon in flight. I must have wondered how all those nuts and bolts now came together as one. What a sight! She must have been only about one thousand feet up and boy, did she roar! She filled the sky! Houses shook, cats gave birth, birds dived for cover, babies cried and mothers reached for the sherry. We all stopped and stared. I was watching aviation in its raw form and obviously something stirred in me. It had an everlasting effect on me. Thus my total devotion to aviation was born. I then had lunch.

Very soon after this BOAC moved from Bristol to the new fancy airport just west of London called Heathrow. So, once again, the family moved. What was different this time though, was that Dad had taken the plunge and bought a bungalow in Wokingham, Berkshire – about 30 miles west of Heathrow. I would imagine that it must have cost under a thousand pounds which in today's world is nothing but in those days was an enormous sum. So we duly arrived at 28, Arthur Road, Wokingham and there we lived for many years and it was the backbone of my youth. I was seven at the time we moved in and the place had only just been built. The year was 1953. Wow, what a memory! Arthur Road became the centre of the BOAC community since many crewmembers lived there. I remember over the road we had a Flight Navigator, Flight Engineer and a Captain.

The best thing was that there were lots of kids of my age to form the 'gang'. We had a large garden with fields behind and I got the bigger bedroom. One up on the sister! One feature I will never forget was the fact that the bungalow boasted a central heating system. Difficult to describe compared with the modern systems, it consisted of a panel about ten feet by eight feet that dominated the kitchen. It was powered by a derivative of coal called Anthracite. It had a furnace-like section that had to be fed with this Anthracite and then stoked all day. The result was that the kitchen was like a sauna. The heat was meant to be sent down ducts to all the rooms. So why did I still wake up in winter with ice still on the inside of the windows and frozen breath? Coats were required to get to the kitchen and then swimming trunks were the order of the day once you got there. The final insult was that Dad designated me to go out to the bunker every day and it was my duty to fill up the coal scuttle to feed the furnace. As I said before winters were cold and this chore became an exercise in Arctic endurance. Just what I needed before breakfast!

Talking about breakfast, obviously it was regarded as the starter of the day and most essential. We had two types of breakfast depending on who was the cook. Mum would cook to order exactly what I wanted and I was in my element since food was very important to me. The downside was when my dad was home it was porridge, porridge or porridge. Now, there is milky porridge, sticky porridge and creamy porridge. Then there is my dad's porridge. The only identification marks for his porridge were that the ingredients came from the same box. The taste would stay with me all day and only Mum would clear this taste when I got home from school. Good old Mum!

I was enrolled in the local primary school. Primary it was but local it was not. It was about eight miles away and entailed a bus journey. This was all right in the winter since the social side of the journey was great with all the 'gang' on board. This brings me to the other, rather less successful side of my life – females. I must have looked a right sight in my short trousers, cap and school bag, trying to be cool in front of the 'gang' but having a sense of curiosity at the same time. In the summer we usually rode our bikes to school. I say 'we' since most of the BOAC kids in my road went to the same school and, in particular, my friend Peter and I would often ride back and forth together to school. The distance seemed irrelevant at the time and often we would ride off down the country lanes to get to school. These lanes ran along by the river some of the way and many a good time was spent lounging on the riverbank trying to do the homework that should have been done the night before.

The converse applied coming home when we would all stop and

talk 'gang' talk on the same river bank. I would get home sometimes well overdue with Mum waiting and then attempting to tell me off but really thankful that the 'bogey men' had not got me. The threat of telling Dad would make the blood drain from my face. Of course, there was Cynthia standing in the background smirking. If I had possessed the power at that moment to make her disappear I would have done. As I said before, my mum was someone special in my life and I loved her dearly but – oh, did I give her agonizing times or what! Sorry Mum! As you can imagine I never did the late arrival when my dad was home. He seemed to look at his watch on my arrival as if he was calculating my transit time from school.

As you have gathered by now food was a big part of my everyday thoughts, together with aeroplanes. Dad was flying on the famous Boeing B-377 Stratocruiser, plying his trade back and forth across the North Atlantic. The advantage of that was that he would bring back food that was not available in the UK. I remember that there was this V8 juice which was prominent in the household. Anyway, you read nowadays or see on TV how the family unit existed in the 1950s and 60s. Well it was just like that with my mum cooking all Saturday for the weekend. Sunday lunch was at one o'clock precisely whilst listening to the Billy Cotton band show on the radio. It was always a leg of lamb with all the trimmings. My favourite!

By this time we had acquired a television – a PYE model with the latest technology. It needed a huge 'X' aerial on the roof plus a start-up time of about six minutes. The programmes were very limited and the only channel at first was the BBC. On Sunday afternoon we went through the ceremony of afternoon tea. My mum really excelled in the food department and saved my life many times prior to me fainting through hunger. Good trick that was!

Anyway back to afternoon tea. It was always accompanied by the ceremonial switching on of the TV with me sitting back with anticipation, a half-eaten egg sandwich hanging out of the corner of my mouth, waiting for the little dot to finally open up into a somewhat murky black and white picture that flickered and danced all over the screen. Dad would approach the machine claiming absolute authority over the adjustment controls. Having witnessed the initial result I knew what was coming next as I continued to devour my mum's lovely egg sandwiches. Today I still have a craving for egg sandwiches but they don't taste quite the same as my mum's. Anyway, to cut a long story short Dad would huff and puff forever with the adjustments and when finally some sort of picture emerged we would hear the presenter, Sylvia Syms I think, say: "There now follows an hour long interlude until the next programme. Thank you viewers."

Short temper rising or what!

Monday was always left over lamb from Sunday with mashed potatoes – yummy! Tuesday, Wednesday and Thursday were generally low key since I had lunch at school. It did not stop me creeping around Mum after coming home from school for cheese on toast. Only done when Dad was away though! There were two meals I detested – yes amazingly enough. They were stew and anything that had cabbage within a mile of it. Stew was tricky because I hated boiled onions. I am sure that any receptacle near the dinner table would be laden with the slimy things by the time I had picked them out carefully with my fork hoping no one would notice. My sister always noticed though – where was my magic disappearing kit? Cabbage was even trickier since it was coloured green. Having said that, by the time it was boiled and generally abused it had a rather emaciated look about it. The only solution was to try and hide it under the fork and scarper off before the game was up. Why were the forks so bloody small when you were a child? Old eagle-eyed Dad would then proceed to serve it up at the next meal.

I wondered if the disappearing magic worked on dads. These particular hate meals always were presented when my dad was at home. I could order 'à la carte' from my mum. Lovely, my mum! Friday was fish day. Not my favourite, but workable. The fish van would drive around the streets of Wokingham. It was an old Morris van if I recall and its arrival in the area was announced by the hooting of his rather strangled horn, obviously exhausted by overuse. All of us kids scurried indoors to get the order of the day plus the money and off we'd go and queue up to buy it. We were the errand boys, you see. The food calendar now brings me to Saturday. Well, the sausages and mash rated highly in my life only just short of Sunday dinner. I would make channels in my mashed potato and fill them with tomato ketchup and then mix it in like cement, much to the disgust of my sister – I didn't care though!

That brings me back to Sunday and so the cycle started again. I must pause at this point to expand on my mum's speciality – Welsh cakes. The origin of these cakes is Welsh obviously but that is all I know. It was a family recipe that combined all the ingredients into something very special. They were cooked on a flat hot plate and resulted in a small cake about three inches in diameter, about half an inch thick. I would seem to develop a homing instinct when mum started the production line. I could be two miles away when suddenly I would sniff the air like a lion sniffing out his prey. I would smack my lips together and bolt home. I am sure my mum used the Welsh cakes as a magnet to attract her son back into the fold. Once home I would hang around her apron strings until they were cooked. Temperatures were irrelevant, as I would make a lunge at the finished product as it left the hotplate.

"Just wait!" she would say in desperation.

Never heard the words, Mum!

School seemed to progress in a sort of fashion. Education is strange, I think. There you have a teacher standing up in front of you and your 'gang' and the last thing on your mind is to listen. Even at that early age I had developed the technique of reading the book later and writing it all down and absorbing it that way. To this day I still do it where needed – no word processor in those days! Anyway the net result was little attention paid at the time to the teacher and more attention paid to the back of the head of the girl in front of with these ribbons in her hair that just beckoned to be pulled. Good for the ego in the 'gang' though. Unfortunately the victim must have known my sister since as the deed was being done up went the cry: "Please Miss – Mullett just pulled my hair."

So off I went on to stand in the corridor again. Now, once banished to the corridor you had to evade the eyes of the headmaster, Mr Denzil, who would often make spot checks for victims. The teacher who had banished you would also make checks as to whether you were still in position. Talk about ducking and diving! Many visits to the toilet followed in order to space the time out until the lesson finished when the punishment terminated. My luck very rarely held out though and Mr Denzil would spot me many a time. He would confer with the teacher and the 'gang' would try and give me encouragement with their eyes. All to no avail, so off I would go like a tame dog following its master to the headmaster's office. The routine that followed was repeated many times whereby a ten-minute lecture would be followed by his three steps to the cupboard and producing this one-inch thick, four-foot monstrous cane. I am sure he had a sadistic streak in him since I felt I could detect a glint in his eyes as he invited me to stretch my hand out.

So there I was a quivering wreck of a boy with my hand out as if I was asking for 'alms for the poor'. He would draw a deep breath and swing this weapon far back behind his head as if he were just about to decapitate Anne Boleyn in the Tower of London. Then there would be the familiar 'swish' sound that I came to hear many times. Contact with my hand was something to be believed. The pain came about two microseconds after the contact – did it hurt? Yes it bloody did! Three on each hand was the order of the day. This was followed by another ten-minute lecture with not a single word registering. All you could think of was wanting him to die a horrible death – mixed with pain so severe it could produce tears, but the mind refused to give in. The final words that echoed in your mind as you left were: "I don't ever want to see you here again or you will get another thrashing – do you hear me, Mullett?"

Not a chance! Funnily enough I was back again and again. After sticking my hands in the nearest fridge I then emerged victorious to face the 'gang'. The girl with the ribbons was never around for fear of retribution. As you can gather I was not a happy pupil. Having said that, the method that I described earlier did produce results: Mum did shield Dad from the worst of my conduct at school.

Thank you, mum!

Unfortunately the truth finally did emerge when the parents were invited to an open evening at school and Dad decided that, being at home, this would be a great chance to meet my teachers.

Big mistake, I thought. Better scarper off and sit it out.

When he arrived at the school and innocently inquired, with a certain Mrs Titely, as to the conduct of his wonderful son, he was then faced with a barrage of abuse and found himself on the receiving end of a lecture that only a schoolteacher can give. I think that the fact I had scarpered saved my life since he was gunning for me from that moment on. Short temper he had but I think that on this occasion he must have burst a blood vessel. Can't think why!

I eventually crept in like a lamb to the slaughter and faced up to Dad. Mum had also got the full brunt of his outpourings for not telling him what was going on. My sister got a load full as well for not forcing Mum to tell Dad. Even the dog got it in the neck, I imagine. The only saving grace with my dad's temper was that it never deteriorated into physical action. Had it done so then my encounters with the headmaster's monstrous cane would have been like a 'walk in the park'. Not a good day in my life! I think I missed my dinner that day.

When I think back it was just school and play in those days. No other worries seemed to surface at the time. Play was the priority in life. We made up our own agenda for entertaining ourselves. TV was still in its infancy and provided a little entertainment for those rainy days. I seem to recall another TV station started up called ITV. It required another array of aerials on the roof to complement the BBC aerial already there. The only drawback was that the programmes were littered with adverts.

"So what!" you might say.

Well, Dad being a staunch BBC man, refused pointblank to install ITV. He considered it vulgar to have adverts on the TV and so it was a 'fait accompli'. All my friends had it but we didn't. Was he rotten or what! No problem for me though as I would often disappear to my friend Richard's to watch my favourite programmes. There was 'Popeye the sailor man' together with 'Olive Oyl' and 'Brutus' on a Friday evening. On a Saturday afternoon at 4pm there was professional wrestling with such names as Mick McManus and Jackie Pallo doing their 'dying swan routine' routine with a radio DJ, Keith Fordyce, doing the commentary. Fantastic it was! Though as I said before the TV programmes were very limited and never really had much of a bearing on my 'must watch' list.

Let me go back to the school side of my life. After the confrontation with Mrs Titely my dad took an almost overbearing interest in my schoolwork. The ceremonial presentation of the homework every night before play was the order of the day. When he was away flying then the pressure was off although my mum did try her best to keep it up – but a son can always work his way around his mum. Had to keep my sister away though! On the subject of sisters, it soon emerged that she was brainy and very diligent in her schoolwork. There is nothing worse than an older sister who is cleverer than you are. All standards are set by them and especially when Dad would say:

"Your sister did this well!"

Or:

"Why can't you be brainy like your sister?"

Where was my magic disappearing set when I needed it?

My passion for aviation continued unabated from those early days at Bristol. When we moved to Wokingham, unbeknown to me there was a local town about fifteen miles away called Farnborough and it boasted an annual airshow. I can remember, back in the early days, me and my mum climbing aboard a bus in the Wokingham town square and going off to the airshow. What a feast of delight was awaiting me. The whole affair was all very leisurely carried out. Mum had made up a picnic for the day. Plenty of Welsh cakes! We sat down on the grass close to the runway only to be separated from it by a rope fence. The aircraft on show were the latest from the UK factories – Gloster, Bristol, Blackburn, Hawker, Supermarine and De Havilland to name but a few. It was quite a spectacle.

I can remember one particular show when, near the end, a sound very similar to that encountered with the Brabazon in Bristol erupted and then this graceful flying boat flew down the flight line. It was the Saunders Roe Princess flying boat I was looking at. She was beautiful and, like the Brabazon, stuck in my mind forever. What a shame she went the same way.

The other insight into aviation came through my dad and his flying back and forth across the Atlantic on the Stratocruiser. Boeing Aircraft Corps built this aircraft. She was quite a machine. From the front looking back she had this double bubble fuselage cross-section with the upper area at the front revealing an enormous expanse of cockpit windows. The tail was also enormous, being grafted on directly off a wartime bomber known as the B-29 Superfortress. The wings seemed to sag under the weight of four enormous Pratt and Whitney reciprocating engines. The propellers seemed like huge paddles, totally incapable of movement. The whole structure was meant to fly like a bird – amazing!

It was not long before my bedroom was adorned with aircraft pictures. There was a publication out at the time called the 'Eagle' comic that prided itself on its centrefold cut-away drawing of some modern piece of technical genius. Quite often it was an aircraft. It came out on a Tuesday if I recall and it was the highlight of my week – almost on a parallel with Sunday dinner – an early dash to the front door to await the thud of the papers plus my 'Eagle' comic. This centrefold was duly extracted and up it went on my bedroom wall. Glad I had the large bedroom. I think that Mum and Dad realized at a very early stage of my life that aircraft were my passion.

When Dad went off to work there he was all dressed up in his BOAC uniform complete with hat. He did cut a dashing figure back then. Mum would fuss about him like a personal valet adjusting this and prodding that. I remember that he had a checklist detailing every item needed for his travels. He would stand there ceremoniously ticking off the items. I am sure 'get into car and drive to the airport' was on the list. We all stood there waving him off as if he was going to war. I know my mum was sad at that point since flying was in those days nowhere near as safe as it is today. Civil aircraft crashes were quite common and always made headlines, as they do today, though not with the same sensationalism that accompanies today's reports.

Then came the day when Dad invited me to go with him to Heathrow Airport. He said that he had to see someone there and would I like to come along? Would I – you betcha! Heathrow was about fifteen miles west of London nestling between two main roads and was about half the size of today's metropolis. The international departure ramp was on the north side and would have enough parking places for maybe 30 aircraft. The other national airline of the day was British European Airways (BEA), based at nearby Northolt. This left Heathrow the total domain of the big intercontinental aircraft. There were the Lockheed Constellations, Douglas DC-4s, DC-6s plus of course the Stratocruisers.

It was then that I realized BOAC was not the only airline in the world. There was Panam, KLM, Transamerica, TWA and many others. I must have looked a right sight with my jaw on the floor and speechless. This was paradise!

As we passed the aircraft ramp I felt a little let down since what else was there to see except the ramp? There then loomed in my sights the BOAC hangars and my jaw hit the floor again. These hangars are on the same site as they are today, on the eastern side of the airport. In fact, the original hangars that housed the aircraft then still house the modern jets of today. I remember my dad parking the car not far from a Stratocruiser that was obviously being readied for flight since it was surrounded by numerous men in white overalls complete with screwdrivers and toolboxes. They were opening and closing panels and kicking tyres. This was the nearest I had been to a Stratocruiser that my dad flew in. The aircraft name of Stratocruiser had been shortened to a more affectionate title of 'Strat'. So there I was staring at this 'Strat' when my dad walked over to one of these men in white overalls and I saw him chatting to him and looking at me at the same time. He then beckoned me over and told me that this gentleman he was talking to would allow us to go aboard the aircraft. I must have stumbled out the words, "Thank you very much, sir."

I was totally overwhelmed as we approached the aircraft on the forward left side where there was a built-in entrance hatch complete with steps. My dad stopped and then turned to me and proceeded to issue instructions as to what and what not to do once on board.

"Yes dad. No dad," I said.

I am sure I added a 'sir' somewhere.

We climbed through this hatch and to the right was a cavernous hold area where all the bags went. Wow, it was big! We then ascended another small staircase and I entered a new, exciting world. There were all these seats, beautifully upholstered, arranged just like cinema seats. They looked thick and luxurious complete with padded armrests that made them look like individual little islands. There were thick blankets and cushions all over them. What a seat! I could compare them with an old style club or business class seat that is around nowadays. The only difference was these were economy seats, as my dad pointed out.

I remember sitting in one and totally losing myself in dreamland. We then walked down the aisle towards the aircraft rear with me gingerly tiptoeing along so as to not touch anything. I will point out at this stage that the First Class section of those old airliners was at the rear, as opposed to today. We passed the Galley where all meals were prepared. So small!

Mum couldn't cook her Welsh Cakes in there, I must have thought.

We then entered the First Class section and the seats there made the Economy ones seem dwarf-like. Was there one seat each or did a whole family reside in one, such was their splendour Dad then flicked a button or something and out of the ceiling unfolded a built-in bed complete with blankets, pillows, mattress and a light.

What next? I wondered.

I just stood there mesmerized by all I had seen.

Imagine 70-odd passengers travelling along in this total luxury, I thought to myself.

We retraced our steps to the front of the 'Strat' where a gentleman was standing just ahead of the Economy section with his back to a door that seemed to mark the front end of the aircraft.

"Would your son like to look in the cockpit?" he inquired.

This was not happening to me! So through the door we went. How can I describe it as an eight-year-old? There were dials, switches and levers all over the place. To my immediate left was a cubicle about the size of a modern aircraft toilet. It had a seat and about two hundred dials, or so I thought, on a panel facing rearwards. My dad proceeded to tell me that was where he sat and controlled the entire aircraft radios. The small table facing the panel in the cubicle was dominated by a large 'thing' strapped down on it.

"What's this, Dad?" I asked.

I had pointed out my dad's pride and joy and the very reason why he was employed.

"It's a Morse Key," he announced.

He then touched it, or rather caressed it, and produced a series of clicks made by the moving arm striking the non-moving base plate.

"I get all the weather and send the position reports with this," he said.

As an eight-year-old it was all beyond me. The only thing that struck me as odd was that my dad spent the whole flight pointing backwards. How strange! The section to the right hand side had a large built-in table at right angles to the front, together with another panel with dials. There seemed to be hundreds of them. This was the Flight Navigator's cubicle.

Wonder what he did, I thought.

The seats in the cockpit seemed to have been transported from the cabin and had that padded luxury look about them. I looked up to the ceiling of the cockpit above the Flight Navigator's station and there was this glass dome through which I could see the sky. I must have said, "What's this, Dad?" about fifty times that day.

Poor old Dad, he must have been exhausted! My dad looked at the dome and said that it was the viewing port for the Navigator to look at the stars. Whatever for, I thought! In the mid-section of the cockpit was an island, for want of a better description, where the seat was also at right angles with a panel containing the largest collection of dials, levers, knobs and wheels I had ever seen.

"This is where the Flight Engineer sits," said Dad anticipating my usual question.

There were red levers, yellow levers, blue levers and finally levers that seemed to have some sort of black and yellow guards over them and labelled 'For emergency use only'.

How would somebody know which lever to pull or dial to read? I thought to myself.

There were so many. Just forward of the island was a curtain that traversed the cockpit from left to right. It was pulled back revealing the pilot's seats.

"That's where the old man sits," said my dad pointing to the left-hand seat.

Whether it registered anything with me then I don't know. It must have meant something since I have described it all in such detail. So why did I have to go to school then? The cockpit décor was black, with all the dials' indications in white. I wondered if I could build a cockpit in my bedroom.

The man in white then appeared and said that we had to leave since they were towing it over to the departure ramp for the evening 'Monarch' service to New York. We retraced our steps to the car and we then watched as they started the tow. The 'Strat' came by the car with the wing tip going right over the top of the roof. What a sight! Thank you, Dad! The journey home was a bit of a blur, with me not stopping talking.

When we finally got home with a very exhausted dad I rushed off and told all my friends about it. The problem was that at the time they never had my enthusiasm or passion for flying. What was wrong with them? Though as it turned out later on in life a few of my friends did get the bug and took up flying.

My schooldays continued painfully at the primary school where the 'goal' was to pass the famous 11+ exam and get on with the next phase of my education. I can remember filing into the Assembly Hall of the school and sitting down at a desk with this crisp white sheet of paper in front of me that was there to be written on with all the answers that were supposed to be in my head.

What's my name? I thought in a panic!

The subjects were basic for the school but, at the time, seemed a long way away from my brain. Anyway, the headteacher came in and started to give out the question papers. There it was in front of me, daring me to open it. I did and speed-read it. The maths questions looked OK. I will point out that by that time my ability fell heavily on the sciences and not the arts. So, back to the maths questions! Fine by me they were, and so off I went and finished them quite quickly.

The next part of the paper was the English prose issue. Well, would you believe it! The question was to write about 'the best day of your life'. My day out at London Airport sprang to mind straight away. So off I went scrawling all about it. The exam came to an end with the bell being rung and we then sat still whilst the headmaster ceremoniously collected the papers, surveyed them and then drifted his eyes over the top of his glasses perched at the end of his enormous nose. He looked at the pupil at each desk, muttered some incomprehensible comment or grunt, then moved on to the next victim. My turn came and he cast his eye over my entry, looked up at me and raised one eyebrow, then moved on uttering nothing. What did that mean? I rushed home and grabbed a handful of freshly baked Welsh Cakes and walked over to the local park, chased by the usual gang of boys all anxious to help me eat them.

The summer holidays were now upon us and I was as free as a bird. This was 1957. Something amazing happened in that July with the family. My dad had, by then, worked for BOAC for many years and he had earned a free staff trip for the family. He announced to all assembled that the family were going off to Barbados in the Caribbean for a holiday in a couple of days. We were to fly out of Heathrow Airport via Shannon in Ireland, Gander in Newfoundland, Antigua and then finally Barbados. The aircraft we were going in was the mighty 'Strat'. Cor! Was this really going to happen?

In due course the family assembled at Heathrow in this single storey building that occupied a part of the north side of the airport. I could compare it with being in your garage with a desk at one end and a couple of posters stuck around the walls. There were no computers in those days and the check-in consisted of a large flat cabin plan on an easel with tags in each seat which the passengers selected and the tags were dutifully extracted and handed over.

Not being in the world of staff travel I just sat and watched all the people checking in. Would we all fit? Why was my Dad not finding me a nice seat? Ah! Now we come to the crunch. Staff travel is based on there being a seat available. I didn't know that then. Anyway, later, when the check-in desk went very quiet my dad rose from his seat and gingerly approached the check-in desk with this formidable lady standing behind it. She seemed to have complete authority over who got on board amongst the pathetic group of staff people all anxious to go to Barbados as well.

As Dad approached he seemed to go on bended knee with his head bowed as if he was paying homage to this exalted lady. Words were exchanged and after a process of paper shuffling, phone calls, counting and scribbling notes she announced that there were no seats available that day and for everyone to go home. Dad's stoop got lower as he reversed away from this altar. The High Priestess had spoken. Being only 11 I did not fully understand what was going on. Were we or were we not going to Barbados? Dad announced that we were not going.

What? Go home! I thought, after all the hype.

We all sat around discussing how we were going to get home and what we were going to do when we got there. I can't recall my exact emotions at the time. Where was Barbados anyway? Mum and Dad's family lived in Cardiff, South Wales and that would take us 6-7 hours to get there from Wokingham by car. Surely Barbados was not much farther. Anyway I had my mates at home. We were actually the only people left there and were just about to leave when the High Priestess beckoned my dad over. Did she want to drive the knife in or what? Words were exchanged and my Dad suddenly stood to attention and swung on his heels and said: "Come on, we are going and we must hurry."

What was happening? Why the change of heart? Anyway, there was no time to debate as we marched down the attached corridor. I can remember the day being rather wet when we walked out to the 'Strat'. There was the aircraft that I had been on just a few months before. At that time the atmosphere was relaxed compared with now. There were people scurrying about in white overalls checking this, prodding that, measuring this and filling up that.

She looked beautiful sitting there, waiting to spring into life and take us just beyond Cardiff to Barbados. We boarded at the rear left hand side and my sister and I were ushered to the front of the aircraft. Mum and Dad were ushered to the rear of the aircraft. I was shown this seat in the front row at the extreme right hand side. I clambered with shaky hands past two gentlemen already seated and strapped in. My sister was ushered somewhere else. Didn't care about that though!

I remember looking out of the window and seeing these enormous engine propellers starting to turn and usher an enormous cloud of white vapour and then settle down in a blurry disc. The next thing was the whole aircraft shuddered and we were on the move. My face was glued to the window and watched every yard go by. We then finally turned into this enormous expanse of concrete which seemed to cover the whole airport. It was long and wide. The 'Strat' seemed to poise like a cat eying a mouse. Suddenly there was this deafening roar from the engines and then, what seemed like all hell breaking loose, the whole aircraft lurched forward and started to roll down this expanse of concrete. I was glued to this window watching everything turn into a blur. I remember that, at a certain point when I thought this concrete would run out, the 'Strat' lifted its nose up and there we were suspended in the air. Suddenly that blur of familiar sights on the ground turned to miniature. Wow!

When eventually I could see nothing discernible below I turned to look at my surroundings. My two fellow passengers seemed engrossed in their own world. Maybe it was because I had not eaten anything for a long time but my stomach suddenly issued a large burbling sound. I then recalled looking out of the window again not trying to think about my stomach. All that did was to compound the problem. Another burble erupted stronger than the first. What is happening here? This is not fun. Yes, you've guessed it. I had the start of air sickness. Then, of course, the next thing was this stewardess placing a tray of food in front of me. I stared down at the contents of the tray and felt the end of my world was coming. Hang on a minute – these bits and pieces look good. I remember gingerly nibbling this sandwich and awaiting my fate. The burbles seemed to slow down in intensity and a somewhat normal feeling started to return to my body. It was obvious that I not eaten for hours and the burbles were a cry for help from my stomach. The more I ate the easier it all became. What a wonderful therapy food is!

Our flight to Shannon must have been about two hours or so. What an indulgence! I could hear the roar of the engines and daylight gradually disappearing. The whole episode was amazing. I can remember it all to this day. Following the indulgence of the tray a somewhat disjointed conversation started with my two fellow passengers. They were actually of West Indian descent but I thought they were from Japan. Don't ask me why! I think the problem there was that I did not recognize any other accent except Berkshire English.

After about one and a half hours things changed a bit with the engine's sound diminishing and the cabin starting to point down towards Earth. Back to the window I went and strained to see the ground. I think the weather was cloudy since nothing showed up at that point. As we got lower this big white fluffy thing loomed up to meet us and suddenly I can remember the aircraft bouncing around.

These white fluffy things, later identified as clouds, must be made of something solid to throw us around like that. My knowledge was somewhat limited at that time! Suddenly out of the window things started to light up on the ground. The miniature world was getting bigger now. I watched as various bits of wing started to unfold. I seem to recall a jolt when the undercarriage went down and then watched as the ground streamed up to meet us. Ah yes, there was this famous piece of large concrete again, only this time it was well beyond Cardiff.

The landing must have been good since nothing is registered on the brain. Anyway, after a short drive around the airport of Shannon we came to a halt and the engines became silent. Nice! So, what happens now, I thought to myself. All was revealed when we were asked to leave the aircraft and go to the terminal for about a two-hour wait before flying again. During the whole flight to Shannon I never saw my mum and dad since they were established at the rear cabin. This cabin was the First Class one that I had been shown months before. As for my sister, she was somewhere around.

The whole family re-united in the terminal and the talk was generally dominated by me firing away verbally. Strange thing this terminal was. There were lots of seats for people to sit around in at one end of the concourse and a huge area at the other end occupied by shops. How strange to have shops inside a building. What did that sign say? 'Welcome to Duty Free Shopping.' Dad disappeared in the direction of the shops. Can't think why. I spent most of the time staring out of the window at the collection of aircraft on the tarmac. There must have been a collection of vintage proportion out there. After some time had passed we were all ushered back to the 'Strat' and I returned to my front row seat next to my new found West Indian friends. I won't dwell too much on the departure from Shannon to Gander, Newfoundland since I was, by then, becoming a bit of a 'vet'. At this stage the night was in full swing. I must have slept well curled up in this spacious seat.

When I woke up there was my dad standing there talking to the stewardess in the gangway. I seemed to recall Shannon being mentioned. Blimey! We had only just left there a couple of minutes ago. Dad spotted I was awake and told me that we were going back to Shannon since the weather at Gander was not good enough to carry on.

To show my complete ignorance at this stage is the understatement of the century. What had the weather got to do with it? Why are we going to Gander anyway? Barbados was only just the other side of Cardiff. Where was Shannon? I thought it was in England.

Anyway the breakfast tray arrived and was totally devoured to prevent any more air sickness. We landed back on the same spot that we had left some hours earlier. This was an adventure indeed. We all left the 'Strat' and ended up back in this terminal with the internal shops. I remember sitting around for what seemed an eternity before any news was leaked to me via my dad as to what was going on. I don't think anyone knew anything. Sounds a bit familiar!

Some time passed and then suddenly we were all rounded up and ushered into some coaches and off we went for a drive around the Irish countryside. Looked all the same to me! A cow is a cow and a field is a field! We all eventually found our way back to the terminal and were informed, for some unknown reason, that a replacement aircraft and crew would be arriving within the hour to enable us to continue our journey. This aircraft duly arrived and we all trooped out to it still wearing the same clothes that we started in back at Heathrow. The whole preparation started again and then off we went to, hopefully, Gander this time.

Amazingly enough we did get to Gander this time around. We were ushered into yet another lounge whilst the 'Strat' was readied for the next part of the journey. On this portion of the journey I decided to do some exploring. I knew Mum and Dad were down the back somewhere so off I went to find them. At a point slightly aft of the wing this rather thick ceiling-to-floor curtain stood in my way.

"Get out of my way," I must have said to myself as I hauled it out of the way.

There were my mum and dad sitting in total splendour in these throne-like seats with their legs outstretched and sipping some sort of bubbly stuff out of very slim glasses. What was wrong with beakers? You could get lots of this bubbly stuff in a beaker. At that exact moment Dad spotted me, gulped, and was about to say something when this rather dapper chap in a white jacket glided over and firmly ushered me back the way I had come, behind the curtain. There then followed a quiet but firm 'telling off' concerning the intrusion of the 'below stairs' passengers into the sanctuary of the First Class and that it was just 'not on'.

What is this? Teachers up here as well! I thought to myself.

Dad followed close behind and stood whilst this lecture continued. After a short while this chap then grinned rather creepily. Maybe his teeth sparkled! Anyway, he asked if I would like to go below to the lounge for a coke. I never knew this lounge existed but there was this small spiral staircase winding its way down into the depths of the aircraft. All three of us descended into this rather ornate lounge complete with little windows on either side. I remember peeping out of one and seeing the underneath of the wing. There were about six seats laid out on either side complete with a bar at the one end. The lecturer fussed around behind this bar and produced a glass with all sorts of things hanging off complete with a silver tray and starchily creased napkin. I gingerly sipped the contents and yes it was coke but why all the fancy bits? Never was like that from the corner shop! He then disappeared again below the bar top and emerged with a crystal style glass with some amber-like liquid in it.

"Here you are, sir" he announced to my dad.

He then went again into the bowels of the bar.

What now? I thought.

A plate then appeared complete with the obligatory starchy napkin on it, plus an assortment of flimsy looking biscuits. They looked like free samples so in I went with all fingers and thumbs working. Within seconds that look only a father can give was fired across the seats. Funny, later in life, my children took this as the trigger point to 'go for the jugular'. When my dad did it, it would stun me in my tracks and if the scene was right would 'turn me to stone'.

My dapper friend issued another creepy grin. Anyway, coke done and dusted and off I went back to my 'below stairs' seat. A short while later Dad appeared again and ushered me out of my seat and led me forward towards the front of the aircraft. This could not be happening to me! We went through yet another curtain – with no creepy grins this time – and stood at the rear of the flight deck. The first thing that hit me was the dazzling amount of light in there. I adjusted my eyes and surveyed a collection of white-shirted people with different gold covered braid across their shoulders. There must have been about five of them, all busy doing something in the allocated areas. The most fascinating was this chap perched on this island that I had seen on that infamous trip a few months previously. As I said he faced the wrong way, being established across the cockpit. Funny, I thought! Anyway, I was moved gently forward by Dad and everybody seemed to spring into life and turned to survey me.

"Hello George," the navigator said to Dad.

Of course, I then remembered that my dad was one of them.

"So this is your son then?" they might have said as a remark.

I stood there trying to take it all in. There I was in the nerve centre of the aircraft, trying to absorb it all, with all these dials, knobs and switches. These were clever people in here. There was a stirring from the front left-hand seat and this chap adorned with four gold stripes turned to face me. This was the Captain. What was said to him I do not remember at the time. My visit must have lasted maybe ten minutes when the Captain shuffled in his seat signalling the end of my visit. They must have ruled as a God in those days. I left through the curtain from whence I came and was deposited back in my seat. Dad returned to the back of the aircraft. Maybe there was some more of that bubbly stuff waiting! Anyway, to complete this flight saga we did finally arrive at Barbados some twenty four hours or so after leaving Heathrow.

Now, Barbados in those days was totally different from what it is today. There were no glossy hotels or resorts around then. The local people were not obviously totally aware of the great tourist invasion that was to come. We were looked upon with curiosity and amusement but with a gentle manner that I think is maybe missing today. Our accommodation was a sort of hotel on Rockley Beach. It was more like a large guesthouse. The owner was a Mr Manning and he greeted us on the doorstep as we arrived in our vintage, smoking, rattling taxi.

So, our holiday started and was it fantastic or what! In front of the hotel across the road was a small beach with large waves pounding away. Mr Manning had a son about my age and soon we became soul-mates. On the beach he produced a spare surfboard. Not your fancy all-singing all-dancing one of today but a simple shaped piece of wood that you put in front of you and placed the concave end in your stomach and held on either side at the top so that the whole lot converted you into a V-shaped 'Point Breaker'. So-called muscles rippled as I stood there waist-high in the waves waiting for the big one. This was all well and good until this half-hearted wave started to brew up some way away and then moved a small distance towards us from somewhere out there in the ocean. It seemed to magnify in size by every yard that it took. My new found friend whooped for joy and would shout: "Here we go".

My knees started to work independently of my legs and threatened to part company with each other. You see, I was never a real success in the water and had a basic fear of it. This fear followed me all my life. The problem here was that I could not show this fear to my friend so just awaited the arrival of this monstrous wave – or so it seemed. As this ten – or was it twenty – foot monster got within about a couple of yards all hell broke loose in the water with the top of this wave erupting into a white mass of seething foam. My knees moved another foot away from my body. Suddenly my friend turned towards the beach and leapt out of the water and triumphantly 'caught the wave'. I was gripped to the spot as he turned. I attempted a turn but this wave that had filled my horizon from the surface to the sky caught me sideways halfway through my pirouette and picked me up like a piece of rag, screwed the board into my stomach and out the other side and threw me in its grip towards the beach. Board, legs, body all parted company at that point and this total mass was deposited unceremoniously close to the beach edge. I had by then had my eyes firmly closed and when all hell had stopped there I was thrashing about thinking I was half way to Cardiff. What is all this sand here! There I was, about two yards from the shore thinking I was drowning. My friend obviously thought that this must be an 'English thing'. Anyway off he roared back into the surf for a few more rides. I followed like a tame dog and off we went again. Was I glad when the session was over!

Dad hired a 'Ford Anglia' car for a couple of days and we toured the island. The houses that the people lived in were built of timber, measured about three yards square and perched all over the hillsides. Some were coloured red, some blue and some yellow. When I think back it was a wondrous sight: all these small homes on the hillside.

The roads were something to be believed, though. There was one main road that ran around the island and small side roads branched off it inland. The problem was these side roads had some sort of surface for about one mile and then thereafter became a track. OK in the dry season but this was the wet season. On the first day Dad, being the master, surveyed the map and stated that if we cut across here via this inland road we would save a lot of time instead of going all the way round. So off we went on this intrepid journey. Yes, we got the turning OK and Dad boldly sped down this inland road through some local villages. The locals looked at us and seemed transfixed at this white family passing through their village.

What are they looking at? I wondered.

Well, just around the corner was the answer. There was nothing but green with no road. Dad went into reverse overdrive but we ended up in the track ruts fit for a tank training grounds and we lurched to a halt. The locals drifted up and continued their transfixed gaze. This must have happened every hour of the day for within a few minutes helping hands pulled and pushed and we were eventually re-united with the tarmac.

"I think we will take the coast road. Much prettier," Dad said as we all breathed a sigh of relief.

Anyway, I have to say that Barbados was magic for an 11-year old. I actually began to master the surfboard towards the end. How about that! We were there for two weeks I think before the great journey home began. We all stood at the airport waiting for the 'Strat' to arrive from Trinidad. Up to that time BOAC aircraft had had a simple white tail with various insignia on it. When the aircraft arrived it was resplendent in the new blue tail which was adopted for many years after that. Looked lovely she did!

There did not seem to be any problems with the infamous staff travel this time so off we went across the tarmac and on our way to Bermuda which was our first port of call for the journey. We arrived in Bermuda late at night and were deposited in the transit lounge where there was a balcony from where I could look over the whole airfield. The United States Air Force had a base there. I remember distinctly the aircraft they boasted in Bermuda was the B-50 Super Fortress which they used for maritime patrols. This was a plane spotter's dream for me.

While I was taking it all in I noticed our own aircraft was having an ever increasing bunch of white overall-clad engineers all gathering about one of the engines and opening cowls and burying their heads into this and that. Nodding of heads followed. Dad wandered over and checked the scene and groaned.

"They said there may be a problem with one of the engine generators."

The cowls were all closed and I thought naively, It must be OK now.

That was far from the truth. We were all summoned to the hall below and this BOAC chap said:

"Ladies and Gentlemen. We are sorry to say but we have a mechanical problem and we are all off to New York to get it fixed soon."

The adventure continued! Anyway we all re-boarded and departed for New York. After a short time we landed at New York airport. I remember being put on this bus and off we went into town or 'Downtown Manhattan' as they say. It was obviously very late at night by now and we all trooped to our rooms to sleep. The next morning I looked out of the window and there was Manhattan in the late '50s with big chequered yellow cabs and rising steam all around. Were the buildings tall or what!

Breakfast was the order of the day. We all joined the queue and collected a tray and strolled down the line of breakfast items. The big mistake was to put me at the rear of the family. It must have been such a selection that in order to not miss out they all went on the tray. The rest of the family passed the cashier with little comment until it was my turn. Dad looked back and saw this mountain of food and must have regretted his family pecking order failure. Dad was not amused. I ate it all though! My sister sniggered. Mum frowned. Anyway, later that day we all boarded the bus again and off we went back to the airport. This time all was good with the aircraft and we finally left for London on a direct flight arriving many hours later. Thus my first excursion into foreign travel and flying ended.

The remainder of the summer holidays was spent much as any other 11 year-old with days spent with my friends soaking up the sunshine. I remember riding my bike all over the place. Being my only mode of transport I spent many hours attempting to fine-tune it. When all failed as usual Dad was forced to come to the rescue and cursed me while he tried to put it all back together. It is amazing when you end up with one nut or bolt missing at the final point. The opposite is also true with one nut or bolt left over as well. Poor old Dad! Towards the end of the summer the results of the 11+ exam arrived and amazingly enough I had made it OK to be enrolled in the local Forest Grammar School for my next stage of education.

Now the next drama arrived. Up to then I had been in short trousers and the enrolment term was approaching. Mum to the rescue again! Into Wokingham we went and out I came feeling totally grown up with a new set of long trousers on board. September arrived and off I went down the road to the Grammar School. Well, you arrive all tarted up in your brand new uniform complete with the infamous long trousers and you assemble in the playground. The first thing that occurs is that the boys one or two years ahead of you assemble to inspect the new boys. You are on parade and the weaklings are being rooted out. So you stand there trying to look tough and macho, quaking in your boots. I remember being allocated a locker and finding it OK but a second year boy was obstructing it. I pushed a bit here and there and next thing Zappo! I was laid out on the floor with this gorilla astride me. My voice went up a couple of octaves and my knees shook. Perhaps I could have bribed him with a Welsh cake. No such luck!

"Lesson learnt. Keep your head down!" I said to myself as I struggled up.

My passion for flying never diminished during this period. The only reason for not elaborating on it was my pre-occupation with trying to avoid trouble at school with other boys. Did I have that sort of face or what?

Now back to the family, with my sister having been enrolled in the local Girls' Grammar School some five years ahead of me and excelling in all subjects. This had the adverse effect on me since my dad, as usual, would use her as the measuring stick for my education. My mum would be my guiding light at this stage with quiet words of encouragement.

I continued with my schooling and tried to get my head round

'Macbeth' etc. I did not excel in the Arts. As for the Sciences I was doing well. Chemistry became my pet subject. How sad can you get? One year later at the grand age of twelve the next new boys arrived and I then became the inspector of the new boys. What a transformation in attitude with my old aggressors. They suddenly talked to me about some poor new boy still in short trousers.

"Hey you – come here!" I would utter.

Chapter 2

– MY TEENAGE YEARS

Two years passed by and, at the exalted age of fourteen, I was on the way and I pretty well knew where. My physical form was looking OK. Put it another way I was not a weed. The voice deepened and I started to get body hair all over the place. This was good stuff. The opposite sex started to interest me as you would expect. What can I say about this wonderful section of the human race? What is that expression – you cannot live with them and you cannot live without them. First there is the intrigue of the physical side. Once enlightened as to what exactly happened between the sexes my feelings were mixed, ranging from:

"Oh my God, my mum and dad had to do it twice to get me and my sister."

To

"I can't wait to start."

I remember me and my friends conjured up this scale from 1 – 10 according to how far you got on the sexual front. Number 10 was the ultimate target. We would meet up on the Monday before lessons at school and proclaim what number we had got to on the previous Saturday night. Imagine at this meeting one of my friends said he had got to No. 10. Discussions went on for days between all of us as to the intimate details of exactly what had occurred. I was fumbling around No. 4 – 5 so I had to do something. Anyway I will return to this subject later.

One thing that was good about the Wokingham area where I lived was the multitude of clubs and youth groups around. One of these was the Air Training Corps (ATC) based at the nearby Royal Air Force (RAF) Staff College at Bracknell. The minimum age to join was 14 years and 3 months. So off I went to the Staff College at the required age and joined up as a cadet. The object of the ATC was to prune the youth of the country for future service with the RAF as a pilot. I was in my element and every Friday night I donned my ATC uniform and rode my bike to Bracknell for the meeting.

The good thing about the ATC was that you did a course of instruction based around flying. This ranged from Aerodynamics to Navigation. This was good stuff and far better than 'Macbeth'. I can clearly remember indulging in these subjects. So life progressed along this vein with boring old school and the Friday night ATC meeting.

The other opportunity was to go flying with the RAF as an ATC cadet passenger. Locally, we had an RAF station called White Waltham which boasted some aircraft that were, in relative terms nowadays, antiques. One aircraft was the Avro Anson that descended from the Second World War complete with fabric covered wings. It was used to ferry personnel around all the other RAF stations in England. When I think back to those days the world was a totally different place. Security was minimal and as a young ATC cadet I was free to go anywhere I wanted and to arrive at the gatehouse of any RAF base and announce to whoever was in charge:

"Please sir, I would like to go flying."

"Wait there, lad," was the usual reply.

This ability to go flying meant that now I had my passport to aviation. I remember when the school summer holidays arrived in 1960 I donned my uniform and biked over to RAF White Waltham for the first time and repeated the well-known sentence at the gatehouse and low and behold I was directed to a small hut adjacent to a hangar with these ancient Avro Anson aircraft parked outside. Boy did they look big! Once inside I stood to attention as I had been taught and saluted everyone. One of the recipients of my salute asked me what I was doing there.

"I want to go flying please, sir," I said in my slightly higher octave voice complete with shaking knees.

"OK. Let's have a look then."

My eyes followed his to a large display blackboard showing the aircraft allocated duties for the day. He seemed to home in on one flight in particular and then beckoned for me to wait there and he would be back. I saluted again! Another person came back with the original one and looked me up and down. I went to do the now well-tuned salute again when he said, "OK, why don't you come along with me to RAF Leeming up in Yorkshire? We should be back about 5 pm."

Anything north of London was in the next world and 5 pm seemed days away. So there I was walking over to this Avro Anson with the two pilots and a couple of passengers. I felt that I was off flying into another world and would be back many days later. I clambered up the steps and was directed to a rather crude, flimsy aircraft seat which was in the first row back from the cockpit. The only problem was that between me and my seat this girder called the main spar protruded about a foot up from the floor and spanned across the gangway. Being totally blind to my surroundings and anxious to please these very senior gentlemen I then found myself totally sprawled headlong in the gangway. Hands were there to ease my transition to the vertical complete with me trying to salute, offer an apology and regain my composure all at the same time. What a sight I must have been! It is amazing what you can remember!

So to continue my first flight in an RAF aircraft I sat in the seat and strapped in and watched everything everyone was doing. The temptation to salute had finally been suppressed. I can remember the bang as the pilot slammed the main door shut. So there I was like a dog waiting for a tasty nibble off the dinner table. The aroma of these older aircraft is like something created out of a melting pot using a variety of ingredients unknown to man. The result is like no other you have ever smelt. To me it was like a drug that needed constant topping up. Whilst I sat there getting my aromatic fix suddenly there were all sorts of whirring sounds and some chat from the cockpit. I will point out that from my seat I could see pretty well everything that was going on in the cockpit. Wow!

Suddenly the aircraft began to vibrate gently and I looked out of the window to see this propeller turning slowly and then starting to splutter and cough followed by a thick cloud of white smoke and then erupting into a blur. The aroma from the white smoke made its way into the cabin and boy what a turn on! The other engine repeated the same routine and suddenly I spotted people outside of the window scurrying around and finally this person threw up a 'thumbs up' to the pilots whilst standing smartly to attention. I nearly saluted! We taxied onto the grass airfield, bumping along and then lined up at some imaginary point and the engines roared into life. Not quite like the 'Strat' but very exciting being so close to the action. We seemed to lurch into the air and looking out of the window I saw the ground turned again into miniature. We were away to the far north and I was settling down to my aroma fix again. The journey was uneventful on the way up to Yorkshire. I asked hesitantly if I could stand and look into the cockpit and the answer was:

'Affirmative'.

What a strange word for Yes, I thought.

To describe the cockpit as old would be an understatement. In today's world it would stand out as 'Relic' and not even a 'Classic'. There were bits of dials all over the place, worn out fabric parts, bare metal bits, all dominated by this array of levers of all colours and shapes. After some time I felt the call of nature and excused myself and walked down to the rear of the aircraft, watching my step over the main spar obstacle, trying to avoid the gaze of what seemed to be very important passengers. Imagine having your own aircraft to flip you up and down the country.

At the rear of the aircraft I pushed aside this curtain and looked around for an obvious toilet. What was this thing bolted to the floor looking like an upturned coffee urn? Blimey, was this it? I gingerly opened the lid and yes, this was the toilet OK. It was bit of a comedown from the palatial ones on the 'Strat'.

Oh well needs must, I thought.

As we approached RAF Leeming I was invited to stand between the two pilots as they prepared for the landing. There seemed to be a lot going on. The chap on the right side seemed to do all the work. He was reading from a small booklet and the chap on the left was replying to his questions. Was this normal? The weather could not have been too adverse or I would have remembered. I stared, looking out of the windows trying to find something that might be familiar like a great piece of concrete. The two pilots seemed to split their time between looking out of the greenhouse type windows and looking down into the cockpit at the instruments. Suddenly a hand went up and pointed to a runway through the windows.

I can't see anything. Where is he pointing? I thought.

Within a couple of seconds everything seemed to happen all at once. Levers were pulled, dials were tapped and then the pilot on the left side started pushing, pulling and twisting the wheel that he had held onto all the flight. Then the chat between them started up again and suddenly a finger was pointed at me as if to say:

"Go away little boy."

This was my signal to go back to my seat and await further instructions. Shortly after that we landed with a jolt at RAF Leeming and it was raining. Memory going full power now! As we moved towards the arrival point I looked out of the window and found myself surveying a collection of RAF aircraft that looked rather strange. They were small aircraft with thin wings but no propellers. These were the RAF training aircraft known as the Jet Provost. They really did look flimsy! There seemed to be a lot of them. The thing that struck me the most was the orderliness of it all. All the aircraft were in neat straight lines complete with bits and pieces on the ground in precisely the same position around each aircraft. Everything was so beautifully shiny. It put our dilapidated aircraft to shame. I didn't care though, since I was fulfilling my dream of flying.

When we were finally ushered into our spot the left hand engine stopped and one of the pilots scurried down the back and tugged away at the aircraft door. When it finally succumbed to his efforts there was a brief exchange of words and the two passengers clambered out of the aircraft and started to walk away. Next thing I knew was that the left hand engine had started up again and off we went back to the runway. Now that was quick! We were soon up in the air again and on our way back to RAF White Waltham. On our way back one of the pilots left the cockpit and shuffled behind the back seats and produced three bags of something. He put one down in my lap and said: "Enjoy your lunch."

Food as well, I thought.

I opened the bag and looked in. There was some sort of sandwich about two inches thick complete with turned up edges. It was very dry and the meat inside looked like an overgrown piece of thick ham cut into a uniform oblong shape. Funnily enough, the complete thing seemed to have been cut and trimmed to a required, regulated shape.

Just like those aircraft I had been looking at. Anyway, having low standards in culinary affairs, I devoured the whole lot. Not bad it was either. After this gastronomic delight I then resumed my watch over the pilots. We duly arrived back home and yes it was about 5 pm. I followed the pilots back to the small office and they turned and said: "You are welcome again anytime, young man."

Off went one of my salutes again. I strolled down to the gatehouse with my bike, on cloud nine, feeling as if I had just experienced Utopia. This whole experience gave me the taste for adventure. I remember that from that day on I donned my uniform as often as I could and rode my bike over to White Waltham to go flying.

It was at about this time that my friend Peter, son of a Flight Engineer, who lived just over the road, got the taste for the flying world as well, and the both of us got together many times to go flying whenever we got the chance. We would also spend a day going to Heathrow on our bikes. It was a 60-mile round trip but nothing for us at the time. It was the summer that Princess Margaret got married. Pete and I went off to Heathrow that day and there on the tarmac we could see four RAF Vulcan bombers which apparently had been dispatched there to fly the film of the royal wedding to all parts of the commonwealth. In those days this was the only method of getting the latest news around the world.

Towards the end of the year Dad had been offered a redundancy package with BOAC or to retrain as a Flight Navigator. The reason for this was that the days of aircraft radio communications had improved so much that there was no need for a specialist in that field. Dad took the option to retrain and so off he went to a training centre on the south coast called Hamble. It was then known as the Air Service Training establishment. Little did I know that that name would mean so much to me many years later.

And so 1961 came into being with me reaching 15 years of age. Life was good to me with the dreaded schoolwork being well compensated by flying with the RAF whenever I got the chance. In the July Dad became a fully qualified Flight Navigator with BOAC. It was an amazing achievement for my dad to come through it successfully. He was 40 at the time and to change to another career was outstanding. What a man!

In the August Dad announced that we were off on another holiday to the Caribbean. The destination this time was Tobago which was situated just north of Trinidad. This time the aircraft for the journey was the Bristol Britannia. This aircraft came from the same stable as the Bristol Brabazon. Its fuselage was circular in cross-section unlike the 'Strat' and boasted about 80 seats. She was affectionately known as the 'Whispering Giant' since she was extremely quiet and graceful in appearance.

The previous route via Gander to Barbados was now a thing of the past. The route via Bermuda and then on to the Caribbean was now well established. Funnily enough I do not remember too much about the flight. All I can assume is that all went well. There did not seem to be any problems over staff travel either. I do recall slipping into this wonderful seat again which, again, was classed as 'Economy'. The only drawback of the outward flight was that we ended up in Trinidad early in the morning and had to wait until early evening to join a local flight over to Tobago.

The aircraft involved was the Douglas DC-3. Now, everyone has maybe heard of the DC-3 or the 'Dakota' in her military guise. So here I was pacing up and down all day waiting to fly again. Eventually the aircraft arrived and we were duly called and off we went. My knowledge of aircraft was beginning to build so I knew quite a bit about this aircraft. It has a tail wheel so sits on the ground pointing upwards at an angle. The result of this is that you have to climb up the cabin inside to get to your seat. Mind you, having flown in the RAF Anson earlier in the summer I was ready for this. I remember clambering up the cabin to my seat. We left Trinidad and after about 30 minutes we landed on the grass airstrip in Tobago.

The island of Tobago is the most enchanting place on the planet and we had a wonderful time on holiday there. We spent most days on the beach at a place called Pigeon Point. The sea was crystal blue and I even got on with my sister. How about that! We stayed in a lovely hotel and every day was spent in total relaxation. I was 15 years of age and my life was wonderful. We befriended a Roman Catholic Priest who joined us on many occasions. All I remember about the place were good things.

OK, enough of this sentimental stuff! I remember being very sad when the holiday came to an end. I had a great suntan and couldn't wait to get back home and show my friends – and maybe the girls. So we left Tobago on the DC-3 back to Trinidad and joined up with the BOAC flight back home. There was the 'Whispering Giant' waiting for us. Boy did she look lovely! We flew to Bermuda and we took our place in the lounge waiting for the final flight back to England. While we sat there a BOAC chap came up to us and said that the aircraft was full and that we would have to be off-loaded from the flight and wait a couple of days for the next one and take our chances again. Dad pondered for a few minutes and then disappeared towards the area where the aircraft crew was assembling. I could see Dad deep in conversation with the Captain and it then transpired that the cabin crew were willing to give up their in-flight rest seats (these seats were designated for the Cabin crew to rest during a long flight).

So it transpired that three of us could be accommodated on the flight. What happened is that Mum, my sister and I would go on the flight and my dad would go up to New York and fly home the next day. Clever old dad! He always made it good. We did indeed arrive in England the next day after a long flight cooped up on the small crew seats. Dad went up to New York and arrived home the next day. He came home on the new, all shiny Boeing 707 that had only just entered service with BOAC. Was I jealous or what!

The rest of the summer holidays were spent biking over to RAF White Waltham and flying in the RAF 'Anson'. I extended my global wanderings to such exotic places as RAF Aldergrove in Northern Ireland and somewhere in Germany that I couldn't pronounce. It was a wonderful summer holiday completely filled with everything that was so right for me.

In the September it was back to school and all that that entailed. I was now in the fourth year and the emphasis was on the exams next year. These were known as the 'O' levels. These were the stepping stones to education that I needed to fulfil my dream of flying. But they were such a bore! The school was situated close to a local airfield called Woodley. They built the Handley Page Herald there. In my early days at school I would look out of the window and watch this aircraft flying overhead. I would then be suddenly brought back to reality by the fierce growl of the master and asked to repeat the last words he had uttered. What a hopeless case I was! To be fair the wandering eyes were as a result of listening to such subjects as 'The Corn Laws of 1804' in an English history lesson.

I was, as I said before, finding my mark in chemistry, physics and mathematics, though. A side issue worth talking about is the famous end of term report plus the results of any school exams taken at the time. The report was a handwritten account of my progress as seen through the eyes of the masters. It covered all the subjects known to man. The exam results were pretty straightforward since they were a finite result of what you knew. OK, History was a total disaster with miserable results. English Literature came in a close second. Consider trying to act out a play by Shakespeare when you did not understand a single sentence that you were reading. The master would despair at my pathetic efforts and drift off into this rhetoric about the failed youth of today.

What is he going on about? It all seems all right to me, was my thought.

The part of the report that always filled me with dread was the box that dealt with the personal side of the equation – or what the masters thought of me. There was also a box to indicate how many times I was late for school and how many detentions I had received. Detentions were handed out to those of us who were, for want of a better phrase, 'out of order'. Some of us clocked them up and did not seem to worry about it. Maybe it gave them some sort of 'street cred'. For me it was the fear of my dad finding out that filled me with dread.

The actual punishment consisted of staying behind after school for 30 minutes in a classroom under the supervision of a master. You could not just sit there staring into space but had to write out as neatly as possible a piece of prose such as 'I will not cause any more disruption during the lessons'. This eloquent piece had to be repeated one hundred times. Now, that is a lot of words to write – one thousand to be precise. My writing was a scrawl at the best of times and to complete the task in the allotted 30 minutes created a total mishmash of words. At the end of the detention period the master watching over us would collect our attempts and we would be told to repeat them at home again so that they could be read by him the following day.

So off I went home to repeat the exercise hoping that neither my dad nor my sister spotted me. Mum was OK. Being late home was soon covered by a never-ending list of excuses. I doubt they believed any of them and just went through the motions of listening. Any thought of going out of the house that evening was gone. I wondered at the time whether my early knowledge of chemistry could be put to use on these masters who dished out these punishments. I could cover the late arrivals at school with a variety of one-liners such as 'The bike got struck by lightning' to 'Got a puncture' to name but a few. Back to the report – what amazed me was how these masters could remember individual names. I suppose they put us all into separate categories and wrote their comments accordingly. So there I was at the end of the school term and duly handed this white envelope by the form master.

"Have a happy break," he would say.

With this envelope in my hot sticky hand how could that be so? I would make my way home slowly and approach the house according to whether Dad was home or not. If he was, then the ceremony of reading would start. Dad would sit at the kitchen table with a cup of tea and a freshly lit cigarette. He would slice open the envelope. I would be standing to attention in front of the table staring into space. Dad would then further prolong the agony with a very deliberate process of putting on his glasses. I think that the lit end of his cigarette would be the first clue as to the unknown contents of the seemingly unimportant piece of paper. If it quivered, scattering ash everywhere, then I would be for the high jump. If it glowed redder than usual then indications were that further research as to the contents were needed based on a verbal interrogation. If it was placed in the ashtray accompanied by a large exhaling of smoke then maybe there was a slim chance of survival.

Invariably it was a combination of all three that happened. This left me totally confused. Dad seemed to home in on the comments as opposed to the end of term exam results plus of course the 'detentions' box. I think he accepted my failure in the arts department for whatever reason. I seem to recall that there was always something for him to chew on. That was the way it was. As I said earlier I never took kindly to someone standing at the front of the classroom spilling out facts and figures.

During the Christmas break from school Peter and I rode our bikes on most days over to White Waltham to see if there was any flying going on. I remember being on my own on one occasion and going on a local flight with just the two pilots on board. I will point out at this point that amongst the Anson aircraft only two of them had two sets of flying controls in the cockpit so that either pilot could fly the aircraft. The aircraft for this local flight was one of these aircraft. I stood in my usual position between the pilots, watching their every move. By simply watching I was beginning to understand how it all came together. The control column that the pilots kept their hands on was the controller of the aircraft. By pulling back it went up and conversely if it was pushed forward it went down. Similarly, if the control column was rotated to the left the aircraft went left and similarly the other way. Although I was learning this at my Friday night ATC meeting to see it work in practice was inspiring to me.

The same was true of the large collection of levers protruding out of the instrument panel between the pilots. These levers had different coloured knobs on the end. They were dominated by a longer pair to the left and seemed the only ones that the pilots used most of the time. It worked out that if these dominant levers were pushed forward the aircraft increased speed and if pulled back the aircraft slowed down. The only confusing thing about it was that there was little change to the noise of the engine whilst these levers were being moved. Anyway, by moving the control column and these levers the aircraft responded accordingly.

Right, so there I was standing on my usual perch when the pilot in the right hand seat got out and clambered past me. Maybe the famous toilet was calling! I remember the other pilot turned to me and beckoned me to sit in the now vacant right hand seat. This was a treat indeed. I sat in the seat and looked around at all the bits and pieces. I strapped in when told to and just sat there gazing out of the window. What a view it was being able to see everything coming up in front of me instead of looking out of the side windows or bending down at some obtuse angle behind the seats. The noise level was pretty high so the other pilot pushed a headset towards me and told me in sign language to put it on. So there I was sitting in the pilot's seat complete with the headset on. I was shown how to use this contraption and low and behold the pilot's voice came through my earpieces loud and clear. I pressed the small button as shown and there was my voice as well. All clever stuff! He then told me to put my hands on the control column gently. I did as I was told and there I was holding onto the controls with sweaty palms.

"OK, you have control," was the order in the earpiece.

He removed his hands from his own control column. So there I was at fifteen years of age flying this aircraft on my own. I was then told to rotate the controls gently to the left. I responded with a rather shaky pair of hands and suddenly the aircraft started to turn to the left. After a few seconds the pilot said:

"OK, now bring her back again."

I turned the controls the other way and off we went back the other way to our starting point. During the whole of this exercise my eyes were super-glued to the controls and I had no idea what was going on outside of this tunnel of vision.

"Right, now look out of the front window and do it again without looking down," the pilot said.

Is this possible? I must have thought.

Anyway I had a go and low and behold it did the same even without me looking down. I was there maybe ten minutes in all trying to do what I was told. Was it successful? I will never know. After a while a tap on my shoulder by the other pilot brought me back to reality and I carefully got out of the seat and he jumped in. I felt like a million dollars!

Christmas in our house was always an occasion worthy of mention. There were two sorts depending on whether Dad was home or not, though I don't seem to recall many times without my dad there. It was a very ritualistic affair. Christmas Eve was spent getting everything in place with the tree and decorations dominating the scene. We all took part in this and the place looked splendid when all was done. As I said earlier the winter season was as it should be, with cold temperatures and usually snow around Christmas time. What a perfect setting.

On Christmas Eve the shops closed at lunchtime so that everybody could go home to their families. The television programme for the Christmas period was something to be revered. It would arrive about six days before Xmas and be treasured like a bible. We were still stuck with BBC only but even that channel boasted some good viewing. In 1961 our television was replaced with one that was a little bit more up to date. I think it was a 'Bush'. For once in our life it seemed to work OK. There was still a long period before it finally produced a picture of any sort of quality though. I use the word 'quality' lightly compared with today's standard but in those days it looked good for the time.

Our road was, as I mentioned before, the residential enclave of BOAC so that on Christmas Eve there was invariably some sort of social function going on for the parents. Not for us kids I hasten to add. So the routine was set with the parents off partying somewhere in the evening. My sister, being older than me by a few years, had her own circle of friends so that left me on my own. I would often creep out of the house and go over to my friend Richard's and settle down with him to enjoy the delights of two channels to watch instead of one. I would get back home before everybody else and wait for the arrivals. My sister was usually first and then would come Mum and Dad. I queried the fact that Dad was pretty happy with life whilst Mum was more talkative than usual. Having sampled the demon alcohol by that time I realized the symptoms. The one thing I would hasten to add is that neither Mum nor Dad ever got out of hand. Just happy!

I suppose that even though I was fifteen at the time and felt grown up on the one hand I did revert to a total child when it came to presents. Looking back I know now that I was terribly spoilt in that department. Anyway, off I trooped to bed all full of anticipation for the following day. The fact that Christmas is a religious occasion was masked by the entire goings on around us. Then Christmas Day came and I would wake early as do all other children and find a stocking crammed with goodies at the bottom of the bed. What is that expression?

"Drivers – start your engines!"

The contents of this stocking were generally a mix of things to

eat and toys. I had by then accumulated a collection of Airfix model
aircraft. These were displayed in an oblong-shaped, clear plastic
bag with a piece of cardboard stapled to it across the longer side
graphically displaying the contents. This stocking usually had at least
two or maybe three of these models so I was in clover. Good old Mum
and Dad. The eating side of the contents I devoured like a person
possessed.

After a while the bed cover was littered with sweet papers and toys.
The only problem was it was still dark outside and there I was raring
to go. I realized the time was only 5:30 am. What a long time to wait.
There was not a sound anywhere. I would then proceed to examine
the models in more detail and maybe make a start at building them
but usually tiredness cut in and back I would go to sleep. Next thing I
was being shaken by Mum or someone since the time was now about 8
am. The scene was surveyed and conclusions reached. Anyway, I would
struggle up and realize that this is the big day. With Dad around the
routine is set. I would arrive in the kitchen frozen as usual and stick
my backside on the intrepid boiler to get some warmth through the
veins. The family would duly assemble in the kitchen and the ritual
would begin. First of all out I would have to go into the Arctic to get in
a bucket-load of Anthracite for the boiler. Now I am bloody cold again.
Dad would then instigate the orders:

"Get dressed first and breakfast second."

We only had one bathroom so getting dressed was a time consuming
chore. Dad would seem to be ages in there. He had a sarcastic streak
I think. OK the dressing part is over. What do I want breakfast for? I
had stuffed my face in the early hours and was feeling a little queasy.
Anyway, Dad would announce that porridge was the order of the day.
Oh no – not his porridge specialty! Think of what the stomach would
do when that arrived on top of the Mars Bar devoured earlier. So we
all had to sit in our places at the table and await the arrival of Dad's
porridge. This all seemed to take ages and I could already spot a few
kids outside with new bikes etc. Anyway, the culinary delight arrived
and we all sat chewing on it. Once devoured then Dad suggested a cup
tea would be good. Groans all round! I know this was his little game
because suddenly he stood up and announced:

"OK, time to open the presents."

The next drama would then unfold. Who would be dispenser of the presents? My sister, who was about 20 at the time, felt that she should do it since she was now grown up. Mum and I never got a look in. We all finally assembled in our respective corners and away we went. Dad usually ended up doing the honours. I didn't care who it was as long as I got the presents. It wasn't a question of greed but a question of let's get it done before it's the night time. Patience is not a virtue of mine. Presents would fall into my lap and be unceremoniously ripped open. I had bath cubes from Aunty Betty and socks from Aunty Melba up there in North Wales. Just like last year if I recall. I would have imagined that this all took about 30 minutes until the end of the presents was done.

"How many has my sister got compared with me?" I would mutter quietly.

Mum would say: "Don't forget to write to everyone thanking them for their present."

So who gave me what? No idea at all. I was looking at a mass of wrapping paper with the odd card poking out. That was going to be tricky. Dad always kept the best to last. He would get up and disappear into the bedroom and emerge with the main present for me. I recall a new bike, handmade work bench, huge plastic model, air rifle to name but a few. Christmas Day in our house was great!

By mid-morning Mum would disappear into the kitchen and gather all her cooking skills to get the Christmas Lunch on the table by one o'clock. So off I went outside to meet everybody and compare presents and generally kick around until lunchtime. So free and easy it was. When the appointed hour for lunch came the road emptied since everyone was on the same timetable. Now, if my mum's Sunday dinner was a mouth-watering experience then the Christmas dinner was super mouth-watering except for these small green things called sprouts. Once again the argument would arise as to who wanted a leg of the turkey. Dad would deliberate for a few minutes before making his decision. I sometimes ended up with the leg and sometimes not. The dinner would last for maybe one hour and by the time it was done we all felt totally stuffed. Then the ritual of who would do the washing up started. To be honest it was pretty evenly split between Dad, Cynthia and me. Mum was awarded the honour of reclining in her favourite chair.

The clock ticked gently on towards an important hour. At three o'clock the Queen would broadcast to the country. She had broadcasted every year of her reign. From 1957 she did this on the TV. We would all assemble in the lounge and on would go the TV waiting for the regal hour. I recall it was quite something to watch the Queen on the TV making her speech. The country still had a very large empire and her speech would cover all corners of it. I remember that as the years went by she got more ambitious with the settings and contents. The Queen's speech would last maybe fifteen minutes or so and amazingly enough all was quiet on the home front. After it was over it was back to the collection of presents you had got. Dad would, by this stage, feel the strain of it all and snuggle down on the settee and drift into a short sharp nap. This routine was normal for him and I repeated it often in later life.

In the early evening Mum would commence the sandwich run. Guess what, it was turkey! And so the Christmas Day would draw to a close in our house with satisfaction all around. The following day, Boxing Day, was filled with routine and ritual as well. The origins of Boxing Day go back many years to the time when, on the day after Christmas, boxes of gifts were given to the poor. In Wokingham on that day the local hunt would assemble at about noon and generally a large crowd would gather to see them off. We would walk as a family into Wokingham to see the riders in the bright red jackets and the hounds all assemble in the town square. The horses were magnificent with their coats all glossy and the hounds all running around in a pack. The master of the hunt would announce the departure of the hunt with a shrill whistle and off they would go. These holiday periods were ones to be treasured forever. Boxing Day was also the wedding anniversary of Mum and Dad so invariably there would be some sort of celebration organised for the day.

Girls were very much on the agenda by now and my movement up the scale progressed slowly. I can recall Christmas arriving and all the festivities that went with it but the ones I remember particularly were the 'parties without the parents'. There was a general planning meeting amongst the boys as to who had a free house on the following weekend. Once established then the planning advanced to the action stage. Girls to organize were number one. Drink was now making an appearance on the horizon. I remember the infamous 'Pipkin', which was an aluminium can about ten inches tall and about five inches across. It had a sort of opening device on the top which defied modern science to make it work properly.

So there we were all duly assembled at the venue and the party started. The old '45' records were placed on an equally old gramophone and out blazed such singers as Adam Faith, Elvis Presley and many other old faithfuls. The music was loud by requirement and after a while the girls assembled on the improvised dance floor and started jigging about. We boys felt that this jigging was not macho enough for us and ended up encircling these creatures who were gyrating and giggling.

Now, the moment arrived for the drink to be opened. The 'Pipkin' was placed in the centre of a table and one of us was appointed to open it up. What we failed to understand was the fact that movement creates an explosive recipe within the can. By the time some older boy had obtained the 'Pipkin' and ridden with it to the house and put it on the table ten minutes or so might have passed. You can imagine the internal pressure that had built up. So the one appointed to open it up stood legs astride in front of it and pushed the so-called opening device in an edge of the top rim. What would happen next can only be described in slow motion. The first piercing of the can would set up a chain reaction of gigantic proportions. The pressure build-up within the can would increase exponentially. With only a small hole on the top of the can to let the liquid escape it would emerge as a thin streak of foam and beer at about one hundred miles an hour (or so it seemed). This liquid streak would destroy anything in its path. Its first target was the boy who was unfortunately doing the opening ceremony. He would be hit square on somewhere between the chest and the head. The penetrating power was enormous. He was totally covered from head to foot within nanoseconds by this foamy, beery, smelly liquid. Of course he took evasive action like someone possessed and the streak continued on its way like a liquid bullet destroying as it went along. Its range was equal to its power and speed. Everybody would be ducking and diving all over the place with vain attempts being made to stem the flow. This only had the effect of spreading the liquid sideways, upwards, downwards, inwards and outwards. No one was missed by this liquid onslaught, least of all the girls who took a fair percentage of the complete contents of the 'Pipkin'. After about ten minutes the flow slowly dropped to a dribble. When you looked around at the devastation caused it was amazing. The home had been transformed in that time into a battlefield. Then the wailing started from the girls who, by now, had been transformed into a gibbering mass of dripping plasma, or so it seemed. The party was well and truly over! Any time remaining was spent trying to reconstruct the inside of the house so as to maximize damage limitation. The windows were opened to try to get rid of the stale smell. This meant that in addition to dripping we were all now bloody cold. So much for the evening of fun and frolics.

So, along comes 1962 and at the end of January I turned sixteen. Back to school and the ever threat of 'O' level exams rears again with just five months to go. So what is the rush, I thought? Having said that I knew deep inside my brain that to fulfil my dream of flying I had to get these exams done and get the required grade to move on. As I said, I erred towards the sciences and found that these subjects were well within my scope but as for English I was falling fast. Unfortunately, English was a requirement to qualify for any flying job and I remember desperately trying to get to grips with such items as proverbs, pronouns etc. Chemistry was my subject and I did excel in it. Top of the class I was! Whereas with English I was languishing down at the bottom.

Then along comes the Easter break so off I go again to fly with the RAF at every opportunity. My progress with the ATC was good. One incident I remember was that my intended promotion in the ranks from a simple cadet to a two-stripe Corporal was looming. However, much to my surprise, my friend was selected ahead of me. What was happening to me? What had he got that I did not have? I was totally gutted and shuffled around blaming everybody. Maybe there was a reason for it. Anyway, Dad spotted the change of mood in me and sat me down to extract the problem. Amazingly I told him fair and square what had happened. He told me to go back to the Friday meeting and present myself to the Commanding Officer and request an explanation as to why I had been overlooked. OK, so off I went on the next Friday evening and did just that. I mustered my best salute. It must have done the trick since one week later I was promoted. That advice from Dad really impressed me.

Then along comes the annual ATC open evening and awards ceremony. This was the evening when all the parents were invited along to see how their little darlings were progressing. The highlight of the evening was the presentation of the annual 'Cadet of the year' trophy by the local Member of Parliament Mr Van Straubenzee. So we all assembled in our smartest of uniforms. The trick for getting the trouser creases razor sharp was to put them under the mattress and sleep on them. Shoes were buffed up and uniform shirts were spotless. When the time came for the 'Cadet of the Year' announcement low and behold my name was called out. Can you believe that? I had only been with the ATC nine months. I was shell-shocked and slowly stood up to a round of applause and struggled as best I could to the stage and there was this MP vigorously shaking my hand. Mum and dad were there and must have felt very pound. The rest of the evening was a bit of a blur. The MP came up to me afterwards and said that the reward for this prize was a visit to the House of Commons in London and tea overlooking the Thames with him as the guide. It was an amazing evening.

As I said before the ATC was designed to groom pilots for the RAF. I must have notched up many visits to the annual Farnborough Air Show by this time and was totally mesmerized by the military fighter aircraft. In those days there were few restrictions on what they did to impress the crowd. One aircraft was the Hawker Hunter. It was an all-British product with sleek swept back wings and looked beautiful streaking about five feet above the ground along the runway about thirty feet away. I can remember a formation of 22 black painted aircraft dubbed the 'Black Arrows' of 111 Squadron performing a perfect loop. It was spectacular to watch. I believe this feat has never been repeated. There was the mighty Avro Vulcan bomber showing its paces as well. This aircraft had a huge delta wing and seemed to

gyrate around the sky like a fighter. It was painted white all over.
What a fantastic sight. The thought of flying one of these RAF aircraft
was on my mind all the time. In those days the RAF was a very large
organization with countless aircraft and bases all over the world. So I
set my heart on joining the RAF when I left school. Must buckle down
to the English though!

Back at school the time was now moving fast towards the dreaded
'O' level exams. It was 'All hands to the tiller' to get ready for these
exams. All thoughts of enjoying the weekends were drowned out by
the schoolwork needed. I seem to recall going for eight subjects or
thereabouts. My sister had sailed through them some years before so
the pressure was on. June approached and the tempo was supersonic.
Then the day came when we all filed into the main hall and gingerly
sat down at our allotted desks for the first exam. With eight subjects to
contend with the brain was bulked out with facts and figures. Sciences
were OK but the others were totally alien to me. French was one subject
on the desperate list. It seemed like an eternity but finally the last
one was done and a great sigh of relief came over me. I mentioned the
French exam earlier since one part of it was to walk into this room
and face the examiner across the table and attempt to speak perfect
French to him. He would ask the questions in French and I would look
into a corner hoping for inspiration. There was none to be found in that
corner. Maybe the other corner might help. A total failure I am afraid.
These examiners had the gift of weeding out the hopeless ones like me
and the confrontation would be cut short. As I left I could imagine the
red pen coming out.

The summer that year and the welcome school holidays arrived.
I had about seven weeks off and I could only describe it as the best
summer holidays of my youth. I was brimming with confidence about
my future. It was to be the RAF. I pondered deeply about the flying I
was getting at White Waltham and thought to myself that if I could fly
there I could go up to any RAF station and do likewise. Not that I was
becoming bored with the flying to date but I had a sense of adventure.
So how do I get to these new stations? The solution was simple. I would
don my ATC uniform and stand at the side of the road and stick my
thumb out and hope some kind driver would stop and help me on my

way. In those days there was little danger of getting into problems or so it seemed. I must have looked a right sight standing there with my thumb out. There were, however, two more RAF stations within bike range of Wokingham so they were worth a trial run. The first was RAF Odiham in Hampshire which was about 20 miles away. No problems on the bike for a fit lad like me. I remember arriving at the gatehouse and asking the standard question. Low and behold I was ushered to a building where all the pilots were milling about. Up went the salute again and this pilot looked at me and nodded when I said:

"I would like to go on a flight please, sir."

The usual survey of the black board showing the activities of the day followed and then he smiled and said: "OK we can get you a flight in a Sycamore."

RAF Odiham was a helicopter station I should add at this point. It boasted a small helicopter type called the Sycamore. It could carry five people including the pilot. The other one there was a large one called a Belvedere. This was a large twin bladed machine capable of carrying up to 18 people. So, I was introduced to the pilot and was led out to this rather ungainly looking machine. I was given a 'Bone Dome' to wear because of the noise that was generated by the engines. This 'Bone Dome' was like a crash helmet with earphones in it. So then I was strapped into the left hand seat. Strange I thought since the Captain always sits there but in the helicopter it is the other way round. I looked around and felt I could touch the ground just by leaning out of the cockpit since we were so near to it. Anyway after a short time and much switch-throwing by the pilot this set of rather flimsy paddle type blades above me started to move in a circular pattern. The whole machine shook and suddenly we went straight up in the air without any moving along the ground like I was used to.

The view was more spectacular than in an aircraft since I was totally surrounded by glass even under my feet. I think the flight lasted about 30 minutes and I can remember descending into this clearing in a local wood and just hovering about one foot off the ground. It was fascinating. The thing that intrigued me was that the controls looked the same as in the Anson but the pilot also held this lever in his free hand as well. I will not go into how it all worked because even to this day I do not understand how it does myself. When we arrived back at RAF Odiham I thanked the pilot and mounted my bike with pride. Another notch in my belt! This outing inspired me to go on further expeditions.

Next in line was RAF Abingdon that was about 30 miles away in Oxfordshire. Now this station had, as its main attraction, a beast called the Blackburn Beverley. I could describe it as having a huge bulbous front end and a skinny rear end. It was built as transport for the RAF to carry tanks and troops into war. Boy was it ugly! In the front end was the space for the tank to fit and then up above in a gallery was the place for the troops to sit. The cockpit was sort of perched on the top. My gatehouse routine was by then perfected and off I went for a flight in this goliath of an aircraft. Space was tight in the cockpit but they found somewhere for me to sit and off we went. We got into the air and then seemed to settle down to a routine of going round the airfield in a sort of circular pattern, landing again and then roaring back into the sky and repeating the process. This was all a bit strange to me. How little did I know about the flying world! So there I was with some three or so RAF aircraft in my logbook.

My final accolade was a visit I made to a United States Air Force (USAF) base, the name of which escapes me. One good thing about being in the ATC was that I was allowed to stay on any RAF base free of charge. Hence I ventured out to somewhere in middle England to really chance my luck. This particular base was in fact leased out to the USAF by the RAF. I have no idea how I knew of it or where it was. But there I was in my uniform with a small suitcase standing at the main gatehouse. This base was huge and boasted an enormous number of American bombers. The one I had my sights on was the mighty Boeing B-52 Stratofortress bomber. This beast is still the biggest in its class today. It has eight jet engines podded four a side under each wing and is just an incredible machine. Many years later in 1991 during operation Desert Storm they flew 35-hour missions out and back to the USA.

Anyway, this aircraft was my target. This time there was no friendly RAF chap but a mountain of a man with an American accent that defied understanding. I said my usual piece and to my amazement he picked up the phone and asked me to wait. After about ten minutes or so this equally enormous American pick-up truck roars up and this officer steps out. He seemed festooned from head to foot in medals and ribbons. I was totally overwhelmed by him and forgot to salute.

"OK, so you want to fly in a B-52 do you?" he said.

"Yes please, sir," I spluttered out.

He beckoned me to jump into the truck and off we went down this never-ending drive. We finally arrived at this splendid array of buildings with very impressive name plates everywhere. I was led into a huge 'Operations Room'.

No blackboards here, I noted.

I was then confronted by a group of USAF pilots who obviously made up a B-52 crew. They were equally decorated with badges, flashes and braid.

"Hey Hank, could you take this fella with you on your flight?"

Was I hearing things or not?

"Yeah, no problem," was the reply.

It transpired that they were off for a training flight somewhere out over the North Sea and I was going along. This was something to be revered. So there I am walking across the tarmac dispersal area towards this enormous aircraft and to think I would be flying in it. We all clamber aboard through a built-in hatch on the forward left hand side. The inside is beyond comprehension in its enormity. I follow meekly towards the cockpit. If I thought the 'Strat' had lots of dials, levers etc this was an understatement. The place was full of them. Some seemed to be put together in an orderly manner but many seemed to be just stuck on here and there. I now had a bone dome on my head and I was shown to a simple fold-down seat somewhere on the left. The flight deck crew consisted of five people and all scurried to their assigned positions. I just sat there trying to take it all in.

The tempo of pace soon hotted up as the aircraft started to come to life. From where I was I could not see too much out of the windows so relied on feel alone as to what was happening. Talking about the windows I was amazed how small they were for such a large beast. Anyway, I felt us move slowly away and the crew member nearest to me had hooked in the earphones so that I could take it all in. The chat was impossible to understand consisting of short sharp phrases but that did not worry me since here I was.

The mood in the cockpit changed up a gear so I assumed we were approaching the runway. The aircraft stopped and one of the crew members started this ritual of pushing this collection of levers forward as if they were welded together as one. Various words were uttered and then I felt the whole aircraft lurching forward. We were on the way. I stared at the dials all moving in unison and suddenly the rumble of the wheels became silent. I was airborne in a B-52. The aircraft seemed to float upwards gently as if destined for the outer limits of the sky. I then felt a turn and strained to see what was happening. My friendly crew member then leaned over and released my harness and beckoned me to stand up. The view was amazing with all the people there doing their own thing in such a relaxed way. I got a view out of the front windows and saw bits of sky and then the English coastline came into view during a turn.

The chatter of earlier reduced to the odd word now and then. It must have been mid-afternoon by the time we reached what must have been the destination area. The tempo picked up and whatever they did for their training started. There were English people on the radio and when mixed with the accents in the cockpit produced a very cosmopolitan atmosphere. I managed a sneak look out of the side window and looked back at the huge wing supporting these four engines. It seemed that the whole of the North Sea was taken up by this wing alone. This 'Training' section of the flight must have taken about two hours or so and as an innocent bystander it seemed quite intense since the aircraft turned this way and that way continually. At the end of this period everyone seemed to settle down and again the tempo dropped.

"Time for chow, anyone?" a crew member said.

My friendly crew member stood up and led me down to the lower deck area. The galley was situated at the rear of the aircraft and to get to it involved travelling along on a sort of cart which ran the full length of the aircraft. The galley was large and seemed to cater for every taste. Totally forget what I ate but compared with those antique morsels on the Anson this was totally gourmet. I indulged on everything on that flight and was very sorry to arrive back to where we had started from some five hours earlier. I now realized that the time was about 7 in the evening. Once again my friendly crew member took me in hand and arranged for me to stay on the base for the night. What an incredible experience. The following day I made my way back home with my faithful thumb by my side.

"Mum, have I got a story for you," I must have blurted out upon arrival.

Totally content with my B-52 outing I settled for the local RAF bases for my flying adventures for the rest of the summer. On one occasion at White Waltham I spotted a small single-engine trainer called a 'Percival Provost' sitting on the tarmac. The pilot had dropped into the station for a day for a meeting of some sorts. My confidence was up so I asked him if he take me up for a spin. The answer was: "Yes. No problem."

So off I went strapped side by side in this small machine. After take-off we went to what could be described as the local flying area allocated to the RAF for local activities.

"OK, young man," he said over the now familiar headset. "Do you fancy doing some aerobatics?"

"Yes please, sir" was my reply in as confident a voice as I could muster.

Now, aerobatics are not for the faint-hearted and consist of putting the body, that happens to be connected to the aircraft by a harness, into the most unusual and strange positions. We went through a sort of checklist and then we were off. The first manoeuvre was a simple loop. What happens is that the aircraft dives down so that all you are looking at is the Earth and then with a mighty heave the pilot pulls back on the controls and suddenly you are looking at the heavens. My body, or stomach more especially, was just catching up with me whilst I was pointing straight up when low and behold the pilot keeps pulling back and there I am pointing at the ground again having been totally upside down, hanging in my harness for what seemed like an eternity but was in fact only a few seconds. We finally get straight and level again and the pilot took a look at me to check that I am still in this world or elsewhere. I am still here in this world but a bit shell-shocked.

He seemed satisfied.

The next one is called a barrel roll. This one is where the aircraft starts off sort of level and then is rotated a complete circle around its own axis. So off we go again. Now this one I enjoyed since I could relate to the ground most of the time. I did not seem to be suspended in my harness at all which I had found to be an 'out of body' experience. There then followed a number of these aerobatic manoeuvres. Some I liked and others I did not like at all. In fact, some were really horrible if I could put it in simple terms. After some 30 minutes or so we settled down to making our way back to White Waltham. The pilot let me fly the aircraft for a while and that I really did enjoy. What amazed me was the aircraft actually stayed in one piece. When we landed I did my customary salute and went off home with another feather in my cap.

As an aside, let me cover some of the national headlines that were around then. In the music world a new group from Liverpool called 'The Beatles' had burst onto the scene. They totally revolutionized the world of pop music. Many more groups followed including a group called 'The Rolling Stones'. You either became a 'Stones' or a 'Beatles' fan. There was a pop newspaper called the New Musical Express that produced the top ten hit single chart. It came out weekly and all schoolwork ceased while we all studied the charts. It was all very serious stuff at the time.

The other subject that burst onto the front pages was the exploration of outer space. Back in 1957 the Soviets managed to put a satellite called 'Sputnik' into orbit around the Earth. I remembered that it was a Sunday morning when I read about it. I was first up in the house and the Sunday Express was jammed in the door. I had a read and there it was plastered all over the front page. My mind did not absorb the impact that this would cause but it stirred my imagination.

Little did I know that the Americans were totally 'caught on the hop' over this Sputnik business. Four months later the newly formed National Aeronautic and Space Administration (NASA) put the first American Satellite up called Explorer 1. This act started the famous space race between the Americans and the Soviets. Don't forget that back then in the 50s and 60s the west was ready to do battle with the east for supremacy of the world. The ability to go into outer space fascinated me and I would gloat over any snippet of information I could get hold of. Imagine the papers reporting in 1962 that a soviet 'Cosmonaut' called Yuri Gagarin had gone into orbit around the Earth and had come back safely. A couple of months later the Americans sent their own 'Astronaut' Alan Shepard up on a short hop of about 15 minutes or so. The space race was hotting up all right. It was not until a year later when the famous American Astronaut John Glenn finally did his three orbits. Also, during 1962 a new American President called John F Kennedy was elected in America. So what you might think, but read on.

As for me, I was enjoying the summer like no other. Flying was mixed with other great activities. One of these was a little known passion I had for horse riding. We had local stables and my sister and I would ride over there together. The deal was that if we looked after the horses for the day then we would get a free ride in the evening. I had no problem with this and became quite adept at clearing out a stable of the muck only a horse can produce. The stables were run by a chap called George and he was affectionately known as 'Uncle George'.

When the time came to the free evening ride we all assembled in the stable yard to be told which horse we were to ride. Now, the stables were laid out so that all the horses were in their own stall separated by a metal barrier facing the wall as you went in. There must have been about two dozen or so all peacefully standing there. On the left hand and right hand ends were two stalls to house the troublesome horses. The one on the right was a fiery redhead called 'Radiance' and it took a lot of handling to keep out of the way of the hooves and teeth when doing the clearing out. So which horse was I assigned as a routine? Yes, you guessed it. The redhead and I were to become an item for the hour's ride.

The other thing that would happen is that the horses and riders would assemble in a field and wait for Uncle George to arrive to lead the ride. Have you ever tried to control a mad beast whose only aim was to kick and bite every other horse around her? By the time the ride was fully assembled you could spot this distant image of me and Radiance somewhere over the other side of the field with me trying to stay upright and the horse determined to get rid of me. So the ride finally got under way and I was usually left trailing behind in some sort of semi-control. The area where we rode was through woodlands with no roads, so if I parted company with the horse then the fall from grace would not be too bone rattling.

Now here's a funny thing! After a while we got on OK and I found that by talking to Radiance things would settle down and some sort of order would evolve. She was very high spirited and strong. She would canter along fine and I would fit into the stride well. Trotting was a bit trickier since somehow you had to match the up and downs of the horse with your own artificial movement. The problem was making that elusive match. If you met the saddle while it was on the 'up' and you were on the 'down' then the result was a short sharp pain in one the most delicate areas of the male body. Then we come to the full gallop. This tested both horse and rider to the extreme. The horse was hell bent on speed and the rider was equally hell bent on trying to stay on and look cool. From the height of the saddle the ground looked a blur below so you gritted your teeth, with maybe a hint of tongue showing, determined to 'hang on in there'.

What was amazing enough was that I think I only fell off once in my riding days which looking back is not a bad achievement. In retrospect I think the reason that I was given this beast was to actually make me ride properly. As time went on the redhead and I found some common ground and the rides became very enjoyable. Mind you these ladies had to be watched.

In the late August I was brought down to earth with a bump since the 'O' level results were due out. The day of reckoning duly arrived and so off I trotted to school to get my results. I opened the envelope with fear and trepidation. After slowly tearing back the various parts of the envelope I peeped inside and took a glimpse at the results. The outcome was that I had passed six subjects and failed two. Yes, you have guessed it! I failed English as you would expect but the other one surprised me. I had failed Geography. I was amazed by this since I had been to a few countries by then. They were not total failures but what you might call borderline ones. The passes were not too bad at all with a Grade one in Chemistry and a three in Maths. I made my way home and there the reception committee was waiting.

"OK, your sister did better so you had better retake the two failures next year," were Dad's only words.

I had expected worse. My sister was now at Exeter University studying Maths so there was a lot to make up for.

The year drifted by with the autumn term at school. In the October an international crisis hit the headlines. It was known as the 'Cuban Missile Crisis'. The Russians had elected to site missiles in the Castro-controlled Caribbean Island of Cuba. John F Kennedy, the US president, was not amused and the world came closer to war as never before. It was very serious and was only defused when the Russian ships carrying the missiles were turned back in Mid-Atlantic and the world could breathe again. I can remember being in a Maths lesson at the time when the master informed us that war had been averted. This all sounds very dramatic but it was real as was revealed many years later when the official notes for the time were released.

As usual Christmas arrived with the usual flurry of parties. These were now being split between those involving me and my friends and those that involved the 'grown-ups'. Either way the festive period was spent juggling between both. The school held a joint dance with my sister's ex-school and that was always a recipe for some fun and frolics. If I recall the area outside just behind the school venue was pretty busy with all sorts of things going on. It must have been cold out there but I think that didn't seem to matter since other things were on the mind. Anyway, the year finally came to an end.

So, 1963 arrived and I attained the dizzy heights of seventeen years of age. I retook the two failed 'O' level exams in the February. The results would not be out until the June.

A whole new world now opened up for me since at this tender age I was eligible to complete a basic gliding course with the ATC. This I did with the venue being RAF White Waltham again. It was carried out over the weekends and so off I went for my first lesson. The glider for the basic tuition was the Slingsby Sedbergh and was a simple side-by-side trainer. It got nick-named the 'Sedbarge' at the time based on its poor performance and almost agricultural construction. It was, however, considered to be of the latest technology of the day.

With no engine, the procedure to get you into the air was simple but effective. At one end of the airfield was a very large RAF winch which trailed its cables across the field to the waiting gliders. The end of the cable was hooked on to the glider and the instructor and I were strapped in. A series of light signals to the winch operator in parallel to shouted commands followed. The first was 'Take up slack' whereby the cable started to straighten out and then when the glider plus contents started to move slowly 'All away' was shouted together with the rapid flashing of the signal lamp. At this point the winch operator hit the 'go' pedal and the glider roared off down the field at ever increasing speed. Instructor and pupil were subjected to a sudden rush of air and pushed towards the seat backstop. The instructor then heaved back on the controls and suddenly we were propelled upwards at about 45 degrees going straight up or so it seemed.

I sat there transfixed, trying to overcome the cold air and get the face back into order. After a short while things seemed to settle down with the glider no longer going for orbit but almost level with the Earth. A lever was pulled somewhere beneath our feet and suddenly we were as free as a bird floating at about one thousand feet above the Earth. It was so quiet and peaceful without an engine roaring away. It was lovely. No time to waste since once up there we had to get back on land and preferably at our starting point and not some muddy field. We gently turned to the right and there we were heading the other way leaving the airfield out on the right side. As with all things influenced by gravity we would slowly drift downwards and the thought occurred to me: not a chance of me sorting this one out!

Anyway, we carried on flying gently in this direction to a point where we had started the flight, passed just under the right hand wing and then we turned right again and descended a bit more until we seemed at a point where the ground seemed awfully close and then we turned right again as if touching the ground and low and behold there was the landing area as we had been shown. Being about two feet above the ground I felt as though I could almost walk it on since we must have been doing about 30 miles an hour. This was my first flight in the glider world and it was great.

As the flights built up then the instructor handed over the flying to me as his name implied. I was here for serious work! One small intrusion in the training programme was the fact that the cable might break whilst climbing up. At one point in my course this was introduced as the one and only emergency that might occur. So there we were confidently climbing to orbit with me in control and feeling pretty good when the instructor would say: "Is that an aircraft over there?"

So my eyes drifted away for a look.

"I don't see an aircraft, sir," I was just about to say when– Zappo! He had pulled the release lever and waited for my response. So there I was climbing up without a care in the world being pulled by this cable and suddenly it was gone. As I said all things attracted to gravity get their way and the glider was no exception. You basically ran out of energy to go up very quickly and, if not sorted out, could take the glider to the point of no return. This would result in a phenomenon called a 'wing stall' rapidly followed by a rather undignified return to Earth. Positively dangerous! What was needed was a sharp push down on the controls to avoid this stall and then once that was sort of under control find somewhere to land within the airfield. Unlike an aircraft with an engine you had to land within the field. All part of self-preservation you know. I must have been OK coping with my first emergency since I do not recall landing in anyone's garden.

So, after maybe ten flights in the 'Sedbarge' I progressed onto the so-called advance trainer. This was the Slingsby Cadet Mk 3. Now this was to my mind a bit of a sporty beast. It was slimmer than the 'Sedbarge' and you sat one in front of the other as opposed to side-by-side. It seemed to slice through the air and was altogether a much more flighty creature. So I continued my weekends at White Waltham until the great day came when the instructor strapped me in as usual and then said: "OK, off you go on your own just as you have been doing so far with me."

I must have gulped, shuddered or uttered some strange word or two. So, there I sit, with all eyes on me waiting for the commands being shouted somewhere out there on the horizon. Suddenly I am off with no turning back. OK the climb up is good and there I am suspended at the end of the cable. I release it and turn to the right just like before.

"Blimey, where has the airfield gone? It was there a minute ago.

CHAPTER 2

Phew, there it is!"

And so I drift in the right direction almost staring at the field.

"Must watch the speed."

"Now where do I turn in for the landing?"

"Ah yes I remember now. There it is."

I must have talked to myself throughout the whole flight. So round I go and end up facing the right direction at about the right height. So now the landing bit is coming up and all my concentration is taken up on this. Maybe a bit of tongue is showing! Suddenly I feel the bump of the grass as I complete the re-entry. I sat there with a big cheesy grin on my face. I had just gone solo. The pick-up truck arrives and drags me off the control column that I was still clutching. I got back to the starting point and my instructor walks up to me and he shakes my hand.

"Well done. Now off you go again but this time when you release the cable do a complete left hand circle and then carry on as before," he said casually.

This was not in the script, I thought.

I only just managed to keep sight of the airfield last time, let alone do some gyration up there. So I was strapped in again and awaited my fate. I released the cable and off I went to the left instead of the comfortable right. I kept going around until I felt that I had done the feat of the century and scanned the horizon for the airfield. This was really nerve-racking. It must be somewhere out there. I remember shouting for joy when I spotted it. I had achieved the impossible.

Now, to do this extra manoeuvre took time and height and the airfield looked a bit bigger than usual. I looked at my altimeter and yes, we were lower than usual. So off I went following the well-trodden road in the sky wondering how I could deal with this height problem. I came to a point a bit short of the usual place to turn for the landing and decided to cut it a bit short and swing in early. Was this was my first ever in-flight decision? It worked OK apart from the fact I must have nearly decapitated people standing around the launch area. I was ceremoniously towed back to the start to a few stern faces but in general quite pleased that I had done the required course. What was amazing was that Mum and Dad were standing there amongst the reception committee. They must have known something was in the air on that particular day. I felt like the king of the heap. I was on the way in the flying world.

In June the results of my retake of the two 'O' level exams came through and to my amazement I had passed them. So now I had eight 'O' levels under my belt including the dreaded English.

Clever bugger I am. Catching my sister up, I thought.

By this time Dad was established as a fully-fledged Flight Navigator on the De Havilland Comet 4. This jet was the product of the De Havilland stable and descended from the infamous Comet 1 which ended its days early due to metal fatigue problems. The opportunity for Dad to apply for a posting to Sydney, Australia for three months was available and early in July off he went on this posting. Mum, my sister and I followed a few days later.

So there we were all sitting in the First Class section of the Comet 4 on our way to Australia. In those days the first class was really quite superb. There was no 'in-flight entertainment' to watch but the sheer ambience was intoxicating. The journey was much longer than today since there were quite a few refuelling stops on the way. I can remember leaving Singapore en-route to Darwin, Northern Australia via Jakarta in Indonesia. While we were on the ground at Darwin the Captain told us that during the approach we had ingested a bird into one of the engines and that we were all in for a night stop in Darwin until the engine could be changed. Another adventure was starting!

We were all taken to the local rest house owned by the Australian airline Qantas. It was a rather basic collection of buildings but it was the only place available. My room was about eight feet by six feet with an old fashioned hospital-style single bed. The next day we boarded a coach for a day out in the Australian countryside. All sounds very familiar if I think back to Shannon many years before. I remember the evening meal in the rest house. Being in Australia the diet was usually based around meat. Really good!

So, after dinner I wandered back to my room having been told that we had to be ready to go flying next morning. I opened the door to my room and there sitting on top of my clothes in my open suitcase was a huge frog. I must point out at this point that I did not like spiders or anything similar. Frogs came into that class. I slowly looked around and found that this frog was not alone. There was another one sitting on my pillow. Things were getting bad! It later transpired that the rest house had been built on a swamp, hence the regular invasion of creatures. OK, so I had two unwanted visitors for the night. I looked with fear and trepidation under the bed and there was the biggest, furriest, ugliest spider I had ever seen in my life. It must have been about six inches across and it just sat there motionless. I beat a hasty retreat back through the entrance door and stumbled to the reception. It must have been late in the evening because there was only this solitary person in attendance. I spluttered out my problem to him and he seemed to dismiss it as if it was a normal night occurrence.

"I wonder where his mate is then?" he said casually.

The thought of going back to the nest of vipers now taking up residence in my room horrified me so I decided to camp out in the reception area for the night. Finally the morning came and there I was sitting waiting for everybody to arrive and get me out of this hellhole. I had persuaded the receptionist to check my room out and pack my case for me. I think I actually must have pleaded with him on bended knee. We eventually left Darwin for Sydney that afternoon – back to civilization.

Sydney is an amazing city dominated by the famous Harbour Bridge or 'The Coathanger' as it was known. It was criss-crossed with waterways and ferries were the main transport to many suburbs. Dad had established himself in a suburb called Manly together with other BOAC colleagues. The way to get there was to go down to the ferry terminal at Circular Quay situated right under the Harbour Bridge and take the famous 'Manly Ferry' to our new home. Dad had met us at the airport so we had our local guide. As we approached Manly Dad pointed out our new home and soon we were installed in a flat in an apartment block called the 'Ambassador Buildings'. So this was to be my new home for some two and a half months.

After a couple of days of getting my bearings I had settled in fine. There was a small shopping parade in Manly with a beach at the far end. I could compare it with a typical seaside town in England except for this strange accent that uttered forth from the local people. Not far from Manly was a headland called 'South Heads' which was a Mecca for people to gaze out across the Harbour towards the city. It was about four miles to walk it from our new home so off I went most days to get my daily exercise. Dad would go off to work on the ferry and we would stand on the balcony of the flat and wave to him as he left the jetty. The same occurred when he came home. The routes he flew were simply up to Singapore and back. What a lovely routine we had. The weather was not too bad considering it was the Australian winter.

After a while I began to think about what else I could get up to. I had packed my ATC uniform and managed to get in contact with the local Australian equivalent of the ATC. I was now a sergeant complete with three stripes on my sleeve. So off I went to the local meeting one evening and joined in the local activities. It was amazing but the meetings were similar to the ones in England and I felt quite at home – apart from the accent, of course. There was even some flying that could be done. This was good stuff! We went to the local Royal Australian Air Force (RAAF) base at Richmond which was about 30 miles away. So there I was flying around the countryside in the back of a Dakota of the RAAF. Another success I thought! I also joined in a visit to the local marine air sea rescue centre and went for a boat trip around the harbour in this monster of a speedboat. It was a great time out there.

Now here is a funny thing! Total change of subject now follows. Earlier in this story I covered the subject of the opposite sex. To date I had got to nine on the infamous list but things were about to change. Amongst the other sons and daughters was a Flight Engineer's daughter who took my fancy. Well, things between us got a bit out of hand and there I was with the full ten on the scoreboard. Blimey I had 'cracked the nut' as they say. What was all the fuss about? There seemed to be lots of fumbling and sounds I had never come across before. Funnily enough we got the taste for it and so began the perfecting of the act itself for maximum enjoyment.

At one time during my time in Sydney Dad got hold of a car and we went exploring the local area. We ended up in the Blue Mountains at a phenomenal collection of rocks called the 'The Three Sisters'. We stayed overnight at a place called Katoomba and enjoyed the spectacle of these amazing formations illuminated at night. After some ten weeks the posting came to an end and Dad decided to make the return journey a bit of an adventure holiday. We all flew to Singapore and stayed with another Flight Navigator posted there and enjoyed a wonderful few days exploring the place.

We then flew to Hong Kong for a few days. Hong Kong was a fascinating place. It was full of hustle and bustle with the local Chinese going about their business. As a seventeen year-old I found it all quite mind-blowing. This was Hong Kong in the 60s. There were no high rises anywhere and the main centre was Kowloon on the mainland with Hong Kong Island only just beginning to emerge as the magnet that it is today. The harbour was twice the size compared with today and filled with Chinese Junks pottering about doing their business. Dad had really pushed the boat out on this one. I remember being taken to Aberdeen Harbour and ferried out to one of the two huge floating restaurants for lunch. What an experience Hong Kong was!

We left Hong Kong behind us and flew to Honolulu via Tokyo in the new Boeing 707. What a way to travel! In my short lifetime I had gone from flying the old 'Strat' to this amazing airliner. In aviation, technology was moving very fast. I needed to be part of it. We arrived in Honolulu for another few days. I don't recall too much about the island so maybe it did not impress me too much. Bit of a casual remark there!

We then flew on to San Francisco on the American West Coast. This was my first insight into the metropolis of an American city at an age that I could appreciate it. What an insight that was. The cars were enormous. The houses were enormous. Everything was enormous. I was in my element in the food department since the portions were enormous. Unfortunately I had developed a bit of a 'tub' since I was not out on my bike everyday as I would have been in England. We arrived back early September in time for school. Ugh!

So off I went back to the autumn term at school. I joined a class known as the 'sixth form'. I was concentrating on the Sciences and got rid of all the arty sort of subjects. I settled for Maths, Physics and Chemistry. The bonus for this elevation to the advanced level in school was that there were periods allocated for private study. School was taking on a different style and I felt totally in the mould for the future.

It was at one of the ATC meetings on 22nd November when I was actually taking the parade of cadets that one of the officers interrupted the proceedings to inform us all that the president of the United States, John F Kennedy, had been assassinated in Dallas, Texas. It later transpired that the nasty deed had been carried out by a Lee Harvey Oswald acting alone. He, in fact, was shot dead by Jack Ruby whilst in police custody two days later. It was one of those moments in history that everybody remembers: when JFK was shot. Back to the Wild West!

Another Christmas came and went and there I was in 1964 at the age of eighteen. I had decided on a future in the RAF. My yearning for that life was to come in the March with a visit to RAF Biggin Hill in Kent to start the application towards the ultimate goal of becoming a fighter pilot. I can remember being ushered into this room and that for interview and tests. A medical was part of it all together with various aptitude tests. I went home with mixed feelings about the visit. In the April I got a letter from the RAF saying that I had passed the preliminary tests and inviting me back later that month for a more comprehensive session. I was over the moon. I was on the way.

I arrived again at Biggin Hill together with about 20 other candidates. We were told that we would have further tests over two days and that some of us would be transported to RAF Cranwell in Lincolnshire for further evaluation. Cranwell was to the RAF what Oxford or Cambridge was to the academic world. This was the ultimate place to go to. After a couple of days we were all invited to an interview to inform those of us that would be going. Well, my name was picked to go to Cranwell. So far so good! This is what dreams were made of. The RAF coach arrived and off we went to Cranwell. We were by now whittled down to about eight of us. We arrived at Cranwell late in the evening and were shown our temporary quarters.

"It all starts tomorrow, gentlemen," were the final words I heard that night.

We were there for maybe three days and got involved with a multitude of tests. I can remember one where we were given a choice of solutions to a tactical problem and asked for our choice. We got involved in playing games on an obstacle course. I seemed to fare OK but did not feel too comfortable suspended on a telegraph pole traversing an imaginary river unable to go backwards or forwards leaving people on either bank stuck. The officers were filling in things on their clipboards all the time. I was number nineteen, I remember. Other tests were based on interviews on a one-to-one basis. I tried to cover up my Berkshire accent since these people were speaking the most eloquent Queen's English. I felt out of place. I remember one interview where this crusty old Wing Commander asked me about my parents. I chirped up by saying that Dad was a Flight Navigator. He seemed to like that but came back at me with: "Excellent. What squadron was he with?"

"What do you mean what squadron? He is with BOAC and I am very proud of him," I replied.

"Oh, not one of us then!" he said dismissively.

Now, that got my back up at that point since I felt that Dad was as good as the rest. I must have betrayed my feelings since the rest of the interview did not go well. He questioned whether I felt I would pass my 'A' levels in the summer. No idea what I said but I am sure he was not impressed. The group I was with all had similar experiences so we spent a lot of time commiserating amongst ourselves. We eventually all departed after these gruelling few days back home with mixed feelings all around. Letters would be posted within three weeks as to the final results. I was not happy and felt that all would be lost.

The other thing that happened at about the same time was that I qualified within the ATC to be awarded an RAF Flying Scholarship. This was a great opportunity to complete a basic Private Pilot's Licence course at White Waltham, all paid for by the RAF. It involved staying at RAF White Waltham over the Easter break and completing a two-week course with the local flying school called the West London Aero Club. The final outcome would be a flying licence to fly privately.

This was a great chance to see whether I had what it took to fulfil my dream. There were six of us who reported to the club on the appointed day. The aircraft used was a rather old basic single engine high wing monoplane called an Auster J1N. OK it was old but it looked good to me. I can remember walking out to this Auster and sitting in the cockpit with this ex-RAF flying instructor. The starting sequence was based on a mechanic swinging the propeller and then shouting to whoever was in the tiny cockpit to put the main switches on. He then gave a mighty heave on the propeller in the right direction and low and behold the engine fired up. The instruments were pretty basic but that did not worry me at all. I was there to learn to fly.

White Waltham in those days was a large field with the active runway of the day marked by a caravan at the start. We had no radios so we had to rely on signals from this caravan as to what we were allowed to do. So we taxied out under the guidance of the caravan's light signals. We would sit next to it and await a green flashing light that gave us permission to take off. So off we went and my flying course had started. The initial part was to get you good enough to go solo. This involved a lot of what we called 'Circuit Bashing' whereby all we did was to take off and circle the airfield and land again and then take off and repeat the process. All the time we were meant to keep an eye on the caravan as to whether we were allowed to land or not. You really had to concentrate as it made the gliding look like a walk in the park.

Occasionally we left the airfield area and practised other things in the flying world. There was a phenomenon in the flying world called a 'Spin' where the aircraft is basically out of control due to a wrong input on the controls. The result is a very stable, circling motion downwards with no escape if you could not recover from it. Up to this point I thought all aircraft just flew as you wanted them to without all these extra complications. As I said, I was there to learn, so I buckled down to it and found I could master these extras with little problem.

Then came the great day when the instructor gave you the signal to go off on your own. Off I trundled across the grass to the famous caravan and awaited the signal to go. I sat there full of trepidation and fear and when the signal came I took a deep breath and off I went on my own. It was only one circuit and landing but it worked out OK and I taxied back in with a grin from ear to ear. Another feather in the cap!

Now you might think that from that point on all would be plain sailing. I was told to go off flying on my own to the local area and enjoy my time as a reward for going solo. I will point out that whenever it was a bit windy the drill was to pull the controls all the way back and to latch them under the adjacent seat belt next to you. Whether it was normal practice or a bad habit I had picked up I will never know. So, off

I go with the controls strapped under this belt since it was a bit windy and then I waited by the caravan for the 'go' signal. It duly came and I casually and over-confidently lined up and opened up the engine power and started the take-off. I was about twenty seconds into the take-off when my left hand must have realized that something was missing. Yes it was the controls that were missing! I looked down and realized my error and grappled with the seat belt to release this vital part of the flight. Meanwhile, by this time I was roaring away across the airfield like some demented maniac. Finally it came adrift and I spiralled into the air like a homesick angel since the controls were set in the fully-back position. I managed to control the flying beast after a short while and all seemed OK apart from a heartbeat out of control and one very hot and bothered pilot.

What happened next is inexplicable. One of the after take-off checks is to apply the handbrake and then release it so that the wheels stop spinning. In my haste to do this I accidentally flicked two vital switches for the engine to the 'off' position and suddenly there was the propeller standing still in front of my eyes like a flag pole. All the noise had gone and I was suspended in time and space with nowhere to go. My heartbeat hit the ceiling again. I quickly realized what I had done and flicked the switches to the 'on' position. Nothing happened so I pushed the aircraft nose down and thought that the only way of escape was to put me and the aircraft onto the ground somewhere. What saved me was that by putting the aircraft in a nose-down position the propeller caught the slipstream and suddenly turned and the engine fired up. What a bloody mess I was! Where was I? No idea at all! Somewhere in Southern England in the air that is all I knew. I managed a slow look around and found the airfield somewhere behind me and there was this chap in the caravan standing on the roof flashing all sorts of signals at me. The signal was to land and go back to the flying school now – not later. His simple, mundane, boring life had been interrupted by the thing called a pilot leaping in the air like someone possessed and then stopping the engine when he felt like it.

"Let's get this chap back on the ground before he kills someone" must have been his immediate response.

I was in a state of shock by this time and I obeyed the signal like a tame lapdog and landed out of reach from the prying eyes of the caravan man and scurried back to the flying school. My instructor knew something was up and came over to me as I fell out of the Auster and literally kissed the earth. I confessed all to him and he just laughed and said: "It's always the second solo that is the worst."

I crawled away to lick my wounds. My instructor was having none of this. So, after lunch I taxied out again in the same aircraft. This time I gripped the controls like someone possessed and approached the caravan again. I wished I had a false moustache on at the time. It transpired that there was a different person in there and everything seemed normal. So off I went for my bit of local flying. Everything went well. I had, in reflection, learned a great lesson about flying. I have never forgotten it to this day.

The course continued and various exercises confronted me. Up to this point I had only flown in the airfield circuit or the local flying area. I came to the point in the course when I had to fly to another airfield. This was known as a 'cross country flight'. It was all part of the course curriculum. I flew with an instructor to some fictitious point about 60 miles away and then returned to White Waltham. It seemed to go quite well and the instructor seemed pleased. The flight was simply based on drawing a line on the map, getting its direction and then plotting how the wind would affect the route. The variable part of all of this was the fact that the forecast wind might not be the actual wind on the day since the forecasting was based on human interpretation plus an enormous amount of variables.

So, the day arrives and I am told to fly to an airfield in Oxfordshire called Thame and back to qualify for this part of the course. I studied the map and finally found Thame and nervously started the planning. The time arrived and off I went. The aircraft chosen was a newer Auster that came with quite comfortable seats and even an electric starter for the engine. This was the Beagle Auster Terrier. This was definitely an improvement on the older type I was used to. When I flew with the instructor previously on the cross-country it all seemed very relaxed but now there was only me to deal with me.

I can tell you it was nerve racking. Was the forecast wind right or not? It was not bad and after about 40 or so minutes I managed to find the town of Thame... but where was the airfield? I wished I could stop in the air and study the map. Not possible! Suddenly I spotted the airfield and looked for directions to land etc. Without a radio the only clues available to sort out the active runways etc of any airfield was a large black display about fifty metres square that had a lot of visual indicators according to the details of the day. The most prominent one was a large 'T' indicator showing which runway to use for landing and take-off. I studied the display and then spotted another aircraft on the runway. All good stuff, I thought! I gingerly went round the circuit and landed and made my way to the local flying club area. I stopped the engine and clambered out and got the secretary to sign the piece of paper I had clutched in my hand. So, after a hasty cup of coffee I departed Thame and headed back to White Waltham. Thankfully the town of Reading was very large and distinctive so the flight back was less dramatic than the one out. I landed at White Waltham and handed in the required piece of paper. All done! The course continued and finally I was awarded a Private Pilot's Licence. The ironic thing was that I was awarded a licence to fly before I had passed my driving test to be able to drive a car solo. I did pass my driving test two months later.

In early May the letter arrived from the RAF selection board informing me that I had been unsuccessful with my application to go to Cranwell to be a pilot in the RAF, but they felt I was more suited to be an engineer and offered me a technical cadetship at RAF Henlow. Me, an engineer! Not a chance! So there I was snookered at the first ball. I was so intent on joining the RAF as a fighter pilot and that chance had gone. What was I to do? I was now within striking distance of taking these wretched 'A' level exams and had got my first refusal at employment. I pondered at length as to the direction of my life. In the end I must have shrugged my shoulders in the belief that something might turn up.

It was not long before the summer holidays arrived. By this time I was well established in the ATC with the grand rank of Flight Sergeant. Up to this point I attended the Friday night meetings regularly with very few absences. Early that summer I was asked to help out with forming a separate smaller section or 'Detached Flight' in the Wokingham area. This I accepted without reservation and together with a friend we started the venture. We had the use of the local British Army hall in Wokingham together with a rifle range alongside. The result was that we accumulated a ramshackle group of boys from the local area and met every Tuesday evening.

The facilities were first class and I soon saw an opportunity to exploit the skills I had accumulated at Bracknell. Amazingly enough, the one skill that I possessed at that time was the ability to perform drill or 'square bashing' as they called it. So there I was on the Tuesday evening in Wokingham with this group of lads whom I felt I could mould into something resembling an orderly group. I feel I must pat myself on the shoulder at this stage since I did just that. The Army hall was huge and ideal for the purpose. The format was simple. We did 30 minutes of drill, followed by 30 minutes of lessons and then 30 minutes on the rifle range. Dad helped out with the lessons since navigation was one of the main subjects. For these boys to go on a real rifle range and fire real bullets was reward itself. As for the drill side the results were amazing and within a few weeks I had the perfect squad to enter into local competitions within the ATC.

In those days the ATC was split up into County wings, then individual town squadrons and finally the smaller detached flights. My small detached flight was part of the Berkshire wing. The powers that be organized various competitions within the wing. So I went with my small band for the annual range rifle shooting competition. We won it hands down! Boy did we feel good! The same happened with the drill competitions and soon we were feared by all.

The other side of the ATC was that the RAF provided an Air Experience Flight of Chipmunk aircraft that were based throughout the UK to provide some flying experience for cadets to enjoy. The Chipmunk was a simple trainer used by the RAF at that time. One of these flights became based at RAF White Waltham. I got heavily involved with this venture as well. It was my job to strap the cadets into the rather cumbersome parachutes and help them waddle out to the waiting aircraft. I then strapped the cadet into the rear seat of the cockpit and let the pilot know that all was well and closed the canopy and away he went for a 30 minute flight. I also issued the cadet with the famous RAF sick bag just in case it all went wrong, gastronomically wise, on the flight. On more than one occasion I would rescue the poor cadet and carry him gingerly back to his seat whilst clutching his lunch remains in the famous bag. The reward for this was a flight of my own in early evening. Little did I know that this Chipmunk would have an enormous bearing on my future employment.

The early summer was spent enjoying myself, doing exactly what I wanted to do. I applied within the ATC to join an RAF transport aircraft on a flight to Europe. In those days the RAF was spread all over the world and I was rewarded with a chance to join a crew on a trooping flight to Cyprus. They even issued me a 'Rail Pass' to enable me to get to RAF Lyneham in Wiltshire free of charge. My trusty thumb was not needed.

I arrived at Lyneham and was met at the station and taken to the RAF base for an overnight stay with the flight set for the next morning. The aircraft was to be the Bristol Britannia which I had flown in before with BOAC. I remember the layout was different since it had a large cargo door at the front left hand side and when I boarded it with the crew there was a military 'Land Rover' vehicle all strapped down in the front area and the cabin started at the midsection extending to the rear of the aircraft. The other thing that amazed me was that all the seats faced backwards. Strange thing I thought since it is always nice to see where you are going. I later learnt that this was standard RAF practice.

So off we went off to an RAF base on the Eastern Mediterranean island of Cyprus. The flight time must have been about four hours or so. I visited the cockpit during this time and simply indulged in my surroundings yet again. I remember arriving there late afternoon and getting to the hotel. I had made friends with the two cabin stewards on the way and they invited me out for the evening. We went into Nicosia and spent the evening strolling around. Both of my new friends had been there when the British Army was fighting the local militia in the run up to Independence some years before so I was listening to them reminiscing about that time. We indulged ourselves with some local food and eventually made our way back to the hotel.

The following day we all assembled and departed Nicosia for the flight home. As we flew over the Alps I got a fantastic view since we were lower than modern jet liners. I can remember straining out of the windows looking backwards at the sight of these wondrous mountains with their snow covered peaks. I eventually got home later on that day full of talk about the flight to my ever-patient mum.

The news at the time was dominated by a girl called Christine Keeler who had got involved with a Cabinet Minister, John Profumo, and some Russian embassy people which created a scandal of enormous proportions. Don't forget that in those days we were at the height of the Cold War with Russia and espionage was rife on both sides. The other side of the scandal was that Christine Keeler and her friend Mandy Rice-Davies were call girls of the day and their activities were rated highly immoral. I think that today it would not even have rated in the Sun newspaper. But in those days some new revelation hit the headlines every day. This was good reading for me since the two girls involved were pretty good looking. The trial ended up in the Old Bailey and the subsequent inquiry brought down the government of the Prime Minister, Harold Macmillan. This was a story that even today cannot be bettered.

Now, here is funny thing how fate played its hand. It was in late May and I was sitting having breakfast with Mum. We had, by now, moved from the bungalow to a maisonette not far away. At least it had a decent heating system and no coal to fetch in all weathers. So there I was munching on my cornflakes and reading the Daily Mail spread out on the table in front of me. I remember looking down at the paper and moved my bowl slightly since I had seen a small picture of an aeroplane. Low and behold there was an advert for the 'College of Air Training' at Hamble, near Southampton, on the South Coast for those people who might well be inspired to fly with BOAC or the European equivalent BEA as an airline pilot. I studied the advert very carefully looking for the requirements. OK I had the 'O' levels and would hopefully get the 'A' levels. There I was intent on flying as a fighter pilot and in front of me was the chance to fly as a pilot with BOAC or BEA. I grabbed paper and pen and sent off that morning for further details.

Here it was already May and the chance to go there was in the August. Time was short. I told Dad that I had applied and he seemed to be happy with that. A few days later the application form arrived which

I duly filled in and sent off. The selection process was split into three parts – an initial interview, a flying assessment and a final interview. Within a week a letter arrived inviting me for the initial interview the following week. Dad was around so he drove me to Hamble for this stage. It was ironic that it was the same place that Dad had re-trained as a Flight Navigator many years before.

The initial interview was based around aptitude tests and general group discussions. The panel that oversaw us came from BOAC or BEA. There was also a psychiatrist who did his bit to establish our character. I was there for maybe about three hours and I seemed fine with the various tests put before me. I must have done OK, as about a week later I got a letter inviting me to go for the flying aptitude test. I arrived at Hamble for the test and to my delight I realized that the aircraft used for this test was the Chipmunk that I had flown in many times with the ATC. The tester was a certain 'Tubby' Fieldhouse. I already had a Private Pilot's Licence under my belt so felt fine about doing the test. In fact, it all went very well with only about 20 minutes' flying done. I had passed this one so the only obstacle left was the final interview.

I arrived again in Hamble for this final test. As I have mentioned before, my whole life was centred on aircraft so I had built up a good knowledge in this field. Before this interview Dad revealed that he knew of the BOAC captain that was to hold the one-to-one interviews but said I should also learn all about BEA since there was bound to be questions fired at me from all sides. This interview was spread out over two days and we were subjected to a few more aptitude tests. One I remember was to keep a dot in the centre of a square on a TV screen with controls that had a built-in delay. Tricky to say the least! On day two we were invited to have lunch with the panel. I think the object of this was to check our manners. No slurping of soup allowed there. After lunch came the panel interviews. I remember entering the room with maybe three gentlemen sitting behind this large desk looking pretty fearsome. I was ushered to the victim's chair and waited for the questioning to begin. It all started in a fairly mundane manner with the usual chat about my schooling and my prospects for the forthcoming 'A' levels.

"How do you feel about passing your 'A' level exams?" was a typical question.

"I feel very confident, sir," I replied.

I had learnt from my Cranwell experience not to put any negatives anywhere. The BOAC captain, who had retired some years before, started asking me questions about BOAC. What routes? What aircraft? And so on. I rattled off my replies parrot-fashion since I knew it all. The BEA captain stirred in his seat and then said to me, "OK, you seem to know a lot about BOAC. What do you know about BEA?"

I was ready for this one and replied in great detail about which aircraft, routes etc. I must have impressed him since he had no further questions and he complimented me on my airline knowledge.

"Was this enough?" I thought on the way home.

All was revealed when two weeks later a thick envelope arrived at home that contained all my joining details for the course that was due to begin that August. All I needed to do was pass the 'A' level exams.

The day finally arrived when the dreaded 'A' level exams were to start. As I said before I was taking Physics, Chemistry and Maths. The Maths exam was a written exam in two parts. We all filed into the hall and went through the ritual of writing our names on the first page. The clock ticked over and away we went. I seem to recall that the questions were pretty straightforward and I got started. One thing I had learnt was that if stuck on a question to go on and then come back to the sticky one. The only problem is that when you are stuck on a question time is ticking by at double quick time. Anyway I finished with about two seconds left. This was the first of two Maths papers I had to sit. One down with one to go!

The second Maths paper was the following day and was one of those abstract ones involving a heading called 'Permutations and Combinations'. Let me try to explain. For example, if six people got into a railway carriage with three seats facing the engine and the other three facing the back of the train how many combinations of seating arrangements could be made. Sounds simple, but throw in the additive that one of the assembled group could only sit facing the engine and two of them could only sit by the window, now it really gets complicated. The mind boggles! Anyway I struggled through that one as well. Physics was next on the agenda and consisted of a written exam paper followed by a practical exam in the laboratory. OK I just about coped with the written paper and then we all filed into the laboratory and stood in our assigned spots and stared at the apparatus in front of us trying to drag the brain into action as to what these things all meant and what we were to do with them. I remember looking totally blank and thinking I was in the wrong laboratory when a glimmer of recognition filtered through from somewhere in the back of my brain.

Got it, I thought.

The master in charge of us came around to each of us and dropped the usual exam paper in front of us staring as he went to each in turn looking for sign of life in these blank faces. He got to me and spotted a glimmer of a smile and must have thought that I was either clever or totally stupid. So, off we embarked on this three hour marathon. Did my brain cells deceive me or was the task set for me as simple as I had thought? I remembered back to my endless notes written down and yes I was right! After about two hours I had done it all. This cannot be true, I thought! One hour to spare – surely not. I went over it all again and yes it was all done. I had done the business and the results were written down in front of me. I gingerly put my hand up and the master stirred, looked at the clock, and then back looked at me with a sort of quizzical look. He wandered up and looked at the answers and then cocked his head towards the door and off I went. As I went he looked at me with a sly grin and shaking of the head.

What did that mean? I thought.

Chemistry was next. Now this was my favourite subject and I have to say I excelled at it both in the written word and the practical. Again, the exam was in two parts. The first was the written one and I remember racing through it and completing all the questions on time. So now we came to the practical exam. Back into the laboratory we filed. I can remember the format exactly. We were given a powder in a small tube that contained four different elements and it was our job to identify these elements by means of heating, freezing, dissolving, mixing or any other method that we could remember. The array of glass containers in front of us was pretty overwhelming but had to mean something in my brain. The master moved like a vampire stalking his prey with his gown flowing behind him. He was a very scary sight.

So we all stood and waited for our powder mix to be presented to us each in turn. I accepted mine and looked at it hoping for inspiration. I waited for the 'Go' signal and set to work. Now, one attribute that I learnt from an early age was tidiness. I can remember Dad checking my room for just that before giving me my pocket money as a reward. So I started on this task and within 30 minutes managed to find three of the elements. This was good stuff. My desk area was tidy and organized and I felt in total control. After another ten minutes I got the fourth element sorted.

The second part of the exam was an experiment that you had to do within the confines of your desk area. It actually seemed quite straightforward and I was all done within about one and a half hours. I looked around at my friends who were trying their best to complete the exam. Maybe I was just lucky and hit the right track at the start. I slowly raised my hand to indicate that I had finished. The teacher looked up and uttered something quietly to himself and then came over. He surveyed my results and sort of nodded and off I went. My friends glanced at me go with a look of desperation. What could I do? I was all done. This was the point I was waiting for with all the exams done and the summer in front of me. I really felt good. Party time! That is, until the results were due.

The summer holidays were spent either flying at White Waltham with the ATC or generally lazing around. I can remember that the weather was classic with long spells of dry and warm weather and only a few days of rain. Dad had accepted a redundancy package from BOAC since the days of even the specialist Flight Navigator were numbered and in future pilots would do navigation as well. This was great shock to him since he was only in his early fifties and felt he was good for a few more years. At that time a number of airlines had arrived on the scene flying older aircraft. One of these was Eagle Airways, based at an airfield near to us called Blackbush. It had a collection of what can be only described as antique aircraft. Having said that it was very enjoyable to bike over there and look at these aircraft.

Eagle Airways eventually became British Eagle and moved their base to Heathrow Airport. They acquired a fleet of Britannia aircraft, mainly from BOAC, and operated routes all over the world on behalf of the UK military, flying people to the far flung countries of the British Empire. For example, in Australia, there was a large research centre run by the British Military that experimented with rockets. This was in a place known as Woomera that was north of Adelaide in the state of South Australia. Dad was offered a job as flight navigator with them so off he went again flying around the world.

Heathrow, in those days, had few restrictions for the public to visit and quite often Peter, my friend and I would bike there and spend the day in the viewing area of the famous Queen's building. I remember sitting down and devouring my lunch listening to the commentary over the loudspeakers and the remark was made that one aircraft was landing every three minutes. Wow! But compare that with nowadays. It was no mean feat to bike there and back in one day. It would finish me off nowadays.

Life was very good to me that summer. Then came the day of reckoning when the exam results were due out. On that day I remember that I was not fully aware that this was D-day since everything seemed normal. In fact, I was not even at home on that morning. I must have been in Wokingham since a school friend of mine spotted me and asked me about my results. Total panic took over! I must have thought it was tomorrow or something like that. I rushed home to get my bike to make steps to get to school. Mum was waiting for me and she had a grin from ear to ear. A neighbour had already taken her to the school since her stupid son was not around. Mum was flashing a small slip of paper in front of me.

"You have done very well in your results," she said with a beaming smile.

I had got brilliant grades for all three subjects: an 'A' in Chemistry with two 'Bs' in the others. I had made it to qualify for the College of Air Training that August. So, I had done the education part and now it was time to move on and get to the flying part. Party time again! I even beat my sister!

One thing that had to be done was to visit Kelvin House, the RAF's medical centre in London to complete an initial airline medical. It was pretty thorough. When it came to the eye test, I failed it. In those days you were not allowed to wear glasses to correct any vision defect. I was very upset about it having come this far. I had passed the interview but not the medical so what would happen?

Dad contacted the renowned BOAC doctor, Dr Alan Sibald, whom he had known all his flying life with BOAC and arranged a visit to see him. He examined my eyes in depth and came to the conclusion that I had got eye strain due to bad lighting conditions when revising for my 'A' levels. He dispatched me to no less than a Harley Street specialist in London for further tests. Dad took me there and I can remember the most thorough of examinations taking place. The conclusion was that, yes I did indeed have eye strain and that the eyes would be fine within a few weeks. He contacted Kelvin House and I was given a clean bill of health. I was ready to go!

Chapter 3

– MY COLLEGE YEARS

So, in the August I arrived at Hamble to enrol in course No. 645. I can describe the college as consisting of a long drive from the gatehouse up to the main office block that housed the administration. Off to the left were accommodation blocks and a swimming pool, followed by the general studies block. On the right at first were more accommodation blocks and the main 'club house'. At the end of the drive off to the left was the way to the aircraft hangar and the centre of the flying side. The airfield itself was grass and extended all the way to the Hamble River on one side. I was to be accommodated in the first block on the right known as Leo House.

We all assembled in the general studies block and waited for things to happen. There were 15 of us on course 645, and two other courses 644 and 646, making a total of 45 of us who qualified to be there. We all came from different walks of life but with one common goal: to be an airline pilot. Introductions over and we moved off to our various 'houses' to get sorted out. My particular course was made up of the following people: Brian Sweet, Ian Metcalfe, Ian Todd, Malcolm Reed, Graham Sheppard, Steve White, Rod Holland, Tibor Solnoki, Eric Smith, Ian Bardrick, Mike Williams, Ian Davies, Tony Partridge and Graham Wright. Brian Sweet and Malcolm Reed both came from the Isle of Wight and were amongst the oldest of us. Ian Metcalfe came from the Midlands. Graham Sheppard was a wild Welsh lad with a good eye for the girls. Steve White came from West Sussex. Rod Holland came from somewhere I forget! Tibor Solnoki was an out and out Scotsman. Eric Smith and Ian Todd were Scotsmen also. Ian Bardrick's origins I forget as well. Mike Williams was from my neck of the woods and we knew each other before going to Hamble. Ian Davies came from County Durham and was the son of a coalminer. Tony Partridge came from Littlehampton which was just along the south coast. Graham Wright, last but not least, came from London. I know this is a bit boring with all these names but as I go along they all will be mentioned from time to time.

By the time we had all sorted ourselves out it was time for us all to get know each other. What better place but the local pub in Hamble known as the 'Bugle'. Our finances were very tight since most of us were surviving on County Educational Grants. Dad was between BOAC and British Eagle at the time and so I got the maximum grant available. It amounted to about five pounds a week for me. Not much you might say but don't forget petrol was about 25 pence a gallon (yes, gallon, not litre) and a pint of beer was about 15 pence. How times have changed!

Anyway, we all got together and introduced ourselves. What was amazing was despite our varied backgrounds we all seemed to get along straight away. There were a couple of cadets (as we were known as) from a course about six months ahead of us and one of them wandered over and said hello. He said that having got here the trick was to stay and complete the whole course. This was not in the script! When some unlucky cadet failed a test or something similar he was asked to leave Hamble. What followed was a 'chop party' attended by all the other cadets on his course to wish him well for the future outside of Hamble. This comment sent a ripple through us and the mood changed. The cadet we spoke to mentioned that they had already lost three cadets in the space of two months. I then realized that this two-year course was no push-over and that I would have to fight tooth and nail to make it through.

This fact was further confirmed when we all assembled the next day to meet our flight and ground instructors plus 'the bosses'. The principal of the College was an Air-Vice Marshall Bates who was of Australian origin. The whole day was taken up with various speakers talking to us about how the course would proceed over the next two years. Various ground rules were laid out. Firstly, we were not allowed any weekends off during the 15-week term. Secondly, we were not allowed to entertain members of the opposite sex in our rooms at any time with the penalty for this being instant expulsion. Various other rules were mentioned but I felt these two were the most significant. After each lecture the final comment would be:

"Enjoy the course!"

This was the understatement of the century! The rules seemed draconian in nature and not what I had expected. The following day we all assembled in the allocated classroom and took our seats. Each desk was laid out with precision, with a variety of instruments ranging from a square looking protractor to a very complicated looking slide rule. We all surveyed the assembled items with curiosity whilst gingerly picking them up and wondering how this worked or what that did. After a short while one of the ground instructors walked in and stood at the head of the class as if surveying his victims.

This is just like school, I thought.

He then passed out the timetable for the term to each of us. What was amazing was that for the first term up to Christmas we would not do any flying but enjoy the delights of ground school covering such subjects as Mathematics, Navigation, Electrics, Aerodynamics, Meteorology, Thermodynamics, Radio, Instruments and Aviation Law, to name but a few. Each subject in its own right was an undertaking. The course syllabus was starting to be revealed and it was pretty formidable. I thought that I had left Mathematics behind me at school but here I was facing the first lesson on that very subject.

The instructors were a mixed bag of ex-industry and ex-RAF people. The ex-RAF ones had a certain amount of character but the ex-industry ones were just plain boring with a monotone voice that sent you to sleep. If I call recall some of them... There was Mr Lee (boring) who took Maths, Mr Smith (boring) who took Aerodynamics. Mr Grant (half-boring) who took Electrics, Mr West-Jones (boring) who took Meteorology, Mr Seymour (a real character) who took Radio, Mr Garrard (boring) who took navigation, Mr Underdown (totally boring) who took aviation law, Mr Wilkinson (boring) who took Thermodynamics and Mr Johnson (boring) who took instruments. The other instructors I cannot recall by name but each one had a characteristic that we remembered them by. I think that the boring title related to the subject so maybe I am a bit biased.

The term slowly drifted on and my brain became saturated. My bedroom was becoming an array of books and bits of paper strewn everywhere in some semblance of order. The comforting factor was that I was not alone. We were all in the same boat. Amongst all the course members I seemed to bond particularly well with Ian Davies and Tony Partridge and soon the three of us became firm friends. This friendship was destined to last well over 50 years even after we all retired. Being restricted to 'camp' for the weekends seemed harsh but actually it was not that much of a chore since we all had the chance to relax and enjoy the local area on our meagre earnings.

We all were pretty fit and got together on the Saturday afternoon to play football on the college playing field. Saturday evening was spent either in the Bugle or at some local social event. The local girls were pretty friendly or maybe it was because we were off to be pilots that interested them. We were down the Bugle one night when there was one heck of a party going on amongst some other cadets. Yes, it was the infamous 'chop party' in progress with the poor chap drowning his sorrows in his beer. Perhaps when someone is terminated then he should go quietly. A chop party didn't seem right. I would soon find out as the course progressed.

The Christmas break was very welcome when it arrived since I found that 15 weeks of intensive classroom study pretty hard. The subjects were so varied and gave me the impression that I was studying for eight or so 'A' levels in one hit. Anyway, I knew that when I went back after the break the flying would begin. I was a bit apprehensive about it all. The word 'chop' was never far from my mind.

I arrived back at Hamble in January 1965 ready for the next term. This included the start of the flying course. The aircraft used was the ever faithful Chipmunk that I had grown up with in the ATC.

Should be OK, I thought.

Soon after the term started we all marched up the drive and turned left at the end to visit the hangar where the aircraft were housed. We were shown into the hangar and there was the Hamble fleet of Chipmunks and a twin-engine aircraft called a Piper Apache. The latter is an early type of light executive aircraft produced by Piper. It looked pretty smooth from where I was standing. At the end on the left hand side of the hangar was a crew room where we all assembled. After a few minutes the Chief Flying Instructor Mr Duff-Minstrel strolled in and addressed us. You could hear a pin drop! The theme of his chat was based loosely around the flying course at Hamble. His final remarks hit home.

"Some of you will fail the course and be terminated," he said in a sombre tone.

It transpired that the course was based on the RAF basic flying syllabus and, since almost all of the flying instructors were ex-RAF, then the only way to go was the route they knew. I will point out that in those days there was no finesse about your performance. The instructors would tell you bluntly how you were doing with none of this modern 'We are to help you' mentality. I have reservations about the modern approach.

A classic thing then was that you were called by your surname only. Amazingly, we never got issued numbers as I am sure that would have been better for them. After his chat we were introduced to our assigned Flying Instructors. They all trooped in and called out various cadet names and off they went into a huddle. Amongst this assembled group of gentlemen was a rather short instructor who was a bit overweight. He seemed to have the air of confidence and cunning about him. His name was John Vickers. He became known as 'Harry' for some unknown reason. Anyway, my name together with Ian Metcalfe's was called out by Harry and we followed him like sheep to the slaughter into some hideaway corner. I was about six feet in height and Ian just short of that but we both towered over Harry which must have intimidated him somewhat. Anyway, I cannot remember the contents of his pep talk excepting words like:

"High standard..."

"I expect..."

"...Tough course ahead."

We all had been issued grey RAF style flying suits to fly the Chipmunk. Ground school was still very much the order of the day. Mr Garrard, the navigation instructor, seemed to spend a lot of time reminiscing about the old war days and how he did this and did that. The collections of implements presented on day one were gradually being brought into use. The slide rule was interesting since, in those days, the calculator was unknown. We all became very proficient in using it. The square protractor was used to plot angles on a navigation chart. The one item that intrigued us was a circular compass rose with a movable scale that itself had a moveable grid that slid up and down. This was the famous Dalton Computer Mk.4 that was used to calculate navigational equations by inserting all the parameters and sliding this and that and getting an answer somewhere. There will more about this thing later on.

Then came the day when we were to start the flying side. Our course donned our flying suits and made steps to the hangar. Just outside of the crew room was a large blackboard showing who was doing what on that day. I saw my name chalked up on this board and waited for Harry to come along and start the business. About 20 minutes later there I was being shown over the Chipmunk with the view to understanding it and all its technical bits. I must have said something about my past flying with the ATC. Big mistake! Here was this instructor, whose job in life was to try and mould me into some sort of capable pilot, being confronted by a pupil thinking he knew it all. Did I live to regret these words!

Anyway, I got to the point where I strapped myself into the front seat of the tandem cockpit and waited for the word from the rear seat. We had throat microphones so talking was fine. The Chipmunk's engine started and off we went taxiing across the grass to the duty runway. Harry did the flying at this point and took off and flew south towards the Isle of Wight. I just sat back and enjoyed the feeling of being back in the air. Hamble airfield was sited just south of the city of Southampton on the banks of the river Hamble – hence the name – and was surrounded by imaginary airways going from east to west and north to south. These airways were known as controlled airspace and in them flew the airliners that were under the control of some remote controller sitting at a radar screen miles away. BEA was one such airline that toiled up and down these airways each day on their way to Jersey for example.

Over the Isle of Wight this controlled airspace restricted us lesser mortals to height restrictions based on whether we were in the eastern or western side of the island. I seem to remember three thousand feet to the west and four thousand feet to the east. In addition there were further restrictions to watch out for. There was a Royal Navy airfield just down the road from Hamble called Lee-on-Solent that served the Navy out of their main base of Portsmouth. We had to avoid this airfield and the City of Portsmouth as the military were pretty sensitive in those days. Just to the north of Hamble was Southampton Airport that had its own controlled airspace to allow aircraft to land and take-off there. To the west of Hamble by about fifty miles was the airport at Bournemouth called Hurn. More restrictions! Now that is all very well when the weather is fine since you can see these off-limits areas but take the case when the weather was murky or cloudy: this was not so easy. In this case a route had been devised to take you out of the Hamble area and safely deposit you out of harm's way to do some flying. Unfortunately it was based on local landmarks that you had to find even when the weather was not good which made things pretty difficult, if you see what I mean. Just along to the east was the RAF airfield of Thorney Island with another load of restrictions. It soon became apparent that the UK was a very restricted place to just take-off and go in a straight line from A to B.

Having now totally confused you let me take you back to my first flight. I was up there over the Isle of Wight (Island for short) enjoying the view when Harry spoke to me:

"OK, you have control."

I took the controls and carried on in the same direction as before.

"I have control," Harry barked over the mike.

Blimey that was quick, I thought!

"When I say that you have control you acknowledge it by saying that you do have control – do I make myself clear?"

"Yes, sir," I must have spluttered, totally taken by the harshness of his words.

He repeated: "You have control."

"I have control, sir," I must have yelled.

Right, lesson number one learnt. Then Harry asked: "Where are we?"

"Over the Island, sir," I replied.

"OK, take me back to Hamble."

So there I was over unfamiliar territory and asked to take the Chipmunk back home. I looked around trying to find inspiration.

Ah, there is water down there, I thought.

Was I getting inspired? Maybe. I spotted a large collection of houses and yes it looks like Portsmouth down there. I looked a bit farther to the north. Yes, there was the naval airfield. Hamble must be just up from there. I see the River Hamble and yes there it is. I had found the airfield! I am a star! The only problem was that all the time I was busy looking out of the window my eye was not on the instruments and so, although I had found the airfield, the aircraft was not at the height or speed that it was meant to be. I took the controls and fumbled around until I had got some semblance of order.

"Better next time, Mullett," was the comment down the mike.

"Not bad for a first outing," he followed up by saying.

As we approached the airfield Harry asked me to identify the runway in use and also to get us in a position to try a landing. We had a radio in the Chipmunk so I made a high pitched call to the tower and then tried to visualize the way to go. No help from the back on this one! I managed to sort of grope my way around the circuit and line up for a landing. The problem was that I was at the wrong height with the airfield looking amazingly small.

"I have control," Harry said.

"You have control, sir," I whimpered in reply.

Harry then put the aircraft into a strange sort of sideslip manoeuvre and we seemed to hurtle towards the runway. With what seemed seconds from disaster he straightened everything out and we seemed to just plop onto the ground. I was totally dejected at this point when suddenly the engine roared away and we were in the air again. Harry turned the aircraft back towards the start point or downwind and called for me to fly it again.

"If you keep at one thousand feet in the circuit then all will work out OK," he said.

So why was I in orbit on the last circuit? I put it down to nerves. Anyway I fly the downwind bit and then turn towards the runway or crosswind and grit my teeth with a bit of tongue showing maybe. I followed the runway like a hawk and also try to keep an eye on the speed and height as well. Finally I make it to the runway and am just about go for the ultimate smoothie when the shout from the back butts in.

"I have control."

I acknowledge this call and then suddenly we are up in the air again without touching down. We get to the downwind leg again.

What have I done now? I thought.

"Right, Mullett, how about some checks before you land this time?" Harry barked at me.

"One day you might forget to put your undercarriage down if you don't do your checks." He followed up with.

So off I went again and, yes, I did remember to do the checks and finally arrived on the ground in some semblance of order. We taxied back to the hangar and switched the engine off. I had been in the air for one hour and I was totally burnt out. I must have lost 10 lbs in weight. I was a dripping emotional wreck.

"Right, Mullett that has got rid of the old bad habits. Now let's start trying to make you a pilot," Harry said.

Here endeth the first lesson.

That evening we all gathered in the clubhouse to chat about our experiences. The clubhouse was the centre of the universe as far as we were concerned. As you entered there was a telephone room on the left and then you entered the foyer. On the left was the dining room. It was under the charge of a Mr Hunt who had to contend with maybe 150 of us all munching at the same time. We were a hungry bunch of cadets and it was more like a chimps' tea party at times. We had no supervision in there so anything went. Bread rolls were the favourite weapons of mass destruction I remember. To the right in the foyer was a corridor leading to the large lounge. On either side were the bar and TV room. Upstairs was the library and snooker room. Anyway we all sat around recounting our first taste of the flying course. The flying instructors were of varied temperaments and then there was Harry. Whether I had been allocated a Mr Nasty or not remained to be seen. We all had mixed emotions about the first day.

We flew about three times a week so within a couple of days I was off again with Harry for another hour's ordeal. I think he knew that I was confident enough with the aircraft but fell into lapses of concentration. I must have kept him on his toes! After about seven or so hours he let me go on my own. Pretty good, I thought. I did my solo OK and drifted over to the Island for a relaxing time just stooging around. I flew back to Hamble and after the landing taxied up and switched off. Harry met me and said very little. Come on, Harry! I was well ahead of the game.

We went into the crew room and sat down and he talked about the rest of the flying course on the Chipmunk which would total about 140 hours. In my mind that was a long time not to drop any clangers and get thrown out. Gradually we all went solo and we all celebrated each other's success. Ground school continued at its own monotonous pace. The ground instructors became targets of our imagination as time went on. Mr Wilkinson, who took us for Thermodynamics, had a defect which we exploited. He was deaf in one ear and we found that if we fired questions at him from various directions he would swivel his head like the proverbial horizontal 'nodding dog'. Mr Lee, who covered Maths, was an absolute total bore and the only mildly amusing thing about him was his very high pitched voice that earned him the title of 'Squeaker Lee'.

The subject matters were now becoming quite intense. The theory of flight was a hard one, I remember. Mr Seymour who took Radio was ex-RAF and must have had a very interesting career. He seemed to be the best of them. He smoked and drank so was OK in our eyes. As I said Graham Sheppard, the wild Welshman, was a ladies' man and soon had all the secretaries swooning around. There was a young post girl called Pam who took my eye but that is another story.

We got issued with large topographical maps of the UK that would be needed soon enough since we were moving into the cross country section of the flying shortly. Together with the maps there was an enormous bunch of official looking documents that covered all the rules and regulations of flying within the UK. We had to try and interpret these regulations and transpose the results onto the maps. I have covered all the controlled airspace restrictions in the local area earlier but when you look at the whole of UK they became a total mishmash of lines, dashes and dots. Each RAF station had a five mile exclusion zone around it. All this added up to a very complicated looking map. The final act was to cover them in a clear plastic material called Fablon.

The flying course gradually moved up a gear and soon we were allowed to fly with another cadet. Great fun! When I flew with Harry, though, it was down to business. The course subject matter was quite intensive. For example, on the eastern side of the island was a small airfield called Bembridge. It was a grass airfield and home to a company that built the Britt-Norman Islander light-utility twin aircraft. The circuit was usually very quiet and Harry would make me do as many circuits as he could to get me to master some sort of task that he had set me. It was very intensive flying and hard work to say the least. Harry never seemed to pause between exercises.

Then came the time when we were detailed to leave the comfort of our local flying area and start the cross-country work. From Hamble there were not too many directions that were away from the restricted areas. The main routes were off to the north-west, flying over Wiltshire and beyond. There was a routine for the flying days. After breakfast in the dining room we would make our way up the drive, turn left and enter the hangar. The flying programme for the day would be chalked up on the board by the crew room and we would all study our various assignments for the day.

I remember seeing the word 'Cross-Country' on the board: I was off with Harry for a flight around the UK countryside. Harry met me and said where we were off to and that it was up to me to plot the tracks and timings etc. This was my first cross country so I very carefully laid the map out and started to plot the route. We were due to fly to the Bristol area and then down to Exeter for a lunch stop and then back to Hamble. After a while Harry arrived and surveyed my results and off we went. Harry was always non-committal about my work or flying ability. He would call me 'Mullett Mark one' or 'Mullett Mark two' according to his scale. I never knew which the better one was.

We took off and then turned north-west and I started the business of trying to fly straight and also read the map on my lap. Difficult to multi-task you might say. The city of Salisbury came up at about the correct time and so the routine continued. I remember the weather was fine and I could see a long way so all was good. We flew over Bristol and then turned south towards Exeter where we landed. A quick sandwich for lunch and then off we went back to Hamble. When we got back I felt pretty good about the flight, but Harry pointed out various items that I seemed to have missed. Good old Harry! By now we were developing a sort of love-hate relationship.

My partner with Harry was, as I said before, Ian Metcalfe and he seemed to be doing OK. We flew together quite often. On the next flying day we followed our usual routine and I found that I was off on my own for a cross country flight somewhere north of Newbury in Wiltshire. I sat down and sorted out the route. The weather was fairly cloudy but did not seem too bad. I had the final approval from Harry and wandered out to the aircraft. Harry's last words were:

"Mullett, watch out for the weather as it is due to rain later with low cloud. If you are not happy, turn back."

Did I take any notice of these words? No, I did not. So off I went in my faithful Chipmunk and started my cross country flight. I was somewhere north of Newbury quite happily stooging along, not noticing the cloud level gradually dropping. There was one thing to always be aware of when flying – how high above the local ground you are. What happens is that you get the height of the local terrain above sea level from the map of an area and then add a certain height factor to produce a figure below which it is dangerous to go for fear for hitting the ground. The altimeter in the cockpit shows your height above sea level so you always have a figure below which you do not fly. So, there I was gradually descending with the base of the cloud getting lower and lower.

The obvious thing to do was to turn around and go home, just as Harry had said. Not me! Like a total idiot I carried on northwards with only occasional glimpses of the ground. At some point I concluded that I was totally lost. Not good with all these airspace restrictions. I turned the Chipmunk around and headed back the way I had come. By this time I was about one hundred feet above the minimum height for safety but I was still drifting in and out of cloud. So what did I do? I went lower still to be clear of this cloud not realizing that the bad weather had built up behind me and virtually cut off my escape route.

I heard a Hamble Apache on the radio and I asked him with a rather squeaky voice what the weather was like where he was. He replied that he was on his way back to Hamble as well but totally in cloud. The difference was that he could tell where he was by use of the radio equipment on board. The Chipmunk had no such luxuries. The only

aid it could muster was to transmit a radio call and hope the control
tower could spot the direction that it came from. They would then
let the aircraft know this direction and it was up to the pilot to use
this information to have some idea which way to head. All this was
dependent on the height of the aircraft in question. Me, I was low
down, so this aid was non-effective.

I was now some five hundred feet below the minimum height and
I was just below the cloud. The view of the ground was partially
obscured by clouds. I was heading sort of southwards but kept drifting
off course. I was totally lost and furthermore well below the proper
height. The problem was that if I climbed up I would go into cloud.
I was staring out of the front of the aircraft looking for inspiration.
I could only see forward maybe one hundred yards since it was now
raining heavily and I was being showered all the time by leaks around
the window seal.

Suddenly something loomed up like an apparition in front of
my eyes. I thought it was a shadow or something but suddenly the
enormity of what it was dawned on me like a great hammer from
above. It was a tall television mast and it was floating past my wingtip
with about twenty yards to spare and the worst thing about it was that
it towered above me. I was transfixed by this sight and slid past it in
a total daze. If I had been twenty yards to the right I would have hit
it head on. If ever you go down the M4 motorway and stop off at the
Membury service station just to the west of Newbury you will see this
mast from the car park. This was the mast that I nearly hit. Imagine all
those complaints of loss of TV picture in the area. They would not have
known that a Chipmunk had wrapped itself around the mast.

Anyway, after this close encounter it slowly began to dawn on me
what I had done. I had committed one the greatest crimes in the
aviation book by going below the minimum safe height. The good
thing was that I now knew where I was apart from nearly ending my
life there. I looked ahead for some sort of break in the cloud and low
and behold I saw the sun peeping through a little way off to the left. I
made for it and suddenly I was bathed in sunlight and all below me was
revealed. I hastily climbed up to avoid the next disaster. I remember
seeing a town below and circled it to positively identify it. Yes it was

Hungerford in Berkshire.

"Right, my boy let's get home to safety," I must have shouted.

The final part of the disastrous flight was fine and I landed and taxied to the ramp. The amazing thing is that although Harry was not there to witness the total shambles of the flight he must have had some sixth sense that told him that I had screwed up. Call that ESP or what! He might have been told by the Apache crew that one of the Chipmunks was in trouble. Anyway, as I approached the ramp there he was, standing as tall as he could with his hands on his hips with a look that could kill. I got out and Harry completely lost it with me. This could be the killing stroke before I was thrown out. After his tirade he said:

"What, if anything, have you learnt from this flight?"

"Never go below your minimum safe altitude, sir," I blurted out.

"Right, good, remember that," he said.

I never did forget it. That evening in the bar I was the talk of the town. I felt pretty stupid because of what I had done. The amazing thing, looking back, was the fact that I was not thrown out on the spot. Harry was pretty angry with me so why not get rid of me? I will never know! In later years when travelling down the M4 I often look at the Membury mast with nostalgia and always get a small shiver down my backbone. There for the grace of ...etc etc.

The remainder of the term went by without too many dramas. I even managed a few cross countries on my own and came back unscathed. Just before the end of term we had our first casualty. Tibor Solnoki was asked to leave. Being our first one to go was a bitter blow for all of us and we gave him a farewell do at the Bugle as was tradition. The other two courses had lost about five between them so we were faring OK as a course. The final count was 39 left from 45 at the end of the second term.

The Easter break was a short one and while I was home Dad had cashed in an investment policy and suggested that it was about time that I had some form of transport. I became the proud owner of a Standard Eight car. It was a basic sit-up-and-beg one with no refinements but it had four wheels and even got up to 60 miles an hour with a following wind. I felt very good loading up my suitcase and driving back down to Hamble. It must have taken the best part of two hours. Dad and I had even hand painted it in a shocking 'Dulux' blue.

I drove it to Hamble where it joined the other equally quaint cars. This was the start of term three and the workload was starting to pile up. The ground school was becoming harder and harder with all the subjects involved. We took the opportunity to form a sort of cadet council under the chairmanship of Dave Hughes, from one of the other courses, and managed to get an agreement that we could have one week-end off a term to go home. This was very welcome to us.

The flying side was settling down with Ian Metcalfe and me getting the usual full verbal assault of Harry from time to time. The best times flying were when you were out on your own over the island. The problem was that there were maybe three or four of us in the area, totally oblivious of where we all were. You might see a small fluffy cloud and decide to do a classic attack 'out of the sun' as our wartime predecessors had done. So there you are thinking you are the mighty Spitfire going flat out towards this cloud from above and someone else was doing the same from some other point and suddenly you were confronted by another Chipmunk about fifty yards away and closing. I think we scared ourselves more times that I care to remember.

One thing that we were introduced to was flying without reference to any outside clues. Sounds simple enough but it is incredibly hard to fly only by looking at the instruments. I can't relate it to anything else. To do this task in the Chipmunk a canvass hood was erected over the front part of the cockpit. Once in place there was no way you could see out of the aircraft. All you had were the flight instruments to look at. These consisted of an artificial horizon, compass, turn and slip, airspeed, altimeter and vertical speed indicators. By scanning all of them then you could keep some sort of semblance of order. They were displayed in a 'T' shape so you could take them all in at a single pass. The secret was to keep scanning them at such a pace that you hopefully kept control of the aircraft. It was very difficult to master at first but then as time moved along it became easier. So you got to the point where you could even take off 'under the hood' once you were lined up. Then along came the punchline. There was another piece of apparatus that was triangular in shape and fitted nicely over the artificial horizon and the compass. Your lifeblood had gone. The two most essential instruments you needed were now no longer there. Now, this was difficult to master if not impossible. OK, so after a time you even managed some sort of order when Harry would put the aircraft into a very unusual attitude and then say:

"You have control."

So there you were, not knowing which way was up and expected to recover to level flight. I'm sure that more than once I ended up pointing vertically straight down with the airspeed off the clock. Eventually I must have presented some sort of control to Harry to get through this part OK. Harry had a habit of carrying a newspaper in the rear cockpit and more than once I felt the swipe of it around my head.

At certain points in the flying course the dreaded flying tests reared their ugly heads. They were known as 'Progress Tests' and were numbered. The way it was displayed on the blackboard was for your name to be written in yellow and not the usual white chalk. I remember seeing my name in yellow and hastily sought to find out who was doing my test. We had some instructors that we were positively scared of and others whom we felt were approachable – or even nice.

'Progress Test One' involved demonstrating to the examiner that you had achieved a certain standard. I cannot recall the content of it but it was pretty daunting. I knew how Harry ticked but there I was with someone else. How would I do? I passed the test OK to my amazement and Harry was pleased. It must have been one of the nice examiners. A few beers were downed that night in the Bugle.

The other thing that occurred during that term was the medical check-up. We all trooped in one at a time to the medical centre for the ordeal. I was OK with the eyesight by now, even passed the test. My flying partner Ian Metcalfe unfortunately failed his medical on his eyesight. As I said before there was no alleviation for wearing glasses in those days. Ian took it very hard but, unfortunately, rules were rules. I can understand someone going through lack of ability but to go for a medical reason was really sad.

Harry met up with both of us and was visibly upset about Ian. He then took us both into Southampton and treated us to a Chinese meal. Harry was an amazing instructor. On the one hand he fired with both barrels for our ability and on the other hand he showed amazing compassion. The whole episode was very sad.

The half term arrived and we all took advantage of a break to go home. My break at home was interrupted by a phone call from the college to say that four of the cadets on their way home had been involved in a car accident at Alton, Hampshire. Ian Bardrick was the driver and somehow he had collided with a coach. He was in a local hospital. The other three were badly hurt but had been discharged. A few of us made our way there to see Ian. I cannot recall the names of all the cadets involved. We all finally got back to Hamble and I seemed to remember that some of the cadets involved in the crash were put back by a course so as to give them chance to recover. Ian Bardrick returned to the college but left shortly afterwards due to the on-going effects of the crash. So, in an ironic blow, we had lost three from our course in total and about eight overall.

By now another challenge confronted us in the flying world. Night flying! As we were on a grass airfield the night flying consisted of a runway being laid out using a collection of flares to mark the runway boundaries. These flares were simply a two gallon oil drum with a lighted piece of material on the top. They were known as 'Goose Neck' flares and originated from the war years. So, we all assembled in the crew room at about seven in the evening and got the briefing for the night's work Harry took me and showed me the ropes for how to deal with this new task. At the landing point was a crude but simple unit that showed you if you were on the right approach angle. It was difficult to see until you were just about on top of it.

Pretty useless piece of kit, I thought.

The Chipmunk was a simple aircraft whereby it had a radio plus some electrical cockpit lighting and that was about all. When you put on the navigation lights then the battery was working overtime to keep up with the demand called upon it. To do this required lots of engine revolutions just like a car. OK for the take-off and flight downwind but when you turned for the final approach and called this fact over the radio, combined with slowing the engine down, all would go black both inside and outside of the cockpit. That was just what you needed at that point in the circuit! So what you did in the end was to get onto the final approach and gun the engine for a few seconds to talk on the radio and see the instruments properly. I never enjoyed night flying in the Chipmunk. At one point Harry came along and took me off the circuit and did some aerobatics. It was quite amazing being upside down at night with all the Southampton city lights shining.

The term slowly came to an end and we all departed for a short summer break. I had completed one year at Hamble and was still there. I was also about two thirds of the way through the Chipmunk flying course with over 100 hours clocked up. Thirty seven of us left out of forty five who started.

We all returned to Hamble after the break with a fresh mind. The next year was going to be crucial for us. We had to finish the Chipmunk course including two more progress tests, start the Apache flying course and do our final exams. A lot to cram in! With only 45 hours left to go on the Chipmunk I felt that it was within my grasp to get through.

Harry was being his usual self and lost his cool with me on many an occasion. I seem to recall him coming into the crew room one day and picking me up and suspending me against the wall. No mean feat for someone of his height. I can remember the other cadets parting the waves as he stormed through like a man possessed. I cannot remember what I had done but it must have been pretty serious for Harry to bodily pick me up like that. How I survived I will never know! Did Harry have some inner faith in me or what?

We lost another cadet from the course. Ian Todd disappeared so we were down to 10 out of 15. I managed to pass Progress Test two and was within striking distance of the end when disaster struck. I was detailed to do the final Progress Test three on the Chipmunk and fluffed it totally. It was a cross country exercise that was my undoing. Can't remember what I did wrong but I did! I did a retake and that was not much better. What I did was to take off with the weather a bit marginal when I should have stopped it before I had even started. What was it that drew me to bad weather and cross countries? This was the low point of my Hamble days, being told by Harry that I was up for the final make or break test the following day. He did not understand where I was going wrong. I remember him and me sitting on the grass and talking for maybe two hours about everything that was going on in my head.

CHAPTER 3

The next day I slowly made my way up the drive with Ian and Tony towards the hangar and wondered what the next few hours might have in store for me. I approached the board and there I was in yellow. I spotted that the examining instructor was one Cecil Pearce who was considered the nicest of all the instructors. Harry came up and we talked for a while about the route I was to follow with Cecil. Then the time arrived for the off. I was in the crew room and in came Cecil. He wandered up and shook my hand. Not normal this! He sat down and he simply told me to forget the previous two attempts and that all he wanted to see was that I was coping with the situation in hand. He outlined the route just as Harry had done.

We wandered out to the aircraft and I looked up at a beautiful day. Was I lucky or what! The route was about 30 minutes to the east and then an imaginary diversion according to the whim of the examiner and then back again. In total about one and a half hours. To go east was unusual since it limited the options of places to divert to. I managed the first leg fine and seemed to find some inner confidence in myself. Harry had told me before the flight to study the map to look at all possible diversion spots. As I said before this route had little scope for anything major so I was ready for the task in hand. When I got to the first turning point Cecil asked me to divert to some place that escapes my memory. Fortunately it was one I had studied earlier so I was ready for it. I took the time out to confirm everything and informed Cecil of the details. He seemed to like what he heard and off we went. I found the second turning point right on time and then plotted a course for home. At this point Cecil said that I was fine and that I had passed the test with flying colours. He then took control and I sat back and let the euphoria overcome me.

When I look back I think that that was the point on the course when I knew I was going to make it through and nothing was going to stop me. We arrived back at Hamble and I was welcomed in the crew room by some of my fellow cadets who had guessed by now that I was going to stick around for a while yet. Harry came in and shook my hand and then said that all was not over yet since we had about 15 hours left to do on the Chipmunk. Harry always had a habit of bringing me down to earth!

The ground school was plodding along as well. A piece of good news was that we were no longer required to study Aviation Law. That was music to our ears. Meteorology was another hated subject. In general the ground school workload was levelling out to a certain extent as compared with the early days. We were starting to get into the jet age, for example, in Thermodynamics where we studied the modern gas turbine engine and not the piston engine. There was an occasion when we were in the classroom when we heard the sound of a Chipmunk approaching to land. Nothing unusual with that you might say except that the engine sound was unusual with a lot of popping and banging going on. It was a fellow cadet, Steve Hill, landing with the engine in not good shape, to put it mildly. This was exciting stuff! That evening in the bar it was the talk of the town. Little did I know that there was something similar brewing up for me.

A few days later I was scheduled to fly with Eric Smith on a flight together early in the morning. At the end of the runway in use was the local school and we all had to take-off so as to not go directly over the playground before nine in the morning for safety reasons. Eric and I strapped in as normal and taxied out at about ten minutes to nine and took off towards the school, bearing in mind the restriction. At about four hundred feet in the air the engine just stopped and all went silent. I thought back to my shambolic second solo immediately. No, I had done nothing wrong this time. The engine had just stopped.

So there I was faced with putting the aircraft down in the school playing fields desperately avoiding the playground. I got Eric to call the tower and tell them what was happening as I was fully occupied with getting back onto the ground safely. I did all the checks correctly. Yes, everything was in the right place. I managed to line up nicely to land with plenty of room to spare when suddenly the engine started. I then abandoned the thought of landing in the school playing field and turned the aircraft away to get back into the circuit to land. I was at about two hundred feet by now and very low so I climbed as fast as I could to about four hundred feet. I was, by this time, over the Hamble river and flying just above the masts of very expensive yachts but seemingly safe. At this point the engine failed again and now I was really up against it. When it first failed I had found a nice field to land in if needed. I was now over the river with no escape and descending rapidly towards the water.

"Eric, tell the tower I am going to put the aircraft down as close to the bank as I can," I shrieked.

Sounds all very melodramatic but it was pretty frightening at the time. So, I was committed to the river bank. At about one hundred or so feet the engine started up again. I will never forget that sound. It was obvious that the engine had a major problem but seemed to go in cycles of stopping and starting. From my predicament over the river I needed to get back to the airfield which was about two hundred yards behind me. I wrenched the aircraft away from the river and did a complete turnabout and headed for the airfield. I was at about two hundred feet by now, heading at right angles to the runway which was just ahead. I didn't care about this as the field was large and inviting.

The controllers in the tower must have got an awful shock to see this Chipmunk appearing from the wrong direction and so low down. The fact was that they were not totally sure of where I was. Was I in the playing field or in the river? No. I was over the field going for a landing. The engine stopped again and I decided that I could land OK so I actually switched it off since it was not needed again. I remember doing one of best landings I had ever done. All that ear-bashing from Harry must have paid off. Eric and I sat motionless and waited for the recovery truck to come over and tow us in to the hangar. By now a crowd of cadets and instructors had assembled for our arrival. Harry came over and congratulated me for getting back in one piece. This was my first in-flight emergency and I had coped with it OK. He then marched Eric and me off to another Chipmunk and said:

"Off you two go again and this time don't break it, OK!" He grinned slyly.

We must have been on the ground only about ten minutes before we were back in the air and off for an hour's flight somewhere.

In parallel with the final flying on the Chipmunk we were introduced to the Link Trainer. It is somewhat similar to the small open aircraft style rides you see at the fairground. The only difference was that these had an enclosed cockpit and sat on their own swivelled supports so that that when inside you actually felt it gyrate about its own axis. The downside was these Link Trainers were electrically connected to an operator nearby who sat overlooking a large plotting table that showed where you were and what's more were you should be.

The establishment was run by a Norman Slipp and his band of pan-faced, sadistic, cadet-hating instructors. I recall a Mr Bryniac, of French descent, who had little grasp of English and who would scream and yell at me to get his point across. They had the power to change all the inputs to the machine. OK, you were in control of where it went but they had control of which way the wind blew. This all sounds a bit overdramatic but remember that in those days we had none of the modern fancy computers available. We had to work out our course of actions in our head and when you felt that you got that right some other spanner would be thrown into the plot. There was many a time when the Frenchman would rip open the cockpit hood and let rip at me verbally. Half of the time I never understood what he said but I had a good idea that he was not too happy with my performance. Harry would occasionally pop in and see how I was doing. Why did he always turn up when my trace on the plotting table was just about to fall off the table? These trainers were introduced before the war and there we were using them in 1965. Call that progress? Anyway we had to struggle with these contraptions until we were deemed to be capable of delivering the goods. Big sigh of relief when I had finished that part of the course.

With about 5 or so hours to complete the Chipmunk course I felt that the end was in sight. We were all roughly in the same position and most of us spent the last few hours enjoying the flying and doing our own thing. I thought I would be doing just that! I remember sitting in the crew room and chatting with Ian and in walks Harry. He strolls up to me and sits down. He had a sort of sarcastic glint in his eye.

"Right, I have an exercise for you to finish your Chipmunk flying. I want you to look at the map carefully and then we will go flying. The difference this time is that I will take your map away and put you under the hood and ask you to take me somewhere," he said as he got up and walked away chuckling to himself.

I wonder if I could resurrect that old disappearing powder I had lined up for my sister many years ago? I now have a new target, I thought.

So there I was studying the map as best as I could and knowing that I had to find somewhere that Harry chose with no reference to the ground to find it. Ian was there and we both looked at the map. I calculated that I needed two more hours to complete this part of the course so that was one hour each way. We looked for obvious places but felt that Harry was too cunning for that. I looked in the Wiltshire area and just for an exercise considered a small town called Mere. It was about ten miles southwest of Salisbury, about an hour away. I calculated the times etc for Mere and wrote them down in my flying suit notepad so that they could not be spotted too easily. After about 30 minutes Harry came in and collected my map and off we went to the aircraft. The hood was erected so that I was only able to fly on the instruments. Harry taxied us out to the runway and then stopped just short and said:

"OK Mullett. I would like you to fly me to Mere in Wiltshire."

I could not believe my luck. The very place that I had worked on had come up. I peeped down at my notepad and stared at my notes.

There really is a god! I thought.

I pondered for a few minutes so as to not give the game away and then announced my proposed track and timings. Harry said nothing as usual. He lined us up and then I took off under the hood and then turned to the northwest towards, hopefully, Mere. I used the radio bearings from the control tower to refine my track. After some 45 minutes or so I reckoned that I was pretty close to Mere. I had run out of radio bearings and so was relying on my own skill. After a few more minutes I announced:

"Sir, I think we are over Mere about now."

"Take the hood off and have a look then," Harry replied.

I took the hood off and looked around. There was a town of some sorts just below the left wing. I took a closer look checking for obvious clues, like a railway station, to confirm my thoughts. It was indeed the town of Mere and I had got there with the odd radio bearing and little else.

"There is Mere, sir," I said with a confident air to my voice.

Harry undid his straps in the back and leaned forward and tapped me on the shoulder and said, "Very well done, Mullett. Relax and I will fly us back to Hamble."

Harry then took control and flew us back to Hamble. I was over the moon with delight. Harry was even humming a tune from the back seat. We landed and then, instead of going to the crew room for the inevitable debriefing, Harry marched me past the hangar, down the drive and into the clubhouse. Tony and Ian were waiting quietly in the wings for a sign. Harry and I turned right and arrived at the bar that had just opened. He ordered two pints and then we sat down and talked. He said that I had now completed the Chipmunk course and that I was ready for the Apache. I actually think that he was relieved that he had got me through. When I think back Harry was the right instructor for me at that stage since he soon found out my weaknesses and strengths and used them to mould some sort of pilot out of me. The faces of Tony and Ian broke into a smile when I gave them the thumbs up.

We had all made it through the Chipmunk course and there was a celebration to be had. From now on we would fly in shirt and ties in what was considered a modern executive aircraft equipped with navigational instruments that enabled us to fly in controlled airspace and even land at Heathrow if called upon to do so. It was midway through the autumn term and we were ready for the Apache. We lost Rod Holland at about this time. He just gave up of his own accord and resigned. Total count was about 32 left from 45.

The amazing thing was that once I started the Apache course I really felt at home. I was teamed up with Tony and our instructor was one Tony Liskutin. He had come to England from Czechoslovakia during the war and became a top Spitfire pilot. His grasp of English was not good but he was without a doubt a brilliant pilot. If you type in 'Liskutin' into 'Google' you will spot his name. As I said before the Apache was the first executive twin to emerge from the Piper Company in the USA. Our aircraft were slightly changed to suit the training role at Hamble. The engines were downgraded in power and only the left engine had a hydraulic pump to operate the undercarriage and flaps. Does not seem to have much significance but read on...

Tony and I settled in well on the new aircraft and were soon getting to grips with the new array of instruments. The object of this part of the course was to get away from the ability to be able to fly but to start to come to grips with flying in controlled airspace and to perform instrument approaches and to really get into the airliner mould. The downside of the Apache was its dreadful lack of power even with both engines going. We were introduced to the phenomena whereby if you stopped one engine you had to be able to maintain the correct speed and direction at the same time as coping with the natural swing and lack of urge when you have the main thrust of the aircraft not right in the middle. In those days the engines were actually shut down totally so there you were fighting this beast all the way down to the ground. We would practise approaches on one engine and then the instructor would shout: "Overshoot."

So there you were putting a lot of power on the only live engine whilst trying to hold it straight with your feet on the rudder pedals and aiming for a speed that would make the bloody thing climb. Seventy knots seems to spring to mind. Anything less you were running out of pedal power and risked banking over and losing control or anything faster you ended up descending into a black hole. As I said before the hydraulic pump was on the left engine so if the right one was shut down there was no problem bringing up the undercarriage or moving the flaps in one of these overshoots. If the left engine was shut down you had to resort to pulling out a handle on the centre pedestal and manually pump this handle with your right hand to do all of the operations. So, I will give you a clue as to which engine was regularly shut down to extract the maximum of pressure on the cadet. Yes, you have guessed it – the left one.

So there you were in one of these overshoots from about one hundred feet over the runway with your arms, legs, feet and hands going all over the shop trying to convince the instructor that you were under full control. The difficult bit was trying to get all of your moving parts to work independently and not in sympathy with each other. Tony Liskutin just sat there and said nothing. Was he a brave man or what? The way they would do it was very sneaky as well. Between the pilot's seats at floor level were the fuel switches which controlled which fuel tank supplied which engine. What they would do was to distract you and quietly put the hand down between the seats and shut the fuel off to one of the engines. About twenty seconds later when you least expected it one of the engines would cough and splutter to a halt. Your job was to get the propeller turned on its axis so as to present the smallest section to the airflow. This action was called 'feathering' of the propeller. You had a selection of red, yellow and black levers to do this action and if you got it wrong then the propeller would not feather and drag the whole aircraft sideways and downwards with you in it towards Mother Earth. At the extreme you could even start to feather the good engine and then where would you be? A bit stuck I would say! These instructors must have had nerves of steel whilst watching us trying to get it right.

On quite a few occasions Tony and I flew together and we would pinch some rolls or similar from the dining room, go flying around munching and generally fooling around. The serious side of the Apache was that we would get clearance to fly to Gatwick and practise the infamous instrument approaches over and over again. In those days Gatwick was very quiet and quite often there might be two or three Hamble aircraft doing these approaches over and over again.

On 27th October that year we all got up as normal for breakfast to be greeted by the news that a BEA Vanguard 'EE' had crashed at Heathrow after attempting a third approach in foggy conditions. This aircraft was a large turboprop airliner seating about one hundred plus passengers and was considered a great successor to the Viscount. Unfortunately it was late in development due to problems with the Rolls Royce Tyne engines and by the time it entered service it was being overtaken by such aircraft as the Boeing 727 and the Douglas DC-9.

This crash brought it home to us how dangerous the flying world can be. It further transpired that the co-pilot who flew each of the approaches had left Hamble some months previously. The suspicion was that the ex-Hamble cadet's lack of experience caused the accident. In retrospect this was hearsay since in those days flight recorders were only just in their infancy and recordings of the cockpit voices were unheard of. The official cause was put down as pilot error with the finger being pointed at the co-pilot. All totally unfair I have to say.

The mood at Hamble was sombre. The ramifications of the accident were soon felt when three cadets on our intake were taken aside and terminated with very little or no explanation. This act was totally out of order but we had to accept it. The sombre mood changed to one of disbelief. So, in a streak we had lost three cadets and were now down to 29 remaining out of the original 45. Not a nice feeling I have to say. Many, many years later it transpired that there was a corrosion problem with the flap position sensors at the time and, just maybe, the flaps had travelled all the way up from the landing position through the overshoot position to deprive the wing of lift, with catastrophic results. This corrosion was not known about at the time and so the finger pointing at the co-pilot's inexperience was the conclusion reached and the college took the full brunt of it.

Anyway, Tony and I continued to fly the Apache with not too many problems and we had a change of instructor to a very nice gentleman called Dai Rees. He was of Welsh origin and was a very relaxed instructor to fly with. As I said before, occasionally Tony and I would fly together. I remember one such flight we did when we decided to fly to Southend Airport. The route was to go around London by flying up the west side and then across the north side and then head south into Southend. We set off with our usual supply of rolls etc for munchies and headed north, keeping London well clear on the right hand side. When we found ourselves north of London with Tony doing the flying and me doing the navigation we decided to fly out towards East Anglia and see what was about.

East Anglia is a very quiet backwater of England with small villages dotted around. Tony spotted a pub that looked all alone and needed a flying visit. We descended down to about treetop height and skimmed over the unsuspecting pub at about one hundred feet. There could have been no time to take our registration on the flyby. Tony climbed up and then asked me to sort him out a course to Southend. I was completely lost at this point and looked around for inspiration. I spotted a light coloured ground feature about ten miles away and generally in the direction of Southend. We flew towards it hoping to get some sort of clue from this feature as to where we were. We got within about three miles of it when I realized that what I had been looking at was a large airfield. I looked at the map and did not see any airfield of notable size in our area except military ones. I looked closer at the airfield and spotted some aircraft dispersed around the perimeter. It then dawned on me that these innocent looking aircraft were in fact V-Bombers of the RAF. We were about to penetrate a sensitive military zone which, in those days, was considered very dangerous.

If you ever saw a light executive twin aircraft turn on its tail then this was it! At least I knew where we were now! We were just about to overfly RAF Marham which was strictly a no-no. Tony and I finally got to Southend and were relieved that no one had reported us or had the RAF descend upon us. We left there and decided to go back to Hamble on a southerly route and ended up flying along the south coast towns at about two hundred feet, half a mile offshore. Tony was always up for adventure. The autumn term ended peacefully and we all departed for Christmas at home, ready for the final two terms in 1966.

We all returned after Christmas ready for the term ahead. Having completed the mind blowing Link Trainer course we then progressed to another instrument of torture. Adjacent to the crew room were two very basic 'Jet Procedure Trainers' (JPTs). They were designed to represent a modern four-engine passenger jet. They could actually simulate flight but never leave the ground. If you looked inside one now you would be horrified to see its very basic layout compared with the more modern types. They were based on the De Havilland Comet 4 performance but any similarity ended there. They were run by a Mr Cope.

A new instructor, Mr Niven, had joined the staff by then. He had recently retired from BEA and was totally disliked by all. Tony and I were assigned this Mr Niven and did he give us a hard time or what! It transpired that he had retired as a co-pilot from BEA under strange circumstances and seemed to have a total loathing of us cadets. When Tony and I had our first session it soon transpired that the JPT flew like a brick and if your nose twitched then it did a loop. I considered this part of the course the hardest of the lot. However, we gradually got to grips with it. The problem was that Mr Niven sat behind us looking over our shoulders with a box of tricks at his fingertips that could inflict a further dose of pain at any moment. The usual point when this was done was when we were distracted by something and then you looked back and all hell had broken loose. The other side of him was that he had a loud voice that shook us to the core when he boomed some order out.

On the flying side all was progressing well with Dai Rees; Tony and I were becoming quite proficient at handling all the exercises. We had some progress tests to pass on the way but even they went well. The ground school was coming together slowly and our thoughts were on the final exams in the following term that would qualify us to leave Hamble fully licensed. The original three courses had now been amalgamated into two courses since we had lost so many cadets along the way.

As the term progressed we were informed that during the Easter break we would be going to fly as observers with BEA on their regular flights so as to get a taste of the airline operation first-hand. Things were starting to build up now. The best thing was that Tony, Ian and I were still hanging in OK. We started night flying in the Apache which involved us leaving the local area and completing some navigational exercise and then returning to Hamble. Just across the Southampton water was the oil refinery of Fawley and that boasted a simple radio beacon so that we could practise the very basic of approaches based on timing from the beacon and descending to a specific height and hopefully look out at that point and see the airfield. The brain worked overtime getting the timing right, the descent right and the direction right. All a bit basic but it worked.

Up the road from our airfield was the Southampton city airport of Eastleigh. In those days it, too, had a grass runway and the arriving commercial aircraft used the Fawley beacon like us to get into Eastleigh. On one foggy morning I was up in the control tower with Ian looking at the weather prospects for flying and low and behold we spotted a twin-engined Bristol freighter emerging out of the fog approaching Hamble with all intentions to land, thinking it was Eastleigh. This aircraft was too big for our small airfield and would have come to grief if it had landed. The controller leapt onto the balcony and fired off what he thought was a red flare so as to warn the approaching aircraft of his predicament and not to land. But what happened was that a bright green flare went up instead of the red one which indicated he was clear to land. Wrong flare! All hands were on deck now and he managed to find the right flare gun and off went the red flare. At about fifty feet the aircraft started an overshoot and lumbered across the airfield struggling to climb away. It all seemed to happen in slow motion and then he was gone back into the murk. It just shows how vulnerable these old radio aids were. I would imagine the captain of the unfortunate aircraft had some explaining to do when he finally landed somewhere.

A small piece about the social side of Hamble is worthy of note now. Around the area were various colleges that had their fair share of young ladies. There was one over at Salisbury that was particularly popular with us. Many a Saturday night was spent coaxing my car over to Salisbury for a night of fun and frolics. The poor old car was really being put to the test and one Saturday night it finally packed up at Salisbury. There were three of us stuck there so we had no alternative but to walk back to Hamble. I believe the distance involved was some thirty five miles. We arrived back at about nine in the morning much the worse for wear. What we did for the chance of an encounter with the opposite sex was not in any text book. Never again we would say! But we did!

In Southampton there were a few clubs that we frequented. Money was always tight but we seemed to enjoy the social side OK. There was a jazz club in Southampton called the Concord Jazz Club and that was a frequent hangout of ours. There was a new local group performing most nights, called 'Manfred Mann'. Perhaps you may have heard of them. The other venue was the Gaumont cinema in Southampton where the latest groups would perform their acts on the UK circuit. I remember seeing Chuck Berry, Tom Jones, The Fourmost, Marianne Faithful, Cilla Black and many others. I do confess I had a thing about Marianne Faithful – that was before Mick Jagger got his claws into her.

We held our own dances in the Hamble village hall once a term and these were well attended by the local girls. Tony had an old Talbot vintage car and managed to get it over to Hamble. The intention was to restore it but with little cash around this turned out to be a fruitless task. It was my poor old car that was detailed to tow the Talbot around the college grounds hoping to kick-start the engine of the beast into life. No luck there except one totally knackered Standard Eight car.

We had three small dinghies on the Hamble waterside. They were generally in a sorry state of misuse but we could usually put one workable dinghy into the water and, under the expert guidance of Tony, would spend many hours floating around the Solent. We even made it to Cowes on the Isle of Wight on a few occasions. At one time, when short of funds we sailed up into Southampton Water and tied up where the great liners were and went into the city. Speaking of the great liners, I can remember ships like the Queen Mary, Queen Elizabeth and the United States drifting past my window in the college on their way to New York. Little did I know that air travel would make them redundant overnight. I will come back to the Queen Mary later on in my story.

It was during this term that we had the first fatality due to a flying accident. The Chipmunks that we had were mainly ex-RAF models. Many years previously there had been a design fault whereby the aircraft could develop a spin manoeuvre that was impossible to recover from. The spin is the most dangerous of manoeuvres for any aircraft and to recover required a very stringent procedure. What the RAF did was add a small strake either side of the tail that prevented this terminal spin from occurring. Unfortunately not all of the Hamble Chipmunks had these strakes installed due to an oversight. What happened was that a cadet took an unmodified aircraft and went off over the island specifically to practise spinning. It was late in the afternoon when we heard that he had what we called 'spun in' and crashed somewhere in the eastern side of the island. It was a very sad occasion for us. When the wreckage was recovered it was put in the hangar right outside the crew room for all to see. A bit cruel to do that I felt.

As the term continued we were informed of our assigned flights with BEA during the Easter break. I was to be an extra crew member on the Vickers Vanguard. I was very happy to be part of a real crew and by the time the term finished I was ready to go.

The Easter break was upon us and off I trotted to Heathrow resplendent in my college uniform and reported to BEA flight operations centre that was in the famous Queen's building situated in the central area. I remember being there on many occasions as a boy looking at all the aircraft from the public viewing area and now I was part of the scene. A few of us were there and we stood around waiting to meet the crews of our assigned flights. My first flight was to Munich, Germany and then onto Klagenfurt, Austria and return the same way. I met the flight crew and introduced myself to the Captain. The two Co-pilots seemed to be a bit nervous and one took me aside and said:

"This Captain is one of the most feared in BEA. He is a stickler for discipline. Don't talk to him unless he talks to you."

He and Harry would get on well, I thought.

Anyway, after a while we were driven out to the Vanguard and climbed aboard. There were no fancy jetways around then with the passengers being coached out in all weathers and then made to climb steps onto the aircraft. The familiar smell of the interior returned to me and I felt I was at home. I followed the crew into the flight deck and was assigned a spare seat known as the jump seat. From there I could see everything both inside and outside. A couple of minutes later a stewardess came in and asked what we wanted to drink. All very civilized I thought. Shortly after that the passengers arrived and off we went on our way to Munich.

Heathrow was a large airport with a maze of taxiways. I wondered how they found their way around. All was revealed by an airport taxi plan contained within a library of books on the flight deck. I kept my conversation to a minimum respecting the words said earlier. So the day unfolded with me watching the crew work together. The only thought that I had in those days was that I wanted to go to BOAC rather than BEA. To date only a handful of cadets had been sent to BOAC after completion of their course. Having said that I really did enjoy the day out on the Vanguard.

When we landed back at Heathrow and were taxiing around I spotted another Vickers product, the VC-10. I wonder! I must have thought to myself. Maybe one day! I flew with the infamous Captain for a couple more days. He actually spoke to me on a few occasions. After these first flights I spotted another Hamble cadet and he said that if you ask the duty controller nicely then you can fly on other types of aircraft. I ventured over and asked if I could go as extra crew on the De Havilland Comet 4B that afternoon to Stockholm. It was all sorted for me so off

I went with the crew and very soon was flying across the North Sea to Scandinavia. There seemed to be a different atmosphere in the Comet but maybe the Captain was a bit friendlier. I did my week with BEA and thoroughly enjoyed it and had a couple of days at home before going back to Hamble for the last term and, hopefully, success.

We all arrived back at Hamble knowing that this was the make or break final push. We had to complete the Apache course that included a man from the Civil Aviation Authority (CAA) examining us to establish whether we would be of sufficient standard to be able to fly commercially. We also had to sit our final exams that also deemed us academically able to attain the Commercial Pilots Licence (CPL) which allowed us to join the airlines. It was all pretty daunting I have to say!

A small interlude came our way early in the term which was a welcome break. Over the other side of the Southampton water was a headland known as Calshot Spit. This was where the famous Princess flying boats were based during their testing period. There were two of them still on the slipway all cocooned up like a monument to the past glories of the British aviation industry. We all went over there to look at the relics. If you recall one flew past whilst I was at the Farnborough Air Show many years before.

We scrambled all over them and it was amazing to see and touch such machines. The flight deck was about 30 feet long and some of the original instruments were still in place. I climbed into the inside of the enormous wing and could just about get to the wing tip. I would imagine that this was available to do in-flight maintenance of the engines. We came away with a feeling that we had just witnessed history. Shortly after our visit they were broken up and gone forever.

The other event was that in the World Cup football tournament, England was playing West Germany in the final. We all crammed into the TV room and were ecstatic with the result. England had won the World Cup. Another celebration was in order. Talking about TV there was a new comedy on the box called 'Till death us do part' with the renowned Alf Garnett. This was very controversial at the time since it ventured onto the subject of colour prejudice. Great comedy though!

With the exams looming the pitch was increasing all the time. I believe that the total subjects involved were about eight so there was a lot to do. The flying was becoming more demanding and as for the JPT course with Mr Niven – enough said! As I mentioned I found that part of the course the hardest to do. Fortunately the weather was good for flying given the time of year so that side went well. Our chief ground instructor was a Mr Nick Hoy. He was feared by all except one of the college secretaries who frequented his company quite often. She must have been blind! I remember being trooped in at the double for an audience with him. He looked me up and down and said:

"Your father was here many years ago doing a Flight Navigation Course and I am sorry but his academic ability was far better than what you have achieved to date."

I knew he had been around in Dad's day and he had warned me about Mr Hoy. Having said that, I was a bit taken aback by his comments. I felt I was doing all right but obviously he knew better. He went on:

"If you don't pull your socks up and start knuckling down to some hard revision then you will totally fail your exams and be out of here with nothing."

Little did he know about my past technique at school concerning how I learnt my work. He did not know that I spent many hours in the library writing it all down as I did at school. There was little I could say but to mumble some sort of reply. He then dismissed me and off I went like a scalded cat.

"I'll show the old bugger, you wait!" I must have muttered once I was out of earshot.

By the time the half term break arrived we were all totally exhausted and there was little fun and frolics going on. This was serious stuff. After the break we returned to be told that the inspectors from the CAA would be arriving the following week for the ministry flying tests. If you passed you were issued with a Commercial Pilots Licence and Instrument Rating. This was the goal! We knew little about these men but their reputation went before them. There was one of them, a Mr Belson, who was particularly feared. Part of the test was to imagine the aircraft had been left out all night in a snow storm and that we had to tell the examiner the various precautions that had to be taken. This was before you had to demonstrate the flying side. Nerves were taut!

I cautiously approached the famous blackboard outside of the crew room to read my fate on the day of my test. There was my name on the board, in yellow of course, together with my examiner's name. It was not Belson so that was a relief. I don't recall his name but anyone from the CAA was, in my mind, pretty frightening. The weather was not nice either. It was raining quite a lot and I studied the weather charts as best as I could to somehow make a decision as to whether to fly or not. Bloody difficult when you have the 'Man' looking over your shoulder watching every move you make. I decided that it was now or never so I said that the weather was too bad to fly. He murmured his acceptance of my decision but said that it was OK for him so off we went out to the waiting Apache with me firing verbally on both barrels about the ice and snow scene. The fact that we were both soaked did not seem to matter.

The actual test consisted of flying somewhere to complete an instrument approach on one engine and then return to Hamble for an approach using the basic aid of the Fawley beacon and land off this approach. Normally we went to Gatwick for this but due to the weather I had elected to go to Bournemouth (Hurn) airport since the weather there was forecasted to be marginally better. As it was it was horrible. In retrospect in was a blessing in disguise since I was under what you might say real conditions and I felt I was concentrating more than if it had been a sunny day. I managed the instrument approach OK in the rain and on one engine. The cloud was very low and when I came down to the lowest height allowed for the approach there was the runway dead ahead. I think he liked it and nodded an approval. We started the dead engine up and made our way back to Hamble with the weather getting worse. By the time we arrived over the Fawley radio beacon there was not much to see. The cloud base at Hamble was below the figure that I was allowed so I said that we should divert back to Hurn and land. He replied:

"Right, what you will do is to make an attempt and if not successful then we will go to Hurn as you quite rightly said. I will take the responsibility for the approach."

So what he meant was that if we crashed he would he accept that it was his fault that I died.

I started this rather basic approach to Hamble not knowing what lay before me at the end. I did a sort of teardrop pattern and then started the final leg, descending to the minimum height all on timings and tracking etc. Boy was I working at it! The examiner was watching every move I made. I think he was looking after his own skin as well. We got down to the minimum height and I started to look out through the rain for the airfield. I saw the river OK and it was in the right place.

"Got it," I shouted.

I managed to find the right places in the circuit and landed pretty well 'on the numbers' as they say. The grass was really soaked and we slithered towards the hangar. As we emerged into the rain he said:

"Well done, you have passed your test."

This was my finest hour!

He then shook my hand and we parted company. I went into the crew room to catch up on everybody else. Ian was there and, yes, he had passed as well. This was wonderful. What had happened with Ian was that he had sat his about one hour before me. He told me that there was a leak in the windscreen that made a small spray of cold water. He said that to cool the nerves and the perspiration he ducked his head into this spray every so often and it did the wonderful trick of cooling him down. He was a wet but happy boy! Tony passed as well so there was plenty to celebrate that night. All we needed now was to pass our final exams and we were home and dry. Simple as that!

Now that this flying hurdle was overcome it was time to get down to the task of revision. I spent many hours in the library writing, writing and writing. All social dates were off by this stage and all you could hear from each room were the groans of cadets pouring over the various manuals. The flying activities had slowed right down so there was not much to be cheerful about. As the term progressed so the nerves got more and more tense. Most of the conversation between us was about some question or other concerning the exams.

As I said before one of the worst subjects was Meteorology. The final part of that course was under the subject heading of 'Climatology'. What it entailed was to study the world's local phenomena weather-wise. For example, the Haboob in the Sudan was one and the Monsoon in SE Asia was another. There seemed to be so much to take in. The exams were set for the end of May so there was plenty to do.

I remember one night when we were all at it in our rooms Graham Sheppard came out of his room and declared that he was off down to the Bugle since he had had enough. This was the trigger we needed and we all downed our books and went off to the pub for a welcome break. Sore heads next day!

The day arrived when the exams were due to start and we trooped into breakfast with various manuals for last minute revision. The exams were being held in the village hall so we all ambled down there after breakfast. I seem to recall the exams were spread out over about five days and it was a very testing time, so to speak. Switching from subject to subject was the hardest part of it. Finally, the day came when we had all completed the endurance test. We were given a day off and then back to the flying and some general tidying up off some groundschool bits. The results would be out in about ten days and so the waiting game had started.

In the meantime we were all called into the general studies block at that time to hear of our aircraft assignments in BEA should we be successful in passing out. To my surprise there was a BOAC chap there who announced that he needed ten cadets to join BOAC and were there any volunteers? BOAC, in those days, still had flight navigators in operation. As I said before the pilots would do the navigation and he would be trained in both roles and become a pilot/navigator. The general feeling was that if you joined BOAC you would become one of those types and not do much flying. When asked for volunteers my hand went straight up as did another nine making ten in all. Perfect! If I made it through I would be joining BOAC and not BEA. This was great!

Results first though! About one week later we all got our results and yes, I had passed all of them together with Tony and Ian. Another great occasion swiftly followed by a great party down at the Bugle. The three of us had made it and I had got my wish to go to BOAC. We had about one week to go before we all graduated and a ceremony was held within a few days with guest speakers as well. The ceremony went very well with various cadets getting awards. I was just grateful to have survived Hamble. We ended up with 28 finishers out of 45 starters. I completed the final flying and bade farewell to the Apache. It was in early July that we all left Hamble excited about our future careers in the airlines.

"Eat your heart out, Mr Hoy. I passed the course, just like my Dad," I shouted as I drove through the gates for the last time.

While I was home for a well-earned break Brian Sweet gave me a call about the possibility of some of us sharing a house in Old Windsor. It was close to Heathrow and would be ideal. No.6 Malt House Close, Old Windsor – and so six of us moved into the Malt House. They were Tony, Ian, Steve White, Malcolm Reed, Brian Sweet and me. The house earned the nickname of the 'Malt House'. In airline terms it was five BEA and me being the sole representative of BOAC. I shared with Tony and Ian shared with Malcolm.

After a few days of partying we were all called to start work. Ian, Tony and Steve were to fly the Hawker Siddeley Trident. This was the latest short range airliner to fly with BEA. It began operations in 1963 and was the pioneer in the automatic landing field. Brian and Malcolm were destined to fly the Vickers Vanguard that I had done some of my route experience on.

Chapter 4

– MY EARLY AIRLINE YEARS ON THE VC-10

As for me, I was to attend the BOAC training centre at Cranebank on the 8th August 1966 for induction into the airline. I arrived there, together with my nine other colleagues and met a Mr Pickles who formally welcomed us to the airline. Consider this: I was 20 years of age and the baby of the group. In his short address he said that BOAC was not too sure what to do with us or where to put us but what he would do is to organize a trip for us to go on as extra crew so as to get the feel of the airline. A little bit disorganized, I thought, but a trip would be good. There then followed a few days of administration stuff.

The uniform section was an old Nissen hut that was run by an Irishman called Paddy. He was bemused at the young age of these new pilots and the fact that our rankings were that of a second officer and complemented by a small single gold braid on our jackets and a similar one on our shirt epaulettes. If you consider that BOAC had not recruited any new pilots, except for a small number from a previous Hamble course, for many years and I would have thought the average age was about 40 to 45 then we were, indeed, a novelty. My 'look see' trip details came through. I was to be part of a VC-10 crew due to fly to Bahrain in the Gulf area. After a two day stop we were off to Cairo in Egypt for another stopover and then to Delhi, India for yet another two days off. The whole trip would take about ten days. These were places that were only in the atlas up to this point and I was very much looking forward to it.

I arrived at the crew reporting office which, in those days, was next to Terminal 3 in the central area at Heathrow. I was all kitted out in my new uniform complete with one small gold stripe on my jacket. The staff at the reporting office were all slightly bemused at the sight of this new, seemingly underage, pilot. I met the co-pilots for the flight and the Flight Engineer. They warned me straight away to be very wary of the Captain since he had a fearsome reputation. This was the famous Captain G.

Not another friend of Harry's! I thought.

After a few minutes Captain G walked in. I am sure that everybody around stood to attention as he walked. I gulped and summoned up the courage to introduce myself.

"Good morning, sir. I am Second Officer Mullett. I am due to fly with you as an observer on this trip," I said trying to be all correct.

"If you have any questions please talk to the rest of the crew and not to me," he said in reply.

I remember those exact words.

So, I did just that. I stood well back whilst Captain G was looking at the flight plan and all the other paperwork. The rest of the crew were just hovering in his shadow and dared not speak unless spoken to. In those days this was very much the normal course of events. The Captain was 'God' you might say and the rest of the crew, including the cabin crew, were there to carry out his wishes whether they be right or wrong. There was no debate!

Anyway, after this rather frosty start I thought that I would keep under the umbrella of the other crew members and enjoy the trip. We all went out to the aircraft. As I got down from the bus I caught all of the familiar smells and sights of an aircraft preparing to fly. The Flight Engineer suggested that I walked around the aircraft with him since that was his duty. He assured me as we walked that I was unlucky to get this Captain for my first trip but not to worry.

"The rest of the crew will make sure you enjoy it," he said with a wink in his eye.

I think that this verbal rendition created in me an immediate affection for Flight Engineers. They were a wonderful breed of men and it was a sad day when they were pensioned off. Anyway, I followed him around the VC-10 and he told me about all the things to look out for with respect to the aircraft. Being close up to the aircraft I realized the Apache was very small in comparison. I would think that you could sit the Apache on one wing of the VC-10 with no problem.

We then climbed the aircraft steps and I stood quietly until invited into the flight deck. As you entered there was, on the left, a seat facing backwards looking at a panel that had some instruments on it. This was the domain of the Pilot/Navigator when he was needed. The next seat faced to the right towards an enormous panel where all the engineering instruments were mounted. This was the Flight Engineer's position. Another seat was on the left-hand side which was my seat. It was the now familiar 'jump seat'. Finally, there were the two seats left and right both facing forward that were occupied by the Captain on the left and the Co-pilot on the right. In all, five crew members could be installed in the flight deck.

There were two types of VC-10 that BOAC flew. The first was known as the Standard VC-10 with 12 first class and 99 economy seats. The best thing about the Standard was that the flight deck was like a ballroom. The second type was the Super VC-10 that has 16 first class and 126 economy seats. To cram in more passenger seats the flight deck of the Super was shortened and to get five in there was a work of art. Fortunately, the aircraft I was on for my trip was the standard type. Total luxury!

I settled into my seat and watched everything going on. In the past it had not meant too much to me but on this occasion it all started to make sense. The checklist routine and the radio calls were what I expected. The training at Hamble was harsh at times but was essential for any would-be pilot to learn and understand. The only difference here was the inclusion of the Flight Engineer. We didn't have those on the Apache!

The role of the Cabin Crew was interesting to watch as well. The stewardesses were the most interesting. I wonder why? The male cabin crew uniforms were similar to what you would expect on a ship. They were dark navy blue in colour, complete with very thin rank markings. The ranks were similar to us starting from a Second Steward working up to First Steward and finally Chief Steward. The girls wore a simple navy blue skirt, white blouse and a simple navy hat. White gloves were in order. The result was a very elegant looking lady. They were lovely! They did not have any rankings but were graded, starting from the most junior or 'C' girl through 'B' girl to the most senior or 'A' girl whose sole duties were to deal with the first class passengers only.

Back in the flight deck the routine of engine start was under way and the first thing I noticed was the total lack of engine noise. This is where the VC-10 came into its own. The engines were all mounted at the back under the tail with two on each side which left all the noise behind. We taxied out with Captain G doing the honours and finally lined up for the take-off. Once on the runway and when cleared to go, the Flight Engineer got hold of the throttles and pushed them all forward together. The engine note changed to a crackly roar which I definitely could hear. The VC-10 then leapt into life and we literally roared down the runway. After about 30 seconds we were airborne and climbing away. What a performer this VC-10 was! About a minute or so later the Flight Engineer pulled the throttles back so that the roar died away to a rumble. He leant over to me and quietly said:

"Noise abatement, my boy."

What is he talking about? I thought.

Again, about a minute later, he pushed the throttles forward again and the flaps were pulled in and we were on our way to Kuwait, which was to be our first port of call before Bahrain. The route fascinated me since I was now out of my UK flying environment and into Europe and beyond. The crew supplied me with route maps showing the airways that we were to follow. The changing voices of the ground controllers as we flew over each country made for some amusing comments by the crew. Captain G just sat in his seat and said very little.

After about two hours the 'A' girl came in with five first-class menus and handed them out to us. We were expected to tick the items we wanted to eat. I surveyed the menu and I must have looked a sight. Up to now I was used to what Mr Hunt at Hamble could provide, ranging from Steak and Kidney pie to Bangers and Mash. Here there were words I had never seen before let alone eaten. Such things as Consommé soup, Steak Wellington, Pan Fried Brook Trout and Caviar spring to mind. I thought of my experience as a boy in the New York breakfast queue and thought I could devour the lot since I was very hungry. The other problem was that there did not seem to be any division between starters and pudding. There were dots and dashes all over the place. My friendly Flight Engineer saw my confusion and helped sort me out with some semblance of ticks on the menu. I was amused that each one had a title on it as to who it was on the flight deck. My title was 'Junior Jet Pilot'.

After a while the menus were collected and shortly after that our meal service started. It was a truly gastronomic occasion. It started with caviar and all the trimmings. I carefully followed the other crew members as to how to deal with it. The taste was wonderful and given the opportunity, even now, I could live quite happily on it all day. Consommé soup followed. The Flight Engineer had told me to put a double tick against the soup. When it arrived it had a taste to it that was a bit strange. I was enlightened about this taste. A drop of Sherry had been added to liven it up. This was good! The third course was the Beef Wellington which was top quality beef in a pastry case and was totally out of this world. There then followed about two more courses with the whole event taking about one and a half hours to complete.

Mr Hunt – eat your heart out, I thought.

The day drifted on and then very quickly became night since we were going eastwards away from the sun and the sunset happened in double quick time. We were about one hour from landing at Kuwait and the flight deck started to stir with books being opened and Captain G briefing the Co-pilot as to how he wanted the approach done and so on and so forth. The Flight Engineer was busy playing with his panel switching this on and that off. We were by now flying over western Iraq and the moonlit landscape looked pretty bleak with very few lights anywhere on the ground. We started our descent and I was amazed to hear the crisp tones of an Englishman on the radio giving us directions. I learnt later that most of the Middle East airfields were run by an English company called Aerad. So there we were flying into a desert airfield run by the English. Strange!

We continued down into what I thought was a total black void when suddenly the lights of Kuwait appeared some way ahead. The whole descent was similar to the normal one that I had done many times at Hamble but just a bit longer and more drawn out. Eventually we began the final approach to the runway. It still really was a strange sensation being controlled by this Englishman and landing in a foreign country. After landing we taxied in to the ramp and shut down. The steps arrived and the first thing that hit me was the heat of the night.

It was about 40 degrees Centigrade at about ten o'clock at night. This was the Gulf at its best! I stood at the top of the steps and just stared at my surroundings. Apart from the lights of the city it was all sand. In those days BOAC had a large overseas contingent of employees who were there to deal with arrivals and departures of the aircraft. We even had our own check-in staff that had been shipped out from the UK. The only locals I could see were the loaders and the refuelling staff. After about 45 minutes the doors were closed and we were off again to Bahrain. I was pretty warm by now. The VC-10 did not have a fancy on-board air conditioning system like modern aircraft and had to rely on ground air conditioning units to keep it cool. The only problem with that was these units often broke down through overwork with the result that the aircraft 'cooked' whilst on the ground during a transit stop. Anyway, we took off for the 40 minute flight to Bahrain. The Co-pilot did this sector under the watchful eye of the Captain. He seemed to do all right.

Could I imagine myself in that position? I thought.

The route took us south from Kuwait past a vast number of oil fields that lit up the night sky. I was fascinated by the sights as we flew along. Once again an English controller guided us into the runway at Bahrain. After landing I was amazed to see a large number of RAF aircraft lined up on an adjacent ramp to the main one. The Flight Engineer told me that apart from being the airport for Bahrain this was also an RAF base. Amazing being so far from home! As we started to get our bits together for the stopover another crew climbed aboard to take the flight on to its next stop. Not knowing a soul I just lurked in the background. The new Captain wandered over to me and said hello and how was I enjoying the trip. What a nice man he was. I was introduced to some of the other crew and took a glimpse at the new Cabin Crew. There were indeed some lovely stewardesses about. Could be fun!

We finally all got off and made our way into the arrival hall to collect our bags. This arrival hall was nothing but a bunch of single storey buildings all bolted together to resemble something like a large hangar style hall. The locals were all bedecked in flowing robes complete with ornate head bands. It was like something out of 'Arabian Nights' to me and, to think I was sitting in London not too many hours before. We all made our way out of the building to a rickety old bus that seemed about 50 years old. We all clambered in and off we went. Captain G had his own car so we were on our own in the bus. Within seconds of leaving I felt a tap on my shoulder and a cold can of beer was thrust into my hand. With the heat that was stifling me through the open windows I downed the can's contents in double quick time. The ride took about 30 minutes and a few beers were consumed. The mood of the crew had now changed from the orderly situation on the aircraft to a bunch of party animals in the time it took to get to the hotel. In fact, we were not in a hotel but a BOAC run rest house as they called it. When we checked in for our room allocation we were each given a brown envelope which contained a wad of local money to be used during our stay there as a crew allowance. The condition of some of the notes was somewhat questionable but it was quite something to get this hand-out. This brown envelope system was simply a method of issuing crew allowances at the time. By this time Captain G had already arrived and disappeared to his room.

"You won't see any more of him until we leave," one of the Co-pilots remarked.

I found it strange that a crew member could disappear like that for the stopover but felt a bit relieved that this particular Captain had gone. The rest of the crew now seemed very relaxed and suggested meeting in the bar in 30 minutes or so. Party time I thought! I presented myself at the bar and were joined by the rest of the crew soon after. There were also other crews there so the mood was very relaxing. I think the saying 'work hard to play hard' springs to mind. The impromptu party went on for some hours and I was, in some respect, the centre of attention since a pilot of my age was a rare sight and worthy of deep interrogation.

Towards the end of the session some of the conversations became a little confused or maybe it was the drink that was playing tricks. I finally weaved my way back to my room. As I left the bar the heat hit me head-on and was quite overwhelming since the layout of the rest house involved walking outside. When I got to my room there was no respite to the heat since there was no such luxury as air conditioning. To describe the room compared with modern day crew accommodation you would have to imagine a simple single bed and bedside table plus a very basic bathroom as being it in total. The lack of any cooling was the hardest to take. I took another shower but by the time I fell into bed I was dripping again. Thus my first night away was an experience never to be forgotten.

I woke late the next morning in a strange sort of way. There I was sitting up in bed dripping again with perspiration and wondering where the hell I was. There was a banging on the door and in comes the local room cleaner ready to start on my room. He spotted this dripping mass in bed and backed away out of the door muttering something in Arabic. I staggered out of bed and showered again trying to clear my head from the excesses of the night before. I made my way down to the reception looking for the restaurant since I was starving hungry by then. Now, if I thought it was hot the night before then the day was something to be experienced. The heat was like walking into an oven. Every bit of clothing stuck to you like Velcro.

By the time I found the restaurant I was a dripping mess again. I found a couple of familiar faces and joined them for a late breakfast. I have to say that I recall that the food was very good and much needed. The conversation ranged from the usual aircraft chat to the latest union problems. I just sat and occasionally nodded or added some simple comment. The nice thing was that I felt I was no longer a novelty but accepted as part of the crew. Breakfast drifted on for a couple of hours and many coffees. One of the Co-pilots suggested a game of squash later on in the day. Not wishing to be a total dropout I said that that would be good. I will add that in those days I was quite sporty and felt that hopefully the courts would at least have some sort of cooling. Wrong!

I rolled up in my kit on time having spent most of the day in the shower. The first thing that happened was that a plate of salt was produced and the Co-pilot said it is good to take a small spoonful to help replace the amount lost during the day. I did just that and then followed him onto the court. It was like walking into a cauldron of hot burning embers. What the heck I thought! I am young compared to this chap and felt pretty relaxed with my game. From the moment the first ball was played I regretted that statement though. I was whitewashed by this older chap He seemed to have the knack of scoring every time without moving too much with me running around like some sort of demented wreck leaving a trail of perspiration in my wake. We played for 30 minutes or so. At that point I couldn't talk and was just about able to breathe. When I finally got back to my room I collapsed in a total heap on the bed and just lay there traumatized. After a couple of hours the Flight Engineer banged on my door and said:

"How did the game go then?"

My reply was unprintable. No doubt my opponent had spread the word that this new young pilot may not live too long due to physical exhaustion and that he was totally trashed. That evening I entered the bar quietly and sat in the corner waiting for the rest of the crew. They all arrived and fortunately not too much was said about the game earlier. We were due to fly to Cairo early the next morning so a quiet evening followed and I hit the heat box again for a restless night's sleep.

I was woken by banging on the door followed by a waiter bringing me in a pot of tea and biscuits and announcing that pick-up was in one hour. No fancy alarm calls here! We all assembled in the foyer and were greeted by the presence of Captain G. I wondered what he had done during the stopover. Anyway, soon we were back on the rickety old bus back to the airport. The VC-10 landed from some point east shortly after we arrived and we walked out to meet the incoming crew. As I stood there at the bottom of the steps I was surprised to see a succession of RAF Hunters taxiing followed by a Vulcan bomber. This was a very busy RAF base by all accounts. I learnt later that they were all part of a large Middle East contingent of UK military assigned to the protection of the Gulf States and, in particular, Kuwait which was under constant threat from Iraq. It was only five years before, in 1961, when British Troops were sent to Kuwait to protect its borders from an Iraqi threat to invade. They made it 30 years later – it goes back that long!

When the pleasantries were exchanged we climbed aboard and got ready for our flight to Cairo. The heat was building up nicely and the ground air conditioning unit worked OK and did a good job cooling down the cabin. I was starting to feel at home and soon tucked myself into my seat and took in the routine. We took off from Bahrain and headed west out over Saudi Arabia. We then had to play musical chairs since the pilot/navigator had to show his skill in navigation. I ended up mainly standing at the back and drifted around the galley area generally getting in the way. Talking of galleys it was quite amazing what the Cabin Crew could do in such a confined space. The forward galley dealt exclusively with the first class section so I watched all these wonderful menu items being constructed from scratch using only the skill of the Steward. Made me hungry just looking!

After about 40 minutes the navigation part had been completed and we all got back to our original seats just as we were presented with lunch. I had never eaten so well in all my life. First class food all the way! About one hour later we crossed the Red Sea and turned north towards Cairo. This was in the autumn of 1966 and all was relatively quiet in the region. There was Israel out to the right and Egypt off to the left. Having left the relatively civilized Gulf Area I was taken aback by the seemingly lack of control whilst descending towards the arrival at Cairo. The English was very poor and we seemed to be flying all over the place following some sort of route based on very dubious radio aids. The Co-pilot leaned over and said:

"There is no fancy radar here in Cairo so it is always total chaos arriving here."

He was right. I was only catching about one word in ten from the controller.

"What did he say?" I asked the Flight Engineer.

"Oh, I think he said for us to turn right or something. The pilots will know what to do," he replied.

In those days the Flight Engineer did not get too involved with the flying side of the aircraft. His job was to look after the engineering bits. Things have changed somewhat from those days. After about 20 minutes of what I can only describe as total chaos we landed at Cairo. The familiar heat barrier stopped me in my tracks as I got to the bottom of the steps onto the tarmac. It was 40 degrees plus and was I feeling it or what! It was a dry heat with little humidity so you did not perspire much. You just baked!

We climbed into the familiar rickety old bus again and made our way to the hotel. The journey, I remember, was a total insight to the

Middle East way of life. The noisy, dusty and crowded roads were, in my mind, like something out of the Middle Ages. As for the cars, they were a mixture of the 'old' and 'very old' variety. I soon learnt that the only essential item, apart from the engine, that needed to work was the horn. The continuous sounds of these horns help to create total verbal chaos. There were donkeys pulling the most enormous carts full of some exotic fruit. There were people crossing the road at all points with little regard to the 'Highway Code'. It seemed that any square foot of pavement had a vendor of some sort established selling some dodgy looking bric-a-brac. What an amazing city this was. I was totally captivated by its charm, if you could call it that. By the time we reached the hotel we were all totally cooked but ready for a night out. Another brown envelope appeared with local money. This was good! We had only come from Bahrain about three hours away and it was about six in the evening. Captain G did his usual disappearing act so we were off and running. The local beer in Cairo is called 'Stella' so the expression was:

"Right folks, we are off for an affair with Stella."

The other crew members knew Cairo well so it was not long before we were established in some local shady bar underneath the date palms and relaxing. This was, indeed, the life for me. I had grown to love the VC-10 and I hoped that I would eventually get to fly one as a co-pilot. The aircraft was an amazing performer considering the temperatures across the Middle East and Africa. The main rival was the Boeing 707. In economic terms the 707 outshone the VC-10 but when it came to the operational side in hot and high airports the VC-10 cleaned up. Besides, she looked beautiful. The colour scheme in those days was simple but elegant. There was a dark navy cheat line along the fuselage which swept under the nose. The upper area was crisp white and the tail was the same dark navy colour. Right in the middle of the tail was the famous BOAC emblem of the 'Speedbird' in gold. The lower area was grey. She looked simply stunning!

Anyway, back to the bar. The evening was hot and humid but did not detract from the atmosphere. It was quite magic watching all the hustle and bustle going on around me. The Stella was going down very well too! Finally, sleep overtook us and off we staggered back to the hotel. On the following morning after breakfast a trip had been organized to go to the famous Pyramids at Giza and maybe a horse ride. I think there must have been about four of us since we all fitted snugly into the beaten up old Ford Zodiac taxi. We extricated ourselves from the taxi, after a nail-biting drive, right by the Pyramids and the sight of the majestic old wonders was overwhelming. We were right on the edge of the desert and there they were commanding the skyline with their absolute precise construction. At the base of one of them was the Sphinx looking very small in comparison and almost model like. A guide showed us around the Pyramids and I found it all quite enlightening. I was glad the tour did not include climbing them since I would have failed miserably.

Just along the road there were a collection of stables. We arrived outside one of them called the 'AA' stables and the boss came running out welcoming all of us to his humble abode:

"Special discount today for the BOAC," he kept shouting in immaculate English.

I am sure that this was his standard patter to drum up business. It was decided that we would go for a ride into the desert to a bar/eatery place called 'Sahara City' about 30 minutes ride away. I declared myself confident in the art of riding. Why did I not shut up at that moment? Out from the stables comes this wild thing huffing and puffing. It took me back to the riding school of my youth and the redhead.

"Good luck on that beast," someone shouted.

The beast and I eyed each other up and down as if ready to do battle. I was hoisted up into the saddle and looked along the neck to the twitching ears and the head that led to a pair of flaring nostrils. The next thing that happened was that the head swung back and the teeth were bared and the target was my foot that was well within his reach. These teeth were yellow and chipped and looked a bit dangerous. I just hauled back on the reins to straighten him out and he pulled back within a whisker of my big toe throwing out a snorting sound that could wake the dead.

"Well done young man. You have got to watch him like a hawk or one of his many tricks will get you. Anyway, Tally-Ho everybody," the boss shouted.

At that point he trotted off and started to climb up the slope right next to one of the Pyramids. I could have leant out and touched them. My horse and I seemed to hit a rapport at this stage since he meekly followed the leader up the slope. So far so good! Once we had climbed the slope we reached the open desert. The boss fired up his horse and off we went. It was wonderful to have such open spaces to ride in compared with the restraints of England. After about 25 minutes of hard riding we arrived at 'Sahara City'. My mount was pretty reluctant to go to the full gallop and needed a lot of coaxing on my part. I thought it strange for such a strong horse to be totally lazy when it came to getting up to some sort of speed. Little did I know!

Anyway, we all dismounted and tied up the horses and sat down at a makeshift table and ordered 'Stella' beer. The heat was very oppressive but I did not feel too bad since there was a fair breeze blowing. 'Sahara City' was, in fact, a ramshackle bar amongst a collection of rundown huts in the middle of nowhere. The time came for us to leave and so I wandered back to my horse and fed him a carrot as a bribe to get me home safely. His chipped, yellow stained teeth seemed to devour the carrot whole and almost my hand with it. I mounted up and ambled around waiting for the others to join up for the ride home.

As we left the area everything changed within a split second when my horse knew that he was on the way home to the comfort of his stable. He did a standing Grand Prix start and suddenly we were at the full gallop with me having no control whatsoever. I just clung on! The desert floor became a blur and the rest of the party were somewhere behind me following this cloud of dust on the horizon. I had never been so fast on a horse in my life and I regretted downing that last beer. My only thought was the slope down by the Pyramids. It is a fact that going downwards on a horse is not that easy for the rider. Surely he will slow down or tire out by then? Not a bloody chance! He was giving it his all and taking revenge on me for pushing him on the way out. As we approached the top of the slope a group of local kids were playing. They scattered in all directions as we tore through them like a tornado and then, without pause, we launched down the slope at top speed. A racehorse hits about 45 miles an hour at top speed but I felt that was like a 'walk in the park' compared with this thing I was clinging on to.

On the way down the slope I gradually slipped forward in the saddle and emerged at the bottom just about astride his neck. As we approached the stables I saw a reception committee of stable workers watching this demented wreck clinging onto the neck of the horse and looking decidedly unhappy. Was he going to stop or will we both continue on into his stable? He stopped all right in about two yards just as we entered the stable courtyard. The laws of momentum come into play now with me not stopping in the two yards allocated and gracefully carrying on in mid-air for maybe another yard or two. Then gravity took over and down I went to meet 'Mother Earth' in a totally crumpled heap on the floor, in a cloud of dust. What a sight I must have looked! I sat there counting my bones as a precaution, checking for breakages. This bloody horse was standing in front of me blowing and snorting and sort of staring at me as if to say: "Good job done. I am off for my tea now. See you later, you stupid Englishman."

This routine must have been normal for this horse since the audience around me giggled and laughed as if it happened every day. I'm sure it did! I struggled up and deposited myself on a chair and was brought a nice mug of tea. The others all trooped in after a short while and enquired as to my health.

"I am fine, except for a few problems with that thing over there," I said pointing at my horse quietly munching away at his hay.

The boss arrived and smirked at me and said: "You must have had a fast ride back because we never saw you. He is a bit headstrong and he loves to get home."

Too right, I thought.

We got back to the hotel late in the afternoon and grabbed a quick bite to eat since we were off early in the morning to Delhi. Apart from the encounter with the mad horse I was totally captivated by Cairo.

The next morning we went off to the airport again together with Captain G and made our way to the VC-10 that was waiting for us on the tarmac. I remember that the ground air conditioning unit was not working and the heat inside the aircraft was unbearable. In the flight deck the intensity was exaggerated since we were surrounded by the glass cockpit windows. It must have been 50 degrees plus in there and made worst by the number of people scurrying in and out. The chaos of the arrival was matched by the scene during the boarding. The amazing thing was that Captain G just sat in his seat and did not show any sign of being hot. Perhaps years of exposure to these sorts of conditions had adapted his body system. As for me I was just about at bursting point which was not helped at all by the aches and pains of my encounter the day before.

We finally departed for Delhi and only then did things start to cool down once we got into the air. In the wing roots of the VC-10 there is an intake that puts the airflow through a large fridge-like contraption that effectively cools the airflow to whatever is selected. This cooled air is then distributed throughout the cabin and gets to work cooling everybody down. This device was amazingly effective and within 20 minutes or so I could breathe again. The initial part of the flight was just as chaotic as the previous arrival with the aircraft gyrating round the sky in three dimensions. The flight was routed northwards over the Eastern Mediterranean towards Beirut, Lebanon and then eastwards over Iran, Pakistan and western India to Delhi. The weather was brilliant and I could pick out all of the features as we flew over them. It all seemed so peaceful down there with little villages dotted around. Little did I know that the whole lot would blow up into a cauldron in the near future and stay boiling for my complete flying career – and beyond.

As we flew over the southern areas of Iran (Persia in those days) I was amazed how desolate it all looked down there. The ground was a permanent sandy yellow in colour with no features that I could make out. We had lunch at some stage in the flight and I was getting well versed with the routine. Consommé with a double tick of course! What I found humbling was the fact that there we were feasting on all this wonderful food and down below there must have been abject poverty with people trying to scratch a living in the desert. Strange world!

We arrived in Delhi at about 10 pm local time and the chaos on the ground was the same as Cairo but with a different race of people. In those days India was what they call a dry state. In other words no alcohol was available to be bought anywhere. Not a nice thought having developed a taste for it from my early teens. One thing I did notice was that all crew members have very large briefcases and I did wonder why.

Now, here comes the trick. Many cans of beer could be stowed in all the nooks and crannies of these oversize briefcases. Surely they would be searched in customs, I thought. What was done was a decoy can was positioned somewhere near the top of the bag and the customs officers would gleefully extract the offending can carefully and then verbally condone the crew member concerned for his crime. A great wad of notepads emerged followed by form filling and various signatures and stamps applied. Eventually the customs officer would pick up a piece of chalk and ceremoniously place his mark of the briefcase and bag and send you on the way little knowing that you had the complete contents of the 'Nag's Head' with you.

Once again the rickety bus was there waiting for us. I am sure that a fleet of these were made just for BOAC crew members to go from the airport to the hotel and back, worldwide. We were only just clear of the airport when the familiar beer can was opened and away we went. What struck me whilst travelling through the dark streets was the amount of local people who seemed to be aimlessly walking around. The other thing was that, even in the darkness, I could make out that there was an enormous amount of poverty. There were people sleeping on the pavements everywhere. As we drove along the scene changed with little signs of the poverty I had just seen; instead were large opulent houses to the left and right. This was obviously the rich side of Delhi. There were still people wandering around though.

We drove into the hotel and were greeted by a fleet of hotel staff all anxious to please. There must have been about 20 of them fussing around us. The hotel lobby was very ornate with all things Indian festooned around. Only 18 years earlier India had gained its independence from the UK but it seemed to be still stuck in a time warp. The Indians are a wonderful race of people and this thought still remains with me to this day. The hotel was excellent is every respect and the service impeccable. Yet another brown envelope arrived full of Indian Rupees this time.

Once our rooms were sorted the word was out that the Chief Steward was opening up his room for drinks. I arrived at his room at the appointed hour and settled down for a few beers. I was amazed where all the booze came from. A well-stocked bar back home would be pushed to stock this sort of quantity. This was my first introduction to the famous 'room party' which would become part of my life. It all starts off in a civilized manner and gradually drifts into a general fracas with maybe six conversations all going on at once. In those days the relationship between the flight crew and cabin crew was second to none as opposed to the 'us and them' scene you have nowadays. The 'room party' was the hub of the crew in those times and cemented friendships between all sorts of people. Invariably everybody turned up for a drink and a chat. Some of the room parties got out of hand but generally they were orderly affairs with the usual struggle to get back to your room at the end. There was plenty of fun and frolics to be had as well which, for a young lad like me, was all part of the game. The stewardesses I can quite honestly say were lovely ladies and full of fun with no hang-ups. Times will change. Coming back to this particular room party in Delhi the topic came up as to what to do in our three days off. I jumped at the suggestion of a visit to the Taj Mahal in Agra which was about two hours' drive away. The Flight Engineer suggested a round of golf and so it went on.

I opted for the Taj Mahal and about four of us assembled in the lobby early next day and were met by a turban-headed gentleman who was to be our driver for the day. He looked like something out of the 'Raj' by the way he dressed and had the most superb moustache. It is amazing when you remember these fine details many years later. Our car was an old American machine but was very spacious and in the boot we had a large stock of soft drinks to pamper us all the way. The only drawback was that the suspension was non-existent or missing and, when combined with the general state of the roads, left the occupants in a total state of shock most of the time. There was no air conditioning so the windows were cranked down which had the effect of drawing in every smell that was known to man. The heat was starting to build up by the time we actually left the hotel. Having said all that it was a great feeling to me to venture out like this.

As we left the outskirts of Delhi we started to see the real poverty of India. We drove through villages that looked absolutely desolate and all the children ran out to shout at us for 'Buckshee' or money. I would think that between ten of them there may have been enough clothes for three of them. It had been raining the night before and that seemed to add to the misery of these places. We eventually ran clear of these villages and settled down on what must have been an 'A' road since the tarmac was more or less even and the potholes were not quite as common as earlier. The smoother ride was good for the body as well. After about two hours we arrived on the outskirts of Agra and drove alongside a river and arrived at a hotel that had been planned for lunch. In India curry is the national dish and my love for it is everlasting. So, it was curry for my lunch, dinner and breakfast if I could. On this occasion I would imagine lamb curry would have been in order. Our driver fussed around us and hovered in the background waiting for the main part of the day.

After lunch we climbed back into the car and then made our way to the Taj Mahal. As we came around the corner there it was. They say that it is one of the Seven Wonders of the World and how right they were. Amongst all the poverty there was this wonderful creation built entirely on the toils of labourers, architects and artists. It was completely constructed of marble and inlaid with the most fantastic designs and figures. Let us pause for a history lesson by quoting the official guide:

'The Taj Mahal was built from 1631-1653 by Mughal Emperor Shah Jahan who got this monument constructed in the memory of his beloved wife Mumtaz Mahal, with whom he fell in love at first sight. The very first sight of the Taj Mahal, the epitome of love and romance leaves one mesmerized. Standing majestically on the banks of River Yamuna, the Taj Mahal is synonymous with love and romance. It is believed that the name "Taj Mahal" was derived from the name of Shah Jahan's wife Mumtaz Mahal and means "Crown Palace". The purity of the white marble, the exquisite ornamentation, precious gemstones used and its picturesque location, all make the Taj Mahal worthy of its place as one of the seven wonders of the world. However, unless and until, one knows the love story behind the Taj Mahal of India, it will seem just like a beautiful building. But, the love behind this outstanding monument is what has given a life to this monument.'

I was completely absorbed with everything I saw. What an incredible sight it was. I felt so lucky to be privileged enough to see it. One of the girls with us remarked she had been before but was still totally mesmerized by it. We all walked through the entrance and slowly made our way up to the Taj Mahal alongside a waterway covered with the most wonderful collection of exotic plants. We must have spent a couple of hours there just taking everything in. We had a guide who explained in perfect English what all the various symbols and artefacts meant. It was very hot by then but that did seem to detract from the sheer immensity of it all. When we left my mind was full of admiration and praise for all that I had seen.

We then went to the famous 'Red Fort' that sits on the riverbank overlooking the Taj Mahal from about two miles away. We climbed to the top of the ramparts and looked across the river and took in the sights. There I was at the tender age of 20 being allowed to see this wonderful place. I felt so lucky! In time we left the 'Red Fort' and were driven back to the local hotel where we had eaten lunch, and sat down for afternoon tea. Now this afternoon tea could not have been more English. You could imagine yourself sitting on the banks of the Thames and not in some faraway country. There were cucumber and egg sandwiches, scones, cakes and tea like no other. No Welsh cakes though! We finally got back to the hotel at about seven in the evening pretty worn out after our amazing day. I think I was asleep in seconds.

The next day it was the local sights of Delhi for me that included the other famous 'Red Fort' in Old Delhi and the market area alongside. The Red Fort was spectacular in its own right and, being on my own, I wandered around at my leisure. The other thing about India is that all cows are sacred. So there you are sitting in the back of a taxi and these creatures just drift in front of you like they owned the road. In India I think they do! It is up to the driver to avoid the animals which makes for a very 'start-stop' journey.

After I left the 'Red Fort' I was propositioned by a young lad whose mode of transport was a large tricycle that sported a seat across the back. He haggled over the price with me for a while and after I felt that I had been done financially, since I was not used to bartering, I climbed aboard and off we went. He was a small chap but he could pull this contraption through the streets of the market with ease. The smells from the spice market area were intoxicating. There were huge sacks of chillies and other spices that I did not have any knowledge of.

As I was pulled alongside the river there were huge great bonfires being constructed on the banks of the river. Strange I thought! It was later revealed to me that these were funeral pyres. Other people's cultures were totally alien to me at that time. The moment I stepped off the tricycle I was surrounded by taxi drivers willing to take me anywhere. It was by now extremely hot with the temperature well over 40 degrees and I had had enough of the sights. I climbed into the nearest taxi and headed back to the hotel. I arrived late afternoon and found out where the room party was that evening and hit my room to have yet another shower. I had been two days on the go in the oppressive heat of Delhi and I was beginning to wilt fast. I had a nice healthy colour on the skin though!

The room party went according to plan and we all went off to a local curry house for a wonderful meal. The following morning I did nothing. I just lay in bed and caught up with sleep. At about lunchtime the Flight Engineer called me for a game of golf at about three that afternoon. How could I refuse! I enjoyed the game and felt that it would be letting the side down to refuse. So, golf it was in the afternoon with about three of us playing. It was pretty hot out there and I remember the golf was lousy. What was wonderful was that you did not have to carry anything and the caddie boys were running around in circles.

"Wonderful shot, sir. Just a little to the right!" they would say as your ball fired off at right angles.

We finally got back to the hotel about seven in the evening and I retired hurt. Besides, we were off in the morning back home. At this point I cannot recall the route from Delhi to London except that the whole trip was an incredible experience and cemented my thoughts as to my future with BOAC. All I hoped was that I would avoid the famous Captain G. I think throughout the whole trip he might have spoken only one or two words in total to me, let alone a complete sentence.

When I finally arrived back at the Malt House the lads were all there waiting for my report. By this time they had all done their induction into BEA and had been allocated their various aircraft course start dates. BOAC called me in and we all had maybe a week of talks by various departments as an introduction to the airline. It transpired that two of us who had left Hamble were about two hours short of simulator time so my good friend Bron and I were sent down to the VC-10 simulator complex to complete the time shortfall. Unlike the wretched JPT at Hamble this was a fully working simulator. I remember the instructor was a bit confused as to what to do with us on the machine so he devised some sort of programme to fly and off we went. Bearing in mind neither of us had ever done the technical course for the aircraft I remember he was quite impressed with our flying ability. Maybe the fact that this machine actually flew like a real aircraft helped. About a week later we were informed that we would all be allocated to the VC-10 and that the course start date was in about one week. I was on the way to all my dreams coming true.

The training centre for BOAC was a little way from the airport towards Hounslow and was called Cranebank or 'Braincrank' to some. This was where all the classrooms and the simulators were housed. In those days it was quite a small place accommodating maybe 100 people at one time. All of us who had left Hamble together were on the same VC-10 technical course plus one extra ex-Britannia Captain making a total of 11 of us. We arrived at Cranebank as requested and were told that the first week would be taken up by the Safety Equipment Procedure (SEP) course and then the technical course after that.

In that first week we covered all of the safety items for the aircraft. On one of the days we all trooped off to the local swimming pool to do the dinghy drill. So there we all were bedecked in our swimming trunks and told to put on the life jacket and climb up to the first diving board and jump in. Not good for one unhappy in the water but it had to be done. Once in the water we had to clamber into this yellow rubberized dinghy and pretend to be in the middle of the Atlantic Ocean struggling to survive. All sorts of other things were dealt with during that week including fighting fires, clambering through smoke tunnels and firing flares. Pretty thorough business I have to say. It transpired that we had to come back once a year to revalidate our SEP.

The following Monday morning we all assembled in a classroom in Cranebank and started the VC-10 conversion course. In those days it was called a 'Chalk and Talk' course with no computer images anywhere. The instructor dragged in a fully working model of one of the aircraft systems and proceeded to go through it in fine detail. The starting subject was the Oxygen system. We were introduced to all the various valves and working parts of the system. The detail was very exacting to the point that I envisaged that I could build the complete system in my garage over the weekend. Each system was dealt with in the same sort of detail. When I think back to those days it was obvious that there would have been nothing that could have been done in flight to repair a system besides turning it off. That was the way it was.

The technical course was spread out over five weeks and all the systems were covered in equal detail. After about the end of week four my head was full of figures and I even knew how the electrics for the landing lights worked. The VC-10 was a very complicated aircraft for its day. Consider a simple item like the windscreen wipers. There were three of them in total and each one had its own self-contained hydraulic system to sweep them back and forth across the screen. They were each actuated by an electrical relay switch from some unknown source. When you switched them off they were parked on the side of each windscreen by hydraulic pressure that came from the main aircraft's system and not their own supply. There must have been pipes all over the place and all this just to wipe the rain away.

The air conditioning system was equally complicated with air from the engines being routed through all sorts of gates and traps before it finally got into the cabin. As with the hydraulic system, it had supposedly two complete systems which joined up at various points to save weight. Anyway, I got to grips with it all and in week five we were all ushered into the examination room to sit the Air Registration Board (ARB) paper to qualify us technically on the aircraft. I passed OK and was ready for the simulator course which was next on the agenda.

The simulators in use in those days were very different to the modern versions. Consider nowadays, if you can visualize a complete flight deck mounted on a chassis of jacks and pistons totally isolated on its own island in the middle of a room, you get aboard via a drawbridge and then strap in. The drawbridge is then lifted and the whole assembly is free to move in all directions so as to reproduce very realistically what actually happens in the real aircraft. The modern simulator is an excellent tool since it is so lifelike.

Now, back to 1966, and the machine we used then. The VC-10 simulator only went up and down. The back was totally open for access and the only sensation of flight was when you pulled or pushed the control column. The electronics to drive the machine were based on an analogue system. A comparison to this is like the old valve-type radio and the more modern transistor one. As a consequence of this there was an inherent lag in performing an action and getting the desired result. Nowadays the visual effects are amazing to the point where you can even see a truck or fire engine out of the window. Back then, the only visual effects was a model runway built on a huge expanse of wood with a CCTV camera suspended over it and free to move across this model according to what was being done in the simulator. Can you imagine the resulting fiasco when you looked out of the window and saw this model runway complete with a spider crawling across it? If I remember this contraption was done away with soon after I arrived since it became more of a hindrance than a help.

The simulator course was based on 12 to 14 details assigned according to your ability to 'do the job'. The amazing thing was that there was no set agenda that could be followed and revised before each detail. The subjects for each detail were totally at the whim of the instructor. This group of training pilots who instructed us were a strange breed. The majority of them had no instructional skills but knew their subject well. They surveyed us with suspicion since we were the new breed of pilot that came from a dedicated flying college and not the military services. I suppose in their mind unless you had been upside-down in a single seat fighter with 'nothing on the clock but the maker's name' we might not able to fly straight and level.

The routine was as follows: you were teamed up with another new co-pilot like myself and met about one hour before you were meant to climb into the simulator and were briefed by the trainer as to what you were to do in the session. We also had a Flight Engineer who joined us. The hapless victim was maybe doing his six-monthly check and had his own trainer dedicated to making his life a misery for the next few hours. So now we had five people involved all crammed into the simulator or 'box' as we called it. The other problem was that the Flight Engineer trainer hardly spoke to our trainer so neither of them knew what the other was up to. For example, whilst we were supposed to be practising an engine fire and failure on take-off the Flight Engineer trainer would throw a bunch of hydraulic problems at his victim and we would suddenly find ourselves with no way of bringing up the undercarriage or retracting the flaps since we had no hydraulic power available as they had been shut down by the Flight Engineer. It was like two completely different sets of people contained within a small area all trying to work their part of the machine.

So, with all these obstacles set before me I duly turned up for my first detail. I was teamed up with a similar ex-Hamble cadet, Alan Lovering, and we were to be together for the complete simulator course. I can remember walking in and facing the instructor for the first time. He had a pair of half-moon spectacles perched on the end of his nose and looked pretty formidable. He motioned us to sit down with a nod of his head. He was busy reading our Hamble notes and seemed completely unaware of his two victims trembling on the other side of the desk. After a short while he placed the notes down on the desk and shifted his spectacles down to the tip of his nose and looked up at us.

"Good morning, gentlemen," he said with a total air of authority that could melt ice. "Welcome to the VC-10 Simulator Course. I can assure you that it will be hard work and I expect your utmost ability at all times."

"Yes, sir," was our collective meek reply.

After this statement was fully understood and absorbed we were then given the formal briefing as to how the course would develop. He kept emphasizing that we would only progress to the next phase when we had attained a high enough standard in the present one. This was going to be a nightmare!

I seem to remember the first detail was based around the New York area and involved various approaches and airways flying. The details were of four hours' duration and we were allocated two hours each. There was no break in the middle as is normal nowadays so the session was indeed very hard. Another thing to note was that in those days the flight deck instruments that were primarily used for flying the aircraft were displayed in the familiar T-shape layout, just like in the RAF Anson from my ATC days and consisted of a collection of dials ranging from a Vertical Speed Indicator, that showed you in 'Feet per Minute' how fast you were going up and down, to a Turn and Slip Indicator, that showed how fast you were turning and whether the aircraft was slipping left or right. I won't bore you with the fine details except to say that there was maybe six of these indicators in the famous 'T' and all were painted black with white needles pointing to various numbers. Nowadays we have a very user-friendly single LED screen with all sorts of colours displayed and computer generated images that makes it virtually impossible to 'lose the plot'. In those days we had to visualize in our minds where we were meant to be and try to put all the needles in the right place to make it happen.

So off we went into our first detail. It was very strange going into the 'box' knowing that you were under scrutiny from that moment onwards. As I said the scene was set around the New York area with the instructor saying such things as:

"OK, let's set up a departure off Runway 13R with a 'Riverhead 7 Standard Instrument Departure' and a 'Hampton Transition' up to 'Flight Level two zero zero' and then a return to the 'Deer Park' hold and a VOR approach on Runway 22L with an overshoot and round for an ILS approach on 31R."

All this was said in one breath as well. Mind blowing! You see, he knew the area well but Alan and I had no idea what was where.

Let me break the instructions down a little. Runways are referred to as a magnetic direction and either the left or right runways. For example a runway heading south and being the left hand one of two is known as Runway 18L where '18' stands for 180° on a compass and the 'L' standing for the left-hand runway. A Standard Instrument Departure or 'SID' is the standard routing after take-off to a fixed point some miles away that represented the start of the route from A to B. The transition referred to the fine-tuning at the end of the SID to get onto the intended route. The Flight Level is the height to climb to on the route. A hold is the point where the aircraft flies a race track pattern based on direction and timing from a fixed point and is designed to keep you in a specific area and absorb any delay before making an approach to land. It is a bit like sitting in the queue at the traffic lights waiting until the lights turn green.

A VOR approach is a rather basic sort of approach using a radio beam that shows up on the instruments as a needle pointing to where it is. For example at New York there is a VOR beacon on the airfield and what you do is to set up the track that is needed on the instrument in question and get the needle to point exactly on this track and keep it there all the way to the runway. There are a couple of variables that are introduced at this point. Firstly the wind is blowing from somewhere trying to push you off this track all the time and it becomes a battle of wills between you and the wind with, hopefully, you winning. Secondly you only know the direction to the runway but you do not know how far away you are from it. This calculation is based on timing using a stopwatch. What it shows is the height you should be at, say 20 seconds, after you have started the stopwatch at a particular point. So, in a nutshell, you are fighting the wind to keep the right direction and the brain is working overtime to try to set up the descent correctly so that finally when you arrive at a certain point you should see the runway in front of you and land. This is all based on the fact that you remembered to start the stopwatch at the correct point and you kept the aircraft on the right track. Some of the tracks did not even line up with the runway by design so when you arrived at the final point or 'decision height' it was off to the right or left. I'll tell you what – it doesn't half focus the mind!

Finally an ILS approach uses a more highly tuned aid that gives you the approach both in height and direction and shows up as two needles waving away at you on the instrument panel. The problem here is that these needles are very sensitive and if you blink one of the needles would drift away and as you went to chase it the other one would wander off as well so you were performing gyrations in the sky trying to get them back into the middle where they belonged. The closer to the ground you got the more sensitive they became. Not easy when trying to 'get it all together' with the instructor breathing down your neck. These characters had a habit of scribbling notes all the time about your performance. They had no finesse at all and just sat there scribbling. They even wrote something down when you were just sat there doing nothing. Just like at Hamble they never developed anything that might relax you even a little bit.

Anyway, we managed to get all the various instructions barked at us in some sort of order and off we went on our first simulator detail. I would hasten to add that a Flight Engineer trainer had joined us by now in the 'box'. He looked us both up and down and said: "Blimey, a couple of kids, eh!"

Don't forget that we were youngsters compared with most pilots on BOAC and so were a bit of a novelty.

I can't remember who flew first between me and Alan, but I have the sneaky suspicion it was me since it was in my character to lead and get it over with. On the first take-off I must have uttered a prayer before committing myself. So we became airborne and I focused the mind on the job in hand. What I remember is that this simulator flew far better that the contraptions we had at Hamble. What a pleasant surprise! It must have mentally relaxed me a lot since the detail seemed to go well. Lots of scribbling though, behind me! I finished my time and then changed over for Alan to do his bit. He had the same result as me with a pretty good performance. I have to say that after four hours in the 'box' we were well burnt out but felt good about it all.

When the detail was finished the Flight Engineer left and gestured a thumbs-up to us and a beaming smile. Obviously we got his approval. The instructor, Alan and I were ushered to a large display in the office at the rear of the 'box'. It resembled one of those plotting charts you see in submarines at the movies. What it showed was our track on a large map of the New York area. Mine was in red and Alan's was in green. We surveyed the map closely and what was amazing was that both our tracks were virtually identical. I wondered if that showed that we were in the right place or had we both made the same mistake? Our instructor studied the map and seemed to be happy since no criticism was uttered. We then disappeared into the briefing room where we had started and he then placed his scribbled notes on the desk and rounded on each of us in turn. He first of all directed his thoughts to me and my performance. He was a stickler for detail and addressed a variety of points where I had slipped up. As his chat progressed he seemed to intercede with an occasional 'that was fine' or 'not too bad'. We both had similar comments and at the end he looked at his notes and paused for a few seconds that seemed to us like an eternity and then took an exaggerated deep breath and said:

"OK. That a good start from both of you! We will move on and start introducing some failures tomorrow."

Immense relief followed and off we went home.

The lads in the Malt House were also going through it with their start in BEA and so the chat was all centred around our various experiences of the day. The thoughts of anything social were far from our minds and it was a case of 'heads down' until this part was over.

Alan and I arrived the following day again for the next detail. We were off once more into the 'box' and we started to suffer the famous 'engine failure' on take-off experience. The VC-10 engines were very close to the fuselage so did not produce much of a swing. Imagine engines that are out on the wing like the famous Boeing 707. The swing on these aircraft is quite marked and required a large input of rudder to balance the aircraft. The rudder was the control that you used with your feet to correct any slipping and sliding that might occur.

Speaking of the 707, BOAC had a fleet of about 20 of these airliners and together with the VC-10 made up the total fleet of the airline. Having two types did create a marked amount of rivalry between the fleets with the 707 crew calling us the 'Iron Duck' and the VC-10 crew referring to the 707 as 'a bunch of rivets flying along in very close formation'. This description seemed to fit since the 707 was built on the principle of riding turbulence by flexing its wings alarmingly whereas the VC-10 was 'built from the solid' and just shook its way through the turbulence. This rivalry continued throughout my career until my retirement and beyond.

Back on the simulator Alan and I seemed to survive each session in not too bad a shape with only the odd hiccup. As each detail was completed it was like the prisoner in jail who marked the wall with a line to show how long he had to go. The whole course must have gone on for about three weeks or so but seemed like an eternity. Then came the final session and not before time. This session was the 'crunch' as far as our training was concerned. Up to this point our instructors had a small amount of praise where they felt it was due. For example, they would say:

"Well, that was not too bad."

Or

"OK, let us move on."

These comments could be translated literally as they appear but to Alan and me they signified that we were slowly being accepted as pilots and were doing pretty well. Compliments in those days were few and far between. Now, this final session consisted of a 'fun packed' two hours where all that we had covered in the previous sessions would be thrown at us in all sorts of shapes and sizes. The added ingredient was that a man from the ministry would be present together with the chief instructor. This combination was a bit daunting as the hour approached. Alan and I walked in like lambs to the slaughter. Nervous is not the word! The chief instructor had a facial expression that resembled someone who must have had a miserable existence. Wow, he must have been fun – I think not. The man from the ministry was equally miserable.

They should have been married, I thought!

The briefing began with both of them consulting our files that had increased in size by then and each nodding or scribbling something down on a massive wad of note paper.

"OK, Mullett you're first," the instructor barked.

I was amazed that I did not have a number stamped on my forehead and would be referred to by that. The briefing followed. We were to be based at London Heathrow for the exercise and would fly a SID with an engine failure on take-off, fly a short route and then return to the hold and land back at Heathrow.

Is that all? I thought.

So we climbed into the box and off we went. In comparison to the previous details this one was quite simple and straightforward. What it was, in fact, was a ministry requirement to validate our flying licence and was of a standard format whatever the type of aircraft flown. It had to be relatively simple and straightforward to cover all types. So, I did my bit and then Alan followed. When all was done we trooped back into the briefing room and awaited our fate. Our instructor seemed to spend many minutes completing forms which had very impressive titles. There were a lot of ticks in a lot of boxes going on so I felt quite hopeful.

"Right Mullett, let's run by you first," he said after an agonizing delay.

"Not a bad performance, but I have a few points to go over," he continued.

There then followed an analysis of every move I had made from arrival to now. Little did I know, but this analysis was really for the benefit of the Ministry man so that the instructor looked good in his eyes. After some time he pushed a form over to me and gestured me to read it and sign in the box as indicated. The first thing I saw was 'Satisfactory – released for base training'. The rest of the form was totally irrelevant and I signed it with a smile on my face.

"I have a couple of points to add," the Ministry man uttered.

Yes, he did have a tongue then! I was beginning to wonder! He droned on for about seven minutes about the finer points of the session with my instructor nodding and inwardly cursing that he missed them and that he had failed to impress all around him. I didn't care since the end was in sight of the dreaded 'box'. Alan got the same as me plus all the talk about what he had missed. We left in total euphoria that we had made it so far. To this day I hate the 'box' but unfortunately it is all part of the package of a life of flying. Checks, checks and more checks!

The lads back at the Malt House had all but finished their course with BEA on the Trident and Vanguard. We had one hell of a party that night! It was very good to hear that all the ex-Hamble cadets in BOAC had all passed the course to date. We had taken them by storm!

There then followed a week or so of waiting to be called for aircraft base training. Nowadays, the aircraft simulators are of sufficient standard to qualify a pilot to go straight onto the route without the need for actually flying the aircraft beforehand. The first time a modern pilot touches the controls is when he is on a training flight with passengers. Back in those days we were required to fly the aircraft before the route flying and this was known as 'base training'. Various venues were chosen for this task. BOAC used Shannon in South West Ireland. BEA used Shannon as well for the Trident but used Malta for the Vanguard.

So the day came when we were called and off we went to Heathrow to fly out to Shannon in a BEA Vanguard aircraft. We took off and headed west out over Wales and Southern Ireland. After about an hour the Captain comes across the cabin address and says that due to the bad weather in Shannon we would be diverting to Dublin and thence by train to Shannon. Bad weather! Mind you it was late November. Anyway we finally arrived in Shannon after about seven hours from the start at Heathrow. We stayed in the Shannon Shamrock hotel which was about ten miles inland from the airport. It was next to the famous Bunratty Castle. There was also a really grubby little pub alongside called Durty Nelly's that served the most exquisite pint of Guinness and became a regular meeting place for us.

It was not until the 3rd December before I was actually detailed to start the base training with an instructor, Captain T. He was pretty overpowering both physically and mentally. He would smoke cigars constantly even to the point when walking across the tarmac to the waiting VC-10. I was sat down in the small briefing room at the airport and once again Captain T was studying my files that by now had grown even thicker. There must have been about three of us victims sitting rigidly to attention in front of him. He closed the various files with a definite movement and then off we went across the tarmac following a plume of cigar smoke that erupted at the head of the column. The VC-10 was a super version with a registration of G-ASGH and sat there in the December sun all gleaming, bursting with energy and ready to go. As I said before, she looked so large compared with the Piper Apache that I had flown some months before. Beautiful sight! We all climbed aboard and took our various seats according to Captain T's plan.

"Ok, Mullett, you can get in the right-hand seat first," he said casually.

"Yes, sir," I must have said meekly.

The doors were shut and all was quiet for a few minutes until the sound of the engines starting up filled the air. This was the real thing and I had to learn to fly this aircraft to the required standard within a short space of time. The chocks were released and off we went. I was sitting gingerly taking in my surroundings in the right hand seat. Captain T suddenly barked at me:

"OK – you have control. Taxi us to runway 24 and prepare for take-off."

I grabbed the tiller, as it was known, and tried my hand at taxing the beast. Blimey, it responded well since when I pushed the tiller to the left the aircraft turned to the left. Amazing! I thought. I managed to line up after numerous wiggles on the centre line of the runway.

"Right – off we go," was the next call from Captain T.

I took a deep breath and then pushed the throttles forward gently. On the VC-10 the Flight Engineer had his own set and very quickly they had a mind of their own and moved briskly to the end of the quadrant and the familiar roar of the engines reverberated everywhere. Since we were at a light weight we moved bloody quickly down the runway with me trying to appear calm and collected but in reality I was clinging on for dear life. We must have been at take-off speed within 20 seconds since I heard the call 'Rotate' somewhere to the left of me. I pulled back on the controls and low and behold we were in the air heading out over the Shannon Estuary.

"Do you want the gear up or not?" was the next call that was fired at me.

"Gear up," I sputtered out.

"Bring the power back to 91% before Mullett puts us into orbit," Captain T barked at the Flight Engineer.

I was oblivious to all around me since I was concentrating on the instruments and nothing else could possibly distract me. After a while I seemed to settle down and took in my surroundings. There I was at the controls of the mighty VC-10 and it was an incredible feeling. It was down to business though. I remember it as if it was yesterday. We climbed up to 35,000 feet to the west of Shannon and performed an emergency descent. This manoeuvre was designed to get you and the aircraft down to a safe height in the minimum time after losing cabin pressure. We then did some steep turns so that I could demonstrate my handling skills. All seemed OK so far.

Next came stalling. Because of the layout of the wing and tail of the VC-10 the stall had to be treated with the utmost caution. The stall is defined as the speed at which all lift is lost over the wing and the aircraft falls away. On the Chipmunk this occurred at about 45 knots (a knot being the aeronautical word for MPH) but on the VC-10 it could be about 100 knots or so. What you did was to maintain level flight and slowly reduce the engine power and try to keep the height by pulling back on the controls. There then comes a point when the air over the top of the wing gets very turbulent and eventually breaks down any lift that might occur. The aircraft then enters the stall and falls away. To recover all you do is to push the nose down and put on the power to get the speed up out of this scene.

With the VC-10 the tail plane is perched right on the top of the fin and this turbulent air can effectively blank the smooth air to the tail plane and the elevators become non-effective. This is known as the super-stall. It is a well-known fact that it is virtually impossible to recover from the super-stall if it is allowed to develop and the aircraft keeps descending until it hits the ground. Only three months before a BAC-111 did exactly that on Salisbury Plain and the crew were all killed including the famous test pilot Mike Lithgow. Since that accident stringent rules were applied to all aircraft that had the aptly named T-Tail layout. This included the VC-10 and the plan was to go to the initial start of the stall and then recover.

The VC-10 had a very sophisticated stall recovery system that consisted of a device that shook the control column or 'Stick Shaker' as it was called. If the stall further developed a device consisting of a piston/ram affair, actually physically pushed the control column forward and forced the aircraft out of the stall thus keeping it well away from the super-stall. This was known as the 'Stick Pusher'. The rules were simple: on training we were allowed to go to the 'Stick Shaker' point only.

So there I was with Captain T doing stalling as an exercise. I held the aircraft level as the power was reduced and waited for the 'Stick Shaker' to operate and then I was expected to push the nose down and apply power and that would be that. The first one was OK and then we put the undercarriage down and extended some wing flaps to put the aircraft in a simulated approach scene. The 'Stick Shaker' started and I was just about to do the recovery when Captain T grabbed the controls and pulled them back hard and the next thing we were looking up at the sky at a crazy angle. Within seconds the 'Stick Pusher' fired away and the controls were wrenched out of our hands and the aircraft lurched downwards and the countryside filled the windscreen. I was out of the loop at this point with Captain T seemingly fighting with the controls but every time he went to pull out of the dive the 'Stick Pusher' cut in and we ended up doing a series of hair-raising climbs and descents. Eventually we levelled out having dropped quite a few thousand feet. The atmosphere on the Flight Deck was very quiet – you could hear a pin drop.

"OK. Lesson complete for today. Let's go home," Captain T announced.

All in all my first outing on the VC-10 was quite memorable. A few drinks were downed that night. The Flight Engineer on the flight joined us and did not mince words when it came to talking about the flight I had just done. As more drinks were consumed his words became more explicit. What a night! Captain T was nowhere to be seen.

I flew a total of three training sessions with Captain T over a period of five days. With the events of the first fight behind me I then had to buckle down to a variety of flying tasks. These ranged from staying close to Shannon Airport or doing various gyrations in the sky away from the airport area. Captain T seemed to be pleased with my efforts since he would put a large tick on my file after each exercise. When flying in the circuit back at the airport or 'Circuit Bashing' as it was known it became more and more tricky. A complete circuit would consist of a Take-off and flying up to about 1,000ft and then turning left or right according to the whim of the instructor and flying the opposite way until we were abeam the end of the runway that we had just taken off from, and then try to turn, descend and slow down all in one so that we arrived in some sort of order at the end of the runway or threshold for a landing of some sort. Once the landing was done the training captain would open up the engine power, re-set the flaps and trim for take-off and we were again up in the air for round two. Of course, we would have various failures to deal with as well just to keep it all interesting. These could range from having one or two engines stopped to half the flaps missing. We had to learn fast or fall by the wayside. Bloody hard work though! After the first week we were all still there. Miracles do happen!

We did get some free time in Shannon which was always very welcome. There were about ten of us in all and quite often a couple of us would go off for a walk around the airport. It was about five miles I suppose and a great therapy. About halfway round the walk there was an isolated cottage where an old lady lived. She must have had a sixth sense when we were passing by since she always seemed to appear 'on cue'. She also seemed to know that we were airline pilots under training and announced herself simply by:

"Are you the boys from the BOAC then?" in her thick Irish accent.

We would then be invited into her humble abode for tea and scones.

"I'm having trouble with my flapless landings," one of us would say.

"Don't worry about those things. Have another scone and it will be all right," she would reply.

The scones were delicious and approached the 'scruminess standard' of my Mum's Welsh Cakes. I feel that could well have been the point of my life where 'middle age spread' started early.

She obviously knew nothing about VC-10s but she became a guru to us. I wonder what ever happened to her...

After a few days a BEA Trident arrived in the circuit and out popped Tony and Ian. It was a bit like a Hamble course reunion. They stayed down the road in a hotel on the way to the local town of Limerick.

Now, there is a place that conjures up everything that is so Irish. Limerick is about 15 miles east of Shannon Airport and on a Saturday night it was the social centre of the area. I seem to remember the St George's Hotel. We had a chance to go there once during our stay. You see, in those days we would spend many days training in Shannon or elsewhere since company costs did not seem to bother the training department and if we sat around waiting for an aircraft to be spare then so be it. Anyway, back to the Saturday night in Limerick. Most of the Hamble cadets under training formed a bond in Shannon with countless tales to tell about how it was all going. To us it did not matter whether we were in BEA or BOAC. So there we all were in this hotel in Limerick with a local band performing good old 60s' Rock 'n Roll and this bunch of would-be pilots strutting around and, as they say, 'checking the local talent out'. We could really shoot a line or two as to why we were in Shannon. I remember that all of the local girls sat on one side of the dance floor and the prospective male suitors sat on the other. Then, as I said, there was this bunch of pilots moving with utmost confidence amongst everybody. Happiness all around! A good night was had by one and all.

Sundays were something else for the local people since that was the day of reckoning with the local Roman Catholic hierarchy. Of course once that was done and heads were unbowed then it was off to the local pub to top up with the local Irish delicacy or Guinness. You see, we never flew on the weekend since BOAC decreed it so. What an amazing start to my career. Talking about Guinness, Durty Nellie's was the place for us. As I said it was in the grounds of the famous Bunratty Castle which was renowned for its Medieval Banquets as a great tourist attraction. In total contrast Durty Nellie's was the other end of the social spectrum and was basically a 'spit and sawdust' establishment and resembled someone's front room. Having said that the atmosphere was electric with fantastic Guinness and crammed with the salt of the Irish people. Sunday was usually the best night. I think, maybe, the fact that the Irishman had offloaded all of his sins to the church that morning and it was time to start building them up again for the next Sunday session.

I would think that there could well have been maybe two dozen of us over in Shannon for the training sessions. There were ten of us cadets plus Training Captains, Flight Engineers and Ground Engineers plus of course one VC-10 sitting out there on the tarmac waiting patiently for the daily abuse by us. The amazing thing was that we were slowly getting to grips with the aircraft and I think the trainers were beginning to relax and starting to consider us as potential Co-pilots and not just a bunch of boys who had not been upside-down in a RAF fighter to prove our worth.

After my training sessions with Captain T I then moved on to night flying with a Captain M I found night flying to be a wonderful mixture of lights, colours and altogether a rather peaceful experience. Having said that, the flying was quite exacting.

Normally the runway would be illuminated the complete length by bright white edge lights and equally bright green ones marking the runway centre-line from the threshold all the way down to the other end. If you followed these green lights all the way to the end they would change colour to let you know you were getting near the end.

The final colour would be red to let you know that you were about to fall off the end of the runway. Taxi-ways leading off the runway would be also marked with various colour combinations. Before you got anywhere near the runway in the air there were a huge array of approach lights sitting on top of posts to help you line up with the runway. They usually started off spread a fair distance either side of an imaginary extended runway centre-line which became narrower as the landing threshold was reached. It was like a horizontal flat cone spread out over the ground. There were other set of lights designed to let you know that you were approaching the threshold at the correct descent angle. These lights sat either side of the threshold and if you were spot on they would show as a set of red and white lights. If you were above the correct angle they would show as all white and if you were low as all red. The secret was to find the red/white and try to stick to it, at the same time making sure your speed was right and you were heading directly down the runway. Of course, Western Ireland had a habit of blowing a gale pretty much every other day so the runway would appear out to the left or right in the windscreen. Chance of rain and gusty conditions always added to the fun. As you were driven to the airport from the hotel with the trainer you sat in the car looking skywards and quietly praying for a nice clear night. Suddenly there would be the vicious beat of rain on the windscreen and you quietly cursed the demon who decreed this act.

"It's going to be a wet night in the circuit. That will make it interesting for you chaps," the trainer would say with a glint in his eye.

Our thoughts varied from pure hatred to total resignation as to our fate.

Now, there is a secret to circuit bashing at night. What usually happened is that the trainer would demonstrate the perfect circuit which was totally depressing to us. The secret was that, as he flew around the circuit we would stare out of the window and look for the odd light on the ground that marked a specific turning point, albeit a house or a small collection of street lights on a crossroads. We would then look at the instruments to see the altitude and/or direction and mentally note it down in our minds. So, the net result was that we could plot the circuit by means of the lights on the ground and somehow get the job done. The only drawback was we assumed that we would always turn to the right after take-off since that seemed logical as we sat on the right side of the flight deck and hopefully keep the runway in sight while we trolled around the circuit. These trainers were a cunning lot and knew all the tricks and I remember being first up in the seat and sat at the end of the runway trying to remember all the ground lights and where they were when the trainer said with a sly grin:

"OK Mullett – let's make it a left-hand circuit shall we?"

My brain collapsed since all my mental planning had just been thrown on the scrapheap. Anyway, sod it, I thought, let's just get on with it. Much to my surprise the first circuit went well and I felt good. As I said before I found night flying quite exciting and relaxing. This feeling stayed with me for my entire career. There is something magical about looking at the stars above on a clear night and seeing the contrast of ground lights below. Anyway, I managed to put in a reasonable performance on my first night flying session. As the night progressed the trainer would ask the Air Traffic Controller to switch off certain approach and runway lights. Life became exciting to say the least. I did two night flying sessions with Captain M and got the famous 'tick in the box'.

The date was now 15th December and I seemed to have been in Shannon half a lifetime, but I was slowly ticking all the boxes needed to get me through the training. Tony and Ian were soldiering on in their Trident and quite often we would be flying in tandem around the circuit. Other airlines joined in as well with KLM and their DC-8 prominent in my mind.

The history of Shannon Airport is interesting. Way back it was the kick-off point for the North Atlantic for the 50s' airliners like the 'Strat' that I had flown in to Barbados many years before. In the river estuary at a place called Foynes there were the remains of a flying boat station which goes back to the late 40s. Can you imagine filling up with fuel and heading west into the unknown with only the most basic of equipment and little knowledge of what might lie ahead?

In the 60s came aircraft like the Douglas DC-7C that were capable of flying from London to New York with no fuel stop required in Shannon.

Aer Lingus was the only exception to this since they were required by Irish law to always stop in Shannon before heading out over the Atlantic until well into the 80s. Hence Shannon went into decline in the early 60s until it slowly evolved as a very good training airport with all the modern aids in situ. BOAC, together with a large number of European airlines, used Shannon for exactly this.

Anyway, back to December 15th since this was the date of my final training assessment with a Captain A and if I recall it was a tense experience with no set programme to carry out. It was based on his feelings on the day. I did seven circuits in all, in various conditions, ranging from three-engine approaches to having no flaps out. There must have been at least three of us new cadets on board and we all took it in turns to try to impress. After my session we did a complete stop on the runway and taxied round to the take-off point for me to be replaced by another victim. As I got up to leave I looked attentively at Captain A trying to seem casual and I remember his words:

"OK, Mullett you're all done. Please send Dyson up."

Could I assume that all was well and that I had passed the training? I wondered.

I just didn't know. Anyway Pete scrambled into the seat and I disappeared out the back to cool down. The seat I had just vacated must have been at about 150°C from my body heat! We all finished our stint in the 'hot seat' and drove back to the hotel to await our fate. At the hotel Captain A summoned us all to the bar and ordered a round of Guinness and pronounced to us all that we were now cleared to start training 'on the route'. Smiles all round, and large quantities of Guinness were consumed that night by one and all.

Bloody hell, they going to let me loose on the route with real passengers sitting behind me! I thought.

Having said that, I would still be under training and going for the final accolade of being a fully-fledged Co-pilot once the 'line training' bit was done. I left Shannon on the 16th December back to Heathrow after completing about 21 hours of real-time training. The lads at the Malt House all seemed to drift in over the next couple of days having survived their ordeals and I would imagine the pre-Christmas party season got into full swing.

The year was now 1967 and I was waiting patiently for my first flight. Life outside of the airline went on. I would go down to Hamble quite a bit to see this girl Pam, who was one of the secretaries at the college I mentioned before. Young love you might call it! This was the start of my adult love life which became a disaster as time went by, but more about that later.

One interesting point about the Malt House was that it became a sort of halfway house for girls travelling back and forth to the teachers' training college in Salisbury which we had invaded a lot when at Hamble. Quite often there would be a knock on the door late at night and two females would be standing there asking for a bed for the night. No problem about that at all! There was also the BEA 'Vanguard Club' up at Heathrow which became known as the Friday night kicking off point for a social weekend. Our local pub was the 'Bells of Ousley' which was visited regularly almost to the point where we had our own table reserved every night. Life was very good!

Now, the difference between BEA and BOAC was that BEA was all tuned up for Hamble cadet training and with me being the only BOAC trainee in the house it felt like I was being left out in the route flying department since shortly after Christmas the others were assigned trips and got going on their line training – but there was me left waiting for the call. In those days our trips or rosters would arrive in the post box. So every day was spent staring at the front door waiting for the postman. Then, one day the famous piece of paper arrived. My first trip was to be on 10th January to Lagos, West Africa via Kano in Northern Nigeria and back via Kano again and Rome arriving back 13th January. There would be Captain W plus three other crew members and little old me. Right here we go!

The 10th duly arrived and off I went to Heathrow complete with a suitcase full of a variety of clothes since I was not sure what the weather would be like. The report time was about 9 am so I must have been there at about 8 am as I did not want to be late for my first flight. The crew slowly arrived and I went through the introductions to one and all. Bear in mind there were only ten of us young second officers amongst what seemed to be much older people. There I was at the tender age of 20 and with only one small gold stripe on my jacket surrounded by this multitude of stripes.

Captain W was a very nice chap. In fact, all of the crew were nice. As I said before the report centre was on the first floor just to the left hand side of the western edge of Terminal 3 in the central area. It was quite small and poky compared with the modern equivalent but seemed large enough to house all the crews on the day. In those days there may have been only about 20 long-haul departures per day. Once you signed in you moved into the flight planning room. Bearing in mind that this was 1967 there were no fancy computers to be seen anywhere; everything was done by hand and checked by the flight crew without even a calculator. Slide rules were the order of the day.

The actual document that covered every aspect of the route, fuel diversion, etc was known as the flight plan. I remember this plan being hand-produced as a work of art with immaculate writing. The fuel calculations were based on kilograms and were subdivided into taxi, take-off, climb, various cruise segments, descent, diversion, holding and contingency sections. In short, enough to get you from A to B and, if needed, divert to C with a bit extra carried for 'mum'. I found the idea of kilograms strange since the UK standard measure was in pounds and ounces. It made it a bit tricky since British and American aircraft were certified in pounds and then converted to kilograms.

We had a pile of figures to remember about the VC-10. Just one was that the maximum landing weight of a standard aircraft was 97,976 kg. Nothing was simple in those days. In addition to the flight plan there were a wad of papers that were known as the communications log which was completed as the flight progressed.

Next in line was another set with all the weather information followed by yet another load with all the latest information about the airports we were going to. We were off to Kano so all the airports on the way were listed and would show, for example, that one of the runways was closed or a radio aid was not working. All in all you would end up with a total package containing maybe 100 sheets of information. No wonder our briefcases were big and our arms long in those days. It was here in the flight planning room that all these documents were checked. One of the other pilots was designated as the Flight Navigator so he and the Flight Engineer pored over the flight plan checking and re-checking the calculations. The Captain and the other Co-pilot would get totally engrossed in the weather and route information papers. I just stood there and looked pretty.

"Don't worry, Gwyn, I will go over it once we get under way as time is always short here," Captain W said to me in a reassuring manner.

What a nice man, I thought.

Eventually all the papers were laid out in front of the Captain and he would have the final say about how much extra fuel he might need since, maybe, the weather was not too clever or not all the radios were working at Kano. This all took about 20 minutes and once all was agreed the wad was stuffed in a briefcase and the Captain would suggest making a move to the aircraft. As an aside it is a known fact that in those days every aspect of the flight revolved around the Captain. He governed everything and whatever he said was considered gospel and he must be obeyed. A lot of the Captains in those days were ex-wartime and flew the aircraft of the 50s and hence were considered a law unto themselves. The modern world of aviation is so different to those days but that was all we knew back then. Amazingly enough it worked well.

As we left the flight planning office we met up with the Cabin Crew for the flight. This was a ceremony in its own right. Their ranks starting from the top were, as I mentioned before, the Chief Steward, First Steward and Second Steward. These were all men. The Stewardesses were ranked as A, B and C girl. Boy – did they look the business! What would happen is that they would stand in line and the Chief Steward would step forward and introduce himself to the Captain and then turn and introduce each crew member in turn. It was quite a ceremony. We all then piled onto the bus – after the Captain, of course – and make our way to the aircraft. Minor chit-chat occurred with the Captain telling the Chief Steward about the route, flight time, weather and total passengers due on board. The Chief Steward would reply by going over the catering schedule both for us and the passengers and when would the Captain feel would be the right time to serve lunch.

The aircraft were, in general, all parked away from the terminal and passengers were bussed out and then boarded via aircraft steps. Nowadays it's mostly air bridges etc connecting direct to the terminal.

Anyway, we finally arrived at the aircraft which was a Standard VC-10 registered G-ARVL according to my log book. As it was my very first trip I was told to just sit back and observe on the way to Kano. Once we got in the cruise and things were quiet I would be put in the right-hand seat and do the communications. There was the usual hustle and bustle around the aircraft with the Captain being the centre of attention.

"When can we board please, sir?"

"Are you happy with the fuel, sir?"

"Catering and cleaning all checked sir and ready for passengers sir."

"We have a small technical problem with one of the radios sir. I will call engineering."

As for me, I kept out of the way since there were people continually rushing in and out of the Flight Deck. Eventually I was ushered in and strapped into the seat just behind the two pilots and right next to the Flight Engineer. The third pilot who had been designated as the navigator sat just behind me facing backwards and set about checking all of his navigational equipment. Since there was always a doubt as to the accuracy of the flight deck clocks a ritual took place before every departure whereby one of the long range radios was tuned into an American station that was responsible for international time keeping. 'Fort Collins, Colorado' was the station name and at every minute it marked it aurally with a sharp 'ping'. So all the flight crew, including me this time, stopped whatever they were doing and with hands on wrists and any clock within 20 yards waited for the famous 'ping'.

"Time-check everybody," was the word and once completed a final check all round was done.

Eventually all the various departure elements came together and we all sat in our seats awaiting the word of the Captain. At this point the stewardess who looked after the first class passengers entered with a small paper cup for each of us which contained an assortment of items like a pen, pack of tissues and a pack of headache tablets. I ferreted around in the cup when the Flight Engineer butted in saying:

"All part of your travel kit my boy."

It was assumed that we all drank tea so it was tea all round. A few minutes later a coach pulled up and out came the passengers complete with armfuls of bags. This was quite normal on this route since London was a Mecca for shopping. In the cabin the overhead bins were totally open unlike nowadays and so were crammed to the gunnels with the shopping. As I said before the standard VC-10 had 12 first class seats in three rows of four seats and 'down the back' 99 seats in rows of six seats. In those days there was not the desire to cram the people in, even in economy, so there was plenty of leg room. I suppose that in the late 60s flying was still a bit of an expensive luxury with no 'Ryanair' mentality.

We now had all our passengers on board and the final item was a hand produced load sheet for the Captain to peruse and sign. This was in itself quite a ritual since not being computer generated but human generated could contain errors so it was down to the Captain to add up the various columns without the aid of a calculator and sign it which effectively transferred the aircraft to him in legal terms. It was a hectic period but all completed with ten minutes to spare before the scheduled time of departure. At this point the Captain asked for the checks to be read out. As opposed to my look-see trip I now knew what was involved from this point on. According to my log book we pushed back off the stand at 1033 hrs and my first training flight got under way.

Being fresh from Shannon where the aircraft was normally quite light in weight G-ARVL was pretty heavy for the flight to Kano but I still wondered at the way it roared down the runway seemingly bursting with energy. Captain W lifted the aircraft into the air with the greatest of ease and climbed away. Then came the famous noise abatement call when the Flight Engineer pulled back the engines' power and the aircraft wallowed for a while. This time I knew what it was all about and followed every move religiously. After a minute or so the noise abatement procedure was announced complete and the engine power was restored and off we went again pointing skywards. Captain W faithfully followed the route to clear the London area and we headed off to Seaford on the South coast and then across the channel and on our way to Kano.

Once we were nicely settled in the climb the autopilot was engaged. This piece of equipment was tailor-made for the VC-10 by a company called Elliot-Bendix. The problem was that they tried to make it so

sophisticated that it kept tying itself up in knots with the net result
that it would disconnect on a whim. Consider the TV sitcom 'Open
all Hours' and the till that bit back whenever touched – then you will
begin to understand the workings of the VC-10 autopilot. When we were
passed to the French controllers I was amazed to hear that most French
airlines spoke in French. English is the international language so why
were they gabbing away in French? The advantage of English was to
establish where other aircraft were in comparison to your own aircraft
and having failed French twice at school my knowledge of the language
was very limited. Don't forget in those days we did not have the
sophisticated displays showing all aircraft near you on the instrument
panel. I asked the Co-pilot the reason and he shrugged his shoulders
and said:

"That's the French for you!"

After a little while the navigator shuffled around in his area and
came up with a pad of rather colourful maps about A4 size and I was
detailed to mark in the route and write in the boxes the estimated time
of arrival, crew names and other bits of information relevant to the
flight. This was then given to the Chief Steward who passed it to the
first row of passengers who in turn passed it back to the next row so
that in the end all the passengers had some idea about where we were
going and what time we would arrive. Compare that to the moving map
displays we have nowadays.

We continued flying over France and left the coast somewhere near
Marseilles and then continued south over the Mediterranean. We had
been in the air some two hours and, as if on cue in sympathy with my
stomach, the same Stewardess popped her head in with cold towels and
the first-class menu with boxes to tick according to what we fancied.
Did I like that bit or what! Four courses of the most wonderful food
duly arrived and were consumed with great relish. Once lunch was
over the captain asked the right hand-seat Co-pilot to jump out and
let me take his place. Here we go I thought! After a bit of close quarter
manoeuvring I slipped into the right hand seat. The view of the 'Med'
was superb from this seat with the water so blue. Enough of this
sightseeing and down to business. At this point the captain got out of
his seat and the displaced Co-pilot jumped in the vacated captain's seat.

"I'm off to talk to the passengers," said Captain W.

That left just four of us on the flight deck and my trainer started
to chat about the paperwork that seemed to be floating everywhere.
There was a lot to learn outside of just flying the aircraft and so my
route training was starting. I will point out that at the time all BOAC
flights used the word 'Speedbird' followed by the flight number when
talking on the radio. After some time I was told to put the headset on
and do the radio communications with the ground controller. Unlike
nowadays we called about every ten minutes with our present position,
our height and where we were going. The controller must have been
Algerian since I had a few problems understanding his accent. After
a while I looked out of the front windscreen at the North African
coastline looming up ahead and on this sun-drenched day it was laid
out for all to see in the windscreen. It looked quite stunning with small
inlets and coves but further south there was nothing but a big expanse
of nothing but sand, the odd hillock and then more sand. How could
people live down there I thought to myself. At this point the controller
called us and said:

"Speedbird XXX, now change to HF 8902 frequency primary, 5604
secondary."

"What the fricking heck is he saying and what is HF?" I must have
said to myself.

The trainer intervened seeing my mouth on my chest and
acknowledged the call. Nobody anywhere had talked to us about this
rather crude form of communications. Now, just to put you in the
picture, radio frequencies are divided into certain categories when
used to talk to the ground controller. For example, when you talk to the
control tower you use the category of 'Very High Frequency' or VHF as
it was known. One above that is 'Ultra High Frequency' or UHF and is
reserved for the military around the world. Both VHF and UHF have
only a limited range of maybe 200 miles. 'High Frequency' or HF is used
when you want to talk to a controller over great distances. The problem
is that the whole world uses HF. To talk to India, for example, we may
use the same frequency as talking to Barbados. The end result is that
when I tuned the rather crude radio to 8902 HF frequency as we were
asked to do then the first person I heard was Karachi trying to talk to

Lahore in Pakistan. In addition to this, the background noise is terrible and there seemed to be about 20 plus aircraft all trying to talk at the same time. Totally bewildered by what I was listening to, I looked at the trainer and he calmly said to try to talk to Algiers when there is a gap in the chat.

What bloody gap? Not a chance! I thought to myself.

So the verbal battle began with me gingerly trying to call Algiers with Karachi still screaming at Lahore. I tried several times without success when the trainer intervened by saying:

"Be positive and keep trying."

I deepened my voice and tried to sound as masculine as possible and had another go. On what must have been my twentieth attempt suddenly there was a rather mushy, barely audible response from the Algiers controller. I must have dropped my pen with excitement when I heard him.

"Go on then – give him your position report before he goes away," the trainer said sternly.

I blundered the details out on the radio and waited for a reply. Total garble followed and I sat staring at the microphone.

"Try 5604 HF frequency," the trainer said calmly.

So I did and the chat was just as bad. Finally I heard Algiers answering an Air France aircraft so I just waited for that chat to finish when I shouted in my deep husky Helen Shapiro tones and they answered and away I went with the chat. I made it after 20 minutes or so. I lay back exhausted when suddenly the trainer tapped the communications log mentioning that we were now at a new position and that Algiers needed to know. Here we go again!

At this point the pilot designated to be the navigator stirred in his seat and announced that he needed to do a heading check before starting his navigation stint over the desert. At this point I will explain in simple terms about navigation in those days. We had the simplest of equipment in the 60s which consisted of two basic direction finders, or ADFs, that pointed to the ground station selected. They originated from the war and in consequence were pretty crude with their two corresponding needles gyrating around a mean point roughly showing the direction of the ground station. I could compare it to the old-fashioned petrol tank dial in a car then varied from full to empty in about 10 seconds. Having said that they did have an advantage whereby the ground stations or beacons could be picked up many miles away. There were two more modern direction finders, or VORs, that did the same but to a greater accuracy but over a much shorter range. The needles were steady and extremely useful for navigation. I remember we also had a simple distance measuring unit, or DME, which was the best of the lot – but there was only one of them.

Once you entered the desert or oceanic region then all of these aids just did not work since there were very few ground beacons around so another device was brought into play. A transmitter in the nose would send out a beam and await its return. Without going into details the receiving side of the device could figure out by the time taken for the beam to return just how fast we were going and how much we were drifting with the wind where we were. What we ended up with was a small dial somewhere down the bottom of the panel showing our speed over the ground and our drift. It was very accurate considering the times we were in.

Now, what the manufacturers had done is to take this drift and speed information and develop a display that, if you put in the intended track and distance, would show how far left or right of track you were. All this is quite boring but the weak link in the display was the accuracy of the aircraft compass system. The compasses of the day were not very accurate as compared with the modern ones but were acceptable then. This returns me to the point when the navigator said that he wanted to do a heading check of the compasses before we ventured too far out over the desert. This procedure involved hoisting a periscopic sextant through a hatch in the ceiling and then direct it towards the sun for example, and use a series of tables to deduct the exact heading of the aircraft and in subsequence any errors in the aircraft's compass system. I won't go into any more details on the sextant scene for the moment since that subject will raise its ugly head later in the book.

So the navigator did his compass heading check and all seemed in order so off we went out over the North African desert with me going through the HF drama every ten minutes or so. HF is still the normal form of communications nowadays; however, though the systems have improved somewhat it still remains the pilot's nightmare.

As we flew southwards the desert seemed to become more and more desolate. The amazing thing was that every now and again an outpost would be shown on the map marked by an ADF beacon. One place I remember is a place called 'El Goléa' in southern Algeria. I strained to look out of the window and could just make out a small collection of sandy coloured houses. Mind blowing it was!

The Captain returned from his cabin chat after a while and re-took his seat with me next to him trying to be all confident until the next HF call. We crossed the southern boundary of Algeria and into the Niamey control area. It is amazing that I remember the route after all these years. This cabin visit by the Captain was part of the routine on all flights. Don't forget that we had no 'In Flight Entertainment' or IFE systems so the personal touch by the Captain was always the order of the day. It usually corresponded to the 'coffee and liquors' part of the cabin service. Since the first-class passengers were first in line as the captain entered the cabin he stayed there most of the time, talking to them about this and that. The Chief Steward would have briefed the captain if anyone of real importance was in the cabin. It really did add that personal touch to the flight and the passengers loved it.

We had now been in the air for some four hours and I was slowly getting to grips with the HF radio. There was still a landscape of sand and rocks out there. Captain W was chatting about the route and all aspects of BOAC flying. As I said before he was a really nice guy and very relaxing to be with and I was absorbing it all as best I could. The Stewardess came in again and it was afternoon tea all round. We were being fed like lords and my waistline was protesting. After about 30 minutes the captain ushered us all to our original seats since we were within one hour of landing at Kano. From my seat I could study the workings of the Flight Engineer while he twiddled and diddled with his panel. Tweaking this and adjusting that.

"Time for a gold plate reading," he announced.

Whatever is he talking about? I thought.

What it was was a large sheet of paper in the technical log which he filled out with every dial reading and every needle position on his panel. In those days there was no other method of recording the aircraft systems except by writing it down. He tucked the completed sheet inside the Technical log which I knew by now was his bible. The Flight Engineers were very dedicated and I greatly admired them.

I studied the approach maps of Kano at this point and came to the conclusion that there was not too much available to organize a normal approach. This was Africa at its rawest. The Captain entered into a discussion with the Co-pilot as to how he was going to handle the approach and landing. The Flight Navigator informed the Captain that he was all done and that there was a beacon which would mark the entry point to the Kano area. I looked out of the windscreen and all I could see was desert and very few landmarks. These were clever guys I thought! Suddenly the more accurate VOR indicator needle started to gyrate around the dial and then rested with the needle pointing exactly where it was expected to be. The wonders of navigation I thought! Little did I know that within a couple of years I would be doing the navigating. The DME showed us about 130 miles away from Kano. The radio had changed from the dreaded HF to VHF and Kano was loud and clear. The weather was read out and showed a temperature of 29°C with no cloud. When we left the UK it had been about 0°C so it was going to be hot on the ground. We started our descent and I looked out of the front windscreen straining to get a glimpse of the airport. At about 15,000 ft on the descent I spotted what looked like a landscape of houses rising thought the haze.

That must be the city of Kano. So where is the airport? I thought.

I looked at the approach map again and wondered if, in fact, there was an airport at all. The VC-10 had, as part of the air conditioning system, two humidifiers that introduced moisture into the cabin to create a pleasant environment. What I didn't know was that the moisture built up and on the descent it 'dropped its lot' in the flight deck. It would start as a trickle and end up like a full blown monsoon. Boy was I getting wet! Anyway as we got lower I started to wonder if we were indeed heading for Kano or some fictitious point in Africa. The Captain and the Co-pilot were looking out of the windscreen as well and suddenly the captain said:

"There's the airfield over there." He pointed with his hand to some blot on the landscape.

I stared at the point he had indicated and saw nothing but desert. Gradually a sort of apparition appeared and I could see a somewhat dusty runway but nothing else.

Surely not, I thought.

Having flown out of Heathrow I was expecting to see a large complex with maybe two runways, outlined in black, and lots of other aircraft around. What I was looking at seemed like a dusty road just plonked in the middle of nowhere. Where were the fancy runway markings and nicely laid out taxiways? Anyway, once the two pilots had agreed that what they had seen was in fact the airport of Kano Captain W spoke a few words to the Co-pilot and Flight Engineer and started to fly the aircraft to some pre-determined point in the sky calling for flaps and undercarriage etc and suddenly there we were in the perfect position to land. Was I impressed or what! The haze was shimmering with the heat and the runway seemed to mould in with the background but when the Captain called for 'Landing flap' I realized we were actually going to land on this dusty road in Africa. We landed at Kano and there I was with the first of my many encounters with Africa. As we taxied into the ramp right in front of the control tower the whole place seemed deserted except for a lone DC-4 in Air France colours.

Blimey that aircraft is from a bygone age, I thought.

As we stopped there was a muted hive of activity as various bits and pieces arrived at the aircraft. Remember this is Africa and the pace is somewhat slower than the rest of the world. First of all the external ground power was plugged in enabling the flight engineer to shut down all of the engines. The aircraft steps were man-handled to the front left hand door followed by a large cart with a large pipe poking out which had the reputation of being an air conditioning unit. Various baggage carts arrived and soon the aircraft was enveloped with a hive of vehicles doing this and that. In those days BOAC kept all the airports totally stocked with its own equipment and was not dependent on any local agency.

The heat hit me pretty quickly and, being a delicate English Rose, I was soon reduced to a steaming blubbering wreckage. I wandered over to the terminal to satisfy my curiosity. The inside was totally devoid of any colour except a light sandy sort of grubby facade. There were no brightly coloured check-in desks and just a few Nigerian people wandering around dressed in white flowing robes complete with a turban style head dress. Even the airline staff looked drab. In those days security was non-existent so I was able to wander anywhere without being challenged. After about 20 minutes I wandered back out to the VC-10 out on the tarmac. I have to say the aircraft looked supreme sitting there outshining its surroundings.

On board the pre-start activities were getting underway and Captain W ushered me into the right-hand seat saying that I could act as the Co-pilot for the next sector to Lagos. My route training had begun in earnest. I sat there looking around and started collecting together all the bits of paperwork under the watchful eye of the training Co-pilot. There were a lot of things I had to do to get myself ready for the engine start.

"Try to establish a routine of your own," the trainer said.

This piece of advice stayed with for my complete flying career. Fortunately we were the only aircraft due to leave so the radio calls were simple and after about 45 minutes on the ground we started to taxi out to the take-off runway. I must have been OK since I was still there in the seat. I read the pre-departure checks and we were ready to go. This time the aircraft was very light so we leapt into the air and away we went to Lagos. The flight time was just over an hour so there was plenty to do. The radio calls were all on VHF which was great. Strange places to call on the way though. Finally I called the Controller at Lagos and got the weather for the Captain. It was slowly approaching dusk as we made our approach. "Landing Flap" was the final call from the Captain and then we were on the ground at Lagos.

The airport was a big improvement on Kano with a lot of green vegetation in the fields adjacent to the airport. The city was much larger and the airport itself seemed to be altogether busier with a few aircraft scattered around. There were some vintage ones and some modern ones. Even the terminal looked a bit more inviting than Kano. As we pulled onto the stand the hive of activity on the ground started again and I sat there watching it all. The Captain must have thought I was OK since he nodded at me and said:

"OK Gwyn. Welcome to Lagos. Now the fun begins."

I remember that as I shut down the radios and generally tidied up there was a distinctive sound of a vintage prop driven aircraft taxiing somewhere nearby. Suddenly I looked out of the right hand window and there was an old Lockheed Constellation of 50s fame parking next to us. It had one engine stopped and had markings hanging off everywhere and looked in a very sorry state.

"Surely that aircraft could not have just landed," I said out loud.

The Flight Engineer butted in by saying:

"Here in Nigeria we are in the middle of a tribal conflict of some sort to do with a break-away region called Biafra. That aircraft has come in from Port Harcourt with a pile of bodies for burial. It's a pretty ugly war."

So here I was transported from the quiet backwaters of Windsor to a war zone in West Africa. Not a nice thought. I quietly finished off what I was doing trying not to look at the Constellation to my right. A rather dilapidated truck passed our nose and I could not help but take notice of it. It parked at the open freight door of the Constellation and there seemed to be a lot of commotion from within the aircraft and suddenly piles of black bags were casually thrown in the lorry as if they were post- office bags. No guesses as to what they contained. What an introduction to the route!!

After about 20 minutes our passengers had disembarked and all of the crew assembled at the top of the steps ready to follow the Captain down onto the tarmac.

"Is it jackets on or off, sir?" enquired the Chief Steward.

This was another ritual whereby the captain decided whether the temperature was hot enough to justify walking to the terminal in shirtsleeves with the jacket over the arm. Caps were not up for discussion I might add.

"I think jackets off would be OK," was his reply.

We then all strolled towards the terminal and entered a different world from what I expected. It was getting dark by now and the lighting was a bit fierce. As we went through the various channels I could not help noticing that all the officials were bedecked in army combat clothing and swinging machine guns around nonchalantly.

"Just stick with us and all will be OK," Captain W said.

You bet I will. I will stick to you like glue and that's a promise. Customs was quite alarming with this young army type chap sifting through the contents of my suitcase using the pointed ended of his machine gun to poke around. With the temperature in the high 80s and about 100% humidity he must have been bemused at the couple of thick sweaters that caught his eye. Eventually we were on the road outside the terminal waiting patiently for our crew transport to arrive when suddenly this dilapidated old bus lurches its way towards us.

This bus must have come from the same garage as the one in Delhi, I thought.

Anyway, we all clambered on and with a great squeal of brakes and clouds of diesel smoke we bumped our way out of the airport.

"Captain, would you mind if we had a beer?" was the cry from somewhere down the back of the bus.

"No problem," was the Captain's reply.

Within a couple of nanoseconds there was the synchronized sound of beer cans being opened. One was thrust in my hand and boy did it taste nice. Nectar in fact! One small point of intrigue for the Cabin Crew was the fact that they were used to older Flight Crew and suddenly there was this young single-ringed pilot amongst us. The journey must have taken 30 minutes or so and the transformation from a very serious and professional crew to a very relaxed laid back group of people was amazing. Having said that the work was done and it was now leisure time. Yes, I was going to enjoy this airline life.

The hotel that we stayed in was the 'Ikeja Arms Inn' in one the suburbs of Lagos. We were due to stay in Lagos for two days. By today's airline standard of hotel it would never have been acceptable but this was Nigeria in the 60s and it was felt to be most convenient for the airport. As we walked into the hotel reception area I spotted a swimming pool off to the right and would have loved to rip my clothes off and plunge in but no such luck. Everybody on the bus had adjusted themselves and the girls popped the hats on. Considering the heat together with the fact we had been travelling for many hours the crew looked pretty smart. As we entered the hotel there was another crew in the lobby who turned out to be the crew taking the aircraft back to

Heathrow. As you would expect I knew no-one at all. The two Flight Engineers discussed the state of the aircraft and generally there was a lot of chat going on. The other Flight Engineer looked me up and down and remarked on my youth.

"Mind you, with two days here and no running water in your rooms and many power cuts you will learn to love this place," he said casually to me.

"What do you mean, no running water?" I said with a fearful look on my face.

"The main water pump has broken. I had a look and it looks like the motor has burnt out, so what you will get is a bucket of water from the pool delivered daily for all your needs," was his reply.

This is not a good start to my career, but what the heck I can manage two days, I thought to myself.

The signing in was again a ritual whereby the Captain who got a higher quality of room than anybody else signed in first and then moved over to the cashier to collect his allowance in local currency for the duration of the stay. Perhaps he got a bigger bucket as well. Anyway, we all walked up one by one and signed in. I looked at the wad of local Nigerian Pounds. It all looked a bit grubby and chewed up but money was money.

Another small word about the allowance scene. What happened is that as you arrived at the hotel you collected local currency to cover the meal costs during your stay and for the flight just completed. For example if you arrived in the early evening as we did you would collect a lunch and dinner allowance for that day plus two complete days. Since we were due to leave after breakfast on the third day and arrive in Heathrow later that day then you were paid breakfast and lunch for that third day.

It was by now about 7 pm and I felt quite tired from the experience of the first training day. However, as the crew completed the signing in someone said: "See you in the bar in one hour."

OK, I felt tired but the thought of a nice refreshing drink appealed and so I strolled off to my room to get tarted up for the evening. To describe my room as I remember it is quite revealing as to the scene in those days, compared with today. It contained a single bed direct from one of those 'Florence Nightingale' hospitals. Drilled out of solid iron it was, with four grand metal legs hanging down. There was no television or radio and the bathroom was extremely basic. There was a small wardrobe in the corner. The paintwork was pretty worn and resembled an old fashioned doctor's waiting room. There was, maybe, a single light suspended from the ceiling together with a huge fan which was the air conditioning. I hit the switch that hopefully would start up the fan since it was pretty hot in the room. The fan slowly started to turn accompanied by a collection of grinding sounds and squeaks. It slowly got up to speed and then started to shake all over and I had visions of me in the bed with the fan directly above breaking loose and screwing me to the floor. The fan was turned off so as to preserve my body. There was no carpet and the floor was covered in a collection of pieces of matting. There was then a knock on the door and the porter arrived with my bag and the requisite bucket of water from the pool. I had temporarily forgotten about the lack of water. It made it all a bit exciting if the truth be known – or was I kidding myself? Anyway, I placed my suitcase down on the floor and opened it up and dragged out what I wanted to wear. After a rather cold experience with the bucket of water I sort of got my act together and ventured out of the room and down to the bar. I gingerly entered the bar and looked for a familiar face. There were none!

So what do I do now? I thought.

There were groups of various colours and creeds in the bar so I made to a point near to a group of English speaking white folk and I leant as casually as I could against the bar trying to be cool.

"Aren't you talking to us then young man?" someone said close by.

I turned only to see the complete crew all giggling away at my expense. How different they all looked out of their uniforms. Stupid boy or what! I spluttered out some sort of apology to all present and shuffled into the group. I have to say the girls looked good out of uniform and well put together.

Don't push your luck on the first trip, tiger, was my thought for the day.

The evening went well with a fair amount of drink being consumed. After a while a rather older plumpish man joined us. He seemed to know everybody. Who was this guy then? Captain W turned to me and introduced him to me.

"This is Joe Harold. He owns the hotel," he said.

This was the start of a good friendship that lasted a few years.

"OK folks, dinner is on the house due to the water problem," he said as only a hotel owner would say it.

I was ready for bed but now we were going to eat! I must keep up with these people! So we all filed into the dining room to a large table made ready for us surrounded by waiters in tailored white jackets. I learnt later that the dining room was famous in Lagos for good food and wine. I have to say I remember the food was very good. The conversation drifted across the table and always it ended up with the latest gossip in BOAC. At one point the Flight Engineer said to me in a serious but drink-induced way:

"Don't forget about the cockroaches in your room."

"What do you mean?" I spluttered still trying to keep cool. They don't have those in Windsor you know.

"The trick is to pull your bed off the wall and rub soap on the bed legs since the little buggers can't get a grip to climb up them to sleep in your nice warm armpit for the night," he explained.

I was by this time all ears and panic struck at the thought of some creepy crawly snuggling up with me.

"When I was in the Navy we all kept one in a matchbox and at night they slept with me to keep off the mosquitoes," he continued.

This was getting better and better. Even the girls stopped and leant an ear.

"Of course the worst thing to do is to leave your suitcase open for them to set up home and invite the entire family in," he continued.

Alarm bells sounded in my head. I recalled that I left mine open to the world back in the room.

What was I to do? I thought

Since the party was getting into full swing and I seemed to have the attention of one of the girls, I decided to order another drink. The evening progressed and the thought of creepy crawlies went onto the back burner. Eventually the dinner was done and we all then adjourned back into the bar. Blimey these people had stamina! At about 2 am after about six hours of socializing a few drifted off to bed. I was torn between going for the kill with this attentive stewardess or staying with the Flight Engineer and my training Co-pilot. I felt it would be the better option to stay with the men as opposed to making a fool of myself elsewhere.

I seem to remember struggling off to my room in the early hours. As I turned the key the words of the flight engineer hit my brain like a sledgehammer.

"Time for action," I said to myself.

I gingerly entered my room and surveyed the scene. Fortunately I had left the light on which seemed to do the trick of keeping the little blighters at bay. All seemed clear but there was my suitcase open to the world for all to venture into. I approached very cautiously and prodded the contents with great delicacy. I needed that gun the customs guy had. It must have taken me a good 20 minutes to check it out. I was not in the best of health at the time and kept forgetting which sock had been checked. Finally all looked clear in the suitcase so I promptly closed it. Now for the bed! My head was hurting now and all I wanted was to sleep but the 'soaping' had to be done. So off I went into the bathroom without thinking too much and there was a king of all cockroaches sitting on the loo seat. This was becoming a nightmare to me as I needed to complete certain bodily functions before sleeping and this monster was in the way. I backtracked to the room door and made my way back to the lobby to complete said ablutions in the bar toilets. Low and behold the Flight Engineer and one of the Co-pilots were still in the bar. Endurance or what!

"Hello young Gwyn, come for another drink then?" the Flight Engineer said cheerily.

I explained my predicament to hoots of laughter, only to be reminded by the Co-pilot:

"Don't forget he has a mate somewhere."

My world was falling apart. Two of the buggers were now lurking in my room ready to pounce into my armpit. I seriously felt like sleeping on the settee in the reception area but that was soon scotched when I considered the ramifications of waking up to a load of hotel guests walking by on their way to breakfast and surveying this idiot slumped in the corner snoring loudly. The only solution was to face the thunder and get those legs soaped. By now, any relaxation in the head after the night's drinking had totally evaporated and had been replaced by a headache of grand proportions. I completed my ablutions with the regulation bucket and made my excuses to one and all and slowly headed back to the war zone. As I entered the room I realized that on this occasion I had switched off the light before going out so when I flicked the light on there was much scurrying and scratching on the floor.

"Two of the buggers, eh! I now have got a complete squadron of the blighters in my room!" I said with desperation in my voice.

I gingerly opened the bathroom door expecting to see a complete family in residence but amazingly enough there was not one of them around.

Maybe they are tucked under the sheets enjoying a night's slumber, I pondered.

"Right, time to build up the defences while there is a lull in the Gwyn v Cockroach war," I muttered.

I grabbed the rather grubby looking bar of soap which resembled the old 'Coal Tar' type and together with the bucket of faithful pool water dragged the bed into the middle of the floor watching every move with the utmost caution in case the enemy had regrouped ready for another strike. I then dumped the soap bar in the bucket and worked up a lather to do the honours on the bed legs. The first leg got the full treatment with what seemed about 30 pounds of soap per square inch.

"One down and three to go," I said triumphantly.

I think if a secret camera had been filming the scene I would have been committed by now since I was pretty well covered in soap and the room was beginning to resemble one of those modern wet rooms. Anyway, I succeeded in doing all of the legs in turn and stood in the midst of the soap suds with a sly grin on my face.

"Right you little buggers! I am now in command of the situation so you can now all just shove off and die," I said with a total hatred of anything insect-like living on the planet.

I was just about to drag my aching body into bed when I thought to myself:

I have just installed the defences but what if the odd lurker has climbed up and is waiting for me to arrive.

So off I went again into the 'seek and destroy' mode, leaving no bedsheet spare of the search. Eventually I was in the position whereby all defences were complete and the sleeping area was clear so I was finally ready to hit the sack. It must have been at least 4 am or something like that. Anyway I noted the route from the light switch carefully and did a final survey of the bed legs, switched off the light and moved like a ballerina to my safe island retreat in the middle of the room. I lay there staring into the darkness at the ceiling and listening intensely for any enemy movement.

Maybe I should sleep with the light on? I thought.

Mind you, to do that required a sprint across enemy territory where they may be already grouping for an attack. Then suddenly it started. A small scratch here and a little shuffle there. I tried to survey the shadows down below the bed with no success.

From where and how many? I thought.

It seemed like there must be hundreds of them all circling the island fortress or maybe even thousands judging by the noise. I must have lain there frozen for seemingly hours, checking my armpits every now and again.

What if they wander elsewhere on the body for a nice kip? I thought, worrying of the obvious place.

Suddenly the noises all stopped as it a tap had been turned off.

What are they up to now? I wondered.

I repeated the curse on all insects and especially the Nigerian Cockroaches wishing for 'hell and damnation' on them all when I must have finally drifted off.

I woke up with a Nigerian standing by my bed looking around at the total chaos. He was the room boy and had come in to clean the room not realizing I was still in it. I looked at my watch and saw that it was late morning so no wonder he was there. He disappeared shaking his head. My first action was to check for any insects of any description around the island. He was right, for the room was a total shambles with soap and the bucket filled with the grimiest looking liquid. I climbed out of the bed and came to the conclusion that my first ever African night stop in BOAC had not gone as I intended it. In fact, it was a total nightmare and what's more I still had two nights to go. I still shudder to this day when I think about it.

I finally got my act together and the room boy returned pretty quickly with a fresh bucket of pool water. Not very nice cleaning your teeth with the taste of chlorine swilling about but, what the heck, it was better than no water at all. The weather was sunny with the temperature in the high 80s already. I re-called the room boy as I left the room and asked him as nicely as I could if he could please tidy the room and leave me a new bar of soap ready for the evening fun and frolics. I made my way down to the pool area and looked around for any remnants of the crew that I might actually manage to recognize. I spied a collection of bodies in one corner and spotted Captain W amongst them. There were about ten of them all laughing and giggling with a table of empty beer bottles in their midst.

Blimey, here we go again, I thought.

Mind you, after the escapades of the night before food was top of my list and as I sat down to join them the pool waiter arrived on cue and I ordered a club sandwich plus the obligatory beer. The reason for the extra numbers was that another aircraft had arrived in the early hours. Most of the new crew were there by the pool. Introductions followed.

Doesn't anybody sleep round here? I thought.

My mind then drifted back to my night and I thought that maybe the best solution was to drink and slumber all day by the pool and stand guard all night. The other crew seemed to be devoid of any cabin crew people so I asked where they were.

"We brought down the Nigerian Airways aircraft last night and that is why there are just us here," someone said.

It was explained to me then that Nigerian Airways leased a VC-10 of BOAC and painted it in their own colours. BOAC flight crews fly it but the cabin crew was all local Nigerians. I seem to remember that they had a BOAC Chief Steward in charge of them on each flight. They also had three of their own Captains fully qualified to fly the VC-10 but the rules state that they must have one of our own training Captains in the right-hand seat.

It seemed to me that all of the crews in the hotel were there by the pool and a lunchtime party was starting. My club sandwich turned up and I tucked into it like a man possessed.

"Did you sleep all right, Gwyn?" my friendly Flight Engineer asked with a slight sarcastic grin.

"Yes, no problems," I replied casually in between bites of my sandwich.

I lied through my teeth so as to not to arouse suspicion of my plight endured in the night war.

"Those bloody cockroaches were pretty active last night. I had to call for the extermination squad twice," someone said.

What was this 'extermination squad' all about then? Have I missed something here? There I was fighting the enemy as a one-man extermination squad unaided when all the time there was help at hand. I asked the Co-pilot quietly and he explained that the hotel staff will come along and clear your room of the little mites before you go to bed. I wished someone had told me about this lot the night before since I could at least have got some sort of sleep at a normal hour.

The stewardesses were all there as well and I noticed that the lady whom I was targeting from the night before seemed deep in chat with the Co-Pilot on the new crew so I mentally licked my wounds and joined in the general chat. Failed again! Since I was a product of the flying college and not in any way involved with the UK Military I found some of the chat hard to follow. You see when a bunch of Pilots and Flight Engineers get together then the talk is mainly about what they did in the RAF or Navy. This was 1967 and the Cold War was still at its height. I was sitting amongst people who had been active in the military flying all sorts of aircraft.

My main interest outside of flying was space flight. The Americans were now poised to go to the moon in the Apollo spacecraft and I found it all fascinating. This didn't have much to do with the ins and outs of the Gloster Meteor Night Fighter as flown by one of the Co-pilots though. Having said that some of the stories were interesting but at that particular time the lack of sleep was starting to catch up with me. I excused myself and slumped into a sun lounger and fell asleep dreaming of the 'Extermination Squad'. I must have slept for a good couple of hours and woke up with a start.

Where the bloody hell am I? I thought.

I could hear laughter and giggles coming from somewhere nearby and spotted that the lunchtime session was now moving into the afternoon tea session.

"Oh, look everybody, the young 'un has woken up finally," someone said.

The beer table was now overflowing with full ashtrays and empty glasses. The Flight Engineer was in full flow relating some tale about when he was in the Navy on an Aircraft Carrier in the Eastern Mediterranean and all hell was breaking loose. I generally found the Flight Engineers amongst the best of the bunch and as I said before I formed a great admiration for them as time went by. I would hasten to add that it was generally the Flight Engineer that would get me into the most trouble during my airline career.

As the sun was setting the congregation gathered decided to up sticks and spruce up for the evening's festivities. As I was pretty well alcohol-free for the day I felt that this was a good to time to hit the cockroaches with the Extermination Squad. I sat in my room and after a short while there was a knock on the door and the same room boy entered carrying under his arm a contraption that resembled one of those squeegee things that you use to seal a window by pulling the trigger. This thing he had was about twice the size and looked pretty formidable. Suddenly I had the utmost respect for this guy since one squirt from this and I could be totally annihilated for he seemed to be swinging it all over the place. He eventually concentrated on one particular spot in the corner of the room where the floor was lifting slightly off and revealing a gap which seemed large enough to transport an army of the blighters. He shoved the nozzle of the machine into the gap and pumped the thing vigorously building up pressure and speed with each stroke. After a while he removed the nozzle and continued his search. This man was becoming my hero and any shadow or possible hole got the full treatment. The smell was pretty vile but better than a full armpit. He then squirted the bed legs where I have done the soaping up the night before. What a star! Eventually having done every possible spot he gestured me into the bathroom and told me in his broken English to always leave the plugs in the sink and the bath. Boy, I was learning fast! He then left and returned with the daily bucket of pool water and so I attempted to get myself in some sort of order for the 7 pm appointment in the bar. Not easy with just a bucket.

"OK for these ex-Navy guys when up the jungle on patrol but not for a delicate boy like me!" I said to myself.

I finally got to the bar at the appointed hour feeling much more in control of my life after the attack on the cockroaches had been seemingly successful. I just hoped the little buggers weren't keeping their head down until the coast was clear. There are some people of questionable ancestry in this world who find insects and the like quite acceptable even to the point that they allow these things to crawl all over their body. I am not in that group and, in fact, if you consider the other end of the spectrum, you will find me sitting on the outside edge. Anyway the two complete crews were assembled in the bar and away we went. The stewardess that I had chatted to the night before was tucked up with the Co-pilot and gave me the impression that things had happened between them during the day. Lucky man!

The evening must have been fine with not too much to report which certainly made a change from the first night. There was an offer running around for a visit to the local Guinness factory on the following day organized by the Flight Engineer leaving at about lunchtime. Having been in Shannon a short while ago I put my name down. As I said the evening went well with the usual chit chat. At least I felt a bit more with it as opposed to the night before. It must have broken up at about midnight. Don't forget most of them had started the party in the afternoon so one could not help but admire their stamina. I had a lot to learn yet!

On my way back to my room I pondered the thought of a second round of anti-roach warfare. I opened my room door half expecting to see the local battalion assembled ready to hit the armpit. What joy! The room was clear of anything that resembled a creepy crawly. The bed was positioned off the wall as I had left it and on the table next to it was a saucer with a green twirl-like piece of clay and what's more it was it was smoking at one end with an aromatic smell and was slowly burning in ever decreasing circles. I later found out that this was a 'Joss Stick' providing a simple way of keeping the mosquitoes at bay. They just did not like the smell. The room boy had even put a small lamp on the table. Life was good and I must have slept a good nine hours.

The following day I actually made breakfast with the rest of the crew. The lovers were there still so I joined my flight crew and listened to the chat. Captain W was, in fact, chairman of the BOAC section of the aircrew union BALPA which actually stood for the British Airline Pilots Association and effectively did all the trade union side of the business. There seemed to be something on the industrial front that was stirring everybody up. It was all about pay and conditions and BOAC and BALPA were in conflict. Just as an aside, in 1967 a senior Captain in BOAC was on a salary of £5,800 per annum and Panam captains were on £8,900. My starting salary was £1,800 pa. Pathetic by today's standards but pretty good at the time. The other chat was about the midday departure to the famous Guinness factory with the demon drink having the local nickname of 'Nigerian Lager'.

I recall about six of us turned up at midday for the outing, comprising mainly the male members of the crews. Now, there's a surprise! We all piled into a rickety bus and off we went down the road. The journey took about an hour and gave me a chance to look at the local scene. It was pretty appalling to see the poverty and the lack of even basic essentials. We went through a shanty-town which was littered with rubbish together with bits of roofing here and there that would be a home for maybe six or more people. Having not been to Nigeria before I was really appalled by what I saw.

How can anybody live like this? I thought.

This was Africa at its rawest. Oil had not yet been discovered in the region and the Biafra war was costing the country dear with the people taking the main brunt of it. We eventually arrived at a sort of industrial area again littered with rubbish and closed up warehouses with broken windows everywhere. The odd local was wandering about, totally oblivious to the surroundings. We passed through a gateway guarded by a bunch of machine-gun armed military guys who seemed to have the average age of about 16.

They must be the lucky ones. They can eat! were my thoughts.

We arrived at a reception area to be greeted by a white fellow who must have been the boss. He was wearing a drab ex-white suit and talked to us as if we were the first white people he had spoken to in years. As you might expect the Flight Engineer was first off the bus and took up the position of team leader. He had obviously done the tour many times. All I remember is a sort of compacted tour in a large factory with loads of bottles parading up and down on conveyer belts seemingly ready to collapse if touched. I was a bit mystified by the pace set by our team leader. I should have thought of the obvious. Guinness is beer and that was why we were here. After the so-called tour we arrived at a bar area. I think that the object of the exercise was to get the tour over within the shortest possible time and then take advantage of the hospitality. So it was Nigerian Lagers all round and I found they tasted nothing like the smooth Irish one from Shannon but it was hot out there and it seemed to hit the spot. We must have been there for a couple of hours when the rickety old bus shambled up alongside ready to take us back to the hotel. OK, not a thrilling afternoon out but an eye opener into other cultures and people.

Back at the hotel it was approaching 6 pm and time for the exterminator to act together with the daily bucket wash routine. The plan for the next day was a departure at about 9 am back to Heathrow via Kano and Rome. The mood at dinner was generally not quite as I had known it from the previous two nights. With an early departure from the hotel and the thought of about a ten hour working day ahead I seem to remember being all tucked up by about 9 pm. I might add there was not a cockroach in sight.

The following morning I was woken by a loud gurgling sound and suddenly I heard water flowing in the bathroom.

"Bloody hell! I am out of here in a couple of hours having endured the bucket and now there is water everywhere," I said to myself.

Having said that, the colour was pretty grim being sort of muddy brown, but I waited for a while and it slowly cleared. The temperature outside was in the 80s as usual so I took the plunge into a freezing cold shower. Once the initial shock subsided I relished the flow of real water and felt good afterwards.

We all assembled in the lobby fresh from our cold showers when

the rickety old crew bus rolled up with the crew who had just brought
the aircraft in. Amongst the other guys was Bron, one of my friends
who I did the technical course with. He was of Polish descent and
built like an ox. We chatted for a while with me doing most of the
talking, explaining about the bucket routine if the water went off
again. The Exterminator was mentioned. We parted company and I
duly clambered on the bus. As we were fussing about getting our seats
Captain W stood and said:

"Folks, I have just had a call from the airport and there are big
security problems all around us. Some Biafran rebels are reported to be
in the area so will be having an Army escort to the airport."

The amazing thing I remember is that hardly anybody stirred and
just carried on with what they were doing. Me, I melted in my seat and
started to wonder if I would ever get home.

Imagine if we are ambushed and I spent the rest of my life locked up
in some jungle outpost, I thought.

With no exterminator patrol either! I added a thought.

As I said, no one else seemed too bothered, so as to not 'lose face' I
casually got a cigarette out and then puffed on it like crazy as if it were
the last. The so-called Army escort was in fact an equally rickety old
army truck from the same garage as our bus. It had about six soldiers
of dubious origin perched in the back.

Fat chance of survival here, I thought.

The journey was spent with me looking out of the window and
scrutinizing every person that was within 20 yards of the road. What
was I looking for? I had no idea since they all looked the same to me.
We must have passed through about six road blocks manned by equally
dubious soldiers. At last the airport came into sight. What a relief!
Another roadblock marked the entrance to the terminal. Once inside I
felt safe. We all made our way to the VC-10 standing majestically on the
tarmac with about 45 minutes in hand before departure.

"Right Gwyn, you can fly it to Kano," said Captain W casually.

"Thank you, sir!" I replied totally gobsmacked at being given the
chance to fly the aircraft.

I sat in the right hand seat and gathered my thoughts. Right, I must
get up a routine. As the scheduled time of departure approached the

Captain leaned over and said quietly:

"OK Gwyn, we have ten minutes to go so off you go and let's get the checks done."

You see, back then when you were given a sector everything was done as if you were the Captain. It started with the call for checks to talking to the Chief Steward, and so on.

A little side point here about the Cabin Crew of that era. Once you were off the aircraft and all duties were complete then socializing was the order of the day and there were no formalities of rank or job distinction. You had a good time 'down the route'. Most crew members met up in the bar normally at about 7 pm and the evenings were invariably great fun. The dress code was different in those days with the male members of the crew usually in an open necked shirt in the tropics and smart trousers. Jeans were an absolute no-no. The girls were dressed as if going out on a date and usually in dresses. There was none of the modern 'Cropped Jeans' and 'hang it all out' tops that you see a lot of nowadays. I am not an old crusty I can assure you but that was the way it was and it was quite excellent. Once you put the uniform on then the protocol set in and all crew members slipped into their assigned positions and treated you with respect according to your position on the aircraft. It was quite amazing how it happened but I have to say it was a really nice feeling. Being with only one ring and quite young did create a few question marks. The 'boy' was reserved for the Flight Engineers and other various 'handles' were brought into play.

Right, well there I was running the show as we progressed through the pre-start bits and pieces and at about 10 am we left the stand for the flight to Kano with me doing the taxiing and calling the shots. I seem to remember being quite relaxed about it all and before I knew it we were in the air and on our way. The flight time was just over the hour so there was no time to be idle and once in the cruise I started to try to get organized for the arrival.

Not having the computer generated display screens resulted in a lot of mental arithmetic and a good idea of exactly where you were based on the dials and needles on the panel was pretty useful. It actually became second nature as time went by but there and then my brain was working overtime. We used a general formula to establish the point on the route from where to start the descent that was based on three times the height plus a few extras. For example if you were flying at 33,000 ft the descent point would be 99 miles away from your destination. If you were planning the landing and the runway direction was similar to the direction of your arrival then you added about ten miles to allow for you to slow down. If you were landing with the runway direction the other way then you subtracted about ten miles. There were a few more factors involved that I won't elaborate on but you eventually ended up with a point on the route from where you wanted to descend.

Of course, the wild card was the chap on the ground. In Africa this was always a lottery since you, maybe, had to get his attention first and then he might ponder for a while and all this time the clock is ticking. The single word that summed it all up was 'Standby Speedbird'. So there I was on my way descending into Kano, with the brain working overtime to try get it right on my first official training sector with me flying. The runway was positioned such that all I needed to do was to look up and there it would be. I needed a little bit of prompting by the Captain as we arrived in the airport area. I must have forgotten that it was a road in the desert I was looking for and not a shiny well defined tarmac like I was used to. I remember looking up and there it was, the famous road in my sights straight ahead. We were at about 2,000 ft so I elected to do a simple circuit just like I had done many times in Shannon. Well, I did it and there was the runway right on cue in the windscreen and I finished off the final bit with a smooth landing.

"Well done, Gwyn," Captain W said as I slowed down to taxiing speed.

I felt chuffed to bits that all had gone well with my first flying sector and sat back in my seat and breathed a sigh of relief once we had parked.

I am on the way, I thought.

We were on the ramp for some 45 minutes and I was to be the co-pilot for the next leg to Rome. The other two Co-pilots swapped roles where the navigation was concerned. I felt sorry for them since neither of them would have a chance to fly the aircraft. I was hogging it all since I was the one being trained.

I was by now slowly evolving a routine and seemed to get ready to go with time to spare. We took off for Rome and I settled back to begin the battle of the HF radio again. This time I was ready for the chaos on the radio waves and became pretty confident in getting the reports through. Looking back I think it is credit to the young mind as to how quickly one adapts to things totally new. As you get older the mind is less willing to absorb new stuff and hence the reluctance to adapt.

Why change things when I am happy as they are now? springs to mind.

The Captain did his normal walk around the cabin after we had had lunch and I settled back into the routine with a certain amount of confidence. The chat on the flight deck was generally confined to the aircraft and how it was performing on the day. This particular VC-10 G-ARVC was the one on lease to Nigerian Airways and was painted in their colours with a green cheat line and an enormous green elephant on the tail. BOAC used it when it was needed, as it was on this occasion. Generally, however, it had a Nigerian call sign and carried the full Nigerian cabin crew. I was yet to indulge on that side of life yet!

We crossed the North African coast overhead Benghazi in Libya. In those days Colonel Gaddafi was not even heard of and both the British and American forces had military bases there. The ground controllers were even English. As for Rome I was studying the layout of the area and was totally mystified by the use of local names to define points of navigation.

"They are European so they must have good command of English, so no problems there!" I muttered to myself.

How wrong I was! The moment I called them I was in an alien world and just stared blankly at the chart trying to relate the odd word spoken in broken English to a place on the map.

Not a bloody chance, I thought to myself.

Just as the controller fired down another set of instructions I could imagine him throwing his hands up in the air when deadly silence was the only reply. The training Co-pilot got a little ratty with me for not listening and understanding him properly.

"If he spoke bloody English I might have half a chance!" was my silent reply.

He intervened quite a few times much to his annoyance and I was sinking further and further down in my seat. By the time we landed I was a total, gibbering wreck. The only words I think I understood was the final call that we were cleared to land. What a complete mess I had made of that arrival. Once parked we strolled up into the terminal and had a cup of cappuccino and the trainer said a few unsavoury words in my ear. The Captain intervened and suggested that I sit back for the final sector to Heathrow and try to listen carefully to try to understand these people. Bloody Italians! They ruined a perfect day for me. Having said that, the other Co-pilot did mention that he still had problems to this day understanding these people. A supporter in the crowd.

Funny, I could understand the scratchy voice deep in the African desert on the HF but not this lot. To my defence I would add that nowadays the inbound route which is known as a 'Standard Terminal Arrival Route', or STAR for short, is defined and can be easily mapped out. These modern routes were all given a name and identified the exact route to get to the runway in use. All you do now is to put this route in the computer and Hey Presto the line shows up where to go. In those days the ground controller would say the complete route over the radio as if in long hand and wait for you to recite it back exactly with maybe an accent or two throw in.

We took off from Rome at about 6 pm and I sat behind the pilots and tried my best to understand the words wafting over the airways. I seemed to catch every sixth word. Must be an improvement from not understanding a single word I suppose. We finally crossed the North French coast at a place called Abbeville. I learnt many years later that this place was on the River Somme marking one of the great battles of World War 1. As we switched the radio to the English Controller I could feel a sense of relief all round since it marked the point where we were nearly home or 'Back in Blighty' as they say.

We landed at about 8 pm and once all the passengers had disembarked we rode back to the crew report area and I started to unwind at the thought of going home. My training file was duly completed with the only adverse comment entered being the approach into Rome.

Fair cop. Maybe I won't go there again on training, I thought.

I travelled to the crew car park and then drove back to the Malt House. This marked the end of my first route training flight in BOAC.

After a few days to recover I found myself rostered for the second training trip in a few days' time. This trip was to Tehran, Iran and onto Karachi, Pakistan. After two days off, the route home was back to Heathrow via Rome. Ah, those Italians again! Captain D plus one Co-pilot and a Flight Engineer completed the crew. The departure was scheduled at 11 pm with a night-flight, arriving in Karachi after about ten hours' duty. The impact of the first trip was still fresh in my mind and I do not recall too much about the departure for this trip.

Now, Tehran is an interesting place both geographically and flying wise. The city lies in a sort of bowl surrounded from the west through north and extending to the east by high mountains. The airport is on the south side of the city and the whole area is generally polluted by smog. From a flying point of view it could not have been placed in a worse position. Because of the surrounding mountains none of the modern landing aids could be installed so you had to depend on the old type ADF beacons as described earlier to find your way. I seem to remember four of these beacons marked our route in. They were not even in a straight line but shaped like a horseshoe with the last one marking the end of the runway. The runway pretty well blended in with the surrounding area and the only real clue was a large monument about five miles north-east of the airport. Also there was an old airfield which marked the point to turn for the final approach. I believe it has been known for aircraft to land at this old airport by mistake. We arrived around dawn and I found it amazing that in this day and age we still did these very basic approaches. Little did I know that in those days many of the world's airports were littered with these facilities only.

This was January and Tehran was very cold with loads of snow around and really quite miserable. I was quite happy when we departed for Karachi. We flew south-east and crossed the border into Pakistan on the extreme western end. The landscape I recall was quite stunning on the route. It was quite mountainous in Iran and then flattened out in Pakistan. I never knew that there was so much sand in the world.

Karachi lies on the south coast of Pakistan and, at the time, was accepted as the capital. From the aviation point of view it was known as the crossroads of the air where west met east. Pretty well all airlines went through Karachi in both directions. The infrastructure left after the famous partition of India had left its legacy with a good understanding of everything in the aviation world. This manifested itself in the airport. It had all the modern aids and two large parallel runways together with a large ramp area. The only thing it lacked was an approach radar system but they coped very well. BOAC had a large base there with engineers and administration staff. There could well have been over 100 people employed there.

Engineering-wise the VC-10 had a spare engine plus a host of other items stored in a large hangar that was exclusively owned by BOAC. Such luxury! It was a well-known fact that here BOAC had a very high calibre of ground engineers working, often with father and son together. This applied to the whole of the Indian sub-continent and quite often when the aircraft was parked for some hours the engineers would perform many tasks. Not easy when the temperatures rarely dropped below 35°C day or night. The place had a real buzz.

Once again we went through the routine of passing through customs and then there I was standing around waiting for the crew bus. At this point the Captain suggested we walk to the hotel.

"How far is it?" I enquired already wilting in the scorching heat.

"You will find out," was his reply.

Why the mystery? I thought.

Anyway, I went to gather up my suitcase and briefcase only to be told that they could stay there and they would be collected. This was getting stranger and stranger. We strolled as a group away from the airport and I tagged along as usual. I remember passing some squash courts on the right after a few minutes and then within a further two minutes or so we turned off the road into a non-descript group of buildings. A dusty old sign was swinging from a pole. I looked at it and it read 'BOAC rest house'. You see, back then BOAC owned its own sort of hotel in Karachi just like in Bahrain and accommodated all of its crews plus QANTAS there. KLM had its own rest house as well just down the road. It was an amazing place and a throwback to a bygone age. When Imperial Airways arrived here in the old biplane known as the HP-42

(Dad flew them in his day out of Croydon) this was the end of the line for the passengers.

To describe the rest house is simple. It consisted of a number of outbuildings that resembled the old single-storey Nissen huts. There must have been about seven of the huts all built around a swimming pool. It was interesting to note that all of the stewardesses were housed in their own block away from the men. This block became affectionately known as 'Virgins' Alley'. Can't think why?! As for the rooms, they were the original broom cupboard with just about enough space for a bed and a small bedside table. There was no bathroom since we all shared a bathroom at the end of our block. It was incredibly basic but since only BA and QANTAS stayed there it was one heck of a social place.

I mentioned that back in Lagos we all queued up for allowances on arrival. Here in Karachi we had none since all things consumed in the hotel were free of charge. Could you imagine that nowadays! The only exception to that was alcohol. Pakistan was a dry state like India with alcohol banned but in the safety of our rest house you simply went to the reception and bought a book of beer vouchers and off you went. The alternative to the alcohol dilemma was to smuggle it in through customs. Many ingenious methods were employed. The best one I think was invented by QANTAS whereby a crew member came through Karachi carrying with him a hose pipe which he claimed was being delivered to a friend in the UK. Little did the customs know but there was cork bunged in either end and the hose pipe produced about two and half bottles of liquor. The other method was to take a short piece of hosepipe that would fit inside your hat rim and fill it with liquor. It seemed to be a game of us and them.

The other thing about the rooms was that there was no air-conditioning and you were separated by a thin wall from your neighbour. As I said it was extremely basic but wow! What a place. We were there for two days so after a good long sleep in my broom cupboard and a good clean up in the washrooms I wandered up to the bar area in the early evening. The temperature had dropped by now to a cool 28°C and I found that very pleasant since the UK was still in the depths of winter.

With regards to the allowance issue there was a solution that by today's standard seems bizarre. In England we had a Labour Government running the show under Harold Wilson and the country was in dire financial straits with a lot of money being shipped abroad and leaving the sinking ship. The government introduced draconian laws that restricted this outflow. I can remember that you were allowed only £50 to take abroad with you on holiday per annum and the pound was continually being devalued. As far as we in BOAC were concerned we were allowed £5 per day for each day away courtesy of the Bank of England. Does not sound much but in those days it went a long way. So what you did was to go to a money changer or local bank wherever you were and wrote out a cheque and got local currency in return. The cheque that you handed over invariably became currency and would do the rounds for maybe two months before finally arriving back at your bank in the UK. I can vividly remember going to my bank at one time at home and being shown one of these cheques written maybe two months previously. It was a work of art with foreign writing all over it and had a whiff of curry about it.

Anyway we all assembled in the bar with our beer coupons in our hand and away we went. With free food we would dine well with the favourite being curry as you can imagine in Pakistan. The star dish was known as the 'Bearer's Curry' and earned the reputation of being the best in Karachi. Apart from us there was always a large contingent of ground staff so the restaurant was pretty busy. The curry by the way was totally scrummy and confirmed my love of it forever. With only airline crew at the rest house this allowed us total freedom without worrying what other hotel guests might think. The pool became the hub of activity late night with all sorts of things going on. I was definitely going to enjoy this BOAC life. The place was magic. I was going to be 21 years of age in a few days' time and here I was having a ball.

When I woke up the next day I must have had a headache from the happenings of the night before. By now it was scorching hot and the pool beckoned me. There was an abundance of cats and dogs at the rest house and, as you might imagine, lots of little ones. They were everywhere. Sitting by the pool was always entertaining with the 'dog vs cat' wars going on all around. Just after lunch the word was out that we were invited to go fishing later that day in one of the large fishing boats owned by one of the brothers of a hotel staff member. Of course, an amount of cash was involved but this sounded good so I signed up. I think that four of us assembled later that afternoon and off we went in the BOAC bus down to the harbour.

The scenery on the way was an improvement on Nigeria but still quite an eye-opener for me. The streets were dusty and full of potholes which made the journey a bit rocky. Karachi itself was sprawled out over a large area and seemed to be full of narrow back alleys with groups of men sitting on street corners drinking tea. One thing I did notice was the fact that there were virtually no women on the streets. This was obviously a male-dominated society. We arrived at the docks after some 40 minutes and stopped by a line of what seemed like fishing boats from a bygone age. They were about 30 feet in length with a single mast right in the middle of the deck. Towards the rear of the open deck was the engine which in its own right was a masterpiece of construction with pipes held together with bits of anything that happened to be lying around. Oil was everywhere. The Flight Engineer surveyed the engine area and shook his head in amazement. The ingenuity of these people was amazing.

Fishing lines appeared and out of the back of the BOAC bus a box full of cold drinks was extracted. They were cold when we left but by now they had hit room temperature. There was a lot of commotion around and in the boat with clanking of chains plus a lot of shouting. The ship's Captain climbed aboard and approached the engine wielding a starter handle in his hand. We all watched with intrigue while he fiddled with the levers and valves on the engine. He engaged the starter handle and started slowly to turn the engine over so as to lubricate the parts. Suddenly, as if possessed by the devil, he broke into a run on the revolutions and then there was a splutter and a bang and the beast sprang into life with a few squirts of water here and a fountain of oil there. A great cloud of thick black diesel smoke erupted somewhere virtually engulfing all of us. The whole boat shook in unison with the engine. It did not exactly spring into life but sort of walked itself into a noisy, vibrating, smoky collection of metal parts. There was another clanking of machinery and gears and slowly we backed away from our berth. We were on our way for a spot of fishing.

Once clear of the harbour after passing the greatest collection of old relics that I had ever seen the ship's Captain approached the engine and pulled a few levers and the engine calmly stopped after a few more protesting gurgles. The silence was wonderful. More clanging followed and suddenly the sail was flapping about whilst being hoisted. These deck hands for want of a better word really struggled with the sail since it looked very heavy. The amazing thing was that they did not even break out into a sweat. I was soaked in sweat and I hadn't even moved an inch from my seat. The sail finally got to the top of the mast and was then secured. There was not much of a breeze blowing but it was enough and slowly we made our way out to sea. There was not a cloud in the sky and the sea itself was calm like a millpond.

The fishing lines were unravelled and some sort of bait was attached and over the side they went. We then sat back and gently moved across the water sipping our warm drinks. It was not long before there was a tug on one of the lines and we all leapt up to watch the result. After a few anxious minutes of tugging and heaving a fish of about one metre in length succumbed to the fight and was landed on board. I have no idea of the name of the fish but it looked pretty good. Maybe it was a small Tuna or the like. Anyway as time went on more fish were landed on the deck. After about an hour we had a good collection sitting there.

"That will do us for dinner tonight. They would be great in a curry," the Flight Engineer said.

You tell me of a hotel in the world where you can go out and catch the evening meal. You could not get fresher than that. We made our way back to the berth collecting a few more fish on the way. Outside the harbour entrance we went through the engine starting ritual and after a great cloud of filthy smoke and the odd backfire we arrived back on the jetty. What I did not realize was that the sun had done its deed on my delicate white complexion and I was rapidly turning a shade of red. I could not go brown like some of these macho film stars and gradually my face turned into a sort of cooked beetroot shade.

Lesson learnt. Next time sun factor 300 for me, I thought.

We loaded the catch into the back of the BOAC bus and off we went back to the rest house. It was early evening so it was a quick sluice down and off to dinner. The cook in the rest house did a magnificent job with the fish and I recall that the fish curry was delicious, washed down with some well-earned beer. Apart from me standing out like a traffic light set to red, it was a great day.

The following day we all assembled for our return to Heathrow via the dreaded Rome and my face was now really itching and starting to blister.

What a sight, I thought! No chance of any fun and frolics in this state, I thought.

Once on board the aircraft the stewardess in the front galley must have taken pity on me and bought me a small bottle of something. I slapped it on my face. Initially it burnt like hell and then seemed to calm it all down. Lovely girl! So far on this trip I was getting well into the swing of things and felt good. The training Co-pilot seemed to be happy with me and so, apart from the deformed face, I felt good.

"Right Gwyn, you can co-pilot it into Rome and I will do the last leg since the Captain has offered me the leg to fly" my trainer said.

Shame it wasn't the other way around, was my first thought for today.

The flight time was about seven hours and thirty minutes so there was plenty of time to practise the Italian language. Captain D was equally very pleasant to fly with so I just sat back and took time out to enjoy the countryside as we flew along. As we passed to the west of Karachi along the coastline towards the Gulf region he related his tales of when he was posted in this area during the war. As I said before most of the Captains in those days flew in the war and I found some of their tales quite intriguing. It helped to pass the time very nicely plus of course the usual sumptuous lunch. We passed over the Gulf region north of Dubai and on towards Bahrain. It is well known that the region is covered with oil wells and everywhere I looked there was the tell-tale sign of the gas burning off with a fiery glow. To this day I have never understood why this is done. Surely there must be some way of capturing this gas?

What a waste, I thought.

After the Gulf we followed a route through northern Saudi Arabia,

Jordan and Syria and entered the Mediterranean over northern Lebanon. The politics of the Middle East was at a sort of stalemate at that time but was simmering away and it seemed only a matter of time before something would happen. It did – six months later.

Afternoon tea was then presented to us with Cornish clotted cream, strawberry jam and hot scones. The waistline was screaming again. How could I refuse it though? No bloody chance when I have the willpower of a moth. There was not a cloud in the sky all the way and life felt good.

That all changed when the controller said: "Change to Rome control."

Come on Gwyn – let's get this over with, was my second thought for the day.

"I have great difficulty in understanding the Italian controllers so it's going to be fun," the Captain remarked.

This was music to my ears hearing that someone else had the same thoughts. As we got nearer to Rome so the tempo increased and I just about managed to cope with the radio calls aided by the Captain and the training Co-pilot. Eventually we arrived at the approach point for the landing and by now I was just about keeping up with the scene. It was a relief when the controller cleared us to land. Once we landed and stopped on the ramp I breathed a sigh of relief.

"Not bad at all, Gwyn. I will put you up for your final check on your next trip. Unless Captain D has any comments," the training Co-pilot said with a smile on his face.

Captain D was happy with my performance with the exception of a few small items. As time went by I have found that even if you feel that you have performed exactly as required there are always a few little bits that the instructor has found. Skilful guys, the instructors.

The sector from Rome to Heathrow was a non-event since the Co-pilot was doing the flying and I was sitting back. We landed in Heathrow at about 7 pm after a long ten hour duty. I got back to the Malt House about two hours later only to find a party in full swing. As I said before my housemates had all joined BEA and they were celebrating the fact that they had all passed out as fully fledged Co-pilots on their assigned aircraft. Ian, Tony and Steve were now fully qualified on the Trident. Malc and Brian were equally qualified on the

Vanguard. This left little old me still waiting for the final calling. The party was in full swing with a collection of stewardesses present. These lads did not waste time! One of the girls was called Penny and she seemed to adopt us all as her personal property and became a regular visitor. She came from a wealthy background complete with a Triumph Spitfire which was considered the tops in sports cars of the day. The party went on until the early hours.

On January 27th 1967 I arrived at the tender age of 21. It was customary to have a big party when that age was reached but I felt it would be better to have it after my final training trip. I was still waiting for the final training roster information to drop on the doormat. It finally arrived showing me off to Nairobi and back via Rome. The date was to be 9th Feb so I had about a week to go. The other lads in the Malt House were all flying pretty much every day. The Trident boys seemed to spend their time going up and down to either Glasgow or Edinburgh and the Vanguard ones seemed to be all over Europe.

In the meantime there were plenty of things to do. Mum and Dad lived not very far away so I did pop over there quite a bit. Dad was still flying with British Eagle, mainly out to Australia carrying UK military personal. The other place on the map for me was Southampton to see Pam. What can I say! At the time all was well with her and things seemed to be just bouncing along just fine. Silly me! The other social spot was as usual the Vanguard club and quite often on a Friday night we would all pile into one of our cars and away we would go.

Finally the 9th arrived and the plan was for a late night departure so maybe a sleep in the afternoon. I found it never really works out like that since when you are told to go to sleep you cannot and when you are told to stay awake all you want to do is to sleep. The Captain was the infamous Captain B. He could be described as a small thin wiry man with a wisp of hair on the back of his head. His looks equalled his character that was altogether pretty aggressive.

"Are you one of these Hamble cadets then?" he barked when I introduced myself.

So what else could I be with one ring and at a very young age, was my thought.

But instead "Yes sir" was my response to this rather stupid question.

"I like ex-military pilots myself since they are much safer than any cadet pilot," he muttered.

He was equally cutting with the rest of the crew. Wow, this was going to be one hell of a trip. Obviously he was well known to the rest of the crew since they simply just kept quiet and spoke when spoken to. He seemed to treat the planning staff with equal venom. I had heard of these types by reputation through the grapevine and here I was flying with one on what was to be a very important trip for me. Ugh!

We got to the aircraft in plenty of time and I got on with doing the checks etc. I had by now established some sort of routine and it was beginning to work. Captain B disappeared into the cabin and seemed to find fault with everything he saw and barked away at the ground crew to come back and fix this and that. He seemed to have no sense of timing as to our departure and I sat there with the training Co-pilot and Flight Engineer with 15 minutes to go and no Captain. The Co-pilot leant over and whispered:

"Don't worry about Captain B Just do your best."

These were reassuring words that meant a lot to me. With about five minutes to go he came into the flight deck and then proceeded to check all of the paperwork meticulously like a professor or doctor who is just about to prescribe some evil concoction. Time went by and then finally he got into his seat. He turned to the Training Co-pilot and said:

"Keep a close eye on Mullett for me would you, there's a good chap."

Nice man! I thought.

It was now about ten minutes after the scheduled time of departure when we finally started the checks. Captain B seemed totally oblivious to all things around him. This was going to be a hard trip. It was the practice in those days for the Co-pilot to read the before take-off checks whilst taxiing, with the briefing by the Captain being done at this stage as well. Checklists in those days were very long-winded and when it came to the item of the Captain's briefing Captain B directed his words to the training Co-pilot and the Flight Engineer and completely ignored the fact that I was there sitting in the right-hand seat and the active Co-pilot.

This guy I do not like, I thought.

The training Co-pilot winked at me which gave me some assurance.

We finally took off some 30 minutes late and his flying ability matched his character whereby he pushed and pulled with no finesse and made the flying very uncomfortable. Once the autopilot was engaged things smoothed out somewhat. I did my job as best as I could. The communications went well since I was now beginning to understand the French accent and the incessant talking by the French aircraft. As we crossed Geneva I picked up the weather for Rome and all the airports around the area and presented them to Captain B He studied them carefully and then opened the landing charts for Rome and proceeded to brief the other two about what he wanted on the approach. At this point I added a small point that I thought was relevant only to be confronted by a stony silence from Captain B I persisted with my words and finally he begrudgingly acknowledged them.

Wow, maybe a breakthrough! I thought.

Having been now twice to Rome on the last two trips I was ready for the Italian chat and actually managed to respond correctly. Captain B seemed to struggle to understand the chat so I acted as an interpreter and in the end I just fed him the instructions and he willingly obeyed. Not much was said when we landed and arrived at the gate. Diplomacy was working out just fine and I just bit my lip and got on with it. We left the Flight Engineer to deal with the refuelling and wandered into the terminal for the routine cup of cappuccino.

As we sat there Captain B started talking to me normally and not totally excluding me. He asked me about Hamble and what the training was like. I answered as best I could and thought that maybe, just maybe, he was beginning to accept me for who I was. We wandered back to the aircraft and started to sort out the departure to Nairobi. When it came to the infamous briefing he even included me in it. I started to relax a bit but felt that one step wrong I was for the high jump.

The flight time was about seven hours so once we took off I settled into the flight as best as I could. It was by now about 2 am and I was feeling the effects of the late departure from Heathrow so I purposely busied myself by doing all sorts of things that maybe were relevant or irrelevant. The effect was to pass the time and soon we were deep over

East Africa somewhere to the north-west of Khartoum. The training Co-pilot seemed happy with my performance and once Captain B disappeared down the back for the normal cabin chat (I pitied the passengers) the atmosphere became very relaxing and finally I started to enjoy the flight. I had never been to Nairobi so with two days there the talk was what we were going to get up to. A game of golf was on the cards. There was a local game park to visit so all looked fine for our time off. The HF was being difficult as usual but I managed to get the messages through. I even managed to negotiate a climb just to the west of Khartoum which seemed to impress Captain B.

The route is quite interesting since it roughly followed the same route as taken by BOAC in the 50s and Captain B mentioned the fact that he started flying on this route on an old aircraft called a Handley Page Hermes. This was really pioneering stuff since the Hermes was a simple four-engined airliner built after the war with the most basic of equipment. It even lacked radar. Just after the climb I looked ahead and saw the most enormous thunderstorms in our path. The radar we had was pretty good and these storms showed up as large areas of solid on the display. This area of thunderstorms was known as the 'inter tropical convergence zone' (ITCZ). Simply put it was in this area where north meets south weather-wise and the net result was to create these towering thunderstorms which lit up the sky every time they fired off a bolt of lightning. At least we had radar to help us through unlike the old Hermes. You could actually end up many miles off track whilst you threaded your way through and it became a navigator's nightmare. To add to it the sun was starting to rise off to the left which took away the stars to navigate by. Our navigator just had to sit there and try to gauge just how far we were off track and issue a heading change to get back to the original track once we got clear of this zone.

The NDB beacons were a bit sparse but there was a well-known one in northern Kenya at Lodwar where the old flying boats used to land. With the help of this beacon and the radar showing up the famous Lake Rudolph in Northern Kenya/ Southern Ethiopia we regained track and with about one hour to go we settled down for the arrival. At this point breakfast arrived courtesy of the cabin crew. The arrival was very interesting since it brought you down the Rift Valley over Lake

Naivasha and then to an area over the highest point of the Ngong Hills northwest of the airport. It was a clear morning and I found it quite mesmerising looking at the terrain as we descended. Kenya was like one big open air zoo with rivers and small settlements all surrounded by rich green vegetation.

This is totally different from West Africa, were my thoughts.

We descended into the airport at Nairobi and landed at about seven in the morning on a beautiful day after a long overnight flight. There was a totally different atmosphere here in Kenya compared with Nigeria. The local people were much nicer and there were no nasty guns poking around in my bag. The Cabin Crew were accommodated in a different hotel to us so we bade them farewell and off we went to our hotel. We were in the famous old colonial hotel known as the Norfolk which lay on the eastern edge of the city. It was made up of a number of single-storey rooms plus a number of bungalows in the grounds where the Captain resided. At the rear of the grounds was a block of rooms built dormitory-style and that is where we stayed. All very basic but the rooms had running water and a comfortable single bed. After the ceremony of the allowances issue we decided to meet up on the veranda or stoop as it was called and have couple of beers before retiring. This calling for a beer before retiring seemed to be normal routine everywhere and I found it was a nice way of unwinding after a trip. Nothing was said about my performance so I worked on the principle that 'no news is good news'.

I slept for much of the day and joined the crew on the stoop for drinks and dinner. We ate in the hotel and the evening drew to a close early since we were off for a game of golf the following morning. Within BOAC at the time there was a club formed by the crew members called the Flying Staff Recreation Club (FSRC) whereby sports equipment was shipped around the world for the crew to enjoy during their various stopovers. It was funded by a simple donation of £1.00 per month which seems very small but with up to 10,000 crew members on the books it funded a lot of equipment. It was run by crew members for crew members. We were all issued with a card that enabled us to access the equipment. Nairobi boasted some stunning golf clubs and we were members.

The following morning four of us assembled after breakfast and off we went to the Royal Nairobi Golf Club. On arrival we were allocated a caddy and I found the course superb. Not my golf I hasten to add, which was pretty rubbish as usual. It was really good to have a caddy since we were some 5,000 ft in altitude and combined with the heat it was just about enough for me. After lunch we made our way back to the hotel and then I found myself ready for a little siesta. This was really the life of Riley! Having no stewardesses with us was a bit of a drawback but nevertheless all very enjoyable. The plan for the following day was to visit the local game park in the afternoon so I had plenty of time to relax by the hotel pool and generally just loaf around.

The following afternoon three of us got together and off we went to the local game park. This would be my first insight into the Kenyan wildlife which is what the country is all about. We entered the park and drove around looking for animals. It was not long before we were rewarded with herds of Wildebeest and Gazelles just strolling along under the African sun. This local game park boasted to have most of the African game, with the exception of the elephant, contained within its boundaries. I was not disappointed since, as we turned a corner, there was a Cheetah sitting quietly in the middle of the road. We spotted a group of cars at one point in a huddle and when we arrived there was a pride of Lions sprawled out in the late afternoon sun under the shade of the famous Baobab tree. When you consider that this game park was about ten miles from the centre of Nairobi it was quite amazing. I can't remember all the animals I saw that day but suffice to say there were plenty to be seen. As we travelled around the sun was gradually setting in the west and we were witness to the wonderful sight of the African sunset. Fantastic it was!

We finally got back to the hotel in the early evening and sat on the stoop for the obligatory beer and then an early dinner since we were off back home next day. My training Co-pilot said over dinner that he was very happy with me and that he was prepared to sign me off as a fully-fledged Co-pilot then and now and he would do the paperwork on the way home. This was music to my ears.

We left Nairobi the next day at about 11 am and made our way north to Rome. The amazing thing is that the VC-10 performs at its best when the conditions are 'hot and high'. The aircraft was originally designed for just this occasion and boy did she perform. As the altitude increases then the take-off performance of aircraft decreases. High temperature has the same effect so there we were with a temperature of 30°C and a take-off altitude of over 5,000ft and the VC-10 performed superbly. No other aircraft of the day could match this performance.

The departure route out of Nairobi took us to the east of Mount Kenya and then followed the Rift Valley to the north. Having swallowed the words of the trainer the night before I felt full of confidence and even the growling of Captain B had little effect. We were flying the route in daylight as opposed to the night time when we left Heathrow so the views were quite spectacular. The main feature was the meanderings of the Nile as it made its way through East Africa on its way to Egypt and the coast. Lunch soon arrived and Captain B did his customary cabin visit. A pile of forms were dumped in my lap for me to read and sign. The words 'Cleared as Co-pilot' shone out in lights. So there I was, a fortnight after my 21st birthday, a fully qualified Co-pilot in BOAC. I felt good!

The training Co-pilot finished his navigation over the North African coast somewhere east of Benghazi and offered to jump into my seat and do the arrival into Rome.

No problem with this offer, I thought.

So I sat back and watched the arrival into Rome and chuckled when the language problem arrived as usual.

"Always the bloody same here," the Fight Engineer remarked.

We eventually arrived at Heathrow just after midnight and I felt that I really wanted to party.

"You've done it, you clever bugger," I kept saying to myself.

I got back to the Malt House at about 1 am to be greeted by Ian and so a few drinks were consumed followed by a well-earned sleep. There was happiness all around.

The following few days were spent completing the paperwork at Heathrow plus a visit to Mum and Dad. I remember one time when only Mum was at home with Dad somewhere out East with British Eagle. We had dinner which sounds normal but there was something not quite right with her. She kept missing the odd thing here and there and sometimes forgot what I was chatting about. Don't ask me what it was at the time but I felt something was wrong. Little did I know what was to happen to my Mum. The Southampton visits to Pam were still a regular occurrence.

My 21st birthday party was planned and Mum came over to the Malt House and Pam came up from Southampton. Pretty good party!

Eventually the famous roster dropped on the mat and there I was displayed as P3 or third in command. My first trip was to be a Nigerian service leaving late night on the 20th February to Lagos with a Captain H. OK I was not too impressed with Lagos but what the heck! I was on my own. The Nigerian services, as I said, were flown by BOAC on behalf of Nigerian Airways together with a Nigerian cabin crew under the guidance of a BOAC chief steward. A word about the Nigerian cabin crew is worthy of note here. Nigeria was one of those countries where ' who you know rather than what you know' was the order of the day and this applied to the selection of the cabin crew so you ended up with a mixture of girls mainly who were mistresses of politicians or people in high places. Yes, they were nice people to talk to but were not the best of lookers. Having said that there were some real characters amongst them. I met quite a few during my spell whilst flying for Nigerian Airways.

Anyway it was a late night departure as usual and off we went to Lagos via Rome and Kano. There were four of us on the flight deck. Being a P3 I sat in the right hand seat for the sector from Rome to Kano so that the other Co-pilot could do the navigation. With three sectors to do and starting late night I have to say it was a hard and long duty. All went well on the trip for me and I found Captain H a really nice guy. Lagos was chaotic as usual with either the water off or the electricity off. Not forgetting the War of the Cockroaches. I got back to Heathrow a few days later and so my career as a qualified Co-pilot began.

I will not bore you with a monologue of each trip that I did that year – suffice to say that I spent most of my time going up and down to Lagos with the odd eastern trip thrown in. What I will do is to highlight some of the happenings. When I joined BOAC there was a split in the flight crew whereby some crews only went west to America and the others only went east or south. This was inherited from my dad's day and it came to pass that at one point an agreement was made with BALPA that the western crews would include Lagos in the rosters. So what! you might say but don't forget that a lot of the so called 'Atlantic Barons' as they were known had spent their entire flying in BOAC going west so for them to come to Lagos was a bit of a cultural shock to them. Some of them took it in their stride but there were a few who were pretty disagreeable characters. I became quite adept at judging the grumpy ones and the nice ones.

With all of us ex-Hamble cadets, or Hamsters as we were known, qualified we seemed to monopolise the Lagos route. It was like an exclusive club for us. I had by now met Joe Harold, the hotel owner, a few times and since I seemed to be a regular on the route he asked me if I could get him some food items only available in the UK. Pork pies, I seem to remember, plus Colman's mustard. The result of this was that normally dinner for the crew was 'on the house' thanks to me.

Another feature of the Nigerian services was the crew catering. Herein lies a tale. It became a well-known fact that the favourite crew meal amongst the Hamsters was the Steak and Kidney pie. The problem was in the aircraft galley. What happened was that the pie was delivered from our catering department at Heathrow all nicely wrapped in aluminium foil and the diligent Nigerian stewardess would put it in the oven still in the foil and then heat it as normal. When she removed it from the oven she would turn it over onto a plate removing the foil and the pastry would end up on the bottom. She then would present it to me complete with a smile. Well, at first this was bit of a novelty but after a while it became a pain and seemed to spoil the taste of the meal. Call me fussy! Whenever I met up with another Hamster it was always the topic of conversation somewhere along the line. Now I was living near Heathrow when I was suddenly struck with an idea. Why not go to the catering section and ask if they could make the pies on the Nigerian services the other way up in the foil so that when it hit the plate it was the right way up.

What a brilliant idea, I thought.

So off I trotted and spoke to the right person. They were a bit bemused but were quite happy to agree to my plan. A few days later I am off to Lagos with another late departure. When the time came for the famous steak and kidney pie I sat there with knife and fork poised and waited. In it came and there it was with the pastry still on the bottom. My face fell. My plan had failed. On arrival at Lagos there was one of my Co-pilot friends and during the chat we came onto the steak and kidney pie issue. What else was there is life except this bloody pie problem?

"Ah, I solved the problem for us. What I did was to go to the cabin crew manager in Lagos with the problem and they issued a notice to all cabin crew that when the pie is taken out of the oven it must be turned twice so as to be presented to the pilots with the pastry on the top," he said with an element of satisfaction.

I explained what I had done. The net result was that the famous pie did about three loops and four barrel roles before hitting the plate. It might seem a bit boring now but at the time it was a crisis. I am not sure if it ever got solved.

In the March I did an interesting trip to Khartoum. We stayed there for four days and then flew to Aden which is now known as South Yemen. This was, at the time, still part of the British Empire and we had a large military operation operating out of RAF Khormaksar in Aden. A few days before there had been a nasty attack against the Argyll and Southern Highlanders regiment under the leadership of one Colonel 'Mad Mitch' Mitchell. The net result was that we were to carry more specialist soldiers than normal to Aden. BOAC in those days was owned by the Government and so we became the link to these lonely outposts on behalf of the Government. When we landed at the RAF base in the early morning I was amazed to see so many RAF aircraft around. There seemed to a procession of Hawker Hunters going by us every few minutes laden with bombs and flying north and dropping them somewhere in the hills. There was a continuous stream of them with the odd Canberra bomber joining in as well. I enquired with the local RAF engineer and he simply said that the RAF was teaching the rebels a lesson concerning giving our boys a hard time. It was quite a sight to watch. There I was in yet another war zone. We left after about two hours and flew back to Khartoum for yet another four days off.

The Flight Engineer had a friend in Khartoum who ran the local brewery. The beer was known as 'Camel' and was pretty awful. In those days the Sudan was not dry so we could freely drink. Trust a Flight Engineer to have a friend in the beer business. We all trooped off the following morning to the Camel brewery. The heat even in mid-morning was pretty unbearable and by midday was up in the 40s. As was customary we flitted around the machinery in double quick time and ended up in the bar area. What a surprise!

We must have been there for a good hour when we were told that a sandstorm was coming our way. This local sandstorm or Haboob I remembered being told about at Hamble in the dreaded meteorology lessons. I looked out to see a wall of sand up to maybe 2,000ft and about four miles away. It was coming our way without a doubt. It was decided to drop everything and rush back to the hotel. It really was a race against the elements with the temperature soaring up the scale the nearer this thing got to us. We just made it back into the hotel in time and as we rushed into the lobby there was a group of hotel workers closing the doors behind us and placing sand bags everywhere. The Haboob hit the hotel within minutes and the sand penetrated everywhere despite the sandbags. It was like being sandblasted with a red hot iron. The heat was wild and we all stood there transfixed as this wave of sand weaved its way across the floor. It was decided the bar on the first floor was the safest place. I can't think why but it sounded good. This was my first encounter with Mother Nature at its rawest. The whole episode took maybe about 20 minutes and then it stopped as abruptly as it had started. I was told later that a VC-10 at the airport was neatly sandblasted on one side only to the point that the paint was peeled off on that side. Such power!

On my days at home I went to see mum as often as I could. She seemed to getting more and more distant and forgetful. Eventually she went to see our family doctor and he sent her to the local hospital in Reading for tests. Suddenly the bottom fell out of my world. My lovely mum had been diagnosed with a brain tumour and was being transferred to a hospital in London. Cynthia by now was married to Robin and lived in Sheffield and so I rang her with the news. She drove down to Wokingham. Dad was somewhere out east, in Singapore I believe, and so I made my way to the British Eagle base at Heathrow and got them to get him back soonest.

After a few days we were all together at home and went to visit Mum at the London hospital. It has to be the most depressing place on the planet. The corridors were dimly lit and when we finally arrived at the Chelsea Ward there was my mum all tucked up in a bed. She seemed confused when we walked in and she struggled to recognize us. This brain tumour hit the main parts and the memory was the first to go. The whole ward was full of patients with various ailments of the same type. I can still visualize it as if it was yesterday. Mum had a series of painful tests and finally we were told that the tumour was inoperable. I cried buckets at the time. This was my mum and she was slipping away from us. All my life until that point was centred on my mum. She was my guide and confidante in all things. It was a wretched feeling. Even to this day I miss her terribly. After a month in hospital it transpired that there was nothing more the doctors could do so she came home.

British Eagle was very good and gave Dad time off to look after her. I visited her many times but each time it got more difficult since her mind was totally gone and she did not even recognise me. God, it was torment for me to see my wonderful mum being like this. I went to the local church that I used to go to as boy and prayed for the end to come quickly for Mum. It was not fair on her to suffer like this. I continued to fly but the problem was that international communications was very difficult since we were not in the age of worldwide mobile phones or Skype so it was always my first call when I got home to see how Mum was. It was not a case of her getting better but simply how she seemed to be coping in her new confused world. Finally on May 5th 1967 she died. It was a terrible day.

I know parents have to die sometime but there is no getting away from the fact that when it happens it is traumatic to say the least. The funeral started in the small church in Wokingham where I had prayed for Mum. We all filed in and there was the coffin. My sister and I held onto Dad throughout the service. Their marriage was one of those old fashioned ones where they stuck together through thick and thin and provided a good family base for Cynthia and me. It was now broken. Afterwards the coffin was driven down the M4 to the Cardiff crematorium for the final farewell. What a day that was. Grieving is a strange thing. I don't think that I fully grieved at the time and it was only many, many years later once I had retired that I fully did. Strange words but true!

It was about one week later that I returned to work. It was my way of getting over what had happened and Dad also went back to British Eagle. In late May I flew with Captain G who I remembered from when I did my familiarisation flight some months previously. Nothing had changed with his attitude even though I was fully qualified. We ended up in Delhi and I found the whole trip pretty hard.

In early June the Middle East finally exploded with the Six-Day War whereby Israel felt threatened on three sides by Egypt, Syria and Jordan and launched an attack on all three countries. It virtually closed the whole of the area down to commercial traffic and BOAC was forced to cancel all services to the area. Israel finally dealt with the attack in style and hostilities ceased after six days, hence the title. The net effect was that I had almost three weeks at home. The training department took the opportunity to call me in for some local flying either at Stansted or Bedford. It usually involved an evening departure from Heathrow with maybe six of us on board to do some circuit bashing. In those days there was great emphasis on our handling skills not just on the simulator but on the aircraft as well. There seemed to be no limit to the training budget. This local flying was in addition to the routine simulator checks that seemed to be planned every three months or so. They certainly kept us on our toes. At the end of June I flew to Tel Aviv and there I was witnessing yet another war zone.

The route network of the VC-10 at the time was quite extensive then with about 30 or so aircraft on the books so gradually I was expanding my own network away from Lagos and flying to some different places. I went as far east as Mumbai which was known as Bombay in those days. Johannesburg featured as well. Nairobi was the main destination in East Africa and had its own network with flights to Lusaka and Ndola in Zambia and Lilongwe in Malawi. Quite often we would stay in Nairobi for a week and do day trips to these places. North of Nairobi in the Rift Valley was a lake called Naivasha which became a favourite day out for the crews. It involved about an hour's drive arriving at lunchtime. This area was part of the colonial white days with a beautiful lake to cruise around in the afternoon followed by an afternoon tea that was totally

English style with cucumber sandwiches and scones. Waistline on the expansion again!

The performance of the VC-10 came into its own as well when flying in the Gulf region. There was then a large UK military presence in the area and they needed us to move people around so quite often we would spend time there just flying up and down the Gulf. I finally made it to Singapore in the August and once again the UK military was ever present with a large base at RAF Changhi on the eastern side of the island. I found Singapore an amazing place with alleyways and little markets all over the place. We stayed in the famous Raffles Hotel which, in those days, was on the water's edge. There were no high rise buildings or large shopping malls. The evenings were equally exciting with an enormous range of eateries. We ended the evening usually in a local area called Bugis. This was the area where it all happened at night. It was infested with the military with maybe a bunch of sailors at one end and another bunch of soldiers at the other end with a group of Marines in the middle. All we did was to sit quietly on the side watching the antics of the evening. The entertainment was further supplemented by a constant flow of transvestites of dubious origin. They would flit from table to table as only they could. When they spoke to us you would be shocked by their deep husky Yorkshire accent. I was certainly seeing the world at a very young age.

In the September there was a serious incident on an aircraft that was en route from New York to London. About an hour into the flight the cabin and flight deck filled with dense smoke. The aircraft landed back in New York and there was a lot of scratching of heads. The source of the smoke was eventually traced to one of the engine components that supplied the air to the cabin. The problem was that if this unit was overfilled with lubricating oil then it had the habit of spilling over and vaporising in the ducts producing this thick smoke. New procedures were introduced which could isolate the problem. All very boring you might say but on one of my flights to Lagos with the infamous Captain B we were just taxiing out at Kano when this young Nigerian steward came onto the flight deck and said that the cabin was filling with smoke very quickly. Captain B dismissed him with a wave of the hand. The Flight Engineer was having none of this and left the flight deck to check. Sure enough the cabin was full of the most acrid smelling dense smoke. Captain B finally stopped the aircraft and it was decided to return to the ramp. This was my first technical incident to deal with and confirmed my faith in Flight Engineers.

Another incident took place in Lagos which I care to forget about. I was the Co-pilot flying with one of the Atlantic Barons and when we arrived there was a large thunderstorm overhead the airport. The normal runway was not available and the Captain elected to land on another runway using a very basic approach aid whereby we had to plan our descent points carefully based around a stopwatch. As we descended to this runway we were about 200ft above the landing limit for this approach when we started to enter the cloud. When we got to the landing limit in terms of altitude we were still in the thick of the cloud with heavy rain beating on the wind screen.

"Decision Height," I called firmly since the rain was noisy.

The Captain totally ignored me and continued below this decision height. There was no way we could see the runway let alone land. About ten seconds later I shouted:

"Overshoot."

I then forcefully pushed the throttles forward and pulled the nose up. The Flight Engineer pushed his own set of throttles with me. We had no choice but to climb away from the runway. The Captain mumbled something and between us we managed to get the aircraft back into the clear sky.

Well, that's the end of my career, I thought since I was expecting the wrath of the Captain.

Remember, that I had only been flying a few months and this Captain many years. About 20 minutes later the storm moved away and we finally landed some 30 minutes later. There was total silence on the flight deck and I expected the worst. When we got to the hotel, again in total silence, we started to check in and the Captain went off to his room. The other Co-pilot and the Flight Engineer ushered me into the bar and ordered three beers. They both assured me that I had done the correct thing and that the Captain was totally at fault for not doing the overshoot at the correct point when I made my 'limits' call. They then told me in no uncertain terms that nothing would happen to me at all and that I could rest easy. Later on that evening in the bar the Captain took me aside and apologised to me about the incident. I think I felt more embarrassed over the apology than he did. Life was full of the unexpected in those days.

In early November I got a letter from BOAC requiring me to attend a Flight Navigation course at Cranebank at the end of November. It was to last five weeks and the object was to train me to be a Flight Navigator, just like my dad. The thought of being grounded for all that time was not well received by me and the other lads at the Malt House ragged me that once I was a 'Navvy' then that is where I would stay for the next 20 years. Little did they know what was around the corner!

So off I trotted to Cranebank with pen and notebook in hand. There are some people who love all this theory stuff but I found it utterly boring. It was like going back to Hamble all over again with me sitting behind a desk and some lecturer giving me grief. A lot of the subjects we had already covered at Hamble and it was just a matter of dragging out the old hand-written files and plodding through them. Having said that some of the subjects were not covered since the emphasis there was to get you into BEA. Without the luxury of modern day computer generated systems whereby you knew exactly where you are within a few square metres we went back to basics that stemmed back many years.

To go into the technical side of the navigational systems available then would require another book to be written. To summarise, there were four main aids that were used by us then. Firstly the use of ADF and VOR beacons that I mentioned before. Secondly we had a long range system by the exotic name of 'Long Range Aid to Navigation', or LORAN for short, which was displayed on a Cathode Ray Tube and you had to twiddle the dials to get various lines to line up and hey Presto you got a figure out of it that you plotted on the chart. Thirdly there was a system called CONSUL that had evolved from the Second World War that required you to don a headset and count the number of dots and dashes you could hear with the result again put on the chart. The fourth and final system was based on looking at the stars or ASTRO navigation and this is where the famous periscopic sextant came in since I had seen it hoisted many times. Loran and Astro were subjects not covered at Hamble so it was back to the drawing board. When we had our introductory lecture we were told that the five weeks would only qualify us to do navigation under supervision on the route and then after that we would be back into Cranebank for another 13 weeks of it.

"Ugh! What a thought!" I said to myself.

The month of December was spent learning about the stars. Dad was really helpful since he was a current Flight Navigator and what was even more useful were all of his notes from when he was at Hamble many years before. I virtually learnt Astro out of the text book. At Cranebank the time dragged on but as Christmas approached there seemed to be a light at the end of the tunnel when we took our final exam to check our knowledge and I managed to get through that. We were to get Christmas free of duty and my first trip under supervision was set for 1st January 1968 to Nairobi and back.

1935 My young Mum

1938 My Dad Imperial Airways DH-86

1948 Bedtime

1948 Tied to my tree

1949 Me and my sister Cynthia

1952 School time (l am 2nd from the left bottom row)

1957 BOAC B-377 Stratocruiser

1957 The Family in Barbados

1960 Me in the ATC

1961 Me and my sister in Tobago

1961 BOAC Bristol Britannia

1963 Mum, Cynthia and Me in Australia

1963 BOAC DH Comet 4

1964 Me as a Teenager

Last ever picture of the Family

1964 Auster J1/N my first solo G-APIK

1964 My First Solo

1964 Course 645 Hamble (I am 3rd from the right bottom row)

1965 Chipmunk Hamble G-ARMG

1966 Piper Apache Hamble G-ARJS

1966 Ian and Me, Hamble

1966 Tony and Me, Hamble

1966 BOAC Standard VC-10 G-ARVK

1966 BOAC Super VC-10 G-ASGC

1969 Me as Co-pilot BOAC

January 1st 1968 arrived and off I went to Heathrow for my first escapade into the art of navigating. The flight was direct to Nairobi and the trainer suggested that we eat early in the flight and then to start the business south of Rome. We did just that and at the appointed hour I started. The trainer did the compass heading check as a demonstration of how it should be done. Being at night then it would be Astro all the way. To summarise the Astro scene, the first thing you had was a collection of three rather thick books that listed every useable star in the sky. There were 52 of them if I remember. This was followed by consulting another publication called the Almanac which basically told you which three stars to use at any particular time. We used three stars since it gave us the perfect fix – or so they were meant to.

Once you read which stars to use then you went into one of the thick books and calculated exactly where it should be at the time when you were going to look at it through the sextant. You did this for all three stars and noted all of the figures on the navigation log. At about five minutes before the fix time you hoisted the sextant and adjusted it to match your calculated figure. You then gingerly looked into the eye-piece hoping to see the star. The field of view was very tiny so you hoped you had got it right. At a specific time you asked the pilots not to turn the aircraft at all since you were about to 'shoot the stars' as they called it. You then stuck your eye on the sextant eye-piece for 12 minutes shooting all three stars. Once done you used a series of tables and the old slide rule and plotted three lines on the chart that all crossed hopefully at a single point. That was where you were! Simple! No time to rest.

The whole exercise took 30 minutes to do and the plan was to do an Astro fix every 40 minutes so there was about ten minutes to spare to have a quick cuppa or correct an error. On a typical five hour navigational stint like we had you might well do six of these Astro fixes and I found it quite exacting work. We were blessed with powerful radar which was useful for ground mapping as well. There is a small range of hills right in the southwest corner of the Cairo region which was nicknamed 'Nasser's Corner'. It was very distinctive in shape and showed up well on the radar. As the sun came up we were over the southern Sudan area and Lake Rudolph was also distinctive as I mentioned before. At that point the NDB at Lodwar started to gyrate and when it settled down it showed us about ten miles left of the track.

Not bad for my first lesson, I thought to myself.

There is something very satisfying about navigation when you get to the other end and find that you were not too far off the intended route. I felt knackered but pleased. The flight home from Nairobi to Rome produced a similar result and I felt pretty good all round with my achievement.

So far in my short career with BOAC I had only flown east or south. The navigational training gave me the opportunity to go west and on 10th January I arrived at Heathrow for my first trip west to Montreal in Canada and ending up in Chicago. The Captain lived in Arthur Road where I was brought up so I had known him when I was a young lad. He has to be the nicest man I have ever met in the flying world. He was very softly spoken and treated all of his crew very well.

We took off early in the afternoon and headed out over Ireland and then onwards over the infamous North Atlantic in winter. The navigation was based around Loran and Consul with no Astro since it was daylight. The North Atlantic plotting chart that we used could be described as a piece of paper where kids had scribbled countless coloured lines all over it creating a masterpiece that all related to something. The scale of the chart was such that you needed a magnifying glass to read the small print. The problem was that all of the squiggles, lines, crosses, dashes plus many more nicks and marks meant something. If your famous plotting pencil was less than razor sharp you could cover a ten mile area in a stroke. My dad was an amateur artist so he revelled in the thought of plotting on this chart. His work was precise whereas mine was half-precise. Whilst I enjoyed my stints of navigation I was a pilot at heart.

Nowadays the North Atlantic routes are well defined on the day and it is a matter of bidding for a particular track that suits you and then entering it in the computer and away you go. In those days every airliner going that way submitted its own track request and it was up to the controllers in Ireland or Scotland to juggle them around and try to please everybody. The net result was that many times you were pushed off your planned route and it was up to the Flight Navigator to sort it all out for the pilots with maybe only minutes to act.

So, we got to Western Ireland and set sail across the 'pond' as we called it. I would imagine that since we had departed in the afternoon after the main bulk of airliners had come and gone the track selected was accepted and I even managed to fit in a compass heading check before the action began. The navigational requirements for the Atlantic were such that with the number of aircraft flying in the area it had to be pretty accurate. Because of this we had to establish a position every 20 minutes so it was all eyes looking down. In addition to the Loran and Consul there were about three ships positioned in the Atlantic specifically there to collect weather data. They were known as Ocean Weather Ships. If, by chance, your track ran close to these ships then they would give you a radar fix. This was, of course, if they knew their exact position in the first place since in those days they relied on the most basic of equipment just like us. It was quite strange talking to a person who was sitting in the middle of an ocean.

I got to grips with the navigation slowly but surely. This was hard and exacting work. Once you had established a position you filled in a small card for the pilots showing a new course to steer and also you let the Flight Engineer know so that he could update the fuel scene. Gone was the luxury of a leisurely lunch to be replaced by a sort of smash and grab raid on the meal tray. We had a table of about 3 sq ft on which to work so space was at a premium. Many times I was seen grovelling on the floor trying to recover a pen or pencil.

As a point of interest the area that we were required to navigate stretched from about 10°W to about 55°W in Longitude or about 1,800 miles. In time terms that equated to about three hours or so. When we approached the North America coastline we had another problem to deal with. There was a line known as the Aircraft Defence Identification Zone or ADIZ line which marked the boundaries of the US military zone and it was pretty important in those days to cross it pretty well on track. The US military had to identify you on radar and then they could confirm who you were. The cold war was still pretty active in those days with the Cuba crisis only six years earlier. We eventually crossed the ADIZ line pretty well on track and so my first Atlantic crossing was all but complete. It seemed strange flying into Montreal since I was born there many years before. We flew down the St. Lawrence Seaway and landed at Dorval airport in Montreal after seven hours or so. It was very cold being in the middle of winter with the temperature well below freezing and snowing.

We were only on the ground for some forty five minutes before we left for Chicago. In those days the flights to North America often involved two sectors since the idea of going direct had not been envisaged like today. Flying into Chicago gave the chance to see my first American city as a pilot. The airport was criss-crossed with runways and even in those days the airways were very busy. The American controllers were extraordinary in their use of English and there was obviously a certain technique to understanding them that I had yet to learn. The list of learning for me was growing by the day. I must admit that once I got to the hotel in Chicago I was pretty exhausted. I did however manage to struggle out with the crew for a beer.

The one problem with time change when you go westwards is that you wake up very early so there I was at 5 am fully awake in the dark and starving hungry. I struggled until 9 am avoiding eating the carpet and joined the Flight Deck crew for breakfast. The American breakfast can only be described as an exercise in self-control. First of all there is the bottomless coffee pot together with a variety of all sorts to feed the body. Here we go again on the waistline! There was a certain language that went with the order like 'two eggs over easy' which was two fried eggs turned in the pan or 'two on a raft' which was two poached eggs on toast. 'English' was a muffin and so it went on. Having struggled with the cult of the breakfast order the final words from the waitress were always:

"Separate checks, guys?"

They must have known us well. What's more they loved our English accent. As far the crews were concerned the breakfast was the highlight of the day in the 'States' since invariably we would be flying somewhere that night. We flew that night back to Heathrow via Montreal again and on this occasion the crossing was made at night so Astro was the prime aid. I seemed to struggle with the pace but got to the other side somewhere over Ireland. My first taste of flying the Atlantic was done and dusted. Bloody hungry though!

A few days later I was rostered to go to New York on the famous BA501 departing at 11 am. This flight number was made famous since its origins go back to 1946 when BOAC first started flying to New York. New York always fascinated me since Dad always flew there in his early days with BOAC and I briefly went there on the way back from the Caribbean many years ago. Departing in the morning put us in the Atlantic rush hour so by the time we flew west of Ireland a major track change had occurred and I was working hard to keep up with it all. I eventually sorted it out and then settled down to the task of navigating the aircraft as best as I could. My instructor kept a close eye on the proceedings to the point of being a bit intrusive. The track was more to the south and so required a longer time for me to concentrate on the task in hand.

The flight time was eight hours and 40 minutes with me doing the business for maybe six of those hours. However I was starting to establish a routine and as the crossing proceeded I felt more and more confident about it all. I was even beginning to cope with the plotting chart and all of its multi-coloured lines everywhere. As I said before I sat facing backwards with just the minimal of instruments to look at on the panel and so spent quite a bit of time straining around to see the 'big picture' as displayed in front of the pilots. The captain was a bit of a stickler and would become irritated if I did not update him every 20 minutes or so. I had to witness the other crew members tucking into a luscious lunch whilst I was still with my head down over the chart. The stewardess who served the lunch didn't seem to understand why I could not multi-task so it was back to the smash and grab raid. Having said that it was a bit decadent scoffing caviar with all the trimmings in one hand and playing with the Loran set with the other.

We crossed the ADIZ line on track so I felt pretty good and signed off from navigating. We had about one hour before arriving at New York's John F Kennedy airport (JFK) so I took time out to enjoy the view and try to understand the chat on the radio. I also took time out to look at the various approach and landing charts for JFK. There were plenty of ILS precision approaches plus a good number of approaches that were quite suitable for us. The last few pages were oddball approaches that seemed totally unsuitable for us. As we approached JFK I listened to the radio as to which approach we were going to use and low and behold it was one of these oddball ones. It involved starting at a point close to a US Navy Base that was about eight miles southwest of the airport. You then followed a motorway, or freeway as the Americans call it, heading north-east for about four miles leaving a racecourse off to the left and then turning through about 80° to the right at about 800ft and landing on the runway. I could not believe that with a modern aircraft we did this sort of approach into a capital airport. It was further compounded with a choice of runways to land on as dictated by the controller at the last minute. This approach had the curious name of a 'Canarsie' approach. The mind boggled. Anyway we did the Canarsie approach and landed OK. It was just before 3 pm when we touched down.

"That's a second lunch allowance for us," the Flight Engineer said with a grin.

The deal in those days was that if you landed anywhere before 3 pm local time in the States you were entitled to an extra lunch allowance.

What a strange business this allowance scene is. Mind you who's complaining? I thought.

Anyway we all got off the aircraft and went through the rather austere immigration and customs procedure and then we all boarded the bus for the ride into town. The ride into town was quite an experience and I spent most of the time looking at everything around me with a curiosity of a cat. We drove past the second main airport, La Guardia, and then on through Queens which is the main residential area of New York. We eventually arrived at the Midtown Tunnel and once through it we were in New York City proper. The layout of the city is based on a lattice work of streets and avenues so as to make up a rectangle the avenues going east to west and the streets going north to south. It is totally dominated by skyscrapers. There was a certain buzz to the place with yellow taxis everywhere and people seemingly in a hurry streaming along the pavements or walkways. Some of the shops looked totally scruffy and dirty but others were full of bright lights and colours and that created an amazing contrast.

We were staying in the New Berkshire Hotel which was on the corner of Madison Avenue and 52nd Street whereas the cabin crew were in the Lexington Hotel down on Lexington Avenue and 45th Street. Once

in the hotel it was agreed to get together and go to the Speedbird Club
which was in the BOAC headquarters on Park Avenue by the famous
Grand Central railway station. The club was all part of our company
headquarters on the 39th floor. When I was christened in Montreal
many years before my godfather was the then finance chief of BOAC
in Montreal. He then moved on to become the finance boss for North
America and worked in the BOAC offices here in New York. When we
arrived on the 39th floor and went into the Speedbird Club I asked if he
was around and sure enough he met us and I felt pretty chuffed that
someone from high places was sitting down chatting to us. In those
early days of flying I was often asked if I was the son of George Mullett
and when I said that I was then the conversation would always drift
back to some story based around Dad. All good I might add!

Anyway we had a few drinks in the Speedbird Club and then off
we went to eat. Eating in New York was quite an experience. You can
go from the glitziest of places to the scruffiest and still take in the
atmosphere which I found quite electric. It took the Flight Engineer
to make the decision. He took us to a place called 'Tads' which on the
outside looked a bit dubious but inside was an introduction to the
New York steak. We had to queue up and select our piece and the cook
hooked it up with a large fork and casually threw it on a large open
grill.

"How do you want your steak done, Bub?" he said as your steak
landed.

We then collected a plate with salad bits etc and a large baked
potato which was known as a 'Baked Idaho' and off we went to await
the arrival of the steak. I have to say that the steak was delicious and
altogether not too expensive. By the time all this was over it was about
midnight in the UK and so off I crawled to bed. My introduction to New
York was complete and very enjoyable. The Navigation training was not
going too bad either.

The following morning arrived with the carpet-biting 5 am
syndrome but finally we went out for breakfast. It was a bit of a hike
down 5th Avenue but well rewarded as only an American breakfast can
be. That afternoon we flew down to Bermuda and back, arriving late in
the evening. On this occasion we all went to a local bar behind the hotel

known as Joe's. In here we mixed with the 707 crews and it was strange how certain tables became the complete domain of the rival crews with our allocated table responding as we saw fit. As I said before there was a lot of rivalry between the two fleets and once beer comes into play then the rivalry intensifies.

The following evening we flew from JFK to Prestwick, Scotland and then onto Manchester. A night of Astro was involved and I started to feel quite comfortable with it all. When we finally arrived in Manchester I felt that I had done a good night's work and on arrival at the Grand Hotel at around breakfast time I felt tired but happy with my lot. We had two nights in Manchester and I have to say it was really good fun. At the time Manchester had the reputation amongst airlines as being the best European night stop around. They were so right! The locals spoke English (of course) and we brushed shoulders with the likes of George Best and Tommy Copper to name but a few. The nightclubs were swinging places and there was many a headache to be had.

On the third day we flew back to JFK via Prestwick again and arrived there in the afternoon just before 3 pm. I was beginning to enjoy the Atlantic routes even if the navigation was a bit exacting. I eventually arrived back in Heathrow after about nine days. I only had a couple of days off and then I was off again to JFK for another session. This time after a day in New York we flew to Montego Bay, Jamaica and then on to Kingston, the capital. After a short time on the ground we headed for Lima in Peru. I was certainly expanding my network and loving every minute of it. South America was, in its own right, quite a unique place. On that occasion we stayed in the Grillon Hotel in the centre of town only to find that the Rolling Stones were also encamped there. Having been a fan in the early days I hoped that I might meet one of them. My luck was in when I bumped into Mick Jagger in the lobby that evening and I walked up to him and said hello. He was quite taken aback with my London accent and he said that they were doing a gig in Lima and would I like some tickets.

"Yes, please," I blurted out.

Suddenly a bunch of tickets were thrust into my hand much to my delight.

"Fancy coming all this way for a Stones concert," was my passing thought.

Gradually the crew turned up in the lobby and suddenly I was very popular with what I had in my hand. I think pretty well the whole crew made it to the bash. The tickets we had were for the VIP area so we were treated well and the music was spot on. We even got to go to the after-show party and our stewardesses were very much in demand. Enough said! Great night though. I think we finally ate at midnight. The food in South America is all about beef and the bigger the steak the better. It is weird to think that people out there eat at about 10 pm onwards and devour a massive chunk of red meat and drink loads of red wine but seem to look pretty healthy. Something strange about that!

The following day some of us took a train ride up into the Andes starting very early and finishing late. I cannot recall the destination and all I remember was that it is very high in the Andes. The scenery was stunning but the altitude really took its toll. It must have been over 10,000 ft when we got where we were going and being a smoker I struggled for breath. I was glad as we descended down the mountain in the afternoon back to Lima. Couldn't show it though!

Finally on the third day our South America holiday came to an end and we departed pretty early in the morning to retrace our steps back to JFK. There was something magic about having a good breakfast and looking out to the right-hand side and seeing the Andes as a panorama of colours. We arrived at JFK in the early evening. It was a bit mind-blowing – when we left Montego Bay the temperature was a balmy 28°C and then about four hours later in New York it was -10°C. Bit of a shock. The trip was by no means over since on the following day we flew to Antigua in the Caribbean for a quick night stop. The trips were getting better and better. I eventually got home to the Malt House after another eight days away.

In the late March Dad retired from British Eagle and had started to befriend a lady called Thirza who had returned to the UK after her husband had been killed in a road crash in Sierra Leone. They lived three doors away from each other and it seemed that Dad had found a bit of love in his life again. Unfortunately in early April he suffered a mild heart attack and ended up in the local hospital in Reading. It was not as serious as was first thought but enough to slow him up. Dad recovered OK and ended up marrying Thirza.

In the late April I was at home in the Malt House and there were a few of us around and we were sitting in the garden enjoying the spring sunshine. Being in the flight path we would always casually look up as each aircraft flew over after departing from Heathrow. I remember hearing this odd sound of an aircraft and we all looked up to see a BOAC 707 flying over with the port inner engine spewing flame all over the wing. This aircraft was in fact G-ARWE and this engine had exploded just after take-off. It was a dreadful sight watching this aircraft struggling with this catastrophic situation. It turned to the left and was obviously trying to get back into Heathrow. As we watched it we saw that the port wing was awash with flames and that they were in dire straits. It disappeared from our sight as it seemed to line up for a landing on one of the cross runways. Something fell away from the aircraft at this point which we later found out was the failed engine and it hit the ground somewhere in Hounslow. The final outcome was that the stricken aircraft landed OK and as it stopped the complete port side of the aircraft was burning furiously. All but five people got out. One of the stewardesses, Barbara Harrison, who had tried to return into the cabin to help the remaining passengers in a selfless act, died. It brought home the fact to us that tragic accidents like this can occur at any time and that was what the seemingly never ending training was all about. Very tragic though.

On a lighter note do you know what I did in May? I got married to Pam from Hamble. What a total dirk I was! I remember going down the aisle and thinking I should not be doing this.

Aeroplanes I could fly but women were to become my biggest failing in life. Anyway, the deed was done and I moved out of the Malt House into a flat in nearby Maidenhead. We went to Rome for our honeymoon and that was that. Having left a party haven in the Malt House I was thrown into the deep end as a married man in Boyden Road, Maidenhead. I will not dwell on that subject too much; suffice to say that it was not a good move. That is all that I am saying about that marriage. At the same time Tony married Margaret and Ian was getting very serious with the lovely Sue.

In the June I suddenly found myself on strike since BALPA, under the leadership of Captain W, had decreed that the company would not negotiate with BOAC over outstanding issues. I was young and gullible and so joined in. The airline was grounded for some two weeks and it was a sobering sight to see all the VC-10 and 707 aircraft parked up at Heathrow. I took a job working for the South West Water Board to generate an income and spent that time mowing the grass at various reservoirs in the area. It was really hard work. After a week of that I then went on to work for National Car Parks at Heathrow dropping people off and collecting them from the various terminals. Not a nice time at all.

Eventually the two parties came to an agreement and we all went back to work. One of the items instigated was the introduction of a Bid line system for the pilots. What it was, simply, was that there were three lists based around your date of joining. They were Captains, second in command (P2) and third in command (P3) and you slotted in accordingly. The resulting effect was that you bid according to your seniority number for trips that you fancied. I remember not taking much notice since I was on the P3 list and quite near the top. BOAC were going to introduce a new service that went to Sydney, Australia via New York, Los Angeles, Honolulu and Nadi, Fiji and the thought of bidding for that trip was quite pleasing. Little did I know what was in store for me.

It was now just under two years since I had left Hamble and the downside was that although we had taken the final exams there that were based on the Airline Transport Pilots Licence (ATPL) before we left, it counted for nothing since we did not have the necessary flying hours to get the full ATPL qualification. It was a requirement of both BOAC and BEA to get this licence since it would prohibit you from further advancement in the airline without it. My side was further complicated by the fact that I had to get a Flight Navigator's licence to advance within BOAC. This was a different set of exams to the ATPL so there I was trying to revise and deal with a new marriage all at the same time. I decided to go for the Flight Navigator Licence on my own since BOAC had threatened us earlier with a 13-week course to spruce us up for the same exams. It was bloody hard work having to forgo any social life and get the books out and revise. As I said I learnt Astro completely off my own back with little help from BOAC saving the information I gleaned from the five week course I had done in the previous December and from my dad of course.

The final day arrived when we all trooped into Acton Town Hall to sit the exams. The subject matter was pretty much the same for both licences with the exception, as I said, that I had different navigation papers since I was going for the full Flight Navigation Licence. In the cloakroom beforehand there were other guys who were in the same boat and the chat was all about the possible questions that could come up. There was a peculiar subject called 'pressure pattern navigation' I recall. It was based on a long equation where you filled in the blanks from the information provided and got an answer.

"Oh my God, I forget to revise that bit!" I shrieked.

"Quick, what's the formula anybody?" I pleaded.

One of the guys rattled it out. I could have kissed him. The problem was that my head was so full of other things that there was no way I could get the formula into my brain. In those days if you smoked you were allowed to continue the habit in the hall at our desks. So, out came the fag packets and a few of us scribbled the famous formula inside out of sight. We all then filed in like lambs to the slaughter and away we went. I remember opening the Navigation exam paper and there was question number one asking us to write down the formula for 'Pressure Pattern Navigation' and to get an answer with the information provided. I think fag packets were opened in unison. Voilà. Question answered! If I didn't smoke then I would have fallen at the first post.

In the September the letter arrived on the mat from the examination board showing that I had passed all of the subjects and I was entitled to apply to the CAA for a full Flight Navigation Licence. Wow, I felt really good. The other lads had also passed their exams so it was party time. Where Pam was I have no idea but she must have been around somewhere. I applied for the licence and it arrived a few days later. On that day a letter from BOAC also arrived telling me to report to Cranebank the following Monday for the infamous 13-week course. Well, I had my licence so no course for me then! I phoned the Navigation office and told them that I had my licence in my hand. There was a stunned silence on the phone and then they told me to come in as soon as possible for them to examine it.

Maybe they think it is a fraudulent copy, I thought to myself chuckling.

Anyway, I made my way to the Navigation office at Heathrow and walked in with my licence in my hot sticky hand. The guys there looked at it inside and out, even holding it up the light.

"Well done Gwyn. We will get you a refresher navigation sector and then put you forward for the final check ride," they said after much deliberation.

In those days we got an allowance of £25 per annum if we got the licence after BOAC had put you through the 13-week course and £50 if you did it on your own as I had done.

"I would like to get the £50 allowance once I get through the final check please," I said smugly.

There was shrugging of shoulders and they finally agreed. I did the required trips in early October and in early November I was issued with the certificate to show that I was a fully qualified Flight Navigator or P3/Nav on the roster.

My first rostered trip with my new title occurred in late November when I flew to Nairobi via Zurich, Switzerland at night and I was the assigned navigator for the second sector. I was full of trepidation since this was the first one on my own and it felt like my first solo flight. I remember checking and double checking the books on the way to Zurich. I had flown with the Captain before and I knew him as a nice guy. I did not let on to anyone that this was first solo and casually pulled out the charts as if I had done it many times before although I was quaking from my boots up. I hoisted the sextant and went about my business. I did my calculations over and over again and low and behold there was the star I was looking for in the viewer.

I managed to get it about right all the way down through East Africa and finally after an exhausting five hours there was the familiar Lodwar beacon pointing straight ahead.

"Bloody hell! I am a genius. Here I am at 22 years of age navigating this big bird," I chuckled to myself.

It was only then that I confessed that this was first sector as Flight Navigator to all around me.

"Definitely a few beers tonight," the Flight Engineer said.

We arrived in Nairobi and got to the hotel late morning. The other airline flying out of Nairobi was East African Airways which was formed by Uganda, Kenya and Tanzania for all services to Europe. They flew VC-10s and a few of the BOAC ex-navigators flew with them. One of these was Dad's best friend Jamie Jamison who lived two doors away from us when I was a boy in Wokingham. I managed to get hold of him on the phone and he joined us in the evening for drinks on the stoop – and so the celebrations of my first solo went on into the night.

On the way back to Heathrow I was assigned to the right hand seat as the Co-pilot so no more solos for me. I did my first Atlantic crossing shortly after that to New York. One interesting point about navigation is that if you take fixes from various sources at different times you have to move them forward or backwards on the chart to equate them all to the same time. If they were all done at the same time then there was no need to do this. If you could imagine me hanging onto the sextant shooting the stars with a headset on counting the Consul dots and dashes plus leaning down with a spare hand fiddling with the Loran set on the panel... I must have looked a right sight.

My third trip was a bit of a nightmare to say the least. The roster fell through the door and I looked at it with mild amusement since it showed me as the assigned Flight Navigator to Baghdad – or so I thought since it read LHR-BGI on the roster.

"Why am I having to navigate to Baghdad when it is a normal sector not requiring any navigation?" I gestured out loud to whoever was nearby.

Anyway I thought carefully about it and thought that there must be a reason for it. The weather in Baghdad at this time of year was pretty cold and miserable and so with three days there in went the sweaters and a large thick coat. So off I trot to Heathrow at the appointed hour and got into the briefing room to find the Captain, Flight Engineer and other Co-pilot all with their heads down surveying the flight plan with much shaking of heads and shrugging of shoulders. I knew the Captain by reputation as a bit of a stickler so I waited patiently to introduce myself. The Captain turned to me and I said casually:

"Good morning, sir. I have no idea why I have to do navigating to Baghdad."

Well, his reaction was a peach. He pushed his glasses down to the end of his nose and turned to the Flight Engineer.

"Well there's a thing. We are flying the inaugural direct flight from Heathrow to Barbados and this chappie thinks we are going to Baghdad!" he said, as only a captain of his reputation could say.

"What's more he is the assigned Flight Navigator to take us there and from what I can see we are very short of fuel on arrival with no en-route alternate airfields around. Plus of course a hurricane is in the way just to add to the fun," he added with a look of despair and mistrust.

I shrank into the floor looking for a large hole to swallow me up.

How could I have been so stupid? was my desperate thought for the day.

I turned to the other co-pilot and he just shrugged his shoulders and told me that he had been off sick for the best part of a year and that his Navigation Licence had lapsed until he did a check flight. So not only did I have to get us there I had to get us back as well. Things were going from bad to worse. I was then invited to look at the flight plan and the first impression was not good. BOAC had rostered a Super VC-10 to do this service and we were, quite rightly, short of fuel when we were due to arrive at Barbados. I checked all the figures as presented and finally plucked up the courage to squeak:

"Sir, there is every chance that we will be the only aircraft in that part of the sky when we head southwest past the Azores so why not try a cruise-climb between 35,000 and 39,000 ft? The winds are forecast to be very light in that area. Also, I see that the weight of the aircraft and passengers shows that we have a full passenger load. Why not wait with the fuel bowser still on hand so that if the load is any lower than what is planned then we can get some more fuel on?"

I will point out at this point that a cruise-climb is the best sort of flight to save the most fuel as opposed to keeping at one height.

I must have stopped them all in their tracks for there was that magical pregnant pause and then the Captain said:

"Good idea. Thank you."

He then turned to the other Co-pilot and told him to sort out the cruise climb on the radio and to the Flight Engineer he told him to keep the bowser on. I think my street credit was slowly returning. Once we were all ready to go the actual aircraft figures arrived and we found we could put on a bit more fuel so the Flight Engineer scurried off to organise it. The route took us out over Land's End in Cornwall and then pretty much in a straight line passing about one hundred miles north of the Azores and then on to Bridgetown, Barbados.

The navigation was pretty standard on the way to the Azores area and the winds seemed to be as promised. The Doppler system described earlier worked fine so all was good for the first three or so hours. The problem was that after the Azores area there were no aids available to use since the bulk of them were centred on the North Atlantic and we were well south of this area, so for the next four hours or so I had to rely on pretty well nothing to confirm our position. The sea state below was smooth since we were now entering the Doldrums in the lower latitudes so the signal from the Doppler just bounced off the sea into Cyberspace. My only real aid was the sun that was to the west of us giving me a single line on the chart with no other line to intersect it to show our position. I had to try to interpret this single line into some sort of clue as to how we were doing.

We managed to get our cruise-climb and the Flight Engineer kept adjusting the engine power settings to match this very gentle but slow climb. The only en-route alternate airport that I could remotely think of as somewhere to go if things went wrong was Bermuda which was quite a way north of us. So all I did was to keep an imaginary line on the chart to Bermuda from where I thought we were until even that proved no use at all due to the distance involved. The weather was perfect with clear skies and not a ripple of turbulence. In the first class cabin were a bunch of VIPs who had been invited by BOAC on this very first flight direct to anywhere in the Caribbean and we had a non-stop trail of visitors to the Flight Deck. We also had the present chairman of BOAC, Sir Giles Guthrie, in the first class as well. Little did they know that the success of the new route was in the hands of little old me who was not even 23 years of age yet!

Bridgetown, Barbados had a single VOR beacon in those days and that had a range of about 180 miles and was the only clue at the end of the flight to confirm that you had indeed made it safely across the South Atlantic. As a Flight Navigator it was your job to let the pilots know when to expect the needle on the VOR compass to start to move to indicate that it was starting to receive a signal and so I plotted a 180 mile circle around the airport and came up with a time. I also asked them to put in a pre-set course into the instrument so that I could gauge how far off track we would end up. I passed the figures forward to the pilots and the Captain got hold of a blank piece of A4 paper and wrote it again in large bold letters and stuck it on the windscreen for all to see.

The Flight Engineer was continually worried about the fuel state and kept bombarding me with questions about our progress. I calculated, using the figures he gave me, that we could divert from our cruising altitude to an airport at Pointe-à-Pitre on the island of Guadeloupe. There was not much else available since Antigua was too far away. I let the pilots know and there was much shaking of heads. I have to say this sector was about the maximum range of the VC-10 with any sort of passenger load and it really did expose the operation. All it needed was a thunderstorm at the destination to hold things up on the approach and off you would have to go to the alternate airport without any hesitation. Amazingly enough the hurricane forecasted on our route never materialised and all we got was the tell-tale sign of high cloud off to the south of the track. Maybe the Meteorology people got the forecast position wrong or maybe I was miles off track.

With about five minutes to go before the estimated time for the needle to start to move, we all stared at the dial with me willing the needle to move. The time came and nothing happened so I turned back to my chart and studied it carefully trying to appear studious.

Have I made a gross error somewhere? I thought to myself.

There I was suspended in space running out of answers. There was a repeater of the instrument on my panel and I stared at it intensely. Having re-checked my work I was convinced that all was in order and that maybe the beacon was working on reduced range. The Captain and

Co-pilot were chatting to the Flight Engineer about the fuel state and what options we had. Suddenly two minutes after the original estimate the needle on my dial flickered and did a complete 360° rotation around the dial. I spotted it and turned around to the pilots.

"The needle has just flickered," I proclaimed as if I had just won the Lottery.

Both pilots were so intent on talking to the Flight Engineer that they had both missed it. All eyes went back to the dial and sure enough it did another gyration and then settled down showing that we were pretty well on track. The DME indicator also started to gyrate and settled down on a figure of about 160 miles from Bridgetown. I translated these figures to my chart and to my amazement we were about fifteen miles north of track and bang on with the estimated times. Boy did I feel great! I had done it and had come through to the other side with flying colours.

After a few moments I gave the Pilots the final course to steer for the airport and then I handed over the navigation to them.

"Well done, Navigator," the Captain said.

There were nods of approval all around.

"Would you mind if I go out and have a few drinks tonight, sir? I feel like a celebration," I said.

"I think I might join you in that," was the collective reply.

We landed bang on schedule and taxied on to the ramp. There was a reception committee awaiting us including a military band and lots of dignitaries. The weather was beautiful with not a cloud in the sky and the temperature a balmy 28°C. What's more we were there for three days. That evening we did go out and yes, we did have a few drinks. The only drawback was that all I had to wear was a thick sweater and winter garb since where had I planned to go on that trip was not Barbados. Yes, bloody Baghdad in the cold but here I was in the heat. I couldn't even lounge around the pool cavorting with the girls. Total prat or what!

The three day stopover was a totally relaxing affair and included an invitation to a BOAC reception party to celebrate the inauguration of the new route. It was quite a lavish affair with champagne and canapés everywhere. No expense was spared. I had a great three days. It was shortly before Christmas and there was a real party mood around. Eventually it all had to come to an end when finally in the early evening of the third day we all climbed aboard the aircraft for our return flight to Heathrow. In general when flying from West to East the winds usually help push you along so in this case there was no real drama with the fuel requirement and being at night presented no problems with the navigation since the stars were twinkling in the night sky. We finally landed at Heathrow and I got a call from the Navigation office asking if there had been any problems on the way to Barbados. I gave them the feedback OK with a few expletives thrown in. That was my last flight in 1968 and now Christmas was upon us.

So 1969 arrived and in the late January I got involved in a bizarre sequence of events in JFK. We had just flown in from Antigua and were enjoying a beer in one of the bars. We must have been there a few hours when some guy walked in looking like the abominable snowman with a complete covering of snow. When we looked out at the scene outside there was a total white wilderness with thick snow everywhere. More crews rolled in and announced that the airport was shut down and all flights cancelled.

When I woke up in the morning it was unbelievable the amount of snow around. The roads were all deserted except for the snow ploughs struggling along. It must have snowed for at least 12 hours non-stop. With no flights out of the airport then there would be no flight arriving so we were stuck in the city. I watched the news and sure enough the airport was cut off and essential supplies were to be flown in by military helicopters. This was not some outback place in Siberia but New York. Amazing! We met another crew over breakfast and they had flown from Detroit, Michigan to Heathrow via Boston, Massachusetts and out of Boston the No.4 engine had failed so they had returned into Boston. Their passengers were put in coaches and bussed to JFK due to the bad weather. The crew managed to fly the aircraft on a three-engined ferry flight to JFK for repair. The VC-10 was certified to do these ferry flights on three engines. They landed in JFK just before the real stuff hit and left the aircraft with the engineers. So there we all were stranded in the city.

After three days of this we did manage to get to the airport and

there was the repaired VC-10 sitting on the ramp ready for us to go
to Heathrow. The passengers included those who had bussed in from
Boston some three days before. The VC-10, with its engines perched
high above the ground, was in its element since the whole airport
was still covered by high snow banks everywhere. No problem there
– so with great aplomb we taxied out to the runway with all the TV
stations filming us since we were the first transatlantic service to make
a departure for three days. We took off normally with the cameras
whirring away and off we set to Heathrow.

At about 10,000 ft there was a rumble and the No.4 engine shut down
just as it had done out of Boston. This was my first in-flight engine
shutdown so I was pretty attentive to what was going on. It was decided
to return to JFK after dumping about fifty tonnes of fuel over the
sea south of the airport. It was a bitter irony that JFK opened up for
arrivals about 40 minutes after our departure and since we were now
on three engines we were the first to land there. The cameras were
whirring away and low and behold BOAC was first to depart and first
to land. Looked good on TV that evening but little did they know that
it was the same aircraft! I felt sorry for the passengers since they had
been travelling for the best part of four days and we were still in the
States.

In the February the Bid Line rostering system was introduced as
per the agreement negotiated months before. I was well placed being
near the top of the P3 list and with a Navigation Licence I was in a good
position to get some nice trips. I was now 23 and well established in
the BOAC way of life. Low and behold I got awarded a trip in March to
Sydney, Australia via New York, Los Angeles, Honolulu and Fiji. The trip
was two weeks in duration and was considered the top trip.

So off I went to New York on the first part of the trip. The rest of
the crew including the Cabin Crew were starting to gel well together.
This trip was going to be fun. The other Co-pilot was qualified as a
Flight Navigator as well so we just split the navigation sectors down
the middle. It seemed that everywhere we went we would get at least
three days off since the route was only flown twice a week. We flew
to Los Angeles within a couple of days and I sampled the city for the
first time. It had a buzz all of its own. We were there for three days

and an adventure lay in wait for me there. The Captain was what you might call, a 'bit of a lad'. In New York he found out that one of the stewardesses was an old flame from years before and they rekindled their friendship in the time honoured way. By the time we had got to Los Angeles (LAX) they were pretty much an item.

On the evening of our arrival there he collared me and told me that the three of us would be flying down to Mexico the following morning and that I was to be a witness to their wedding. The mind boggled at the thought since it was obvious that they were already married to different partners. Apparently, in Mexico no questions are asked and all that is required is a passport. Well, the next day off the three of us go to Mexico and yes, they did get married under Mexican law. Wonders never cease! We got back late that night and there was a party to celebrate. The whole crew was out to play. On this route it was decided to keep us all together as a crew for the whole 14 days. The funny thing was that when we all got back to New York then we had a different crew to go to Heathrow. I wonder why?

We left for Honolulu and within five hours we were off the plane again for another three days layover. Honolulu was an America holiday island and so had all the quirky bars and night spots going so I was really ready to enjoy myself. The 'newly married' couple announced this fact to the hotel manager as we checked in and his response was to allocate them the honeymoon suite for the stay. What a party room that was! I was beginning to see the 'method in the madness' of the newlyweds. This was beginning to be one heck of a trip. After three days of basking in the sunshine and partying we flew to Nadi in Fiji. What a magical place that was with palm-fringed beaches and glorious sunshine. The newlyweds did the same deal with the hotel and low and behold another huge party room came our way. I would add that I enjoyed myself as well but that would be telling.

I felt really relaxed since the UK was still in the throes of the last of the winter and out here it was sunshine all the way. The navigation was simple and straightforward and to fly for about five hours and then get off for three days was amazing. We eventually wrenched ourselves from Fiji and flew to Sydney, Australia. Australia was, in those days, a very austere region to fly into with their procedures very precise and correct. As we arrived mid-morning we had a wonderful view of the city totally dominated by the Sydney Harbour Bridge. Our hotel was very close to the harbour and the memories of my short time spent as a 16 year old with the family on a posting came flooding back. The Australians are a strange breed whereby they seem to have an attitude problem when talking to us English types. I have the feeling that it stems back to their historical relationship with the UK. You know what? We had yet another three days off and I took time out to go on the Manly ferry and walk up to the 'heads' as I had done many years before.

This was the end of the trail for the Pacific route which was by now becoming known as the '591 through the west' where the 591 refers to the BOAC flight number. We finally left Sydney and retraced our steps back across the Pacific at the same leisurely pace. When we got to LAX on the way home I was called again by the Captain and off we went to Mexico again – and low and behold the two lovers got divorced. The mind totally boggles. What a scene! There was one hell of a divorce party that night. In JFK, as I said before, we swapped crews and now I realised the sensibility of that action by the company. Could you imagine the wives and husbands waiting in the cold at Heathrow for their partners to arrive after two weeks away in the sunshine and watching the odd nods and looks amongst a crew that had been together for some time in the sunshine? Not good for morale methinks! I eventually got back home after a wonderful two week holiday interrupted by a bit of work. Magic it was!

The news in 1969 was pretty interesting. In the February Boeing flew the new 747 aircraft on its maiden flight. Here was an aircraft that dwarfed all others in size. It was a monster! BOAC had ordered a number of them for delivery in 1970. At Cranebank they placed a disc on the outside of the building somewhere on about the fifth floor to show the height to the top of the tail. I watched the flight with interest but until it got back on the ground I could not get a feeling for the size until I saw people scurrying around it. In the March the Anglo-French Concorde also flew its maiden flight. It was amazing that the French and the English were working together since they were bitter rivals in the technology world. Having said that the French did manage to get the 'e' put in the name. In the May Apollo 10 did a complete orbit of the moon in preparation for the first moon landing. On a more morbid side the first HIV case got diagnosed in America. There was a lot happening in the world in 1969.

When I got home off my '591 through the West' I got a call from the training office that I was ready for a promotion check flight for upgrade to second in command or P2Nav. I was pretty pleased that I was up for this promotion. In those days you were invited in writing for this sort of thing and it was not your right to expect it. I duly arrived at Heathrow with about five of us Hamsters and we flew off to Shannon for the night. The check flight was very exacting with some tricky flying needed and combined with the fact that it was a really miserable night weather-wise. We all managed to convince our masters that we were worthy of the promotion and passed OK. So there I was with the exalted title of P2Nav and what's more I now had two stripes on my sleeve with the rank of 'Acting First Officer'. I did not think at the time about the ramifications of moving onto the P2 bid line scale since I thought that there was lots of flying to be had. How wrong I was!

I was now at the bottom of the P2 list and the choice of trips was very limited. I got very frustrated with my life and what was happening. In the April and May I flew maybe twice and one of these was a day trip to Tel Aviv and back. I looked at all my options and the fact that I was a Canadian prompted me to contact Air Canada and check out their scene. I was invited to Montreal for an interview and they offered me a position of Co-Pilot on a DC-9 on the odd days of the week and navigating a DC-8 on the even days of the week. This appeared to be the other end of the spectrum to BOAC. In the end I stuck with BOAC and I am glad I did. In June things started to move a little and I did a couple of trips so I felt happier about it all. Things were not good at home so I was desperate to get away anywhere. Dad seemed to settle in well with Thirza and they moved into a bungalow back into Arthur Road.

In the July I finally got a long trip out East to Hong Kong which was another place I had not visited yet except for a fleeting visit as a 17 year old. It was only now that I could fully appreciate its magic with markets, back alleys, hustle and bustle plus what seemed like millions of Chinamen running all over the place. We stayed on the mainland in Kowloon at the Park Hotel on the Eastern side. The island of Hong Kong had not been totally exploited by then and all the action was in Kowloon. The eating was amazing with many street stalls around. I remember visiting the place on our way back from Sydney so I apologise for describing it again; besides I was much older. Even when I finished flying it still held a magic all of its own. It was there in the Mariners Club that I saw on the television Neil Armstrong set foot on the moon on July 20th 1969. Now, what did he really say?

Back home Pam and I moved in the July to a small bungalow very close to the airport and we tried to sort out our marriage which was only just over a year old. Maybe I was too young or selfish in attitude, I don't know, but I found it very hard to settle into the marriage. When I was away on trips I didn't seem to have any morals. So, in reality, I was not the best behaved of people. In my defence the life of a pilot is very artificial when you are 'down route' since you stay in good hotels with a bundle of local money in your hand surrounded by young crew members and after a few drinks all sorts of things can happen. I was not a wild one but rather I would say average in that department. The irony of it all was that the boiler had no doubt packed up minutes after you left and the kids all had chicken pox whilst you were sunning yourself on some beach. However it was the life I chose and when I look back I think I earned my sun lounger on the beach due to hard work. What can I say!

As the rest of 1969 evolved I found that I was doing a variety of trips all over the world. I never did another '591 through the west' much to my dismay though. Some highlights did occur worthy of mention. Towards the end of the year I was on standby through the night when, at about midnight, the phone rang only to be told that I was needed to go to Frankfurt, Germany and on to Nairobi since the scheduled aircraft had broken down in Frankfurt. So off I trot to Heathrow and climb aboard with a standby crew and off we go to Frankfurt. We landed at about 2.30 am and picked up the stranded passengers and set sail for Nairobi. As we approached the North African coast I opened the drawer to get all the star books out and guess what! The cupboard was bare!

"Golly, Golly Gosh," I said or something similar to that.

The Flight Engineer swung in his chair with a quizzical look. I recovered my composure and got up and casually walked into the forward galley.

"Has anybody seen my star books and Almanac?" I asked the cabin crew.

"What's that, a new sort of cocktail?" was the sarcastic reply I got.

The Captain was of the grumpy variety so this was going to be tricky. I had fortunately flown the route a week ago and if I remembered the winds were pretty much as forecasted so I decided to maybe bluff my way to Nairobi. Pretty irresponsible thing to do but I felt that to return to Europe based on the fact that the Flight Navigator had forgotten the books would be a capital offence in BOAC. So I settled back in my seat and pondered how to go about the Astro bit. I looked at the location where the sextant was kept and low and behold it was empty so I was totally snookered. My only saving grace was that it would be light in about two hours and that I would not be able to use the stars anyway. I had to assume that the compasses were good but I was sure if anything was untoward I would have known about it by now. So I took a deep breath and stood up and announced to the all-around that I had goofed. The Captain shifted in his seat and shuffled a few papers around.

"Well, you better start making excuses to the Navigation office then and I hope you are right about those winds. The Doppler seems OK at the moment but once we get more south it will go offline," he said with a grunt.

Fortunately we had quite a bit of extra fuel so there was room for error and I watched the Doppler do its bit and managed to evaluate what the wind was where we were and it seemed as per the forecast.

"So far so good," I muttered to myself.

The Doppler then stopped working as predicted and I just pottered around my charts trying to envisage all the options. Did I mention earlier about a bunch of rocks in the corner of the Cairo region called 'Nasser's Corner'? As we approached the area the radar painted a beautiful picture of them and by a bit of imaginary plotting I deducted that all was well and we were just about on track. The thunderstorms of the Inter-tropical Zone loomed up ahead and I sat there noting the heading changes both in direction and time. I then calculated a new course. Lake Rudolf showed up as predicted, shortly followed by the good old faithful Lodwar beacon.

Lucky Jim, I have got away with it and we are pretty well on track, I thought to myself.

"The problem is that your chart goes back with the aircraft to Heathrow and to the Navigation office and they will ask questions. We can get a replacement Sextant and the books from East African Airways OK but you will have to spend the day in Operations making up the Astro fixes, so don't bother going to bed," the Captain said as if to say all will be hushed up if I did just that.

So that's just what I did for the day and by the time I was finished I was burnt out. The aircraft did a local flight to Lusaka and I caught up with the crew complete with a Sextant and books in my hand with strict instructions as to what to do with my rebuilt chart on the flight back to Heathrow. I managed to escape the wrath of the Navigation office.

Another amusing ditty was navigating to Lagos in the middle of the night on one occasion. We had a Nigerian Captain and he was busy flying around some thunderstorms and I was as usual sat facing backwards in my seat. The Autopilot control was on the control pedestal between the pilots and for turning it had a large sort of wheel that, when you returned it to its central detent, the aircraft flew straight and level. On this occasion he did not quite get it in the detent and left the aircraft with about 5° of left hand bank angle remaining. He then fell asleep together with the Co-pilot. The Fight Engineer was busy with his engines and I had wandered into the galley for a cup of tea which took about 20 minutes or so. I then returned to my seat and casually looked around to check all was well when my eyes fell on my repeater compass I could not believe what I saw.

"What the heck are we heading north for when we are on our way south to Lagos?" I said out loud.

The Flight Engineer swung round and looked at the compass and we then both turned to the two sleeping souls up front. I saw that the aircraft was in this gentle left turn and, yes, we were indeed heading north. I looked at the Autopilot control and saw that the wheel was slightly out of the detent. I leaned forward and got the aircraft heading the right way. At this point both pilots woke up and were completely unaware of what had happened.

"Don't worry Captain. Just add 20 minutes to every time you have on the log," I said casually.

"OK, thanks for that," the Captain replied.

I am sure that neither of them were completely aware of what had happened and why the Navigator was hastily setting up an Astro fix. I then settled down to my Steak and Kidney pie whichever way up it was.

In the September I really goofed in the navigation department. We had departed from Bermuda to Heathrow and the navigation started straight away after take-off since the island had no beacons to use. The Doppler unit was unserviceable and of no help. I gave the Pilots a course to steer and settled down to do my first Astro fix after about 40 minutes. I plotted this fix on the chart and saw that we seemed about ten miles south of track. I didn't think too much about it and settled down for the next Astro fix set for about 30 minutes' time. This time the fix showed us about 30 miles south of track. I still did not take any notice thinking that maybe the sextant was in error. Workman blaming his tools springs to mind! The next fix showed us about 60 miles south of track and it was time to sit up and take notice. I got my ruler and put a line through the positions and traced it back to Bermuda and low and behold I realised that I had given the Pilots the wrong initial course and we were indeed way south of track. I took a deep breath and leaned forward and said:

"Captain, I have goofed. Please turn left 60° now. We are way south of track."

There was a Flight Deck conference as to what had happened and I said that it was my mistake and I would try to get us back on track soonest. The Captain was not amused and told the other Co-pilot to go back and check my work. Yes, I had really goofed and this was confirmed by the other Co-pilot. I really did struggle for an hour or so since it was approaching daylight soon and only one more chance for an Astro fix. After about 20 minutes of virtually heading north I announced us back on track and gave out a new course. This was treated with a large amount of suspicion. I was pretty thankful to see the coast of Cornwall appear on the radar and breathed a big sigh of relief. The Captain was still not amused. I can't blame him though! I did hear that someone else did the same as me but ignored the error and ended up landing in Lisbon, Portugal.

There but for the grace of God go I, was my passing thought.

In the November I got involved in a very harrowing experience in Lagos. Up to this point Nigerian Airways had leased a Standard VC-10 from BOAC with our crews flying it. In the October they purchased a VC-10 G-ARVA outright from BOAC. It was to be crewed by their own people and also some Pilots who had retired at that time from BOAC and went to work for them. In the November this aircraft had arrived at Lagos from Heathrow in the early morning hours and crashed north of the airport whilst attempting to land. All passengers on board were killed including a BOAC crew who were travelling as passengers in the cabin. I flew the next day as scheduled and carried a UK Board of Trade accident investigation team and they invited me to go with them to the crash site. I did not know what to expect but was curious as to what a crash site would look like.

We finally arrived at the site and the scene was quite overpowering to see. There was nothing left of the aircraft except for a few bits of tangled metal and the odd wheel lying around. The aircraft had cut a neat groove through the trees like a scythe before coming to rest and catching fire. The site was sealed off by soldiers to protect the remains. In my naivety I was expecting to see a VC-10 lying there in bits and all I saw was a nothing. Aluminium burns to nothing when ignited. I won't go into any more details of what I saw except that I was shaken to the core and whenever I hear of an accident similar to this the memory of this sight always comes flashing back to me. It affected me for a long time afterwards.

So 1969 came to an end with my marriage just about sustainable but my flying world was very exciting. We moved out of the small bungalow and I bought a place in a village in northern Hampshire called Ellisfield and we moved in at the beginning of December. This house was really in the sticks, surrounded by woodlands and fields. It was at the head of the Candover Valley and I have to say the location was stunning. We even got ourselves two cats and a German Shepherd dog called

'Ramma'. I was fast becoming a country yokel. My only regret was losing contact with Ian and Tony. Ian had married Sue and moved to the Windsor area and Tony went back to live in Southampton with Margaret. I actually spent New Year's Eve in Trinidad enjoying the Carnival. Pam seemed quite happy with that and headed to her parents in Southampton.

So along comes 1970 and I get to the exalted age of 24. I now have the rank of First Officer and so I am slowly climbing the ladder. In the January the first commercial service by a 747 aircraft was flown by Panam arriving at Heathrow from JFK. I can remember taxiing out close to the 747. It was enormous and dwarfed every aircraft around. To watch it take off was extraordinary with crowds of people along the airport fence waiting for a glimpse of it. I continued with my flying as a P2Nav and found that the training office was being less demanding. I had to deal with the simulator checks that were every three months plus a medical check every six months. The other thing to complete was the annual flight route check which involved having a check Captain sitting behind me complete with a clipboard and a pen that seemed never to stop writing. You could say we were kept on our toes.

In early April Apollo 13 was launched and was set to be the seventh manned mission in the American Space Programme and the third one intended to land on the Moon. The lunar landing was aborted after an oxygen tank exploded two days into their journey crippling the service module upon which the Command Module depended. It was announced by a simple radio call:

"Houston, we've had a problem."

Despite great hardship caused by limited power, loss of cabin heat, shortage of potable water, and the critical need to jury-rig the carbon dioxide removal system, the crew returned safely to Earth a few days later after having done a loop around the backside of the moon. I remember everybody was glued to the TV during that time. In those days there were no fancy computers to deal with the calculations involved in getting back to Earth and it was all done by slide rules and guesswork. In Rome they even had a mass said for the safe return of the astronauts in St Peter's Square. It must have worked. Heroes all!

Things were happening in the aviation world that were making headlines with the main occurrences being hijacking. It was mainly confined to the United States with an almost daily frequency.

"Take me to Cuba," was the most used phrase.

The Middle East was still the No1 trouble spot and various extreme terrorist groups were coming out of the woodwork. The 'Popular Front for the Liberation of Palestine' (PFLP) and 'Al-Fatah' were the most prolific amongst them and their symbol was a red head scarf. On many occasions going into Beirut these guys would be strutting around the airport lounges armed with weapons of all descriptions. It was most weird but we became quite used to it. European airlines were trying to come to terms with hijacking and how to prevent it happening. Up to this time airport and airline security was minimal and these hijacking events started the ball rolling in the name of 'Airport Security' which is still with us today.

The Europeans did not in fact do a lot to protect its airlines and in early September it all happened and the world stood still. An El AL flight out of Amsterdam to JFK was carrying a terrorist called Leila Khaled plus an accomplice. Shortly after take-off they attempted to hijack the aircraft. In the ensuing gun battle on board the Captain diverted to Heathrow. On arrival Leila was the only survivor of the pair and was taken into custody by the British police and that triggered a series of events that was to set the scene for years. Within days a Swissair and TWA aircraft had been hijacked and flown to an old RAF airstrip known as Dawson's Field in northern Jordan. A Panam 747 was also hijacked and taken to Cairo. The Middle East was littered with hijacked aircraft. The group responsible for this were named 'Black September'. At the time I was on the sick list suffering with a bout of the flu. It was only a matter of time before a BOAC aircraft would be taken and sure enough a few days later a super VC-10 G-ASGN out of Bahrain was caught and it too landed at Dawson's Field to join the other two already there. When I looked at my roster which I had had to cancel because of my flu I realised I should have been the Co-pilot on that flight. Lucky escape! I loved the flu at that point.

After about a week of negotiations the passengers were released and driven to Beirut for safety. A few including the flight deck crew were held in various locations in Amman. It was about this time that I

called in fit and no sooner had I done so then I was told to assemble at
Heathrow to be part of a crew to fly an empty aircraft to Beirut and to
stay there until orders to fly the hijacked flight crew home. Beirut was
teeming with all sorts of military types strutting around. I watched
the released passengers from the hijacked aircraft arrive in busses and
then board a flight out of the area. I was really seeing life in the raw.
Amongst the types at the airport there were a lot of locals wearing
the tell-tale red head gear and it was obvious these were the terrorist
group PFLP. They seemed to have total freedom of the airport, such was
the politics of the day in Lebanon.

In Jordan King Hussein launched an offensive against Black
September and eventually the flight crew were released and driven to
Beirut. They were a very weary bunch of guys when we greeted them.
It was then that a strange thing happened as we took them to the
aircraft. There was a row of these PFLP guys waiting for us and they
shook hands with the released crew as if they were saying 'goodbye
and have a nice day'. It was most bizarre! They all got a hero's welcome
when we landed back at Heathrow. The aircraft that remained empty at
Dawson's Field were blown up a few days later starting with the VC-10.
It was really a sad ending for that aircraft. The ironic thing was that
in the Engineering department of BOAC there was a dilemma at the
time since the VC-10 tail plane was in need of a major overhaul which
would ground each aircraft for at least a month. So, within a few days a
Cargolux CL-44 which had a modified interior capable of holding a VC-
10 tail plane was dispatched to Jordan and picked up the tail plane from
the wreckage left in Dawson's Field. BOAC had now got its tail plane.
Leila Khaled was eventually released from custody and one of the most
famous hijack events had ended.

Regarding the 747 aircraft, BOAC got its first deliveries in the October
but there was a big conflict with BALPA and the company as to the pay
scales for these big birds under the title of 'Wide Body Pay'. BALPA felt
that more money should be forthcoming for flying the 747 as opposed
to the VC-10 and 707. As a consequence of this the first three aircraft
were parked in the hangars for all to see. As it was it was a blessing
in disguise since the Pratt and Whitney engines of the 747 developed
major faults and BOAC made good money leasing out the engines of the

three parked aircraft.

As for my personal life it was sort of drifting along. In hindsight it was as much my fault that things were not good. The bedroom scene had all but disappeared and that I found soul-destroying. Maybe I was immature in the ways of marriage or, to be more exact, in the workings of a woman. A Flight Engineer said to me once:

"Women are wired differently."

How right he was! I will go to my grave with that quotation written on my tombstone.

I was very much in love with the area where we were living and had many longs walks with Ramma and sometimes the two cats came as well. We had a Forestry Commission site just down the road and many an hour was spent just strolling along. I could see that Pam was becoming bored with her life there but what could I do? I think I was more in love with aircraft than another human being. We just sort of blundered along.

The year ended with not much to report on the marital scene but the flying world was going well. I was collecting flying hours well and the routes were good together with a good social life down route. I had nothing to complain about.

So along comes 1971 and I had been in BOAC for some five years and well established as a Co-pilot. One of the general thoughts with BOAC and BEA was the fact in BEA Hamsters were getting into the position of getting a command within about eight years and so both Ian and Tony must have been getting itchy feet and looking around at the various options to get the command. In BEA there was, in theory, much more opportunity to do this since there were a lot of sub-divisions to go to. One of these was to fly in Scotland on the twin- engined Avro 748 or the four-engined Vickers Viscount. In BOAC there was only the VC-10 or 707 to choose from. When I joined the airline there were many Co-pilots who had been in there for maybe up to 15 years so I was well down the pecking order and the thought of a command did not enter my mind too much.

In 1971 there was a large exodus of wartime Captains who had all reached the exalted age of 55 and so there started a large training programme to upgrade these long serving Co-pilots to Captains.

There were a large number of failures when the training started due to the very high standards set by the training department and so the company was eating through the list of possible victims at a high rate. Whilst this might seem totally irrelevant now, quite of few of the failed Co-pilots took early retirement and so I was moving up the scales rather fast which, in turn, gave me a better choice of trips.

The news that year was interesting to say the least. In the February Rolls-Royce went bust. What had happened is that they had developed a new engine called the RB211 designed to be flown on the new Lockheed Tri-Star which in turn was their answer to the 747. They developed a material known as 'Hyfil' which was light and would be used in the construction of the blades of the engine. Several engines on the VC-10 were reworked using this new material for testing purposes. It was brilliant in concept since it made the engine so much lighter than previous ones but what they did not envisage was how the blades would handle an ingestion of birds. It so happened on a flight out of Entebbe, Uganda that an aircraft flew into flock of birds and one unlucky fellow flew into one of the test engines. The engine just exploded causing an extraordinary amount of damage to the surrounding structure. I think that the aircraft was grounded in Entebbe for some weeks before being cleared to fly again. By this time the contract with Lockheed was all signed up with a fixed price contract but the use of Hyfil was no longer an option. Rolls-Royce was forced to turn to Titanium which was very expensive and so the contract did, in effect, bankrupt them. In the end the government nationalised the company to save it. The RB211 went on to be one of the most successful engines made and its variants are still being produced today.

The other thing that happened in the February was that the UK went decimal. Up to that point we were dealing in pounds, shillings and pence with such quirky names as 'half a crown, Florin or Three penny piece' and suddenly it was all based on the pound being equally divided into one hundred bits and overnight the financial world as I knew it had changed. It seemed to be a good excuse to hike up the prices and we all suffered somewhat.

By the middle of May an agreement was reached between BALPA and the company over the issues of the 747 and so courses were planned for that month. By chance, I bumped into a fellow Hamster Pete Dyson whilst on my travels and he said that we should put our names down for the 747 and that is what I did. I did my last flight on the VC-10 to Chicago at the end of May after just under five years of flying the beautiful beast.

Before I leave my beloved VC-10 I must tell you about a couple of trips I did with the infamous Captain G On one occasion I was with him in Nairobi and on the day of departure it was normal to go the local food market where the fruit and vegetables were bloody scrummy. The prize fruit was the pineapple which was pretty well unknown in England and we usually ended up with a large basket delivered to the hotel in time for the pick-up in the evening. It was normal to ask the Captain, out of courtesy, if it was OK to carry the fruit but Captain G was just not around to ask. So the complete crew got to the airport and then Captain G arrived with his own basket of fruit.

"Nobody approached me about the loading of fruit so it will all be offloaded and only mine will travel," he barked.

As the crew bus moved towards the waiting aircraft struggling under the weight of all the baskets the atmosphere on board could be cut with a knife.

"Sir, we were unable to find you all day," I piped up on behalf of the crew.

"I have said that the crew fruit will not travel on the aircraft and that is final," was his curt reply.

He actually got out of the bus and walked over to the crew hold and made sure that the only fruit to go on board was his own. So there was this pile of sad looking baskets sat by the aircraft and just the one miserable basket in the hold. It was customary for the Flight Engineer to leave the Flight Deck just before the doors were closed to check that the all the panels were closed up. The stand we were on required us to do a sharp right about turn before taxiing for the runway and as we did this turn the Flight Engineer tapped me on the shoulder and beckoned me silently to look out of the right-hand window and low and behold there was this solitary fruit basket flat-packed on the tarmac with tyre marks embedded on it. No wonder the aircraft was difficult to move in the first place since it had to climb a fruit basket first. Have you ever struggled not to giggle when you know that it is out of order? I struggled to Heathrow with a grin from ear to ear. The arrival at Heathrow was conducted like a military operation whereby the Flight Engineer scarpered off quick and got the fruit loaded well deep into the boot of the bus with only the crew bags showing. Once we got back to the crew report office we all evaporated into thin air with our fruit baskets tucked under our arms. I was certainly not going to be around when Captain G found that his fruit basket was missing. Sweet justice I thought!

The other occasion was when we were flying from Delhi to Tehran when Captain G. gave me the sector. He had the habit of handing over the aircraft just as we were lining up for take-off and so off you went with the radios all set up the wrong way round which I found really annoying. The landing I did in Tehran was pretty rubbish to the point that we only just managed to walk away alive. Anyway, in the hotel in Tehran he did his usual disappearing act and I ended up in the bar late at night having a quiet last beer. I was on my own except for a young South African chap of about my age. We got chatting and it transpired that he was a Co-pilot with South African Airways (SAA). What they were doing in Tehran I have no idea! Anyway the conversation drifted onto Captains and I sort of got a bit verbal about Captain G and his cranky ways. I was describing my crash landing on arrival in no uncertain terms when there was a shuffling of feet behind me. I had failed to notice that Captain G had arrived in the bar and was standing a few metres behind me. I was just about to issue another tirade about Captain G when a voice boomed out:

"The landing was not that bad, Mr Mullett!"

My heart fell through the Earth's crust and I swung round to be confronted by the man. My drinking friend did a quick 'Exit stage right' and so there I was on my own with Captain G.

"Would you like a beer?" he said.

To say 'no' would have been the wrong thing to say even though I was desperate to disappear down an imaginary hole and never come up again.

"Thank you, sir," I spluttered out.

So there I was trying to create a normal conversation with this person that I had been raving on about to a complete stranger.

Did he hear the lot or just a snippet? was my thought.

The beer seemed to be of the self-filling variety since the more I gulped it down the more that was left in the glass. It had to be the largest beer I had ever drunk. Funnily enough, he never said a word about my ranting. I do not recall what we talked about but it was an endurance test of the highest order for me. Eventually the ten-gallon beer was drunk and I excused myself and made to the sanctuary of my room. Nothing was said the next day either which made it all very strange. Maybe he was going to get me fired on arrival at Heathrow but again nothing. Lesson learnt about my big mouth. Keep it closed! Never did though. I was amazed that I had survived in the airline to that point since I did have the habit of getting a bit noisy and verbal after a couple of drinks.

Chapter 5

– FLYING THE BIG ONE

As for the 747 this was to be a whole new ball game for me since this was a Boeing I was going to fly and I was so used to the quirky ways of the VC-10. I was assigned the second course in BOAC for the 747 and started the technical part in early June. The format of the course was very different from the old 'talk and chalk' system I had back in 1966. What happened was that we were all assigned as an individual crew and sat in front of a classroom mock-up of the cockpit as a pair complete with a headset and a slide show to cover each subject. My Captain was an ex-707 chap and looked down on the fact that I was off the VC-10.

"Once a Boeing Man always a Boeing Man," was his proclamation when we first met in the classroom.

The aircraft was, at the time, the latest in technology and I have to say did impress me with its systems. To simplify it in real terms it had four engines with four hydraulic systems, four electrical systems and so on. In fact it had about four of everything. The main difference was that it had an Inertial Navigation System (INS) which had been developed for the Apollo moon shots. Once you told the INS where you were it could take you anywhere you wanted to go in the world at the push of a button. At a stroke it killed off the Flight Navigator. It was even responsible for most of the flight instruments. That was the 747 in a nutshell. It took a bit of brain power to understand the INS but I made it through the technical course OK.

At the end of May I settled down for the Simulator Course. Bearing in mind that the VC-10 Simulator was pretty basic in concept and operation due to its age the 747 Simulator was mind-blowing in comparison and showed me the advances made in the intervening years. What was a pleasant surprise was the fact that the programme for this part was very well defined from what I was used to. This was a great improvement and marked the change in the training world to what it is today.

My first view of the simulator was quite amazing. There was this machine sitting on an island in the middle of its bay supported by an array of hydraulic pipes and pistons that seemed to keep it suspended in space. To get onto this island we literally walked across a drawbridge and entered the machine. The drawbridge was then pulled up and there we were suspended in space. The instructor hit a few buttons and the whole thing started to move under our feet and assume some sort of level pose. We all strapped in and away we went with the machine seemly gyrating around its axis so as to create a motion or feel for us. The artificial visual system was equally good and gave you the real feeling that you were actually flying the aircraft. It was quite brilliant I have to say.

The one big difference between the VC-10 and the 747 was that the latter had the engines on the wing so if one failed the swing was very noticeable as opposed the former where you hardly felt a thing. We were also teamed up with a Flight Engineer for the complete course so at least we could get to grips with the various exercises together. There must have been about 12 sessions in the box with each one creating its own problems to solve. I remember finding the engine failure on take-off the hardest to manage but I did eventually master it. There was amusing incident when the Captain wanted to see how it would perform if two engines failed on take-off.

Typical flash ex-707 pilot, I thought to myself.

The instructor agreed to try it out. As we were getting ready for the take-off out of Heathrow the instructor glanced at me and winked.

What was that wink for? I wondered.

As we rolled down the runway the left hand outboard engine failed and the Captain threw in some rudder to hold it straight on the runway. About two seconds later the right hand outboard engine failed. The net effect of this was that there would be no asymmetry at all since both engines had failed on either wing hence no rudder required. The Captain took his eyes off everything and first of all shoved with all of his might the rudder one way. This made the aircraft slew off to the one side. Just as we got airborne he thought that he had got it wrong and reversed his rudder input and shoved it the other way to the end of the travel. The net result was the aircraft started to do a pirouette in the sky and gently fell back to earth into the middle of Hounslow High Street according to the visual. During all of these gyrations the instructor was thrown off his seat and disappeared down the back of the box somewhere with his headset sort of stuck up his nose and legs all over the place. As we hit the ground then the machine just shut down and we were left in total darkness with the Captain totally bewildered as to what had happened and his ego somewhat dented. I must admit the visual was very realistic and had my respect from that moment on.

The simulator course finished in the middle of July and I sat at home waiting to be called to go base training at Shannon. By this time BOAC had six 747s flying but they were all plagued with engine problems. It was lucky if two aircraft were serviceable at any one time. Because of this there were crews stuck all over the place and more were needed desperately but to do this it needed a serviceable aircraft for base training. Because of this I sat around for maybe two weeks awaiting the magic phone call. It finally did come through and in late July I went up to Heathrow to fly to Shannon that night. I reported to the training office and there were about six of us ready to go. The Trainer had only just got qualified on the aircraft so it was a case of the blind leading the blind.

The 747 was parked in the maintenance area and as I approached the size of it confronted me. It was enormous and seemed to occupy the whole ramp area. Everything about it was big from the tyres to the tail plane. We climbed up the steps which seemed never-ending. Captain S had told me that I was to sit in the right hand seat for the flight to Shannon so after climbing another set of stairs I eventually found the flight deck and clambered into my seat. I remember looking out of the window and looking down at what appeared to be toy town. People were in miniature and the cars seemed like dinky toys. Other aircraft stood out like Airfix models. The taxiways looked like little pathways. Anyway we all took our seats and started up. Captain S taxied the aircraft out to the take-off runway.

"OK Gwyn, you can take us to Shannon and we will get some

exercises done on the way," Captain S announced.

I taxied onto the runway and we seemed to sit astride it and away we went. In the air I was pleasantly surprised how well the aircraft flew and how good the simulator was. It was once quoted to me: "If you just fly the cockpit like a Cessna then the rest of the aircraft will follow."

How true that was! The INS worked like a dream and took us precisely to where we wanted to go with no 'ifs and buts'. As I said this was the complete finish of the Flight Navigator and would establish the aircraft as a 3-crew aircraft. I am sure Dad would not agree with me but times had changed above and beyond.

We arrived in the Shannon area and, as usual, the weather was pretty dreadful but off we went straight into circuit bashing and by the time my spell was over I had done six landings. The only real difference between the 747 and the VC-10 in the landing scene is the fact that on the 747 you feel like you are landing about six floors up. The Flight Engineer was fully involved in the flying side of the operation on this aircraft and it was his duty to call out the heights above the ground as we landed. We had three radio altimeters that were extremely accurate when near the ground. He would call '50ft, 30ft' and what you did was to start the landing flare somewhere in the middle. I have to say the 747 landed beautifully due mainly to its superbly soft undercarriage and aerodynamics when close to the ground. Anyway I finished my stint and another victim was brought forward and so it was about 1 am when we finally finished our session. We stayed as usual in the Shannon Shamrock so Durty Nelly's it was for a beer or two.

The next day I flew again with Captain S to do some altitude work and circuit bashing again. The programme was set out precisely which was a big improvement all round from the VC-10. On the evening of the second day we were assembled in the hotel bar when the Hotel front door opened and in walked the Flight Manager, Captain R, and the Flight Training Manager, Captain B, as if they had just parachuted in. These two were the bosses of the 747 fleet and were considered a formidable pair. The problem lay in the fact that on the first course there were some pilots that they felt were not suitable for this new shiny aircraft and so they had become known for being quite ruthless in clearing them out. The bar fell silent.

I wonder who they are after this time? I thought to myself.

Everybody looked around in a sort of nervous frenzy. The following morning I was detailed to fly with the boss Captain R and boy, was I nervous. Together with me was an ex-707 Captain. The detail started with me doing the usual circuits and after about one and half hours of this we landed with a full stop landing and I was hoisted out of the seat and Captain R said: "OK, off you go and send up the Captain but please stay in the cabin during his detail."

I had no idea as to whether I was doing OK or not so I meekly disappeared into the cabin and ushered the other Captain to the flight deck. I wandered about the cabin during his detail and wondered at the size of everything. There were seats for 329 passengers in three classes. First class was right at the nose and seated maybe 16 passengers in total luxury. The first class galley was at the rear of this cabin and even featured a microwave cooker. There was then a set of stairs that took you to the upper deck which was kitted out as a lounge for the first class. Just behind the first class galley was the club cabin with smaller but still roomy seats with maybe 40 seats in all. The club class galley was next and then the remainder of the aircraft was devoted to the economy class in ten-seats-across arrangement and resembled a hall of people. There were so many seats and it seemed to be unbelievable. This was a huge aircraft without a doubt. I settled down in a first class seat and thought about what might be happening up in the flight deck with the other Captain. From what I could tell we were not in the circuit and by the motion of the aircraft he was being put through the hoop. After about one hour we landed and taxied to the ramp. The Captain emerged from the flight deck in total silence and looked totally washed out.

"I'm going home tonight," was all he said.

Captain R followed after a short while with little expression and simply said to me; "Tomorrow we do some more circuits."

That was that. It was the first time I had witnessed another pilot being chopped in BOAC and it was not a nice experience.

The following day I did some circuit bashing with Captain R and it seemed to go OK but how was I to know? We kept doing 'touch and goes' and finally he announced that the next landing would be a full stop.

Have I made it or not? was my thought.

We landed and taxied around to the take-off point by which time I was expecting the next victim to replace me and either way I was burnt out and needed a break.

"Just one more circuit should do it for you," Captain R said to me.

I then had to rise from the ashes and perform just once more. It had to be the hardest bit of flying I had done to date. I think he knew it as well. I did manage it OK and we landed for another full stop and as we taxied around he said:

"OK, you're fine for the route. Off you go and send the next one up."

This was music to my ears. I had cracked it again.

"Bloody good," I thought to myself.

I sat down at the back while the next Co-pilot did his bit. As we were downwind on one of the circuits the aircraft started to climb and turn east away from Shannon. I walked onto the flight deck to be told that although we had six 747s flying we were in the only one serviceable and it was needed in Heathrow to fly that night. So, two hours later, we landed at Heathrow and taxied to the ramp. What had happened is that one of the five was stuck in Rome with an engine failure, two were in New York with the same and the fourth was somewhere else in the world with a problem. There was one in Heathrow having an engine changed so we were told to wait for that one to take back to Shannon later. We sat around for maybe five hours and finally flew back to Shannon and finished off the flying. We finally got to the hotel at about 7 pm after a long day. I felt good though, as did the other guys with me. We completed the paperwork and off to Durty Nelly's we went to celebrate. The next day we flew back to Heathrow and I waited for the first training trip.

In early August I started my route training with a flight to New York and back. Having come from a background of conventional navigation it was amazing to watch the INS in action. All I had to do was to enter the co-ordinates of where we were before we moved and then where we were going and away we would go. It was perfection to watch. As we entered the Atlantic region we spotted a Pan Am 747 on the same route 2,000ft above us about two miles in front of us. We both flew in virtual formation as if tied together by an invisible umbilical cord.

The cabin crew for the 747 numbered about 16 or so and there was suddenly a change of direction in their world. A new rank had been established for the boss of the cabin crew known as a Cabin Service Officer (CSO) and he had four stripes on his jacket albeit slightly slimmer that the Captain's. Unfortunately in some cases that gave him the illusion of power and being in charge of a large number of crew members started to create a great divide between the Flight Crew and the Cabin Crew. It was really sad since on the VC-10 we were all a close knit family.

"CSO stands for 'Chief Sandwich Orderly' in my books," was a quote I had from a Flight Engineer.

Enough said! The other thing at that time was that the Cabin Crew had developed their own management structure and for the first time they were independent of the Flight Crew management. This was the start of the 'us and them' syndrome. Anyway, we flew to JFK in our new-fangled machine and I felt quite at home on the beast. It was quite amusing how the sheer size of the 747 seemed to drift into the background as time went by.

Coming back to the INS the drawback at the time was that you could only insert nine positions at any one time plus the fact that they had to be entered as Latitude and Longitude so if you omitted to insert a new one when it got to the ninth it would turn the aircraft and go back to the start. If nothing had been entered it would then fly the aircraft to a point south of Lagos, Nigeria that equated to Latitude of zero, ie the Equator and a Longitude of zero which was the line through Greenwich in East London. This was known as the '747's graveyard'.

We landed in the early afternoon just before 3 pm so as to get our extra lunch allowance and all was well. In Jo's bar behind the hotel another table was allocated to the 747 crews so the rivalry hotted up again with three fleets now having a go. The following afternoon we flew the 'Bermuda Shuttle'. The engines were still playing up so I was lucky that all was going well in that department. We flew back to Heathrow on the third evening and so my first trip was completed successfully.

Back home BOAC and BEA were going through a change that would affect us all. It was decided to create a new airline that combined both of us and would be known as British Airways (BA). In the autumn the new airline came into fruition. It was decided to adopt a new logo and uniform and we were known as the British Airways long-haul division. It did not really affect me too much at the time but being loyal to BOAC it did grate a bit that we were going to lose our famous blue fin with the gold Speedbird symbol in the middle of it. It looked really elegant. The new colour scheme was pretty colourful with a white top on the fuselage complemented by red and white cheat lines. The words 'British Airways' were plastered along the side of the fuselage and low and behold the Speedbird symbol was up there as well. The Cabin Crew went through the change as well and gone were the smart shirt and blouses of the girls to be replaced by a simple pink or blue dress with a zip up the front. Of course, some of the girls had the zip half pulled down if they were that way inclined and that made life a bit more interesting. All of this would take at least two years to implement so it was a right mix for quite a while.

I did one more trip to JFK with the infamous Captain R who was pretty overbearing in all things flying wise. At this time there were a predominance of Captains from the 707 and if I thought there were some strange ones on the VC-10 then this lot made them look quite normal in comparison. I finally got cleared at the end of August. As far as the routes were concerned we only went to JFK and Bermuda. Life was pretty much routine with the bid line not applicable so I virtually went once a week to JFK until the end of September. More aircraft were then delivered and the route structure started to open up with Toronto, Canada and Manchester getting on the list. And so 1971 came to a close with me having done maybe 50 Atlantic crossings.

1972 arrived and the route network of the 747 started to expand rapidly and on 3rd January I flew the inaugural flight to Nairobi via Rome. As we flew over the desert I wondered how I had ever survived navigating this route since all I did now was to enter the various reporting points into the INS and that was that. I keep coming back to the INS since of all the advances in technology this was the one single thing that changed the course of aviation. Overnight it dispensed with the fourth crew member on the Flight Deck which was financially a great plus in aircraft operating costs. It was a lesser known fact at the time that the 747 with every seat filled was cheaper to run than a full up VC-10 even though the 747 was still being paid for and the VC-10 was totally paid for.

After a stay in Nairobi of a couple of days we flew the second ever service to Frankfurt. Having enjoyed the wonderful power of the VC-10 this beast seemed to struggle totally. In those days we did the take-off calculation by hand using a graph to get the maximum weight that can be used for the conditions on the runway. As I said before Nairobi Airport was in the 'hot and high' category where the VC-10 was supreme. With the 747 we used up every bit of runway for the departure. The engine instruments were displayed on the front panel with the engine 'Exhaust Gas Temperature' (EGT) the most important dial since it was generally the first indication of an engine problem. I recall that the maximum allowable temperature for take-off was 930°C and if that was exceeded an amber light would illuminate on the dial. On this particular take-off I remember all four amber lights were on and the Flight Engineer was getting very agitated. The problem was that if he slowed the engine down to extinguish the light it had the effect of taking a lot of power out of the engine and that screwed up the take-off performance so we had to live with it. Not easy for a Flight Engineer to accept. Bearing in mind we weighed something over three hundred tonnes on this take-off it was a wonder that we got airborne at all. Once we staggered into the air then, as usual, the air temperature would increase for various reasons and we seemed suspended in the air neither going up nor going down. After what felt like an eternity the Vertical Speed Indicator showed a very small climb and very slowly the aircraft started to go the right way.

The engines had another limit to contend with now, due to the fact that they could only keep full power on for five minutes, so after being strapped to the runway for about one and a half minutes this time limit arrived all too quickly. What we did was to keep full power for maybe eight minutes so that at least we had a chance of going somewhere. Although the Flight Engineers had learned to live with these excursions they were not too happy with what was happening. Apart from anything it shows the built-in robustness of these modern big engines. Eventually we got the flaps in and got some sort of a climb out of the beast and settled down for the flight to Frankfurt and on to Heathrow.

At the end of January I ventured off to the Far East via Tehran, Bangkok and Hong Kong. Bangkok was new to me and I was intrigued. I remember landing and looking out to the left-hand side of the runway and seeing a line-up of United States Air Force B-52 bombers. These were the main bombers employed in the Vietnam War that the USA was waging against the communists of North Vietnam. There must have been at least one hundred of them parked there looking very menacing and aggressive in their dark camouflage.

At that time Bangkok was used as the main departure base for the bombers and in consequence the city was full of American servicemen enjoying what they called 'Rest and Recreation' or 'R and R' for short. The market area that dominated the city rapidly turned into a haven of bars and 'girlie' places where the local ladies would display what girls display to attract these American servicemen. The area became known as Patpong or the red light district. It was, in simple terms, a 'meat market'. I have to say it was a pretty wild place for us but had that undercurrent of sleaziness about it. The sad bit was that it was very difficult to estimate how old these girls were and how they ended up there. If you do some reading about Thailand you will understand and maybe get the answers.

After a couple of days in Bangkok we then flew to Hong Kong routing directly over the huge American base of Da Nang in South Vietnam. I noticed that as we left most of the B-52s had also departed to do what they had to do. As we turned towards Honk Kong just off the Vietnamese coast we could see a myriad of contrails to the north-west of us. No guessing who they were!

In Hong Kong on about the second night there was a lot of commotion in the harbour and from where we were we could see a large ship burning from stem to stern. It was in fact the ex-Cunard Liner Queen Elizabeth. She had been sold off to a Hong Kong businessman some months before and there she was burning in the harbour like a giant funeral pyre. We had in fact moved to Hong Kong Island by this time and from where we were we had a bird's eye view of the whole episode. It was very sad to watch her go like this. It transpired later that there was a suspicion that it was arson since the insurance money was quite tempting. She was eventually towed out to the Western entrance of the harbour and lay on her side for months. At the time we were still doing the famous visual approach to the airport and she became a landmark for a long time. As an aside it was quite spectacular to do this visual approach in a 747 since at about 700ft you had to do an 80° right turn to line up with the runway for landing. It must have looked frightening on the ground seeing this new big monster gyrating overhead.

After Hong Kong we flew to Sydney, Australia via Darwin in Northern Australia. I can't think why we did that but maybe there was an operational problem that required us to drop into Darwin. We came back to Hong Kong the same way and eventually after about 12 days away we ended up in Tehran expecting to go home. The alarm call woke me as usual followed by a call from the Captain who said that instead of going home we would be doing the whole trip out to Australia again due to an aircraft technical problem somewhere in the world. I eventually got home after 26 days out of the country. That was some trip! My next trip was already in the system so after two days at home off I went away for another 14 days to Australia again. It was no wonder my marriage was being strained to the outer limits. When I look back I can now see all the signs of total breakdown but at the time I was oblivious and seemingly ignored it all.

The news in 1972 was quite startling beginning with the 'Bloody Sunday' shooting in Northern Ireland in the January. In the June there was a horrific air crash involving a Trident aircraft just after departure from Heathrow. The Captain was a very vocal figure within the airline and a difficult person to fly with. He had control problems shortly after take-off with the aircraft entering the 'Super Stall' which I mentioned way back and came down within a few yards of the reservoirs at Staines. Altogether there were 118 fatalities including the crew. A very sad day for aviation and particularly for me since both Tony and Ian were both established on the aircraft as Co-pilots. Various recommendations came to light at the time and were acted upon.

In the August the new dictator of Uganda, Idi Amin, decreed that since the Asians in the country had British passports he would deport them all out of the country and it was up to the British to take them on. Diplomatic feathers were ruffled but in the end Britain had no choice but to comply. An airlift was commenced and I got a bit involved helping to fly these wretched people to the UK. In the September there was a massacre at the Munich Olympics where terrorists had got into the rest quarters of the Israeli team and there was a lot of killing. It was the first time that Western countries had had a terrorist act on their soil and was a marker for future acts.

In the October the first Airbus A300 flew and marked the beginning of a very successful range of aircraft to rival the Americans. In the November the UK sent the Royal Navy (RN) to Icelandic waters to protect our fishing fleet and came off worse when the Icelandic gun boats did a lot of damage to the thin-hulled RN ships which became a bit of an embarrassment back home. I clearly remember a RN Frigate with a great lump of concrete hanging over the bows. Whatever would Nelson have thought? In the December the last moon landing was completed successfully and the Apollo programme came to an end.

As for me I worked very hard during the year due to a shortage of fully trained Co-pilots plus the fact that the route network was expanding fast. The 747 was proving itself a world beater in mass transportation and airports were struggling to keep up with demand. A typical example was Singapore where we used the old airport at Paya Lebar which only had capacity for two 747s at any one time. It was usually us and Qantas so it was full power ahead to build the new airport on the old RAF Changi airport site that had been left vacant by the British military. Consider now that this new airport can handle up to 80 large aircraft at any one time. Nothing startling happened in my world except that the famous bid line was introduced and for the first time I was able to get most of the trips that I had bid for. I actually spent Christmas at home that year to try to make amends to the marriage but I cannot remember if it helped or not. I think that at the time it was heading southwards at an alarming rate.

So in comes 1973 which marked my sixth year in BA with my flying on the 747 continuing apace. I seemed to find a niche route in going to Australia via Bahrain in the Gulf and Singapore or Hong Kong. I would be away for some 12 days or so which suited me. The engine problems seemed to be abating after a big upgrade programme with the result that the schedules settled down somewhat. I spent a lot of time in Australia on these trips covering all the major cities from Perth in the west to Brisbane on the east coast. Occasionally we would fly to Auckland, New Zealand. In fact at one time my social life in Australia equalled or exceeded my scene in the UK. Less said about that the better methinks!

Back in the UK I had a very sad occurrence. Ramma, my faithful dog, had to be put down due to an ear infection. He really was my best friend and when I was coming home off a trip, even before my car got anywhere near the house, he had a sixth sense and would run to the gate barking like a crazy animal. I can remember one time in the middle of the night there was this enormous racket outside of the back door and there he was bristled up and ready to let rip. I eased the back door open and let him loose. He charged out at the gallop and within a few seconds charged back in at the same gallop. I peeped out and there was a fully grown mother badger ripping six bells out of our dustbin since she had cubs to feed. He must have realised that in a duel he would have come off worse, hence the hasty retreat.

Bloody wimp, I thought. Having said that the badger looked pretty mean. The dustbin was destroyed.

Shortly afterwards Pam and I decided to move to Southern Hampshire to be nearer to her parents and so we bought a house near to a place called Wickham. It was a large house with an enormous garden and soon its upkeep became a challenge. The garden measured 50 metres in width and 400 metres in length which was really awkward to deal with. The house itself was lovely and was right in the middle of forestry land so once again I was in my element being a country boy at heart. The act of moving did seem to revive the marriage a bit so maybe there a glimmer of hope. Having said that, I was still married to my aircraft and was away a lot of the time breezing around the world. One thing that is relevant to the flying world is that you become totally oblivious to what day of the week it is or, in fact, what season it is. You might depart on a flight on a Sunday in the middle of winter and just a few hours later you were basking in the sun somewhere.

By the way Jan 1st marked the day when the UK entered the European Economic Community (EEC) under the leadership of Prime

Minister Edward Heath. Technically we were all classed as Europeans but I had my doubts about that and still do. In the March the Vietnam conflict ended with the Americans retreating and covering their tracks.

Within BA I was going through a strange phase whereby I was brimming with confidence and might class myself as a bit arrogant at times. I think I felt I had achieved a lot and was untouchable. It was not really my character but anyway it kicked back on me on one particular trip. We were on our way to JFK and somewhere west of Shannon when the Captain engaged me in a conversation about how he thought the airline was doing and that all the crews were happy with their lot and what did I think about the recent changes to the management structure. Without thinking and failing 'to engage brain before operating mouth' I said a few derogatory words about the present management set up.

"You don't know who I am, do you, young man?" the Captain replied sarcastically.

I then realised that I had gone a step too far. I knew I was for the high jump. I had never met this Captain before and I had no idea what his position was.

"No sir, I don't know who you are but I have a feeling that you are management," I said, resigned to the fact that I had dropped myself in it.

Nothing was said and I noticed the Flight Engineer was burying his head into his panel more than usual. After a while the Captain disappeared out of the Flight Deck.

"You have just insulted one of our Flight Superintendents and he is not happy with you," the Flight Engineer informed me.

I think at that moment I knew my arrogant phase of life was getting me into trouble and I had to change. A few days after that trip a letter arrived asking me report to the Flight Manager in uniform and not to be late. I duly reported to the office to find that the Flight Manager had been called away and that I would be seen by a Flight Superintendent. I sat down in his office and was read the riot act as to why should I not be fired from BA and I would now be subjected to reports for the next three trips, and if not satisfactory then I would be fired. I left with my tail between my legs and thought long and hard about what he said. I was on trial for three trips.

This was in April and I scanned my next trips carefully as to who the Captain would be. The first trip was to Toronto with a Captain S who was a Canadian. I had never met him before. On the return sector he opened the form about my conduct and studied it intently.

"Bloody management! Always out to trap us!" he said out loud.

"Gwyn, you seem to be OK and I have no complaints and I will give you a glowing report."

"Thank you, sir," I said with a feeling of relief in my voice.

One down and two to go, was my thought.

My next trip was to Singapore via Bangkok with a Captain H and that worked out OK. He had recently run off the end of the runway at JFK in a rainstorm through no fault of his own but had endured the wrath of the management so he was very sympathetic towards me. The end result was another good report.

Two down and one to go, I thought again.

My third trip was to Boston, Massachusetts with a shuttle to Detroit, Michigan. Sounded simple but the Captain was a well-known ex-707 man who, apart from his lack of ability to converse, was reputed to be a bit of a nightmare in the flying department. Just to add to it we were destined to do a route check on the shuttle to Detroit and back with another well-known Captain who was loathed as a route checker. So the scene was set for this route check showdown. On the way to Boston I seemed to impress him but it was difficult to see any reaction from him. He was obviously very nervous of the impending route check so now there were two of us on edge. The Route Checker arrived the following day and the next day we all set sail to Detroit. The weather was not very good either so it was all mounting up. The Captain flew the first sector and I bent over backwards to help him and say all the right things. In fact the flight went better than I expected and we landed spot on time in Detroit.

"That's fine, Captain. Let the Co-pilot fly it back to Boston," said the Route Checker.

The Captain breathed an invisible sigh of relief and so off we went back to Boston with me doing the business. We landed OK and after we had parked, the Route Checker produced his famous clipboard and ticked off a few items. They always do! The outcome was that we had both passed and that he thought we were well up to standard. Relief all around!

On the way back to Heathrow the Captain pulled out the form on me and passed it over and said:

"Thanks for all your help on the Route Check. Please fill in this form and I will sign it."

I did fill it in with a lot of glowing words that suited my thoughts. I handed it over and he never even read it but just signed it. A few days later I got a letter from the Flight Manager's office saying that I had completed my three-trip report and I could consider the matter closed. I learnt a big lesson there!

In the May a new gadget was born in the shape of a mobile phone. It was very experimental and did not even impact on the media save for a small mention. Little did they know! Don't forget in those days we did not even have a PC, let alone the Internet.

A new route had been added to the 747's repertoire, to Tokyo, Japan via Anchorage, Alaska. I was now moving up the seniority list at a fair rate so I was able to bid successfully for one of these new trips. Within BA we had a very structured allowance system as described before but the Anchorage route was without a doubt one of the more lucrative routes since Japan was, in those days, an expensive place to eat and so the allowance was pretty good together with at least five days stopover in Anchorage. I did one of the early trips and off we went up north to 'go over the pole' to Alaska. As we were climbing we passed through the wake turbulence left by another aircraft when low and behold the No. 4 engine suddenly hiccupped and started to overheat. This was a common feature of that make of engine and was known as a surge. The only course of action was to shut it down and that is what the Flight Engineer did. This was my first in-flight engine shutdown on the 747 which, considering I had been on the aircraft some two years now, was not a bad record compared to some people. So there we were at about 20,000 ft on three engines seemingly thinking about dumping lots of fuel and returning to land at Heathrow. How wrong I was! After consultation with the company engineers on the company radio it was suggested that we have a go at a relight or restart of the engine.

"Don't forget that there is $128 US waiting for us in Anchorage as the allowance," the Captain jokingly remarked.

So we had a go at a relight and low and behold the engine started up OK and after a few minutes we advanced the throttle and it worked 'like the brochure'. The Flight Engineer pondered how he was going to write this up in his Technical Log but the Captain simply smiled and asked me to get the clearance and off we went to Anchorage. At this particular time there was an industrial dispute with the Canadian Air Traffic Controllers and Canadian Airspace was closed. Using the magic of our INS we routed right over the top of the Geographical North Pole. The weather was clear all the way and the views were spectacular. Seeing all this ice and snow weaving contours below and so crisp and white was absolutely magic. The best bit was that we were sitting above it all in air-conditioned comfort where, at the flick of the button we could warm up or down as we fancied.

I mentioned earlier that the relationship between us and the Cabin Crew started to head southwards with the advent of the 747 and things were now going from bad to worse. I could never understand how this could be since we were all pitched in together in the same tube going from A to B but it did! Instead of the First Class menu being presented to us as I had known it on the VC-10 we were just presented with crew meals as and when they felt like it. To even get a cup of tea was a major exercise. In my opinion it all stemmed around the chief or CSO in the cabin. I would go for a wander around the galleys when I knew things were quiet and found the individual crew members very pleasant to talk to. Once the CSO got involved then the social chat evaporated and on more than one occasion he or she would attempt to create a barrier to the effect that anything outside of the flight deck was their domain and I should keep out. I have to add that amongst the Flight Crew community we had some pretty disagreeable characters that did not help the plight of a young Co-pilot like me. On this particular flight we had the sort of crew that I was talking about. The Captain was clearly 'Anti Cabin Crew' and the CSO was clearly 'Anti Flight Deck'. Here was me in the middle trying to be nice to everyone. Not an easy job.

Back over the Arctic I found that the visibility was outstanding remembering that in those days there was very little pollution in the region. As we flew southwards down over Alaska you could almost envisage the polar bears roaming free down below. As we descended into Anchorage the views again were mind-blowing with a hint of green down below since it was springtime. When I read the weather out to the Captain I noted that the visibility reading was something in the order of over 100 miles such was the clarity of the air. The time change put us at about midday local time and so once established in the hotel I strolled around the local area to get a feel of the place. There were no skyscrapers to be seen and I felt that I had stepped back in time. The Cabin Crew were accommodated over the road in a separate hotel so they did their thing and we did ours. Oil had only just been discovered in Alaska so the place was teeming with oil men whom I have to say are a race apart. I would call them gentle giants for want of a better description.

That evening I went out with the rest of the Flight Deck crew and enjoyed a feast of a meal since we were in seafood territory. The most famous was the 'Alaskan King Crab' with the legs of these creatures being up to two feet from tip to tip. Afterwards the crew took me to an old 707 haunt, the 'Alaskan Bushman's Company' that boasted good beer and lots of entertaining ladies. Bit of an eye-opening experience that was. Enough said! Sleeping was a bit tricky since it was daylight for most of the night. The following day was spent on a local tour bus and by chance I bumped into a couple of the girls from the Cabin Crew so the three of us teamed up for the day. The tour took us to north of the city into the local nature reserve where we encountered moose roaming freely and the most wonderful scenery. Lunch was organised sitting in the spring sunshine by a river just taking in the views.

The three of us got on very well and when we got back to the hotel they suggested that I came over and joined them for a drink in their party room. What a revelation that was, with more booze there than a well-stocked hotel bar. It was obviously all nicked off the aircraft by the Cabin Crew. I had with me a couple of beers bought in the local 7/11 and so I declined the offer of a drink. I knew that a certain amount of drink disappeared from the aircraft but this collection defied belief and really 'took the biscuit'. Some of my crew were there plus the obnoxious CSO who seemed to take great exception to my presence. It was all very embarrassing since he seemed to have a total hatred of Pilots and directed his conversation to the masses present within my earshot. I did not rise to the bait on this occasion and confined myself to a small group of the girls including the two I had been out with. In addition to the booze, aircraft food appeared from nowhere and I was quite horrified that this was their dinner.

"It's all right for you Pilots earning all that money and going out to eat everywhere. We have to save our allowances just to live," was one of the comments from the CSO.

"We never had this on the VC-10 you know!" I replied.

There seemed to be a muted muttering in reply to my comment. I think after I finished my beers I left the unhappy scene much to their relief. Times were changing fast in the Cabin Crew world. Up to about 1970 there were strict rules about who was employed. For example the girls were not allowed to be married and their contract ran until they hit 35 when they finished. From this year on they were allowed to be married and the contract was extended until they were 55. Whilst I agree that this in itself was fine but what it produced were girls who took on mortgages and had children which took all the fun out of the job. OK, we were paid well but that was the duty of BALPA to negotiate this.

The following day we flew to Tokyo, Japan. The route was again a feast for the eyes as we flew south-west from Anchorage and saw the magnificent Mount McKinley rising to over 20,000 ft, being the highest peak in the USA. We flew down the Aleutian chain of islands that cover the southern area of the Barents Strait's waterway. We crossed the International Date Line and promptly gained a day. As you travel westwards the local time goes backwards and when you go eastwards it goes forwards. At exactly the opposite side of the earth relative to the 0° Longitude line the time balances out either by gaining or losing a day. Sounds simple but it can make your body clock go haywire.

I had never been to Japan before and I was looking forward to it. We landed early in the morning at Haneda Airport in the middle of Tokyo and what amazed me was how many people could live on such a small area of earth with everything seeming to merge into everything else.

The trains ran right alongside the road and the traffic just poured out of every entrance and exit. We stayed at the Tokyo Prince Hotel which was rated the best hotel in the city. That evening I woke up wondering where I was and what the time was or in fact whether it was morning or evening. Bloody time change! Now, you would think that we would go and eat at some real Japanese style restaurant but the Flight Engineer steered us to a place he knew that was in the famous Ginza area of the city. He took us up two flights of stairs and down some shady corridor to a place called 'Uncle Michaels'. It was a small non-descript bar infested by all airline crews staying in the city. You could not move in there but did it have a buzz to it! The place was run by an elderly Japanese couple and the speciality of the house was noodles with a fried egg on top. What can I say! It was bloody delicious! Lots of beer was drunk as well.

The following day it was decided to go out of town to the Mount Fuji area on the famous high-speed bullet train. It was quite an excursion with about six of us in the party. The high speed bullet train fired us off at breakneck speed about an hour out of Tokyo and then we moved over to a slightly smaller local train that took us to a station where we boarded a train that literally tacked back and forth up the side of a hill and dropped us off at a cable car station. We all then climbed into the small cabs of this cable car, bearing in mind the Japanese people are quite small and we were not! The cable car traversed across some sulphur fields with the smell of rotten eggs radiating everywhere.

We eventually arrived at the side of a lake and there we all piled into a boat for a leisurely float across the water. This was quite an adventure considering none of us spoke a single word of Japanese. After about one hour in the boat Mount Fuji came into sight and was quite spectacular. The ex-707 people in the group fell silent and the Flight Engineer offered a few words of explanation by stating that some seven years before, a BOAC 707 had crashed not far from where we were sat. It had broken up in mid-air whilst climbing out of Haneda on its way to Hong Kong due to severe air turbulence. Even to this day a ceremony is held every year in the village close to the crash site. It actually happened some four months before I joined BOAC. We finally docked at a small village and arrived at a small restaurant for lunch. All I remember was the fish were quite happily swimming about in their pens until we arrived. We eventually got back to the hotel at about 8 pm so a quick beer and bed.

On the following day we all assembled for the return flight to Anchorage in the late evening. During the flight we lost a day to put us back on Alaskan time. Dawn broke and in the sunlight we made out the outline of Mount McKinley and worked out that we were more than 500 miles away, such was the incredible visibility in those days. After we landed in Anchorage whilst waiting for our bags to come off the conveyer belt it was by coincidence that the three Flight Deck bags arrived first.

"Typical bloody Flight Deck collecting their bags first," the CSO murmured to a small band of Cabin Crew resulting in a lot of nodding of heads in agreement.

Unfortunately I heard it and I saw red. He was a total moron as far I was concerned together with his band of admirers. I have to confess that in those days I was a bit fiery and very headstrong. I waited until things were a bit quieter and the CSO was standing on his own in the customs queue when I sidled up to him and let him know that it was time for him to quit these outpourings and general nastiness since I had enough evidence from the party room in his hotel to get him sacked and unless he started being nice I would shop him without a single thought. That brought him up sharp. I think the fact that I threw in a few expletives to drop myself down to his level totally gob-smacked him. It did the trick!

The following day we went as a group up to the Denali National Park where we got a magnificent view of Mount McKinley this time from a different viewing point. There were plenty of moose around and, would you believe it, right in the middle of the park by a river was a McDonalds so it was burgers all round for lunch. That evening was quite quiet since we were off to Heathrow in the early hours.

On our flight home as we flew over the Arctic we witnessed one of nature's phenomena with the Northern Lights dancing all around the aircraft. The theory is that ionisation produces these lights and, depending on the atmospheric activity, they can be quite subdued or, as I witnessed them that night, incredibly bright and almost coming inside the aircraft itself. It all must have lasted a good 20 minutes or so and it was quite mesmerising.

As the dawn arrived we were starting to head south towards Scotland and the radio altimeters suddenly leaped into life. Bear in mind that these altimeters only work close to the ground so at 35,000 ft there was no way they should work. They seemed to settle showing something about 500 ft below the aircraft and it was certainly not ground. The Captain, who was ex-RAF, seemed to think that a Russian military aircraft was just below us and sitting in our shadow. So what we did was to turn one way to see what would happen. As the aircraft turned I strained to look below us through the Flight Deck window and sure enough I saw the right wing of a large turboprop aircraft. It was a Russian TU-95 Bear reconnaissance aircraft and as soon as we moved he dropped down and veered away. It was all a bit melodramatic and a bit scary. I read somewhere later that the Russians patrol this area frequently and use civilian aircraft to hone their interception skills. Rather an exciting sector this was turning out to be. The CSO was really nice to us during the flight, I should add.

In the June of 1973 the Russian TU-144 supersonic aircraft crashed at the Paris Air show. It was nicknamed the 'Concordski' and there were various rumours as to the cause but it resulted in a setback for the Russian supersonic travel scene. Boeing had, by this stage, abandoned the supersonic aircraft project leaving the Anglo-French Concorde as the only front runner. In the October the Yom Kippur war started with Egypt and Syria attacking Israel, resulting again in the closure of airspace around the Middle East and causing the usual disruption to air traffic. It was interesting to note that the Russians flew many supply missions to Egypt and the Americans did the same with Israel all controlled by the British military radar on the island of Cyprus. As the war progressed Israel was pushed back somewhat before finally winning the day. The oil-producing states, mainly in the Gulf, started embargoing countries supporting Israel and the first oil crisis hit the world with the cost of a barrel of oil rocketing. The result of this left many airlines struggling to survive financially. Ironically, the resultant price was nothing like the cost nowadays and there was no 'fuel surcharge' facility to help.

I continued to amass flying hours at a good rate during the year and also picked up a lot of sectors for myself since we generally flew with a 3-man crew. Australia was still my favourite haunt and most trips lasted about ten to 12 days. My home life was still just about hanging together by a thread. I have to say at this point that my flying was very much routine. Having said that, I did have a bit of an adventure in Singapore as a result of an encounter with one of our stewardesses. I had met this particular girl on a previous trip and we seemed to hit it off in all the right places. It worked out that I was in Singapore for three days at the same time as she was in Kuala Lumpur (KL), Malaysia so I suggested that I could pop up to KL and stay with her for the three days. Why is it that we men are driven by anything but our brain?

Anyway, off I trot to get the local Singapore Airlines for the one hour flight and arrived in KL within minutes of her aircraft arriving. So far so good! I met up with her in the airport and scrounged a ride to the crew hotel with the Cabin Crew and set up camp with her. She was pretty exciting and we had a great three days together. What can I say! Anyway I was due to fly that evening to Sydney, Australia and so I bade her farewell and arrived at the airport in KL at about 2 pm for the scheduled flight to Singapore which would allow me plenty of time to get to the hotel and get ready to go.

As I strolled into the departure lounge I saw the words 'SQxxxx cancelled due to shortage of aircraft'. In those days there were only about four flights a day. I was now in panic mode! The next service was totally overbooked and since I could only get on if there was a spare seat I was totally snookered. Out of the corner of my eye I spotted another flight going to Singapore belonging to Malaysian Airlines. So I went up to the desk where the flight was showing and managed to swap my staff ticket to go on this flight provided that I would sit on the flight deck jump seat. No problem there, I thought. We walked out across the tarmac to a rather old, tired and tatty looking Fokker F-27 and I clambered aboard just managing to squeeze in to the tiny seat between the pilots. We took off OK and I started to relax since I felt that I would arrive in plenty of time. How wrong I was! Within about ten minutes of getting airborne we were on the way down again and landing at some small airfield on the Malaysian west coast. When we stopped I asked the Captain how many more stops and when would we get into Singapore.

"We make about five stops before getting to Singapore at about 7 pm tonight if all goes well." he said as if I should know this.

My brain worked overtime and suddenly I realised that if we got in on time then I had about 30 minutes before I should be departing to Sydney.

"Now come on boy, get a plan and soon!" were my thoughts together with the first beads of sweat running down my forehead.

We took off again after what seemed like a lifetime on the ground and sure enough we were back on the ground within minutes at another desolate airfield in the middle of the Malaysian jungle. Fortunately I had my BA Briefing sheet in my pocket so I asked the ground staff if I could use the phone in the office. I managed after many attempts to get through to the hotel in Singapore and asked for the Flight Engineer's room hoping and praying he would be in. He answered in a very tired tone.

"This is Gwyn here, in a panic. Please get the pass key and go to my room and pack my entire suitcase. Tell the Captain that I am with friends and will see him on the aircraft. I have got my briefcase with me. I will buy you the biggest beer you have ever known when we get to Oz," I pleaded with him.

"Where are you now?" he asked.

"Don't ask. I am, at the moment, up the jungle without a paddle," I replied trying to be as cool as a cucumber.

I rushed back to the F-27 just as they were shutting the doors and crawled back into my cramped little seat grovelling an apology at the same time. I nearly saluted! We took off and then landed again soon after. I spent the complete time staring at my watch. Why is it that when you want the world to slow down it speeds up? At about 6:30 pm we crossed the Straits separating Singapore and Malaysia By this time I was a total wreckage and was timing everything to the second. I had explained my predicament to the Captain and to be fair he did try to speed things up.

I hope the aircraft is late tonight, I thought to myself knowing that the serviceability of the aircraft was not good.

Not a chance on this night; as we made our approach there was the 747 sitting there on the tarmac with all the usual pre-departure activity going on. After landing I asked the Captain if it was possible to get a parking bay as close to the 747 as possible. This he did manage to do and, as the door opened, out I shot at the gallop toward my aircraft. I knew that the crew bags were loading in the extreme rear hold and so I continued the gallop round to the rear of the aircraft. The conveyer belt was still in position so I just climbed aboard and sailed gracefully up the rear hold. As I clambered in there were two very startled loaders staring at me. I gestured to them for the crew bags and then ripped each one aside to find mine. It is amazing the strength you find when in a panic with 20 minutes to go before departure. Had the Flight Engineer done his part? Yes he had, as I spotted my faithful old Globetrotter. So then I stripped off in the hold to the amusement of the two loaders and threw my uniform on and literarily threw the remaining clothes back in and leapt for the door. I am one of those people that do not like heights and there I was some 30 feet up and what seemed to be a very narrow gangway to get me to the tarmac. Again adrenalin took over and I danced down the gangway like a ballerina. It was now 15 minutes before departure as I bounded up the aircraft steps and swept past the Cabin Crew. I must have looked a right sight since I still had the labours of the day sweating off me. I stopped by the aircraft toilet for some sort of clean up before walking onto the flight deck with head bowed.

"Nice to see that you work for British Airways from time to time," the Captain said with sarcastic grin.

What had happened is that the Flight Engineer had spilled the beans about my escapade to the Captain and he actually saw the funny side of it. They both watched my mad dash across the tarmac with great amusement. We actually departed on time and once we were en route I did a full clean up in the toilet and then I passed out asleep for an hour or so.

Multiple beers to be bought here! was my final thought.

This sort of dash across the tarmac could not happen nowadays with the modern security procedures. Chances are that I would have landed up in jail. My final comment about all of this is to point out that this was all because of a woman!

And so time passed and we arrived at December and in England the miners decided to go on strike. As a result of this the Prime Minister Edward Heath called for a three-day working week plus countless power cuts. It did not affect my flying too much but at home it was pretty miserable with the power cuts. It was a pretty ugly time on the industrial front with confrontations daily in the mining areas. The miners were led one by Arthur Scargill who was the last Trade Union leader who worked in the old-fashioned ways in my opinion. Christmas came and went, and with the power cuts at their worst together with my marriage problems it did not create a wonderful atmosphere. So ended the year 1973.

The following year, 1974, produced much of the same flying routine with few dramas to report. I got a third stripe for my uniform and was now known as a Senior First Officer together with a nice pay rise. In early January I did an Anchorage/Tokyo flight and discovered there what it was like to live and work in temperatures down to -40°C. Bloody cold, that is all I can say! I was now 28 years old and found that I was moving up the seniority list quite fast so my choice of trips was getting better and better with, again, Australia being my number one destination. In those days we covered every major city down under and I would spend maybe one week just pottering around Australia. It was all very leisurely back then.

In the March a Turkish Airlines DC-10 crashed just North of Paris and was the first of the big jets to crash with over 250 dead. It was established that a freight door opened in flight causing the crash. It did emphasize that when a large capacity aircraft goes down fatalities can be high. Back in Britain Edward Heath called for a general election over the miner's strike and lost out to Harold Wilson who got the dispute resolved with his famous 'Beer and Sandwiches' meeting in No 10 Downing Street where he resided. The Labour Government of the day did have a heavy left wing leaning and industrial strife was widespread throughout the UK with the end result of wiping out many of our traditional manufacturing industries, a classic example being the car industry which floundered, taking many famous brand names with it.

Also in March another hijacking occurred when a VC-10 flying from Beirut to Heathrow was taken and landed in Amsterdam. On the ground everybody was evacuated and the cockpit was set on fire using alcohol out of the bar. The aircraft, a Super VC-10, G-ASGO was totally written off and is still somewhere in a museum in Holland. Everybody got out though. By late March the oil embargo imposed the previous October was lifted and airline breathed a sigh of relief.

I have to say at this point that there was not much to report for 1974 except that I had learnt my lesson regarding the KL dash and just settled for a more sensible life. Maybe or maybe not, I cannot really remember, but it sounded good. The only other thing of note in the news was that in the August President Nixon resigned over the Watergate scandal. He was a bit of a rogue but I kind of liked him.

In the November we had another VC-10 hijack which did turn out a bit traumatic. What happened was that one of our aircraft was in a transit in Dubai and four hijackers of dubious origin stormed aboard dressed as cleaners. The problem was that once on board they found that there were no pilots around so they threatened the passengers and very bravely the Captain and his crew left the terminal and climbed on board and followed their instructions. It was ironic that we were on the ground in Bahrain on our way back to Heathrow at the time and were held awaiting developments.

The VC-10 departed Dubai and flew west towards Beirut and we were requested to slot in behind them and keep the operations people in BA up to date as to what was happening. It was very strange and quite weird seeing their lights just ahead of us and knowing what was happening. They descended towards Beirut and we kept the radio monitored. We then heard that the airport at Beirut had been closed and vehicles placed on the runways. They then climbed away from Beirut and headed out along the North African coast. We lost our tracking job at this stage and continued on our way to Heathrow. They landed at Tripoli, Libya departing shortly afterwards and eventually landed at Tunis, Tunisia.

At this point the hijacking turned ugly for, within 24 hours, the hijackers had killed a German businessman and thrown his body out of the front door onto the tarmac. Their demands were the usual release of Palestinian prisoners in exchange for the 'hostages'. The various governments gave in on this occasion and flew the released prisoners to Tunis and the hijackers released all of the passengers but kept the Flight Crew on board for a further 24 hours under very difficult conditions, with explosives being placed on the console between the pilots, and the hijackers seemingly ready to die and take the crew with them. After some very tense negotiations by the Captain they finally gave themselves up to the authorities and so the aircraft and crew were saved. I remember chatting to the Co-pilot later on and it was obvious that the whole episode was quite terrifying. Generally, I don't think a week went past without a hijacking somewhere.

On Christmas Day Darwin in Australia was devastated by Cyclone Tracy that totally wrecked the city. We were in Sydney at the time doing a shuttle flight to Melbourne when the news struck. I remember Sydney being extremely hot at the time and a dust haze was everywhere. All air traffic was stopped whilst the aftermath was being evaluated. Qantas flew some 747 aircraft into Darwin with relief supplies and evacuated people. I believe that they put over 500 people in the 747 at a single stroke. We did a second shuttle to Melbourne when things eased up a bit. New Year's Eve was spent in Sydney at the famous Sydney Auto Club with all the fun and games that went with it.

And so 1975 arrived with a master headache. On 2ndJanuary we were supposed to fly to Hong Kong and eventually we got the clearance to go since it appeared that the Royal Australian Air Force (RAAF) seemed to think that Tracy had disappeared off the east coast and was well clear of our track. The track to Hong Kong put us just to the east of Darwin and as we headed north we heard a RAAF aircraft reporting in that they seemed to have lost Tracy.

"How can you lose a cyclone?" the Captain said with a sarcastic tone in his voice.

Just to the east of Darwin is the Gulf of Carpentaria and as we flew northwards towards this area we spotted on the radar the perfect picture of Cyclone Tracy. Our radar was particularly good and the tell-tale high clouds showed up like a horizontal corkscrew. The wind at our height slowly increased in strength and showed up with a speed of some 150 knots from the west.

"I think we have found Tracy," was the common statement from the fight deck.

We did not have the fuel to go around her so we strapped everybody in and penetrated the high cloud with a bit of trepidation, expecting heavy turbulence. There was not a whisper or ripple save for a very high wind reading. After about 15 minutes the cloud cleared and the wind speed dropped to zero within a few miles. We were right in the eye of the cyclone.

"Tell the controller that we have found the centre of Tracy if that helps the RAAF," the captain said with a grin.

As we entered the high cloud again the wind had swung round to the opposite direction and increased sharply in speed. Still there was not a ripple of turbulence which we found quite amazing. We cleared the Gulf of Carpentaria and left Tracy behind and made our way to Hong Kong. It was quite an experience to fly through a cyclone and not feel a thing.

A Flight Navigator's nightmare with that rapid change of wind direction, I thought to myself chuckling.

After a short stay in Hong Kong I flew back to Sydney. We were about 24 hours behind the normal schedule leaving Hong Kong since an engine had to be changed in Hong Kong. After about three hours we were cruising down the western side of the Philippines and everything was normal. An ashen-faced steward came onto the flight deck and showed the Captain a note that had been found in one of the toilets. It said that there was a bomb on board and was due to explode at a specific time which was in about two hours.

Well, that woke us up I can tell you!

The Captain went off with the steward into the cabin to check out the area.

"Gwyn, please find me an airfield where we can land before this thing is due to go off," he said as he left.

In those days not too many airfields were equipped to take the 747 so the task was not going to be easy. I got onto the radio and asked the controller for information. We hit the language problem and so I abandoned that route. I made a call to any aircraft in the area for help and a friendly Dutch voice came on line. In those days KLM flew the routes for the local airline 'Garuda' with a stretched DC-8 aircraft. He came up with an airfield called Zamboanga which took one of his aircraft once a week but needed the road to be closed off the end of the runway to take-off again. It was about 100 miles east of us and we could be on the ground before the deadline. At this point the Captain returned and listened to my findings with interest.

"If a DC-8 could land there so could we, but we might as well write the aircraft off as they would have to take it apart to get it out of the place," he said.

We then entered into a discussion as to the best course of action and eventually we decided to divert to Darwin which was about two hours away. So, it was down to me to get the radio all fired up with the Australian controllers as to our intentions. That was not an easy task considering we were using the infamous HF frequencies so I switched to the emergency frequency and low and behold the whole world answered me. This frequency is only used in a situation like ours and all ships, control centres and even 'Ham' operators listen in. The first to reply was the Australian controller questioning why we were on this frequency. I explained that we diverting to Darwin due to a bomb scare and we would be there in about two hours. Because Darwin had been hit by Cyclone Tracy only days before the facilities available for our approach would be mostly missing, having been destroyed or uprooted. That was no problem for us though since we had the fancy INS system working well and the rest would follow.

Back on the flight deck it was decided to descend to about 6,000 ft and then depressurise the aircraft so that if anything did happen it might just blow a hole in the fuselage and that was all. All a bit dramatic you might say but in those days it was all the rage to blow up airliners. So there we were at 6,000 ft flying over the South Timor Sea heading for Darwin to land. Back on the radio the Australian controller informed us that a Royal Navy ship that was plodding back to the UK was in the area when the time was up according to the note in the toilet. What an amazing co-incidence that was.

As we approached the time, about 100 miles off the Australian coast, we put on all our lights and low and behold there were the lights of a ship just ahead of us. We assumed it was the Royal Navy out there and flashed our lights to which the ship did the same. On the radio the ship came in loud and clear and wished us well in our misfortune.

While all this was going on the Flight Engineer remarked that the time when we were all due to die had passed and we were all still alive. It was a false alarm but had to be taken seriously since, as I said, we were in a particularly volatile period when to bring down an airliner was considered a sensation by the evil people.

We landed at Darwin and were surrounded by the Australian military since they had taken control following the cyclone. They had the dogs as well all champing at the bit and so once all the passengers had disembarked they were let loose on the aircraft sniffing out anything that looked out of the ordinary. The terminal was a bit of a shambles but it did the trick. After about two hours the Military lot declared the aircraft safe and we loaded up what remained of the airport fuel supply and flew to Sydney after some 15 hours on duty. At Sydney the press were all over us and we hit the front pages of the Sydney Morning Herald with the usual stuff:

"Heroic Captain saves many people from a fiery grave by skimming at wave-top height to the safety of Darwin."

All we wanted to do was to go to sleep for ever. I finally got home after some 20 days away.

In the news not very much happened in 1975. Maggie Thatcher deposed Edward Heath as the opposition leader in the February and so heralded the Thatcher area. Also in the February there was a horrific tube train crash at Moorgate with over 40 people dead. And the Irish Republican Army (IRA) were freely setting their bombs off on the UK. I can remember coming out of London one day, being held up in traffic on the Lower Crompton Road and just crawling along past a hotel on the left-hand side when, about two hundred yards past it, there was an almighty bang. When I looked in the rear view mirror there was total chaos since the IRA had just exploded a bomb in that hotel. Not a nice feeling!

As far as the flying was concerned it was very much routine on the 747 and I just plodded through the rest of the year with the usual mix of trips. On the home front things were falling apart big time. What was the point of trying again and again when there was no future in it? It does need a special sort of woman to be married to a pilot and I didn't have it in this one. Pam actually went out and got herself a job with

Avis, the car hire company, in Portsmouth towards the end of the year and disappeared every day to work. We did have, by that stage, two cars with one being an old Mini which was designed to be used for going and coming from the airport. The other car was a MGB two-seater sports car which was my pride and joy. Unfortunately I invariably ended up driving the Mini and Pam flashed about in the MGB. My fault I suppose but, then, I was not that strong when it came to trying to say what I wanted. I usually took the easy option to keep the peace.

As the year progressed I started to feel uneasy about her work scene and I began to suspect that Pam was getting up to no good. Who was I to talk considering everything but I did keep it out of the home front whereas Pam seemed to revel in dropping small hints about whom she had met. Portsmouth was a military city with all the trappings that came with it. Funnily enough I did not get too upset about it, with no emotions either way. I think that when that sets in then there is no other way to go but downwards. Her parents' home was only about ten miles away and I did get on with Pam's parents very well. She had an Aunty who lived West of Winchester and we would go over to them quite often and I would disappear down the pub with the husband and mix it with the farmers over a few pints. It was times like that when all seemed OK between us. Funny world!

In the December of that I year I did do a trip to Bombay and met one of our girls who I have to say did have an impact on me. We just hit it off straight away and we really enjoyed each other's company. We met again on the same trip in Sydney and furthered our friendship somewhat. We lost touch after a while only to meet up many, many years later, unfortunately at her husband's funeral. He was a pilot so she did marry one of us. His demise was very tragic. Her name was Lisa. And so 1975 ended.

Well, 1976 started like any other year but little did I know what was in store for me as the year rolled on. I was now quite high up the seniority list and was, as they say, on 'Page 1' of the bid line package that arrived every month. I had now been in BOAC/BA for ten years and I was 30 and life was good. It started to dawn on me that maybe I was in line to get a command. In BEA the normal time to command was about eight to nine years but that seemed to have slipped a bit with Tony and

Ian still on the Trident with maybe two years to go.

In the January Concorde did its first commercial flight from Heathrow to Bahrain since the Americans had banned it due to the noise factor. By this stage the Americans had no equivalent supersonic passenger aircraft so knowing their protectionism they used the noise factor as the tool for banning the Concorde operating in the USA. As for me my track record on the 747 was pretty good with only one in-flight engine failure to date which itself was a record since the engines were still failing quite regularly despite a huge upgrade package.

All that changed whilst flying from Bahrain to Heathrow in January with Captain E. There we were just pottering along over Istanbul, Turkey with Captain E down the back somewhere. We had just climbed and the aircraft was at its heaviest weight for the altitude when the No.4 engine just seized and stopped within about five seconds. The throttle lever on the centre console pulled itself back to the idle position on its own pretty forcibly. Consider this engine whirring around at one minute and then suddenly stopping. The resultant torque shook the aircraft quite aggressively and we yawed to the right suddenly due to the loss of power of the right hand outboard engine.

So there I was with the Flight Engineer having to cope with the power loss, yawing and vibration all at once. We had to descend straight away since the aircraft was too heavy to stay at that height. It all sounds a bit dramatic and a bit over the top but I can assure that it was very character forming at the time. Anyway we started to descend and I got the yaw under control and even the vibration ceased so we were back to some sort of normality. Captain E arrived shortly after that and we settled down to continue the flight at a lower altitude. Obviously the engine had suffered some sort of catastrophic failure to do what it did.

It is an odd situation whereby the overall fuel consumption on three engines is not dissimilar to four engines so all options are available as to where to go. In our case it was decided to continue to Heathrow. The only thing you have to watch out for is the fact that if you lost another engine ending up on two engines you definitely had to land sooner rather than later plus the fact that you had to be aware of any high ground around. As it was, there were plenty of airfields on our way home and no real high ground to worry about so the decision to go to Heathrow was fine. When we got close to Heathrow we got a priority approach since the weather was not too clever with snow showers and gusty winds. We landed OK anyway and the Engineers reported that the engine had bent the support brackets and it was amazing it had not actually fallen off. That showed a lot for the strength and design of the 747.

In the March something happened. I got a letter from the VC-10 Flight Manager inviting me to a command course commencing early May. In those days you did not apply for a command course but were invited and those who they felt were not suitable were not invited. Simple as that! So there it was in black and white. Wow, I had been accepted. My acceptance hit the road within nanoseconds. There were to be nine of us on the course and all but one were Hamsters. Mind you after a couple of days I thought long and hard about it and realised that although it was fantastic being invited to attend the course I still had to pass the bloody thing.

The deal was that we would have to do the complete technical course again since I had been away from the VC-10 for more than five years. That would be followed by 14 sessions on the dreaded simulator. If you got that far you then went for base training in Prestwick since Shannon was not usable due to the IRA problem. This base training was reputed to be really tough and not for the faint-hearted. In past courses it was the base training that finished off many of the candidates and was known as the 'chopping grounds'. If you survived that bit then you went onto route training which was again reputed to be extremely hard. The problem I had was that I was only 30 years of age and the big question was whether I would be accepted at this young age.

I did my last flight on the 747 at the end of April and the ironic thing was that we were forced to shut an engine down on the way into Bombay. On this occasion it was a bit more sedate than the last since the engine very slowly ran out of oil and we were all ready for it.

Chapter 6

– THE VC-10 COMMAND COURSE

On May 8th I reported to the training centre at Cranebank to start the command course. All nine of us assembled in a classroom awaiting the arrival of Captain S who was the Flight Training Manager of the VC-10 fleet. He would give us an introductory chat as to how he perceived things would evolve for us. I can remember the entire collection of fellow Hamsters on the course – they were Jerry Latham, Pete Dyson, Ed Murray, Dave Tolley, Richard Blandon, Peter Lumb and Alan Lovering. We also had a chap who had failed the 707 course and was attempting the VC-10 course. There were nine of us in all. We had an issue of a fistful of VC-10 manuals at our respective desks for a bit of light reading before going to bed. After a while Captain S walked in and stood in front of the gathering of victims and surveyed us slowly, nodding at the odd one he had flown with.

"Good morning gentlemen and welcome to the hardest course you will ever do in your flying career," were his opening words.

Nice start! I thought to myself.

He formally introduced himself and then proceeded to break down the course into its gruesome components.

"At the end of each stage we will discuss amongst ourselves as to your progress and whether, in our opinion, you are then OK to continue to the next stage," he continued.

This was all very much matter of fact stuff and designed to focus our minds as to what lay ahead.

"In conclusion, gentlemen, I see nine of you here in front of me but I expect only half of you to make it through and become Captains."

What! Only four and half of us will survive, I thought sarcastically to myself.

When he left there was deadly hush in the classroom with everybody lost in their own thoughts, me included. This course was going to be hard and long. We spent the rest of the day completing paperwork with the technical course starting the following day. Being in deepest Hampshire I stayed with Pete Dyson on more than one occasion. It was good since he lived in Teddington which was not far from Heathrow and it also kept me out of the marriage circuit which was rapidly going down the toilet fast.

The technical course started OK the next day and we were all pleasantly surprised that all the Super VC-10s had been retrofitted with the INS system that was on the 747 so there was no need for a Flight Navigator as had been the case before. There were only three Standard VC-10s left in the fleet. One of these was G-ARVM that was used exclusively for training. What a luxury that was! G-ARVH was operated by the Royal Emiri Flight in Abu Dhabi and G-ARVJ was based in Doha for use by the Qatari Royal family. Both VH and VJ were reconfigured in the Royal Flight layout as used by the Queen when she travelled abroad. The course was a reminder of the various systems that were employed for use on the VC-10 and it started to refresh the parts we had all but forgotten. There was no requirement to sit a ministry exam but BA made sure that we had to do one of their own special exams. This was the trend of the whole exercise. Towards the end of the technical part we had various briefings from the training department as to how the rest of the course would unfold. The other problem I had was that having been brought up in Bristol and Wokingham my accent resembled a bit of a mix of London and surrounds and did not really fit into the 'Queen's English' category.

Difficult to change at my age but I will make an attempt to speak a bit better, I thought to myself.

It reminded me of the time when my mum despaired at my accent and tried to put me up for elocution lessons. She failed!

I eventually got the technical side completed and then had a few days off to prepare for the dreaded Simulator course. As I said it would consist of 14 sessions with each one getting more pressurised with a final check as the last detail. This was the start of the real course as I saw it since from now on I would be marked as 'suitable' or 'not suitable'.

The format had changed for the Simulator course whereby we did a two hour session followed by two hours off and then another two hour session. If you included the pre-flight briefing and the post-flight inquest then you were on the go for maybe eight hours. Not a nice thought. The other point was that we worked alone with a normal line pilot in the right-hand seat as opposed to pairing up as before, hence the four hours in the box were all yours. The only luxury was the fact that the Flight Engineer was not under check so no funny happenings in that department. At least the programme was mapped out for us so I could really get to grips with what was coming up next. The object of the exercise was to get the approval from the trainer to carry on – or, in simple terms, to get that 'tick in the right box'.

Day 1 arrived and I enter the world of the Simulator and start the ordeal. I did not really know what to expect in the box but the first couple of sessions were not too bad. I had to get used to the workings of this old machine since it was so different from the 747 one that I was used to. The company had equipped the Simulator with a rather basic visual system which was a bit scruffy but workable. The trainers seemed to be of a more tolerant breed with most of them being younger than my first encounters in 1966 so maybe there was a certain amount of latitude.

By the third session I was getting to grips with the VC-10 and its ways. The Flight Engineer was far more involved in the operation than before even to the point of reading the checklists and generally joining in with the briefings. As I said the co-pilots were normal line pilots and seemed to understand the pressures of the command course since one day it would be their turn.

Once four sessions were completed then it was assumed that I was totally up to speed with the aircraft and from session five onwards the pressure increased four-fold with the object of getting us to act and behave like Captains. The philosophy employed in those days was that the Captain was King of his domain and that what he said was gospel and not to be questioned. There was none of this Crew Resource Management (CRM) around in those days. I found that I felt quite at ease in the role of King and so moved forward session by session, slowly but surely.

It was session eight that was the most gruelling. I got a call the night before from the trainer for the next day to let me know that apart from him and the three of us there would be a CAA inspector present plus a second inspector being checked out. The Flight Engineer was under check since we were the only session available and to oversee the whole pantomime would be the Deputy Flight Training Manager. That made a total of eight of us in the 'box' and six of them would be watching my every move.

They must be having a laugh. The Simulator will never get off the ground with that lot on board, I thought.

Anyway, I approached the briefing room the next day feeling that this could either be my finest hour or a total disaster. The thing was that the briefing room was not that big and in it were crammed this hunting party. I felt like a condemned man going to the slaughterhouse. The briefing started and once I had cleared all the frogs from my throat I responded to the questions and added the odd comment where I felt that it might be needed. I did make the point that I felt it unjust that the Flight Engineer's check should be done on this session since I had enough on my plate. Sympathies were passed around and a collective shrugging of shoulders met my comments.

"Just concentrate on the task in hand and we will see how it goes," the Trainer said finally.

I entered the torture chamber and set about getting myself organised for the task in hand.

What the heck! I can only do my best, was my thought for the day.

My Trainer was next into the box and quickly whispered in my ear:

"Just try and relax, Gwyn, and you will be all right. You are doing all right so far."

Words of encouragement were just what I needed and I got them. Anyway, the session got underway and just to humour the hunting party I said, as part of my pre-take off briefing:

"This machine could well have a problem lifting off since we are full up of passengers."

A muffled titter was the response I got. At the end of the first session of two hours I was pretty knackered but quite happy with my performance. I had no idea as to the feelings of their Lordships so off we all trooped off for something to eat during the enforced two-hour break. It was approaching midnight when my followers and I trooped into the coffee shop and there was a 707 crew sitting there contemplating their navels and were quite amazed when eight of us minced in. A few sarcastic comments were exchanged which was quite normal and so I had to sit there and endure small talk with the others. In a quiet moment the trainer said:

"Gwyn, you are doing fine so just keep going."

Maybe I have defied gravity and all will be OK. When we all trooped back into the box I whispered to the control column asking it not to let me down and do as it was told. I can't recall the exercise in detail but I would imagine that being number eight it was full of engine failures and bits missing here and there. I finally got to the end of the session and felt absolutely burnt out. We all climbed out and marched in single file into the briefing room for the dreaded de-briefing. Each one had a clipboard and as I sat in the chair with the imaginary spotlight on me I dutifully pulled out my notebook and armed my pen ready and poised to write down the comments as they arrived. It looked good that bit but usually it ended up in the bin once clear of the training centre since hopefully you had passed and that was good enough. The trainer then proceeded to go through the session as to my performance in the finest hair-splitting way since he was under check himself by the CAA. As it went along I duly wrote it down in my notebook and after about 25 minutes he summarised it all by saying:

"Overall not a bad performance, Gwyn, considering the pressure you were under. Everything was fine excepting for the points I have just gone over."

At this point I felt quite relieved that I had not done a bad job. A smile came over my face but was cut short by the CAA inspector who was being checked saying:

"Captain Mullett, I am happy with the trainer's assessment but I have a few points of my own to add."

My notebook was opened again and I jotted down his comments for posterity since it seems that I had passed OK. My trainer also pulled out his notebook and took notes since he was the one being checked by the CAA. After about 15 minutes or so he finished with his comments with both notebooks filling up. At this point the CAA man, who was checking both my trainer and the other CAA chap, started up:

"Just a few points of my own if you don't mind."

Three notebooks were opened and off we went again. They must have known that I had had enough but it did not stop them warbling away. Finally he finished and I went to get up when the Deputy Flight Training Manager piped up:

"I would like to add a couple of comments if I may, gentlemen."

I had not even seen him since he was lurking about in the background. Maybe four notebooks got taken out at this point but all he said was:

"Gwyn, I would like to say that your performance was very good tonight despite having us all watching you. Well done!"

Blimey, this was the deputy boss saying these kind words. Perhaps I might get through this course. The meeting broke up and as we all disappeared, the trainer said quietly to me:

"Well done, Gwyn. By the way, they were impressed with the way you took notes during the interrogation."

"What can I say? I need a new notebook. This one is full," was my reply.

I now had five more details to do on the box but after the dramas of the last one I felt that I could now handle anything thrown at me. I went into the next session and must have given the impression of total confidence since it all went very well and the comments from the trainer were very favourable. I feel that you get to a point when doing this sort of course when suddenly you feel good and know in your own mind that all will go well. I must have reached that point. The next four details went exactly the same.

The last session was to be the final reckoning and the Flight Training Manager took it. It was a scenario whereby we were to be an ordinary flight out of Heathrow with many problems thrown in to test your resolve and command ability. I cannot remember what the problems were but I do remember that there was a real obscure one that really needed a lot of thought. I must have sorted it OK since at the end of the first session Captain S gave me 'the nod' as they say and that the second session would be dealing with engine problems and so on, all based around the session at Prestwick. I found that he was very helpful in that part by pointing out all the things needed for the base flying. When we had finished the final session the de-briefing was quite short and quite relaxing. I was off to base training at Prestwick within a few days.

"Fricking heck, I am on the way," I said to myself as I drove away from Cranebank.

I was staying with Pete and when I got to his place it transpired that all of us had made it to Prestwick and so it was celebration time.

In 1976 my football team Southampton beat Manchester United 1-0 in the FA Cup Final with a goal by Bobby Stokes early in the second half. Southampton rocked!

In late June I flew up to Prestwick as a passenger on the training aircraft G-ARVM or 'VM' together with the rest of the Hamsters. I think that the fact that we were all together as a group led to quite a jovial flight with lots of banter. The only downside was the presence of the trainers who were to put us through our paces once we started this part of the course. We also had a bunch of engineers to keep the aircraft flying throughout our stay. We were all accommodated in the Adamton House Hotel which was about three miles from the airport. The bar was pretty lively that night as we all settled in. We all knew what we were up against but at that moment we didn't seem to care. We were brought down to earth when Captain S announced that the flying programme was pinned up on the board in the lobby. We surveyed it just like we used to at Hamble and there I was destined to fly the next day, in the afternoon. My trainer I knew and seemed like a pleasant fellow so I felt that I was off to good start.

On the following afternoon the crew for my detail assembled in the hotel lobby and off we went to 'VM'. It was quite unreal that we had an aircraft totally dedicated to training but there she was all alone waiting for us on the ramp. We clambered aboard and I sat in the left hand seat which was still pretty strange for me. OK, I did it on the simulator but to actually sit there on the real thing was quite weird. We taxied out and departed for a bit of local flying down to the southwest of Prestwick just to settle in and get the feel of it all. So far so good! We did a few steep turns this way and that way and then a few gentle stalls – unlike my experiences at Shannon in 1966 – and then flew back to

the circuit for a few touch and go's. I had a problem with knowing the
height to actually start the landing since the 747 was a lot higher off
the ground than the VC-10, so at the start I was trying to land at about
100 feet up as opposed to about 30 feet. The trainer took the controls
and demonstrated how to do it properly. He was so smooth that he
could put the rear wheels of the main undercarriage bogey on first and
then the front ones with two distinctive bumps. The landings took a bit
of getting used to but after about circuit number five I sort of got the
hang of it. After two and a half hours we landed and taxied in and went
back to the hotel.

"That was fine, Gwyn. From now on in it will be assumed that you
know how to fly the VC-10 and the real work now begins," were his only
words.

I flew the next day in the morning with a rather obnoxious Trainer
whose first question was:

"Are you ex-RAF or ex-Hamble?"

I knew that he had all the information in my thick training file that
he had tucked down beside him.

"Ex-Hamble, sir," was my reply with a quizzical look on my face.

"I personally think that the best Captains are those who are ex-RAF
types," he announced proudly.

Obviously he had been upside down in a Hunter, unlike me who had
only been in that position in a Chipmunk at Hamble by accident.

This set the tone for the day with him picking holes in everything
I did. Maybe at this stage I did need to tidy things up but I had only
just done one session on the real thing but he didn't seem to give
me a chance. Anyway I slowly started to get things right but he was
knocking my confidence a lot by his constant nagging.

I wonder if he is like this with his wife, poor cow! I pondered the
thought as we drove back to the hotel.

Back in the hotel we Hamsters would gather every night in the bar
to compare notes as to how each of us was getting on. It was becoming
obvious that one of us was not doing well even at this early stage.
The problem was that he was a bit of a drinker and would disappear
off to his room and do whatever drinkers do. We all knew of his
problem over the previous few years and what put him there was

one of life's mysteries. The company was not aware of his situation until we were all together in Prestwick. I find it extraordinary how a person can cover this sort of thing up. As for the rest of us there were mixed feelings and the euphoria of getting to Prestwick was slowly evaporating. We all agreed that the trainer that I had just flown with was a bit of an oddity. Someone knew of his background amazingly enough. In the RAF he was a Sergeant pilot having been turned down as an officer and he ended up flying some two-engined heap of junk around the UK. How he became a trainer on the VC-10 one could only guess. Perhaps his sister's best friend's next door neighbour's husband knew someone who knew the secret.

On the following day I ended up in Keflavik, Iceland for some unknown reason doing circuit bashing. The Trainer for the day had about four of us on board so we each took our turns in the 'hot seat'. It was a chance to compare our skills and each of us seemed at about the same level so I felt pretty good. There was a real spirit of camaraderie amongst us with a mutual feeling of wanting to get us all through the base flying and deal the statistics a cruel blow. We even devised a plan to help us do the approaches at the correct approach angle. What would happen is that when the main precision radio aid was switched off on my side the trainer would keep his working but hidden by a screen so that we could not glimpse across and cheat. What we did was to put one of us in the centre seat so that he could see the live radio aid on the right-hand side and casually lean across and tap the trainee on the left shoulder if he was above the correct angle and on the right one if he was below the angle. It worked a treat! The Flight Engineers knew what was going on but said nothing and just sat back with a smile on their faces.

Bloody youngsters, they must have thought.

As far as the weather was concerned it was the famous summer of '76 with beautiful blue skies and not a cloud in sight. Temperatures were in the upper 70s all the time so overall it was perfect flying weather.

I had now done three details and, apart from the 'sergeant pilot' episode, I seemed to coping quite well. As for the entertainment side there was not too much to offer with the exception of the fish and chip shop in Monkton which was just down the road. There was definitely a shortage of females but then I was not there for that side of life – it would have been nice though. Generally the trainers were a nice bunch of chaps with the odd exception and we would all gather in the bar of an evening. I felt that they had their own 'hit list' of possibles, maybes or no hopers by their general chat with us in the bar.

The next session arrived a couple of days later which proved very interesting. Just off the coast is a small rock sticking out of the water known as Ailsa Craig which rises to about 300 ft. My trainer suggested a flight around it at 200 ft to have a look at it. A bit of exacting flying was required by yours truly and I duly performed it OK. There you are at 200 ft with about 45° of bank on with the trainer staring out of the window on his side oblivious to me fighting the aircraft tooth and nail to do the job. He seemed to be suitably impressed and suggested we fly down to Shannon in Ireland for a few circuits so it was all a bit of a leisurely outing. When we returned to Prestwick and got to the hotel the news was that the 707 chap had been sent home together with the Hamster who had the drink problem. That was two gone within five days. The atmosphere in the bar that night was a bit subdued, to say the least. We did expect these two to fall by the wayside but it happened so quickly since I had breakfasted with them both that morning and by lunchtime they were on their way to Heathrow.

The following evening I was lined up for night flying and duly presented myself at the appointed hour. The Trainer was the famous Sergeant pilot so I was a bit dubious as to how the session would unfold. He made the usual comment about his preference for Ex-military types as opposed to us Hamsters as we drove to the airport.

Nice start! I thought.

As we lined up for take-off that evening I had the feeling that this session would not go well. Maybe it was intuition or that my nerves were coming to the surface. As we turned downwind my favourite trainer asked the tower to switch off all the approach lights, the angle of approach system and the precision approach radio. Considering this was my first circuit at night this action was pretty grim and no introduction to night flying at all. What was he trying to prove? Anyway I did make a bit of a mess of the approach ending up high and fast which is a no-no so we did a second circuit which was not much better. I had lost the edge by now which, considering I felt very much at home at night, was not good in his or my eyes. As we got airborne for the third circuit he muttered something about me not being able to fly the aircraft at any sort of standard so I said:

"Captain, would you please show me the correct way of doing things since I am not doing it very well?"

That stopped him in his tracks and he said with great aplomb:

"You have no idea where the correct approach angle is so I suppose I will have to show you."

At this point the tower asked us if we still wanted all the aids still switched off and before the trainer had a chance to reply I said:

"Please leave all the aids off as before, thank you."

This obviously rattled him.

What the heck. Let's see how he does, I thought, since I had the suspicion that he was 'All mouth and no trousers'.

I settled down in my seat and watched his flying whilst we were downwind abeam of the runway. It was not very good and less accurate than mine. As we turned onto the final approach he was all over the place and he even forgot to ask for the final flap setting. He was high then low, fast and then slow. At about 500 ft I asked him if he wanted the final flap and the landing checks to be completed. This totally threw him and we then sort of arrived half way down the runway with a great thump followed by a mighty roar of the engine reversers operating together with harsh braking. As we turned off the runway right at the end and started to taxi back I said:

"I'm sorry, Captain, but your circuit was worse than mine and your final approach was dangerous since we could have quite easily run off the end of the runway."

What made me say it? I will never know. Maybe it was a case of 'operating mouth before engaging brain' again but there it was.

"Young man, you are here in Prestwick for us to judge your ability as potential Captains not the other way round. Your performance tonight was well below the standard I would have expected at this stage. This session is terminated as of now and I will be referring your file to the Flight Training Manager with my recommendations," was his curt reply.

Lots of expletives came to my mind but I just shut up and thought hard about the meeting which would take place with the boss.

When we got back to the hotel the bar was buzzy as usual and so I wandered in with my face on the floor. Fortunately there were only Hamsters in the bar at this stage so I told them the tale.

"You said what?"

"You are in deep trouble."

"Not like you, Gwyn!"

Now, our files were kept in a cupboard in the lobby and to get to them would be a disaster if spotted by any of the trainers. The cupboard was kept under lock and key with the reception staff. As far as they were concerned the files were as secret as the Cold War itself. As the evening moved on we became a bit more relaxed, as they say, and then my favourite trainer came into the bar having first deposited my file in the famous cupboard and tried to engage us in conversation. He left after a solitary drink. The Flight Engineer then arrived as well and joined us.

"About time someone gave him a mouthful. Shame it was on a command course," he muttered to us.

As the evening wore on my thoughts turned to this file of mine that was in the cupboard.

"Look chaps, I want to read my file and the question is how to go about it?" I quietly said.

The Hamsters all huddled around a table to plan what can only be described as a military operation. A torch was found and with about three other trainers left in the bar it was decided to distract them somehow and for me to crawl on my hands and knees across the floor below their viewing level and get into the cupboard. The only problem was the key that was behind the reception desk on a hook. We did notice that at this time of night the desk was pretty well unmanned and I could pinch the key quite easily. To get back I had to wait for three taps on the cupboard door and retrace my steps. We synchronised watches and off I went. I got the key OK and then dropped on all fours and, at the set time, crawled across the floor for about six metres and got the door open. In I went with torch in hand and closed the door behind me. I found my file and then read the comments of the Sergeant

Pilot about me. It was pretty scathing and was well biased to my background not being military. He even considered my accent totally unsuitable for the role of Captain. His recommendation was that I be terminated and sent back to the 747.

"All this because of a lousy couple of circuits that were loaded against me! Not to mention his feeble effort," I said to myself.

This was then followed by load of expletives suspecting his family origins. After about 20 minutes the door opened and there was the Flight Engineer standing there with a stupid grin on his face.

"Right you, the trainers have all gone off to bed and I want you in the bar now!" he bellowed.

I meekly emerged to cheers from my fellow Hamsters and we all adjourned to the bar. The Flight Engineer bought me another beer to add to the few that I had already consumed.

"Look Gwyn, this guy is not a very nice person at the best of times and I think he is a bit off his head since he seems to thrive on creating these sort of happenings. I have seen him do it before," he said.

"What's more, the bosses know all about him and how he keeps his position as a trainer is a bit mystifying, so tomorrow when you are hauled up before the boss just say what you think and what he will most probably do is to let another more senior man have a look at you. If you need any support I might be able to pitch in for you," was his closing statement.

"Time for another beer!" I proclaimed.

I thought long and hard about it and decided along those lines when I see the boss tomorrow. I had not got this far to be dumped by one bad report. The drinking went well into the night and I got a very drink-induced sleep that night.

I struggled up in the morning and just made breakfast feeling totally out of sorts. As I slurped yet another gallon of coffee the boss walked in and pulled up a chair and, complete with a cup of coffee, sat down opposite me.

"Gwyn, you look like you have been dragged through a hedge backwards," were his opening words.

Here we go, I thought.

"Must be the coffee, sir," I said meekly.

He then stirred his coffee carefully and said:

"Look, I have had an adverse report about your night flying The problem I have is that I have followed your progress throughout this course and looked back at your complete file from when you joined the fleet and I have found nothing that shows to me that you are in anyway sub-standard. I consider that this session where you fell down a bit as a one-off. Maybe your nerves showed through or maybe there was a clash of personalities with you and the trainer. I had a word with the Flight Engineer and it appears that you were thrown in at the deep end a bit quick and that you were not very nice to the trainer."

Was that glint in his eye I just spotted? I thought.

"Anyway, one of my more experienced trainers is going down to Shannon tonight with a couple of you for night flying so I have suggested that you tag along and see how it goes for a few circuits. All he needs to see is about three circuits flown well and he can tick off the night flying bit."

This was his final word as he got up. He then leaned over and shook my hand and said: "Try and get some sleep today and it would be good if you don't turn up looking like a shaggy dog. First impressions always help."

So back to bed I went and slept for most of the day. At about 4 pm I got my act together and arrived in the lobby in plenty of time to go off to the airport. This particular trainer can only be described as a real gentleman with a superb reassuring approach to the training. I only found out afterwards that he was also known as the 'chopper' since his word was enough to fail a pilot when the boss needed a second opinion. Anyway we all toiled off to the airport and climbed aboard 'VM' and took off and headed for Shannon. There were three of us due to do night flying and I would be the third victim. The weather at Shannon was pretty grim with quite a low cloud base at about 600 ft and gentle Irish rain falling. I wondered if night flying would be cancelled but in retrospect the bad weather was a real ally to me since it made the circuits a mix between the totally visual thing and the full instrument approach one. After the second of the victims did his bit satisfactorily we stopped on the ground for a meal. Once eaten, I clambered into the left hand seat and had a few moments of talking to the machine. As I said the weather was pretty grim and we could only fly to the south side so I had a good memory bank of the various turning points. We went through the start OK after which I started to taxi down towards the runway.

"Gwyn, would you mind stopping the aircraft for a moment," the trainer said.

So I duly stopped.

"You know what Gwyn, it is useful at night when taxiing to put the main taxi lights on since it is nice to see where we are going. I tell you what, you relax and I will finish the taxiing and do the first circuit for you," he said quietly.

Bloody hell, my nerves must have been at breaking point and I did not even know it. The trainer did the first circuit and, considering the weather, it was quite brilliant and a wonderful display of flying. As we got airborne after this first circuit he handed it over to me. It was all down to me now. I had one of my friends sitting in the centre seat for the prompting bit if needed. Anyway the first circuit went like a peach. All I did was to mirror his first circuit. As we turned downwind again just underneath the rain clouds the trainer said:

"Gwyn, that was really nice considering the weather. All I need is couple more like that and you will be done."

That was the sort of encouragement I needed and the next two circuits went pretty well. After the last one the Trainer said:

"That was really nice. I see you got control of your nerves finally. Now let's go home to Prestwick."

It was at this point that I realised that the Sergeant pilot was a total waste of space in the training world and that my confidence was such that I knew I would get through this part of the course. All it took was a little encouragement and away I went. As we were taxiing in at Prestwick I was asked to stop again on the taxiway. The main taxi lights were on so what was the problem? Once stopped the trainer did an extraordinary thing. He opened his window and then opened my famous training file and extracted the report written by the Sergeant pilot and tore it into little pieces and threw the remnants out of the window. Nothing more was said and so there was I on top of the heap again. Drinks all round!

As I said earlier the social side of Prestwick left a lot to be desired. However, it all changed when the following night a few of us went into Prestwick and ended up at the Golf Links Hotel. It was a Saturday night and by tradition there was no training on the weekends so we were free to roam. Hence the visit to the 'Links' and it was really hopping with people. I think they were celebrating something and the Scots need only the feeblest of excuses to party.

The beer was starting to flow when I spotted a couple of young ladies sitting all alone so my mate and I decided to inflict our charms on them. What happened was that I sat next to one of the ladies and we hit it off straight away. She was a teacher by profession and I found her quite intriguing. She said she was divorced which narrowed my vision somewhat. She lived locally and I was starting to envisage all sorts of things in my grubby little mind. Anyway the evening moved on and my mate moved on to pastures new and I found myself alone with the teacher. Mavis was her name. We decided to move on as well and ended up at the local chippie scoffing fish and chips. I know how to treat my women! We finally ended up in her place drinking coffee and just enjoying each other's company. Mavis had two children – a boy aged five and girl aged four. I eventually got back to the Adamton House at about 4 am and curled up my toes and slept a very contented guy. It had been agreed that Mavis would pick me up the next day, being a Sunday, for a drive out to a local loch or lake for a picnic with her kids. As I said, this was the summer of '76 and every day was sunny and very warm.

I got picked up at about midday and off I went to play happy families down at Loch Doon. It was a real treat to have female company around even if it was interrupted by:

"Mum, I need the toilet!"

"Mum, I've cut my thumb."

"Is it time to go home yet?"

I cut away from the usual bar scene in the evening and took Mavis out to dinner at the Marine Hotel in nearby Troon. We were getting on extremely well, even too well at this stage, but what the heck! My home life was a total waste of space and here I was hanging on her every word. I won't go into the rest of the night's activities – suffice to say I got back to my hotel with the larks and a big grin on my face.

On the Monday it was down to business in the flying world. I was down for an evening detail to Shannon for some approaches. When I looked to see who the trainer was I fell out of my boots since it was the famous Sergeant Pilot.

Bugger him! I can handle anything he throws at me so here we go!

Funnily enough I did not have any of the previous nerves about him and, as I said, I was on top form and brimming with confidence.

In the late afternoon I met up with the crew and we left for the airport with a stony silence. The Flight Engineer was the same as the one I had on the fated session and he tried to engage the trainer in some sort of conversation. My guess was that the infamous trainer had been given a bit of a telling off by the boss. Anyway we climbed aboard 'VM' and flew down to Shannon. As we started our descent I picked up the weather which was its usual rain and low cloud. At this point the trainer decided to make it interesting by shutting down the two right-hand engines to simulate a double-engine failure. Wow, things were beginning to hot up! Shortly after that he said:

"Right, I would like you to do a 'runway reversal approach' on runway 24 for a landing on Runway 06."

He had to be kidding! Let me explain what the 'runway reversal approach' is all about. At Shannon the main precision instrument approach is set for a landing on runway 24 or to the south-west. This is usually set this way since the winds generally blow from the southwest. In those days generally only one runway was designated in this way. Now, if on the odd occasion the wind is from the other way or north-east but the cloud is too low to do any sort of approach then the procedure we had then was to fly down the precision approach aid for runway 24 and at 400 ft we would level out and then fly at that height the full length of the runway. As the landing threshold of the reciprocal runway, in this case runway 06, disappeared under the aircraft nose then, we would do an immediate turn to the right of 80° followed straight away by a turn to the left so as to line up on the threshold of runway 06 and land. Sounds simple but consider this is all done at 400 ft with the wind blowing you away from the runway and maybe rain and cloud. Now add the factor of having two engines shut down on the unfavourable side and things could really get exciting.

Right, you bloody sergeant pilot, I will show you how it is done! was my thought.

I briefed the Flight Engineer to watch me like a Hawk and in particular the airspeed. I tipped him a wink so that he understood that he was welcome to help me with the airspeed by using his own throttles. I flew down the precision approach aid as perfectly as I could with only the first stage of flap hanging down and at 400 ft, just below the cloud, I levelled the aircraft and flew down the runway. Fortunately the wind was pretty well calm so that was at least something in my favour. As the threshold for 06 disappeared under the nose I swung the aircraft quite forcibly to the right with a bucket load of power to hold the airspeed. This was not a time for looking after Granny down the back with delicate flying. Once I had arrived at the 80° point I reversed the turn sharply and swung the aircraft to the left and concentrated like never before on watching the height, airspeed, angle of bank and looking out of the left hand window for the runway. As I came to the point at right angles to the runway threshold I saw the runway clearly just below the cloud and asked for the next stage of flap. At this point the airspeed was good together with the height and if I carried on round to the left as I had been doing the runway threshold would be exactly where I wanted it. As I straightened up the turn there it was, spot on.

"Landing flap and the checks please," I said triumphantly. All this was done at about 200 ft.

I eased the VC-10 onto the runway right 'on the numbers' as they say and gently brought the aircraft to a halt with about 500 metres to spare. We then turned off the runway and stopped to start up the two dead engines. The trainer did not say much at this point but eventually said:

"Not too bad an approach I suppose."

"Not too bad you say. I thought it was brilliant considering the situation you put me in. I would say that in these conditions it was pretty dangerous to do that sort of approach, even on training," was my curt reply.

I stared at him waiting for some sort of response when the Flight Engineer chipped in:

"Not for me to say but I think young Gwyn did a very good approach and I don't think the boss would be too impressed with the fact that it was done in bad weather with two engines shut down."

I liked the 'young' bit. At this point the trainer shifted in his seat and mumbled that, yes, it was a pretty good approach and should we have some dinner. After dinner I jumped out of the hot seat and another victim took over. It would appear that I had done my lot for the evening and I felt quite relieved. We eventually got back to Prestwick in time for a good drink at the bar. Funny enough the sergeant pilot packed his bags and went back to Heathrow the next day.

Bloody good riddance, I thought.

Having said there were other equal demons waiting in the wings which I would meet before this part was over.

I then had a couple of days off and spent most of it with Mavis since it was the summer holidays for her and we made a few trips to Loch Doon to soak up some rays. I was really beginning to enjoy her company and my mind was working overtime as to how to get out of my pathetic marriage. I had now been in Prestwick for some ten days and was about two thirds of the way through base training. On the Wednesday I did some more flying, this time with the boss, and all seemed to go well. I was, as they say 'cautiously optimistic' that I would get through OK but there was always the 'curved ball' to watch out for. It was also nice to know that everybody else was doing fine so the atmosphere settled down to a pleasant routine. I flew only once more that week with a new trainer that had arrived and I found him a bit overbearing. He was the one who was the overseer on my mammoth simulator session and loved the sound of his own voice. I flew with him on the Friday.

"Are you ex-Hamble or ex-RAF?" was his opening chat with a very condescending manner.

"Ex-Hamble and proud of it, sir," was my monotone reply.

Are they a bunch of thickies or what? I thought.

To try to fly well was a bit of an effort with him and his responses were a bit negative but I did get a few boxes ticked with him. I think he was a generally miserable chap who maybe seemed to rule anywhere outside of the home. I pitied his wife. I had now only about two more sessions to do until the dreaded final check. The weekend arrived and I high tailed it out of the hotel and stayed with Mavis for the weekend. Really good it was.

On the Monday I did a session with the boss again whereby we flew a navigational exercise around Scotland. We rarely got above 1,000 ft. The views were pretty good. It was a very relaxing session and we finished with a couple of precision approaches to Prestwick. By this stage I had a pretty good feel of the aircraft and was developing the ability to totally command all around me which is what they wanted. I now had one session to go and on the Wednesday I completed all the pre-final items except for crosswind landings and was deemed to be ready for the final check assessment session. The reason for the crosswind exception was the fact that this summer there was generally no wind, not even a breeze, to conjure up the minimum requirement and it would have to wait.

The final check was more like an exercise in working out the best course of action to take when faced with a situation. For example you are en-route from A to B and something happens in the middle. Do you divert to C, go on to B or go back to A? Whichever one you decide will be fraught with dramas since other things will happen and you could well end up in D. 'VM' went unserviceable on the proposed day of my check and was out of the circuit for most of the day and well into the next day so it all stopped for us all. To cap it all, the regular VC-10 service from Manchester to New York via Prestwick needed a part of our aircraft to send it on its way so all in all we had a couple of free days and then came Saturday so it was free holiday for us and I spent most of the time with Mavis. This was now getting quite serious and a bit frightening at the same time. On the Sunday evening I got back to the hotel to find that my final check was scheduled for the Monday since 'VM' was up and running again. I was due to meet my checker at breakfast for the briefing.

We met up as planned on the Monday only to find he was the replacement for the sergeant pilot and seemed to be of a similar character.

Never mind, I will give it all that I have got, I thought as I gingerly joined him.

He actually had his wife with him and asked if I would mind if she came along for the ride.

"No problem, provided that your wife is OK with the safety equipment," was my rather condescending reply, not wishing to be caught out by anything.

"That's OK, Gwyn, I will give her a briefing once we get on board," he replied.

"Anyway, the situation you have is the scenario where there is a train crash in Manchester and we have to fly a team of doctors down there as soon as possible but the aircraft has too much fuel on board here and we would be too heavy to land normally. To remove the excess fuel would take two hours. The extra fuel amounts to about five tonnes.

"What would you do?" he said, with a hint of drama – which may have been said to impress his wife.

I pondered the scenario for a while and then uttered my solution:

"Since we are five tonnes overweight I would not attempt to remove it due to the length of time it would take. I would fly down to Manchester at the lowest level possible since the aircraft would burn up lots more than if at its normal altitude and arrange with the ATC at Manchester to give me a long approach to get the aircraft to the maximum landing weight on touchdown."

"Would you consider going down at the normal altitude and actually getting rid of the extra fuel by dumping it overboard as we flew along?" he replied.

"No, since I consider fuel dumping as an emergency procedure not to be planned and, besides, what if the dumping system failed to work correctly?" I replied trying to be as professional as I could.

"Right, that sounds good to me so let's go," he said.

So far so good, was my thought.

When we got to the aircraft it was actually overfueled so apart from being an exercise in make-believe I was actually going to have to get rid of about five tonnes of fuel.

What a waste of fuel and money, I thought.

Anyway, once everybody got on board and the checker's wife had been briefed we started up and taxied out for our early morning excursion to Manchester. If you look on the map of the area from

Prestwick to Manchester you will see that we fly over the Lake District and the lowest height to fly is about 5,000 ft. So I elected to fly at 6,000 ft which hopefully would do the trick. The theory behind this it that for any aircraft to fly economically it selects a height taking into consideration many factors and results in the minimal usage of fuel and therefore less money burnt. The moment you go away from this height then the fuel consumption goes up quite remarkably and you burn more and the expense goes up. Hence my plan was to fly as low as was practical and get the aircraft weight down for the landing.

It was beautiful morning and the views were spectacular on the flight down. Not that I had much time to really enjoy it all since I was talking continually with the Flight Engineer as to how the weight was going. I mentioned way back that the magical figure for the landing weight of the standard VC-10 was 97,976 kg and this was the figure I was aiming at for the landing. As we approached Manchester the Flight Engineer announced that we were about a ton over the maximum landing weight and so I asked Manchester radar to vector me so as to give an extra 20 miles to the landing. This all might seem pretty boring to relate but I was working my brain to a standstill to get it right. I put the undercarriage down early so as to create a lot of drag to get the engine to turn faster to get rid of the last ton. After about five minutes the Flight Engineer announced that we were about half a ton over and so I felt that I could get that down if I put the flap out early as well. As we turned onto the final approach I looked back at the Flight Engineer with a sort of pleading look in my eyes and he proudly announced that we would be spot on the figure on the landing. That was just what I wanted to hear. The only thing to look out for was the notorious hump in the runway, which was the undoing of many a pilot, and I would be OK. I did manage to avoid the hump and landed exactly on the correct point and slowed to a halt and turned off the runway with a sort of smug expression on my face. I had delivered the goods as required.

"Not bad at all, Gwyn. Why don't we stop for a cup of tea and then go home?" the Checker said.

We stopped at a convenient spot and the Checker's wife kindly made the tea and so we sat quietly supping. The VC-10 has a small flip down table on the window side of the instrument panel and has a hole for the teacup.

So what, you say!

Well the downside is that it obscures the nose wheel steering tiller when in the 'teacup' mode and is really designed for use when airborne. Anyway, we were stopped on the taxi with the table down and all was well. After a short while the Checker suggested that we moved forward a few metres to let another aircraft by. I stowed my table so that I could steer the aircraft but the Checker left his table down. As we moved forward I said:

"With all due respect, sir, would you please stow your table since you are unable to steer the aircraft if, for some amazing reason, I fall out of the loop."

Was this some sort of game he was playing or what? I thought to myself.

He muttered a couple of words and managed to put his teacup on the floor and stowed the table. It all sounds quite trivial but it was the games that they played and the secret was to join in the games. We finally departed Manchester on our way back to Prestwick and within a few minutes the usual routine of problems were thrown at me. So we ended up on two engines and one of the hydraulic systems was out of action so it was a real bookwork exercise sorting out the various restrictions. The main one was the calculation of the landing distance needed with the problems we had. The Checker did the calculations very laboriously and came up with a figure that showed we were in fact some 200 metres short of runway length with the prevailing wind. There were various additives to the calculations and so I took the decision that we had enough runway if I came into land right on the correct speed and used reverse thrust. The calculation allowed for the speed to be fifteen knots too high on landing and no reverse thrust. Not ideal but bear in mind it was the only solution to land where we intended to. The checker accepted my decision reluctantly and I made sure the speed was spot on as we landed. After landing we taxied in to the ramp and he said:

"OK, Gwyn, off you go back to the hotel since I have another session to do and I will see you later."

"OK, but before I go, can I have a drink in the bar to celebrate or not?" I replied gingerly.

"Yes, you have passed but there are some items we need to go over and I will give you a full debriefing once I am back in couple of hours," he replied.

That was enough for me and I skipped down the stairs like a fairy. He could give a two-hour debriefing and I would not care. Once back in the hotel I hit the bar and started on the beers.

"Bloody hell everybody. I have defied the odds and made it to hell and back!" I said as I entered the bar to anybody that happened to be listening within earshot.

"Well done Gwyn, let me buy you a beer," the boss said rising from his morning coffee.

"Thank you, sir," I replied.

A couple of the other guys came in and the beers started to flow. Out of nine of us, five had passed the base training with two on their final checks very shortly. Not bad for a bunch of Hamsters who had never been upside down in a Hunter. By the time my checker arrived I was getting well stuck in and when he beckoned me into the lounge for a debriefing I felt very relaxed and could only grunt the odd reply. He did love the sound of his own voice and droned on for about an hour interrupted by me popping off to the small boy's room every now and again just to keep alert and awake. Finally he asked me to sign the final check report as confirmation of my 'pass'. His other session of the day was to pass another Hamster so only one to go and we were all done.

"Right Gwyn, I doubt if anything I just said sunk in through your alcohol-soaked brain except to say that you did OK and all that remains is for you to get some cross-wind landings and you will be ready for the route training part," he said casually.

"Oh yes, I had forgotten that bit; so presumably I just sit at home and wait for a call?" was my reply.

Right, back to the bar I went and we partied for the rest of the day. In the evening Mavis came over and joined in our celebrations since the final last Hamster got cleared that afternoon. It was quite a party I remember. The deal was that we would all stay for the weekend and then all of the crew at Prestwick would fly down on 'VM' on the Monday. How civilised can you get!

Once again the weather was glorious over the weekend and I enjoyed every bit of it with or without Mavis. Having said that we both drove down to Loch Doon for a leisurely picnic with the kids on the Saturday. I was starting to enjoy the company of both the kids, Colin and Jacqui, a lot and for the time I was there in Prestwick it was happy families. I didn't press Mavis on the subject of her ex since I did not want to intrude on her private life. She knew all about the disastrous state of my marital affairs. Anyway the weekend was a pretty relaxed affair and by the time Sunday night came along I had clocked up three weeks at Prestwick and just about 20 hours flying on 'VM'.

On the Monday morning in early July we all climbed aboard the VC-10 and flew down to Heathrow. The three of us who did not get the cross-wind landings done were told to go home and wait until somewhere was found in Europe that would do the job and get them done. What they did not tell us was that every week we had to do a local training flight to keep our hand in just in case we had gone off the boil in the intervening period.

Back home the scene was worse than ever due to the fact that another additive to the equation had arrived in the shape of Mavis. Pam confessed that she was becoming very friendly with a Royal Marine whom she had met while working in the Portsmouth office of Avis. How far was the 'friendly bit' I did not know but I was not too bothered about it at the time. She even had the cheek to invite him over while I was at home and the three of us would go out for a drink. Amazing!

I was becoming really frustrated and bored waiting for the call to do the cross-winds and spent most days looking at the weather on the TV just in case. I got a call about two weeks later to go to Heathrow for a local training flight to Stansted that evening. I was with Peter Lumb and the trainer was the one who did my final check. I did the take-off and flew it to Stansted and ended up with the usual mix of failures to deal with. I have to say that it was all a bit demanding and not that enjoyable. Pete Lumb did his bit and boy was he good, much to my dismay. Funny thing was that when we flew back to Heathrow in the early hours Peter announced that he was resigning from BA and going off to fly with an airline in the West Country called Brymon Airways as their Chief Pilot. Nothing stranger than folk! So that made us six out of the nine surviving with only one and a half to go.

During the July there was the famous raid by the Israelis on Entebbe designed to release a load of Jewish hostages that had arrived there on a hijacked airliner. It was an amazing feat when seen from a Pilot's point of view since they had landed in a blacked out airfield with no aids at all and rescued all but one of the hostages with only one casualty amongst the Israeli forces. President Idi Amin was not amused. God bless him!

As for me I sat at home yet again basking in the never-ending sunshine dreaming of a wet and windy night. Once again a week later the call came to go for a local training flight with the same trainer so once again I was put to the test as to my ability for all to see. By this time I was really hacked off with it all.

After a month at home I got a call from the boss saying that he had found some cross-winds in Keflavik and that three of us would hit the trial that night to, hopefully, get the final tick in the box. We assembled at Heathrow that evening and climbed aboard good old faithful 'VM' and off we went for a three hour flight to Keflavik. As we approached the area the weather was pretty bad with the runway in use lying north to south since the wind was blowing a gale from the north plus low cloud and rain. OK, cross-winds I wanted but this was a bit extreme.

The boss got the tower to release us to use the east to west runway for training. I sat in the flight deck whilst the first victim went through his paces. The weather was right on the limits with respect to the cloud base together with the cross-wind limit as well so it made for some interesting approaches. We were each required to do three approach and landings. I was last and by the time I got into the seat it was red hot from the physical exertions of the previous two. The one thing the VC-10 falls down on is the fact that the roll control is very heavy plus the wing is clear of any engines hanging down so it catches every gust. So, when you are faced with a strong cross-wind, you need biceps like Arnold Schwarzenegger to pull the aircraft straight for the landing. This was a night like that. You would follow this rather basic guidance system down the ILS precision aid shoving and pushing the aircraft so as to keep right on the nail for the approach path and at about 300 ft you would then look out and see the runway through the rain out of one of the side windows since you were crabbing to the left or right. The airspeed would be bouncing all over the place and the temptation was to turn the aircraft early to land and then find yourself struggling to stop you landing in the field alongside the runway.

I managed to do the three landings and the boss seemed happy with me. I felt totally exhausted and what was left of the biceps ached like mad. We then stopped for dinner on the ramp and enjoyed the delights of Icelandic cuisine. No expense was spared considering the aircraft was flown all this way to get us cleared for the route. The whole night's expenses must have run into thousands of pounds. Who cared though, since I had ticked the final box and was now ready to tackle the route side of the training. I flew it back to Heathrow under the watchful eye of the boss and finally got home at about 6 am, a tired but happy soul.

I had now been on the command course some four and a quarter months and finally on 27th August I got back on the route for the final hurdle – and believe me it was becoming an endurance test. Unfortunately I had no support at home which made it doubly hard to keep focussed.

My first training trip was out of Manchester to Montreal via Prestwick and return to Manchester the same way and on to Heathrow. The trainer was a Captain S who turned out to be a very nice guy and quite relaxing. It still seemed strange to assume the left hand seat from the start and to be amongst the youngest on the crew. I remember the CSO giving me a quizzical look since all communications were directed at me who was many years his junior. The stewardesses seemed to be impressed though. Nice that! The sector up to Prestwick was pretty simple since I had done the route on the base training. As we taxied in at Prestwick there was 'VM' with the next lot of victims doing circuits. I felt relieved that the base bit had been done.

As I said before BA now only operated about 12 Super VC-10s and all had been retrofitted with the INS system similar to the 747 so I felt very much at ease in that department even to the point where the trainer was asking me questions about it since he was new to its workings. We departed Prestwick and set sail across the Atlantic towards Canada and Montreal. It was ironic that my birthplace was to be my first night-stop.

The atmosphere amongst the crew was exactly how I remembered it when I flew on the VC-10 before as a Co-Pilot and made a refreshing change to the scene on the 747. The flight was pretty well uneventful and was marked by a good lunch and an afternoon arrival into Montreal at the new airport of Mirabel that was about 30 kilometres north of the city. This new airport was part of the modern world whereby noise was becoming a massive issue with airports located convenient to any city centre and so these 'White Elephants' airports were built at vast expense in the wilderness away from the city expecting people to travel all the way out to them to go places. Mirabel was a classic example and ended up with only about ten movements per day totally defeating the cost of it all. Anyway we landed OK and so my first training session went well and that night the fleshpots of Montreal were studied very carefully out of the bottom of a beer glass. What was really nice was the fact the whole crew came out which just never happened on the 747. Happy days were here again!

We had a day off in Montreal so I took the opportunity to revisit my roots and made my way to Dorval and into Neptune Boulevard to try to find my old house where I had spent my early years. I walked down the street in the summer sunshine until I spotted the house on the left-hand side. It was quite amazing since I had no recollection of it in my own memory and relied on a couple of old photographs. I was standing on the pavement staring at the house trying to visualise myself living there when I noticed an old man behind me mowing his lawn and so I walked up to him and said:

"Good afternoon, sir, have you lived here a long time?"

"I have lived here since 1942," was his reply.

"Do you remember when the Mulletts lived over there at all?" I inquired.

"Yes, I remember them very well. They had two children, didn't they? Don't tell me you are the boy that used to be tied up to that tree over there?" he replied.

"That's me all right, only a bit older," I said with pride.

You could have knocked him over with a feather. What a memory he had! That was the end of his lawn mowing and he called his wife and before long we were sitting on his porch enjoying a beer together.

His memory was amazing since he related tales of all the happenings when I lived there. He even remembered the occasion when I got free of the tree and shot off down the road to the lake since he was one of the posse who set out in hot pursuit to round me up. After a while he got his car out and drove me to the local recreation centre and showed me the wall that had all the memorabilia about the North Atlantic Ferry Organisation that my dad was part of. There, amongst it, was a picture of all the people who took part including my Dad and my Godfather. He was himself involved on the ground at Dorval servicing the aircraft before they departed for the UK many years before. He asked about my mum and dad and I related the sad ending for my mum.

"Your mum was a lovely lady," was his comment.

That bit did choke me up I have to say. It was an incredibly nostalgic afternoon and he eventually dropped me off at the bus station. I got back to the hotel in the early evening and joined the others for a quiet dinner since we were off back to the UK the following evening.

The return flight followed much the same routine, flying to Prestwick and on to Manchester where we arrived at about mid-morning. It was a shame that we only had 45 minutes in Prestwick otherwise I would have made tracks to see Mavis. Anyway after about an hour in Manchester we flew the aircraft to Heathrow as a replacement had arrived. On arrival at Heathrow Captain S gave me a good write-up in the file and wished me luck with the remainder of the training. What a nice guy he was! I eventually got home in the early afternoon and collapsed into bed for a well-earned sleep.

I was home about one week when the call came for the next flight in early September which was to be a long one out to the Far East to include Hong Kong and Tokyo. Captain M was to be the trainer. I had not heard of him so I assumed he would be one of the nice guys. How wrong I was!

I reported as normal and found Captain M to be a bit intimidating.

"Right Gwyn, I see we have a long trip together so a good opportunity to go over all the manuals and check your knowledge during the night stops," he said.

Yes, it had to be done but this trip seemed like it was going to be hard work. The first day's work took us through Tehran and onto Delhi for two days off. As we flew over Germany the trainer looked down and said with an air of superiority: "I was stationed in Germany years ago flying 'English Electric Lightnings' against the Russians."

Oh dear, he was one of those ex-RAF types who relished his military background and what's more he was a fighter pilot flying the pride of the English Aircraft Industry, was my thought.

Not that I am against these people but we were now flying civilian aircraft and the fact that I descended from Hamble should not affect their judgement. I engaged him in conversation about the Lightning since I was quite interested in the aircraft and also to try to melt the ice between us. We transited Tehran OK and then made our way south-east to Delhi where we arrived late at night. Normally as a Co-pilot I would turn a blind eye to a few beers off the aircraft for the ride to the hotel having negotiated the India customs but as I was under training I asked the Chief Steward to do anything like that very discreetly so as to not cause a scene. I think the trainer was on the lookout for my handling of the indiscretions that were part of the normal routine on board.

"No problem Captain, I will keep it all under the carpet," he said.

This was the first time I had been called 'Captain' and it felt good. We eventually went off to the hotel. Once there, the trainer declared himself off to bed and so I had a chance to let my hair down a bit in the Chief Steward's room with a well-earned couple of beers. The Flight Engineer was the brother of a Hamster who was on my course at Hamble. Amazing co-incidence! I did get on with him very well so the trip would surely have its lighter moments.

At breakfast the next day the trainer collared me and suggested that we met up at lunchtime by the pool to go over one of the many manuals that we had on board. He must have had the complete library with him. So I duly turned up at the pool with not a cloud in the sky and all the stewardesses prancing about in the water or splayed out on a sun lounger looking rather nice. I sat down at a table with the trainer and ordered a soft drink so as to not seem to him a lunchtime drinker. He pulled out one of the manuals and proceeded to itemise its contents in the smallest detail and fire questions at me; some I could answer and some I could not. The idea of any aircraft manual is for reference when you need to answer a query. I am not expected to learn every page by heart. The trainer obviously did just that and I found that he enjoyed catching me out over something trivial. Maybe he was right and I was wrong but I find that if a subject or procedure is committed to memory then that is when mistakes can occur. I have, over the years, seen just that happen. The lunchtime session went on for quite a while and it was very difficult to concentrate with all the distractions around me but I had to try. After a couple of hours he announced the session complete and suggested that I learn up on a couple of items and we could review them later in the bar. What!

The two days passed in much the same vein and I had no choice but to 'go with the flow' with his method of training. I even skipped breakfast the next day so as to not meet up but low and behold he called me in my room giving me about ten minutes to see him at breakfast before the restaurant closed for lunch. If you remember back I did say that my method of learning was to read all about it and write it down and this still applied. What I did not want was a lecture every day and then a 'question and answer' period. Besides, I had done it all in the ground school and passed the exams at the beginning of the course.

As we assembled in the operations department at the airport for our flight to Hong Kong we were told about a mid-air collision between a BA Trident and a DC-9 over Zagreb, Yugoslavia killing 176 people. I immediately thought of Ian and Tony and managed to get the BA Ops guy to let me know the crew names. Neither Ian nor Tony had been involved and I felt relieved but nevertheless shocked at what had happened. It was a very sobering thought that life could be extinguished in an instant. The flight to Hong Kong went well albeit a bit quiet considering the shocking news we had heard. The arrival into Hong Kong was based on, as I said before, the older rather basic approach using a couple of beacons and flying around the western tip of Hong Kong Island followed by the large turn at low level to land on the runway. Having been quite a few times on the 747 I was ready for all the pitfalls that can happen on the arrival and I managed to perform a reasonable approach and landing. Mind you the trainer still found a few bits to spout off about. The hotel for our stay was on the Island overlooking Causeway Bay and was a vast improvement on the previous hotel on the mainland. The area was pretty social and it only took a gentle 20 minute stroll and you were in the heart of the bars and clubs. This time round we only had a day clear and of course the trainer took time out to grab me for a lesson for want of a better name.

On the second day we continued the trip, flying to Bandar Seri Begawan, Brunei which was an old British Colony in Malaysia from where the fight against the Indonesian insurgences was based during the Malaya Emergency in the 60s. After a short transit we then flew to Colombo, Sri Lanka. This island was perched off the southern coast of India and was full of charm and beautiful beaches with our hotel sitting right on one of the best beaches. Dad used to rave about Sri Lanka when he visited there on the Comet 4 and he was absolutely right about its magic. The only thing it lacked was a good precision approach aid and was a bit character-forming when the tropical monsoon rain was falling. Apparently it did have a precision aid installed but the rats continually gnawed through the cables. They must have got a perm from the electric cables each time they took a bite. The weather was ideal for lounging about by the pool and generally surveying the scene but the trainer was having none of it so there I was once again sitting like a pupil and answering the teacher. I was getting strange and curious looks from the rest of the crew and I am sure they saw the anguish in my face as all I wanted to do was to get amongst them. The Flight Engineer was the cruellest by raising his glass of beer out of eyeshot of the trainer.

I'll kill him one day, was my viscous thought for the day.

On the third day we flew back to Hong Kong and the sector went fine and I got the approach spot on.

"OK, I can sign your Hong Kong clearance for you together with Tehran on the way out," the trainer said thoughtfully.

"Thank you, sir," I replied relieved that at last we were getting somewhere.

On the network you were required then to have a visit with a trainer to New York, Tokyo, Hong Kong and Tehran so as to obtain a clearance to fly on to these places as a Captain. There was just New York and Tokyo to go. We only had a short night stop in Hong Kong and the

trainer decided that he would go off to bed since we were off on Cathay
Pacific Airways the following morning as passengers to Tokyo. It was
about 7 pm so I grabbed the Flight Engineer and said:

"Tonight's the night to have a good fun time since I can sleep it off
on the flight the next day."

Well, we did have a great night. We went over to the mainland since
we knew the haunts better and there we linked up with another VC-10
crew and the party started. Just after midnight we all made our way
back to the ferry terminal to take us across the harbour to Causeway
Bay and the hotel. This was where the trouble started since the ferries
had all packed up for the night and the only transport available
was a small boat or Sampan with a 99 year old women at the helm
with this rather dilapidated oar sticking out of the back to propel us
forward and steer us in the right direction. Four of us piled aboard in a
somewhat dishevelled shape and off we went across the harbour. As we
drifted this way and that under the guidance of this old lady and her
dilapidated oar the lights of a Royal Navy Warship came into view and
one of the group declared:

"I am ex-Royal Navy and the bar will be open on board so let's get
this lovely lady to drop us off alongside."

The old lady started shouting this and that until a nice crisp 20
dollar Hong Kong note was put in her hand. As we pulled alongside
I hadn't appreciated just how high this Royal Navy ship was. Not
being one for heights I started to sober up fast. There was a bit of
commotion on the deck with sailors peering down at this bunch of
blokes alongside. The ex-Royal Navy man amongst us was actually a
Flight Engineer and confirmed my theory that these breed of men were
responsible for many of my wildest adventures in the world of aviation.
After a bit of Navy banter up we went up this sort of gangway to be
greeted by what must have been the Officer of the Watch and the Flight
Engineer and he was consulted over some old ship that they might have
been on together at some stage way back in history. Maybe it was HMS
Victory at Trafalgar. The net result was that we were ushered forward
and into the heart of the ship and, low and behold, the Officer's Mess
or bar loomed into view and drinks were ordered courtesy of the Royal
Navy. It was assumed that we would consume our drinks 'Navy style',

ie bloody strong! By about 3 am I was well happy and needed my bed. It was agreed that it was time to go and instead of a dodgy old Sampan we were treated to the ship's courtesy tender and this bunch of idiots struggled down the gangway and fell into the small craft in a total shambles.

"To Causeway Bay if you please, young man," was the order of the morning and so off we went.

We were eventually deposited on the quayside and managed to get to the hotel more by luck than judgement. I think I had about one hour in bed when the call came through to get up and report downstairs for the passenger flight to Tokyo. I was in a very bad way and struggled at every move with the dream that once on board I could collapse and die quietly in the corner. What I had failed to grasp was the fact that the Flight Engineer was only entitled to Economy Class since he had only been in the company a couple of years whereas I was entitled to First Class. My trainer was on top form since he had slept all night and there was this wreckage slumped next to him in the most comfortable of seats you could ever imagine. After take-off breakfast was served and I did it no justice. The trainer announced that once breakfast was out of the way we could go over some aspects of the Navigation Manual that he felt was relevant. By the time breakfast was finished I was a snoring dribbling heap in the seat and any teaching had to be abandoned for the day. Great! I actually woke up to the sound of the undercarriage going down prior to landing in Tokyo. The trainer was not amused!

What can I say? was my thought.

We did have some three days in Tokyo and the trainer made up for my lack of attention big time by pursuing me at all times for this and that. I have to say I felt bad about Hong Kong but it was one hell of a night. By the time we departed from Tokyo I was a bit more in favour since he decreed that we had covered all the manuals to his satisfaction and I would get a tick in the box for that bit plus the fact that he would sign off my Tokyo clearance based on the departure. The ticks were coming along quite nicely. In Hong Kong again and a quieter night was attempted. The problem is that Hong Kong just speaks 'fun' since it never sleeps and there is always some venue to amuse one all night. We had the same cabin crew up to that point so it was natural to all go out together and invariably we would end up in 'Joe Bananas' with loud music and lots of drinks followed by a stroll down Lockhart Road back to the hotel and maybe breakfast.

After a couple of days we flew to Colombo again and then onto Abu Dhabi, UAE in the Gulf for a night stop. Having dispensed with the reading of the manuals the trainer kept firing questions at me off the top of his head. We eventually left Abu Dhabi for Heathrow after some two weeks away. As we flew over the Lebanon the trainer went into a verbal overload of how he had single-handedly defeated the Egyptians when Britain was engaged in the Suez crisis many years before. This was the time when Britain, France and Israel went to war against Egypt when President Nasser of Egypt had decided to nationalise the Suez Canal.

"What aircraft did you fly then?" was my innocent question.

"By that time I was on the Canberra bomber running a squadron," was his reply.

This was followed by a complete rundown of how he managed to do the most courageous of attacks against all the odds. It was non-stop self-praise. OK, he did do some heroic stuff but please do not ram it down my throat the fact that I only went upside down in a Chipmunk once or twice at Hamble and, as I said before, usually by accident. Anyway I arrived at Heathrow and his write-up was not too bad although it took about an hour or so on the ground to get that point across. Apart from the episode in Hong Kong I felt that all was going well and the light at the end of the tunnel was starting to glow.

I eventually got home to the usual dramas. I did confess that there was someone else in my life. The amazing thing was the response from Pam. She took it really badly and cried a lot. At this point I have to confess a complete lack of understanding of the female brain. There she was giving her all to some Royal Marine and making it pretty obvious that I knew but when the boot is on the other foot then all hell breaks out. Bloody strange lot!

I had about a week off before the next trip so spent it catching up on the house chores like mowing the lawn. I still spent most of my time driving the beaten up old Mini. In the news the first NASA Space Shuttle appropriately called 'Enterprise' had been launched from a 747 test bed to glide back to earth. A new era of space travel had begun. The other amazing bit of news was the introduction of the 'Quickie Divorce' whereby for about £16 a couple could bypass all the red tape and legal costs and, based on certain criteria, obtain a divorce by post you might say. Things were looking up OK.

My next trip was with a Captain J and was a ten day affair around the Middle East. He was a really nice guy and we flew from Heathrow to Baghdad, Iraq for a two day stopover. In those days Baghdad was a normal Middle Eastern city with bright lights, good restaurants and night clubs. All a little different today methinks. My flying side seemed to be becoming quite comfortable and I was feeling very much at ease in my new role. Once again the whole crew acted as one and we generally went out as a group for all things social. After the two days in Baghdad we then flew on to Kuwait and Abu Dhabi for another two days off.

This trip was really very leisurely. Not once did the trainer ask me about the books since he has seen the various ticks on my file. From Abu Dhabi we did a shuttle to Muscat, Oman in the middle of the night and then back to Abu Dhabi for yet another two days off. It was generally a feature of the Middle East in those days that the British still had a lot of influence so most cities sported a 'British Club' where you could drink and eat unperturbed by any countrywide religious restrictions. Anyway, after the rest in Abu Dhabi we retraced our steps back to Baghdad and finally on to Heathrow. At this point Captain J let me know that I was doing very well and after maybe two more trips I would be up for the final check.

It was now October and my sixth month of the course completed. After a few days I was off to Abu Dhabi again via Jeddah, Saudi Arabia with a certain Captain S who was a right character. He did not even bother to open my file and created a very relaxed, even jovial, atmosphere on the fight deck. At that time we had a Standard VC-10 based in Abu Dhabi as part of the Royal Emiri Flight and on board our flight we had the wife of the resident BA Captain. In those days a complete crew would ship out to either Doha or Abu Dhabi and be the resident crew for maybe three months. She came onto the flight deck at one point and Captain S recognised her as an old flame from way back.

So there was the pair of them canoodling around the flight deck like
a couple of re-united lovers with me and the Flight Engineer watching
the spectacle with amusement. She stayed with us all the way from
Jeddah to Abu Dhabi and as we descended we heard the call sign of
'Emiri 1' departing. This was the call sign of the VC-10 and the trainer's
eyes lit up even more when he heard the Captain making a radio call.
He let the wife know that she would be on her own for a while and
two complete set of eyes lit up. That was my stopover sorted. Anyway,
at about 2 am on the first night there was furious knock on my door
and there was my trainer standing there looking very dishevelled and
worse for wear.

"Bloody Emiri 1 arrived back after a two-hour air test and the
Captain is after my blood," he said with panic in his voice.

"And what's more, he is a big chap," he added.

"I need to camp out in your room for the night since he has staked
my room out with intent to get hold of me," he stated as if there was no
debate.

So there were the two of us trying to sleep in a large double bed with
two lots of snoring units going full blast. It was really romantic and if
the room boy came in as they sometimes do with total disregard to the
'Do not disturb' sign what would he think?

A couple of gay pilots, maybe?

My reputation would be in tatters and the cleaner on the fifth
floor in Hong Kong would know within seconds such is the speed of
the jungle telegraph. So what I did was to creep out once the snoring
machine next to me was at full volume confirming a comatose Captain
and got dressed and wandered down to the reception and sat around
until the breakfast room was open and then drank coffee after coffee.
The resident Emiri Captain strolled in and asked me if I knew where
Captain S was and I pretended not to know. It transpired that he was
off with one of the Sheik's sons to Paris in an hour so I just chatted as
normal until he drove off to the airport. His wife then turned up and
was looking a bit worse for wear and sat with me for a while. I called my
night visitor in my room and he crept into the breakfast room looking
very sheepish and thanked me for the use of my bed and that he had
had a great night's sleep.

That's nice, I thought having had maybe four hours' sleep.

Fortunately we departed the following day back to Heathrow via Muscat and the coast was clear and I got a super write-up on my file. It transpired that I had one flight to JFK to do and then I would be up for the final check.

It was towards the end of October when I met up with Captain T for the flight to JFK and hopefully my final clearance before the check flight. He greeted me with the news that we had two CAA inspectors on board with one checking the other and again me in the middle. This would make five of us in total in the cockpit and it would be a really cramped affair. I suggested that one of the inspectors would have to have a seat in the cabin for the flight and only visit the Flight Deck for the minimum of occasions.

"They are actually here to check my training ability with you and also to check your ability so I think we should let them do what they want to so as to not upset them," Captain T said with an air of resignation.

When we met the Inspectors I realised that they were the same two that had sat in with me on that infamous simulator session some months before. It transpired that they had been tracking me all the way along since I was of such a relative young age.

"Bloody hell, here we go again," I muttered to myself as we all exchanged licences to check each other's qualifications.

Captain T was a really nice chap and took me aside briefly and said that all was well with my file and just to do the job normally and all would be good. The weather at JFK was not too clever so we studied the Flight Plan in order to squeeze on some extra fuel which could well be needed at the end. The cost of fuel was now starting to make an impact on the economics of the airline and so fuel was continually being trimmed to the bone. For example, only a few years before we would plan to arrive at JFK with sufficient fuel to divert to Montreal plus a handsome contingency to cover the route phase. We now had a local airport in the New York area to divert to if necessary and maybe a stretch to Boston if really pushed.

On the Super VC-10 the manufacturers declared that the fuel consumption guaranteed to BA was not quite there and the aircraft used more fuel than calculated. The main reason for this was the fact that the aircraft was built 'Out of the solid' as they say and was heavier than calculated. To give you a comparison if you took all the fuel off and weighed the basic aircraft it turned out to be about seven tonnes heavier than the 707 was but with the same passenger capacity. This fact equated to more fuel to carry this extra weight. One smart idea was to create a fuel tank in the large vertical fin at the rear to get about another three tonnes of fuel on board. They followed this up with a simple balance calculation whereby taking some of the fuel out of the fin after take-off it could balance the aircraft better which might help improve the fuel scene. The Flight Engineer did the calculation as best he could and whilst I can recall it not making much difference, it looked good.

So there we were trying to justify some extra fuel on this particular flight to JFK since the last thing I wanted with the CAA breathing down my neck was to find myself short of fuel.

"Look, considering the situation and this weather plus strong Atlantic winds I am opting for enough extra fuel to give us plenty of scope when we get into the New York area. I am happy to talk to the Flight Manager when we get back to explain my decision," I said with an air of exasperation.

"No problem with me at all. That is exactly what I would have done," Captain T said with a nod of approval.

The two CAA guys nodded and so we now had a mutual nodding party. So we all went out to the aircraft and went about our business. We had a full load of passengers and a good cabin crew and it all went well with an on-time departure. The Atlantic crossing was pretty uneventful with me attempting to 'cover all angles'. There was a significant difference with flying to the States as opposed to the East based on the fact that the weather, routings and clearances could all change within minutes and you had to have a certain basic knowledge of the local scene in as much as the situation may need you, as the Captain, to make good sound decisions. This was all serious stuff but remember in those days we did not have the luxury of modern day systems and communications. The philosophy of BA at the time was that, once you left Heathrow, then you were the focal point of any down-route changes and is was up to you to hopefully get it right.

So, back to our flight. As we continued down the Eastern Seaboard towards JFK, the weather was not looking too bad with the chance of thunderstorms rating pretty high on the agenda which is what we had been expecting. It was bit of a squeeze with the five of us in the Flight Deck and luckily there were a couple of spare seats in the first class so the two CAA guys enjoyed the luxury of the first class lunch and gave us some breathing space. After the lunch Captain T did the rounds of the cabin so for a good part of the time there was room to breathe.

All that changed as we passed the Boston area with about one hour to go with the full squad tucked up complete with all eyes and ears on me. Captain T was very good in his role as Co-pilot feeding me all the information that I might need. It was at about this time that a massive thunderstorm passed over JFK and headed our way. It did some damage to the radio aids at JFK but were soon back on the air. We opted to do a re-route to the South so as to avoid the storm. One thing about the American controllers which is excellent is that they try their level best to help you out if they can. I asked the Chief Steward to close everything up and that for everybody to strap in since the ride here on in was going to be bumpy. Anyway we got our southerly routing and what's more a few other aircraft followed suit and so there was this trail of aircraft all going to JFK following us.

The storm that had now passed through JFK had created a backlog of arrivals so the delays to the approach were beginning to build up which, in my mind, totally justified the extra fuel that I had asked for back at Heathrow. The sky looked pretty vicious up ahead but we avoided the worst using our weather radar. One advantage was that the storms were going from south-west to north-east so we could get a sort of trend by checking the weather to the south-west of JFK at say, Baltimore, and see what was on the way. It is always a bit of luck when you arrive in these conditions as to whether you will land in between the storms or in the middle of one. From what I could see we might be in the lucky zone and so we started our descent into JFK. At times we had no choice but to go through the bad weather and it was quite a rocky ride. The VC-10 rides the weather well with the only disadvantage being that the fuselage tends to nod up and down since the wings are a long way back.

On the Flight Deck it seemed to be irrelevant that I was under training since we all mucked in with the operation checking fuel state, aircraft state, weather state and the state of the ground facilities. A few aircraft ahead of us had diverted already due to low fuel state since most of us had arrived from Europe and fuel was always tight. We got to the holding area and were told that we must stay there for about 20 minutes. That involved flying in a racetrack pattern for the allotted time. Being in the basic days of instruments it was a fine art to keep the racetrack tidy with the winds blowing all over the place. As we went round and round we looked at all the options in case the weather caved in again and we had to divert to Boston or somewhere that way. These storm systems that invade the Eastern Seaboard are notorious in strength and direction and could very easily render maybe two good airports out of action at the same time. The tempo was certainly heating up!

After what seemed like an eternity the JFK controllers gave us the approach clearance and so we moved onwards and downwards towards the runway. Just to add to the fun the runway in use did not have the usual precision ILS system but rather a basic VOR system so we had to work the approach path using the distance indicated from the runway and the height that we should be at. To add to the fun I was flying manually and being tossed around by the turbulence. As we turned onto the final approach path we did a final fuel assessment and decreed that if we could not land then we were on our way to the North-east with no delay. The radar was belting away and showed a new storm cell about five miles south-west of the runway and it became a race between me and it as to who was going to arrive at the runway first. I won by the skin of my teeth! As we taxied off the runway all hell broke loose as the storm broke right on top of us. Once clear of the runway we parked up for the duration of the storm. We had the airport to ourselves by this time since the authorities had closed it until the weather cleared. I reckon I had earned my four stripes out there in the 'parking lot' and by the time we eventually got to the gate I was pretty well burnt out. As we shut down there seemed to be a hush on the Flight Deck from all five of us.

"I don't know about you lot but I need a drink!" was my only comment worth saying.

It was generally agreed between all of us that the end result was pretty good irrespective of whether I was under the watchful eye or not.

"So much for the company screaming at us about carrying extra fuel. We needed every drop today. Good operation, Gwyn. Now let's get at that drink," Captain T said.

The Cabin Crew was very quiet as well, having been thrown about as we were. Once we go onto the bus the Chief Steward quietly asked me if it was OK for a beer at the back of the bus. I pondered for a few seconds and declared an open bar for anyone on the bus including the 'two Ronnies' from the CAA. That broke the ice and the journey to Manhattan became a very social affair. Another nodding session followed sealing their approval that this young potential Captain was doing the right thing. Me, I was fast asleep with a half consumed Fosters can of beer just hanging off my fingertips.

We had a day off in New York so the Flight Deck crew met up with the Cabin Crew for the evening of the following day and we all had a few drinks and a great meal at the local 'Tads Steak House' and had a mini celebration that at least the weather had improved to become a balmy autumn evening. By this time, the two CAA guys had high-tailed it to Heathrow so the pressure was off for the time being. Captain T explained that I had to one more sector acting as a Co-pilot on the return to Heathrow so the pressure was really off and the beer flowed.

The following day we set sail back to Heathrow with me doing my 'support crew' bit and we arrived in Heathrow in the early hours. Captain T went through the entire file on me from the beginning to end checking and double checking that I had covered everything and then announced:

"Right Gwyn, you have ticked all the boxes as far as I can see except the 'big one' which will be your final check on your next flight. I will let the boss know."

"Right," I said, gathering all the enthusiasm I could muster.

"Chances are that it will be a straightforward flight to Bahrain or somewhere like that. They only need one sector flying and a second one as the co-pilot and you will be done," he replied.

"Right," I said again.

I had an agonising week waiting until the roster fell through the door. It was a bit of a surprise and consisted of Heathrow to Addis Ababa, Ethiopia via Paris, France and back via Khartoum. I had not been to Paris or Addis so this was going to be fun. The Checker was Captain O whom I knew to be a really nice guy.

So on the 22nd October I reported to Heathrow and met up with the crew for the check flight and was pleasantly surprised to find that Captain O had not been to Paris either so it was the 'blind leading the blind'. I had by now become quite proficient at getting the pre-flight bits done and on schedule Super VC-10 G-ASGP taxied out for the short flight to Paris. After departure we were faced with a one hour flight to the new Paris airport of Charles de Gaulle. It was a bit hectic since this was a BEA sort of sector and unusual for us. The French being the French had inbound routes designed to avoid all the noise sensitive areas which made the flying side a bit exacting.

We landed OK and that was where the fun began. The terminals consist of large circular affairs and a one way taxiing system in place based on the fact that if you were arriving you went clockwise around the terminal and if you were departing you went anti-clockwise. So we entered the clockwise stream and missed the entrance to the gate on the first pass and asked if we could just double-back. 'No chance' was the answer so off we went again for another circuit and just made the entry to the gate this time. Anyway all very minor but since we were both unfamiliar to the airport all was forgiven.

For my final check I only required one sector but Captain O suggested that I flew it to Addis since Heathrow to Paris was too short for him to sign me off. I had no problem with that so we once again got all our bits done and off we went through the night to deepest Africa. Addis Airport is an interesting place with the runway laid out on the top of a hill so that on all sides the ground fell away which made it a bit tricky to judge the landing coupled with the fact that we were about 7,500 ft high so the odds were bit stacked against us. In the end the arrival was not too bad and as we came to a halt on the ramp Captain O said:

"That's fine, Gwyn. Two nice sectors so I will sign you off and all you need is to be a Co-pilot for me up to Khartoum in a couple of days and you will be done."

"Right," I said with a big banana style grin on my face.

After the standard couple of beers and a good sleep the complete crew assembled in the bar for the evening. We went to a restaurant well known to airline crews and had a bit of a rave up. We ended up in some nightclub swinging the night away. I really felt that I had arrived at the end of the rainbow and it showed. Addis in those days was very safe with none of the political dramas of today. The following day was generally spent recovering from the night before and saw us all in a huddle around the swimming pool on soft drinks. The evening was a bit of a quiet affair since we were off early the next day back home. Hopefully this will be my finest hour. In the morning we all assembled and off we went to the airport. The flight to Khartoum went like clockwork with me doing my support bit well enough for Captain O to say after arrival on the ramp:

"That is the end of your course, Gwyn, or rather 'Captain Mullett'. From now on you are on your own. Congratulations and well done. All you have to do now is to decide who does the next sector."

At this point he leaned across and shook my hand followed by the Flight Engineer.

"It'll be a bit tricky flying with such a young'un barking orders at me!" the Flight Engineer said with a grin.

"By the way, Gwyn, I did some checking and you are the youngest Captain in the long haul side of BA since 1949, so you have done very well."

"Thank you, sir. It has been a long haul. In fact, it has been six months and 20 days to be exact. There will be the party of all parties when I get home. Be my guest and fly us to Heathrow," I replied.

The grin remained for some time and when I got out of my seat for a stretch the Cabin Crew chipped in with handshakes and kisses all around. The girls remarked that I was very young to be a Captain and I replied by telling them to look out in the future if we fly together again.

Another fricking miracle, I thought as I clambered back into the left-hand seat for the final sector to Heathrow.

We eventually landed back at Heathrow in the early evening and when we handed in our various items there was Pete Dyson who had just passed the final hurdle as well. It was decided that instead of going home I would stay with Pete and we could do our celebrating together. It transpired that of the nine of us at the start five of us had made it through OK which was pretty much as forecast. When we got to Pete's, phone calls were made and it was agreed that a few of us would get together the following evening at Ed Murray's place in Sunningdale for one heck of a bash. I didn't see the point of going home anyway since there was no real support there and, besides, Pam had moved on and was playing around with most of HMS Invincible by then. I rang Mavis and made plans to go up and see her soon. She was very pleased for me considering that she was all new to the airline world, let alone Pilots.

We hit Ed's the next night pretty hard and partied on through the night. Eventually after about three days of partying and catching up with the rest of the Hamsters who had made it through I managed to make it home and found the usual atmosphere too much to take and left the next day and flew up to Prestwick in the back of a BA freighter. There did not seem to be a problem with that arrangement with Pam. Mavis was chuffed to bits when I rolled in and I waited at her place for the first flight as a real Captain to come along. By coincidence my good mates Ian and Tony had got their commands at about the same time. Ian ended up on the Vickers Viscount flying around the UK and Tony got his on the Avro 748 flying around Scotland. The three Musketeers had all made it together.

Chapter 7

– MY LIFE AS A VC-10 CAPTAIN

I didn't have to wait long before the first roster as Captain arrived. It was to fly from Prestwick to Toronto via Montreal and return the same way after a day off in Toronto. The funny thing was that I was already in Prestwick so I thought that I could just stay there and meet up with the crew when they arrive from Heathrow. I thought wrong! BA decreed that I travel all the way to Heathrow to sign on and then travel all the way back to Prestwick via Glasgow to make things all correct. Who was I to argue! Not on my first outing anyway.

So off I went very early to Glasgow and flew down to Heathrow on the shuttle flight just to sign in the book at the crew reporting office. The Co-pilot was John Cater who became famous as a training Captain on the 747-400 many years later. The Flight Engineer was Peter Grant whom I had known for some time. Two great blokes though. I decided not to let on that this was my first trip in command to add to the fun. We all met up together with the Cabin Crew and all flew back on the shuttle flight to Glasgow and then by coach to Prestwick arriving in the early evening. The whole day had been filled with travelling. We stayed in the Marine Hotel in Troon and Mavis joined us for dinner. Neither John nor Peter cottoned on to the fact that this was my first as Captain with my shiny new stripes on my jacket. Incidentally my official rank was 'Captain, second Class' and I was entitled to have the four stripes stitched on my uniform jacket but only half way round, such was the protocol of the day. I didn't care though since they were on!

On October 29th 1976 in the late morning Super VC-10 G-ASGK arrived on the Prestwick ramp from Manchester and she was all mine to take to Montreal and Toronto. It felt really strange with the ground people all fussing around and coming up to me with the usual problems, addressing me as 'Captain'. The Cabin Crew were really nice and the Chief Steward comes up to me with the question:

"Sir, do I call you Sir, Captain or Skipper?"

Right my first big decision of the day had to be made.

"Skipper would be fine on board, but Gwyn when we get off the aircraft would be nice," I said as if my life depended on it.

There, that was easy! I thought.

"Now for the minor decisions like the weather, fuel, aircraft state etc."

We departed on schedule and as I took off and flew west out over the Island of Arran it felt like doing my first solo all over again. Wow, it felt good! We had no problems getting the track and altitude that we requested since we were well north of the normal tracks of the day.

"When do you feel it right to serve lunch, skipper?" asked the Chief Steward after about an hour.

This felt good and I was enjoying the freedom from the training shackles.

"There is no turbulence up ahead so I would get the meal service going at your leisure," I replied.

"Right, Skipper. Oh, by the way, we have a delicious lady in 2A whom I am sure would love to have the Captain dine with her" he chipped in.

"I am on my way - hold the first course!" I said with a grin from ear to ear.

John and Peter settled in to hold the fort whilst I skipped back and settled in the seat next to this luscious blonde and we had a great lunch and banter for at least two hours. This was indeed the life! Not bad for someone who could not speak the Queen's English properly. After lunch I strolled back onto the Flight Deck and was confronted by Peter who said:

"Can we ask you when you finished your training and what trips have you done as Captain? John and I have money on this."

"Right, I've been caught out by you two. This is my first one, so look out," I replied.

"Bloody hell, a virgin," Peter said with a grin.

"We will have one hell of a party in Toronto then. Do the Cabin crew know?" said John.

"No, but I suppose that you will tell them at some stage," I said.

"Too bloody right I will," Pete said.

So the cat was out of the bag but what the heck! I had come this far and all was well. And so we continued on towards Montreal. A short while later the second steward, Patrick, from down the back appeared on the Flight Deck and uttered a strong condemnation about the behaviour of the Chief Steward towards him and how he was out to get him. What it was, in fact, was a lover's tiff since they were both of the same leaning. He continued his rant asking me to talk to the Chief Steward and, in effect, sort out his love life.

"Bloody hell, they never told me about this on the course," was my comment as he scurried off the Flight Deck.

Within seconds the Chief Steward, Paddy, appeared and demanded to know what the 'bitch' was complaining about.

Nice way to refer to one of the crew, I thought.

Anyway, I struggled to try to put a reasoned argument forward since this situation was not one I was familiar with. In the end I said for the two of them to stop bickering and do the job in hand and sort out their differences on the ground. The Chief Steward huffed and puffed his way out of the Flight Deck and the three of us sat back chuckling about it all. I then disappeared down the back and gave the same edict to Patrick. On my way to the back of the aircraft Paddy asked me if Patrick was all right and should he go down the back to comfort him. The emotional workings of these sort of relationships were, and still are, beyond me let alone the Man v Woman scenario!

Anyway we finally made it to Montreal and landed OK and once we got onto the gate I breathed a sigh of relief that my first solo went off OK except for the drama with the 'girls'. The weather was kind to me as well and after 40 or so minutes we set sail to Toronto and landed there on a beautiful late afternoon autumn day and so I had completed my first trip in command and it felt very good.

We did have a bit of a party that night and I took the time out to phone my step sister Angela and her husband Roger who lived in Toronto and they joined us for the celebrations. The 'girls' from down the back had made up and were all over each other. I think we all ended up in some shady bar in the city until the early hours.

The following day was a day off and was spent mostly in bed recovering from the previous night's excesses. In the late afternoon we all gathered for the return flight to Prestwick via Montreal. Once again the weather was nice to me and the flight went like clockwork. Once we arrived at Prestwick we all piled onto a coach and went over to Glasgow to take the shuttle down to Heathrow. I suppose I could have stayed with Mavis but I felt it was time to go home and try to get things sorted out. I got home in the early evening to a very icy reception which I found amazing, since Pam was playing the field with the Royal Navy – but maybe I was not allowed to by her rules. Considering that this was my first trip and we were both playing away why the long face? Really ruined the day it did.

I then had some holiday due and spent it at home. Now that was a fun two weeks if ever there was one! Pam was working every day in Portsmouth and obviously resented me being around. I think the fact that Mavis was so far away started to dwell heavily on me. Having said that, there was one particular night when I went off to the pub on my own for a drink and when I came out at about 11 pm I took a long breath and decided there and then to drive to Prestwick and see Mavis. Fortunately, at the time I was in the MGB which made my impulsive mood easier to execute. I will point out that I had had very little alcohol but maybe just enough to make this mad decision. So I climbed in and off I went. I can remember that there was a football match on the radio to listen to for the first couple of hours. It was England v Chile. I think we lost. Now there's a surprise!

At about 2 am I hit the M1 and it was pretty clear that the brain was getting tired. Various pit stops came into view and I did take a few breaks to replenish the coffee intake. At about 4 am the M1 finished and I drifted onto the M6 and then onto 'A' roads and crossed the England/Scotland frontier at about 6 am. I must have been mad to do this but at that point I felt the goal was slowly coming into sight. At about 8 am I rolled up outside Mavis's house and it coincided with the kids getting up and having breakfast before school. As the curtains were pulled back one of the kids spotted me and next thing a very dishevelled Mavis struggled out of the front door and there I was having breakfast with the kids. What a crazy man!

We did have a very nice day together but in the evening I decided to drive all the way back to Southampton such was my impulsive nature.

So off I went again all the way through the second night driving home. I must have been going through a minefield of emotions at this point. As I have said many times flying is one thing and women are another. I could not wait for the end of my leave and get back in the saddle once again.

It was at about this time that a good friend of mine, John Penwill, who was a fellow 'Hamster', was on his command course on the VC-10 and seemed to be having a few problems on the base training at Prestwick. He had been sent home to have a few days off before going back up to Prestwick. He lived not far away so I went to see him to try, in my small way, to help him. I found him mowing the grass and I felt sorry for the motor mower since he seemed to be taking all his aggression out on it. We sat down and went over his problem as much as we could.

At this stage I was quite friendly with the fleet training secretary and I made a phone call to her to see if I could get the 'Inside track'. She was really helpful and I relayed her words to John and he made his way back up to Prestwick to attempt to complete his base flying with a clearer head. He made it through the base flying OK which was great. On one occasion when he was flying the route training bit we coincided and I had suggested that before any flight to have a good meal so that would be one less distraction. So off I go round to John's for breakfast before we both hit the road to Heathrow. Bridie, his wife, was a lovely Irish lady and the breakfast she served up was fit for a king. There was nothing missing. She took me at my word and stoked us both up with enough food to feed an army. We both waddled to the car and off we went. John passed his command course a few weeks later. Good lad!

My next trip was a long one out east to Kuwait for a night stop via Baghdad and then on to Colombo for a few days off and then down to Johannesburg, South Africa via the Seychelles, finally passengering home on the 747. So off I went in early November on my travels again. Compared with women this side of my life was really settling down well and the trip turned out to be a very social one since we kept the Cabin Crew all the way round and so fun was had all over the place.

Colombo was a particular favourite of mine since we were generally the only people in the hotel together with the VC-10 crews of the RAF who had a regular run to the Far East. In the RAF the VC-10 was known as the 'Shiny Ten' and attracted the more mature sort of Captains so when we bounced into the bar eyebrows were raised. Invariably there were up to three crews staying there and so it was a party every night by the pool. It was unfortunate that in the lobby was a magnificent model of the VC-10 on a stand. It must have measured about five across and at the end of the night it was quite often removed and launched into the pool under the pretext of ditching trails. In the morning the pool attendants would be seen pulling it out and drying it out and remounting it in the lobby ready for the next trials.

After about ten days away I eventually get home pretty exhausted. I have to say I was really enjoying my new status. At home Pam and I started serious talks about our marriage and what could be done, if anything, to save it. One thing we did decide was to move house and within a short period of time we had moved to a house in the northern suburbs of Southampton.

In the news in November President Carter was elected as the President of the United States. It did not mean too much to me but as world events unfolded it was dramatic four years for America.

I had about ten days off and would you believe it the training office called for me to go for a local training flight one evening on 'VM'. Apparently this was normal with new Captains so off I went for a session one evening. It all seemed to go all right and as we got back to Heathrow it transpired that we also had to do a Simulator session as well within a couple of days. I did feel a bit aggrieved over all this attention since I had only had the command about one month. The trainer casually remarked that it had been known for new Captains to be 'chopped' even when promoted since we were basically on probation for the first six months. I never knew all of this so it was a bit of a shock to the system. However, I did the Simulator session after a couple of days and once again I was cleared to continue as a Captain.

I got back to the flying in early December with a couple of Western trips and then ended up in Cairo for Christmas Eve flying back home on Christmas day. The VC-10 fleet was now down to about ten aircraft so the infamous bid line system was suspended and replaced by simple rostering which was good for me since I was very junior on the fleet. I got my come-uppance however over the New Year when I spent six days shuttling between Manchester and Prestwick. After each short flight we stayed there for a day and then repeated it the next day. I did have New Year's Eve in Manchester but it was a bit muted since I was due out the following morning to Prestwick at about 10 am. Mavis got my full attention when I was in Prestwick which was really nice and relaxing. So ended 1976 that for me had been an amazing year. However, on the emotional side it had been a real rollercoaster – but this was nothing compared to what was about to unfold. Read on!

So along comes 1977 and the amount of flying increased since the retirements of the old wartime Captains had moved up a gear. My trips took on a great variety of routes and one minute I was in the States and then the next I was somewhere out East or in Africa. With the increased numbers of 747s joining BA I found that our stopovers were getting longer which made the route flying very enjoyable and relaxing with very little times when I was totally burnt out due to tiredness. As far as the VC-10 was concerned the fleet was becoming a family since most of the Captains were now of my variety and meeting up down route was good fun. I think that on at least two occasions I was in the envious position of being the youngest member of the crew. This fact I played to my advantage as you could imagine. Boy was I having a ball! Although I was still technically married we both did our own thing and I maybe went home for a couple of days per month to catch up with all things domestic.

In the news in January Commodore launched the first home computer, the 'Commodore Pet' in Chicago quickly followed by the BBC computer launch in the UK. In the March there was a terrible aircraft accident in Tenerife where a KLM 747 taking off collided with a Panam 747 that was still on the runway; 583 people died that day and this still holds the dreadful record as the worst of all accidents. Both aircraft had diverted to an unfamiliar airport due to fog and after a series of communications breakdowns the collision occurred.

Also in March Mavis, together with her friend Terry and his girlfriend, came down to London to stay for a couple of nights. It was Terry who organised it since he was going to Barbados on holiday. I have no idea of his connections but we stayed in an apartment right in the centre of the London next to Soho with all the trimmings to go with it. It was very enjoyable to be able to walk maybe 50 yards and there you were in the heart of the entertainment area. Clever guy! After a couple of days Mavis and Terry's girlfriend went off back to Scotland and I went off flying. I do not know what happened between Mavis and me after the stay in London but our relationship just seemed to peter out. Maybe it was the logistics of the distances involved or maybe it was me. Who knows!

In the May I heard the sad news that one of our instructors at Hamble had died in a 707 landing accident in Lusaka, Zambia. His name was Jim Collier and he had left Hamble a few years before to fly this fated 707 Freighter. What actually happened was that the tail fell off due to metal fatigue as the crew selected the final flaps for landing.

Also in May I did a bit of an epic flight out of Bermuda to Mexico via Freeport, Grand Bahamas. As we flew from Freeport on the final leg to Mexico with our usual minimum fuel scene thunderstorms built up as we approached and then we were told that the airport was shut. I opted to divert to Acapulco on the southern coast of Mexico. We had to climb up out of the Mexico area over some relatively high mountains and in doing so managed to surge one of the engines. It was a well-known fact that the engines on the Super VC-10 were prone to high altitude surging but to witness it for the first time was a bit of a shock. The Flight Engineer was under training at the time so the lesson was learnt. The engine recovered OK in fact and we landed in Acapulco in the early hours to a deserted airport. Having no ability to speak Spanish we had great problems with the ground staff to explain that we needed to stay for the night. We eventually made it to a hotel after a lot of negotiating and we did have a bit of a room party to celebrate our arrival. Any old excuse will do!

In the morning we made our way out to the aircraft with our passengers and this is where it became interesting. As we asked for start-up there were various comments on the radio as to our shape and engine layout.

"Who makes that aircraft, Boeing or Douglas?" some smarmy American voice said.

"This machine is built by Vickers Armstrong of Weighbridge,

England and is the pride of the British Aviation Industry," I replied to all interested parties.

As we taxied out then the chat got more inquisitive.

"Does she fly well then?" was one comment that really got to me.

At this point I asked the Control Tower if we could do a low circuit of the famous Acapulco Bay and then a 'Fly by' of the tower before setting sail to Mexico.

"Permission granted," was the response.

Well, the VC-10 flew like a bird around the bay at a relatively low altitude and the final 'icing on the aviation cake' was the low run over the airport and then pouring on the power and climbing away 'like a homesick angel'. Wow it felt good!

"What a beautiful sight. God bless you, Mr Vickers," was a comment heard on the radio.

I hasten to add that it was totally forbidden to do anything like this but the recording systems on the aircraft would never have picked it up. We eventually arrived in Nassau via Mexico to a bemused crew who were taking the aircraft on to Heathrow. That trip was a bit different to the normal one.

Also in the May one of my Hamster friends had left home for a Stewardess and so I made a point of visiting the deserted wife but then away I went again into a romance of short duration. I even stayed with her a few times between trips. I can remember playing happy families and seeing the cult film 'Star Wars' with her kids at the local cinema. What I did not know was that she was in fact having a fling with the local builder. So, that romance got assigned to the scrapheap by the end of June. I should have stayed in the clouds to be safe!

In the July, by chance I met up with one of our Japanese Stewardesses by the name of Koko. What happened was that local girls were recruited in various countries to add to the international flavour in the cabin. We had Jamaican, Indian, Pakistani, Chinese and Japanese stewardesses. They were collectively known as the 'national' stewardesses. With a few days off at various places out east there was plenty of time and opportunity to get social with them. This is where Koko came about. I would meet her when she came to Heathrow and she had the ability to work her rosters around wherever I happened to be in the Far East. Not having the famous Bid Line then it was not too difficult to get the Eastern trips that I wanted.

The problem with Koko was the clash of cultures between West and East. She would meet me in Tokyo and adopt the complete Flight Crew and look after us royally. I do confess that I was a bit dishonest about my marital status. Her ideas were based around marriage and it came to a head when I met her once in Tokyo and she took me home to meet her parents. Whilst in my eyes there was nothing wrong with that the opposite was true where she was concerned. The idea was to show me to her parents with the view of marriage.

It was, however, an amazing evening, with Koko's father, who was a retired Sumo wrestler, and me sitting cross-legged on the floor and being served the weirdest of food by Koko and her mother. At the end of the meal the father let out an enormous belch which signified his total approval of the food. I nearly jumped out of my skin when he did it. I stayed for the night which proved pretty interesting in its own right. There I was struggling to sleep on this hard mattress on the floor with the sound of the father snoring like a trooper a few feet away behind a bamboo screen which marked the boundary of the bedroom. In fact all the bedrooms were separated by these skinny bamboo screens.

I was just about asleep when there was a movement at the side of the bed and there was Koko clambering into my camp. What could I do but to take her on board and we moved beyond the cuddling stage with both of us desperately trying to keep the noise down. Not an easy job! Anyway, as things moved up a gear then suddenly the snoring from beyond the screen stopped abruptly and my heart leapt many multiple beats. I suddenly envisaged the wrath of a father bearing down on me with a Samurai Sword in the killing position and me ending up in the pot for breakfast. Well, it took the wind out of my sails and any amorous thoughts went straight on the back boiler. Koko seemed unmoved by the silence from next door so maybe it was expected or something like that! All activity ceased at that moment and I had to shove her out of the door to return to the land of the living. What a night that was! We did still continue to be an item for the next few weeks but no home visits please. In the end Koko must have realised that I was not the marrying kind and opted for a Panam Co-pilot and my Japanese season ended.

In the August I had my first major incident on the aircraft. We had just taken off from Tokyo towards the north when right on the 'rotate' speed No. 3 Engine caught fire. The Co-pilot was Dick Long and the Flight Engineer was Lance Varty and as the fire indicator lit up we did the drills as if we were in the simulator and I turned to the right out over Tokyo Bay, much to the dismay of the Controller, since I wanted to avoid the city centre and in particular the famous Tokyo Tower which would have been right in our path had we carried straight on. The fire took a full 30 seconds to extinguish which just stopped us firing the second bottle. We tidied up the drills and then considered what to do. We opted to dump some fuel and go back into Tokyo. There were some thunderstorms in the area and we needed a professional translator to speak to the Controllers about where and when to dump fuel without the onset of the chance of being struck by lightning from the nearby thunderstorms.

We eventually landed back into Tokyo, being chased down the runway by half of the city's fire engines with little Japanese men in silver suits leaping about all over the place as we came to a stop. On the VC-10 it was authorised for an ordinary line Captain like me to do a ferry flight on three engines to an airport where the broken engine could be replaced. Hong Kong had the spare engine so after we had transferred the passengers to another airline the complete crew climbed aboard and off we went on three engines to Hong Kong arriving in the early evening. By the time we got to the hotel it was cocktail hour in the famous Dickens Bar at the Excelsior Hotel and so we all assembled for a well-earned party.

It was amazing the power that the Captains had in those days to run the show to the point that we decided the course of events after the 'Tokyo Incident' and did not once have to talk to any management types to get this and that permission. We just did it and then let Operations know what we were doing. Funnily enough it worked! I finally got home after some ten days away.

While I was home I was taking Pam to work one day when the radio cut in with the news that the pop icon Elvis Presley had died in Memphis, USA.

CHAPTER 7

One of our trip schedules took us to Dar es Salaam, Tanzania for a five-day stop over. It was like a five day mini-holiday with the hotel right on the beach and good fresh food everyday including locally caught lobster with a price tag in pennies. What happened there was that on the second or third day we would do a shuttle to Blantyre, Malawi leaving at about 10 am and getting back at about 4 pm. Gentlemen's hours you might say.

Dar es Salaam was also the haunt of Lufthansa with their 707 and since we both were on a small fleet within our two airlines we frequently met up with the same German crews on arrival. Lufthansa also had the five day holiday with a similar shuttle to us but to Mauritius and back. As each crew departed for the airport then the gauntlet was laid down as to who could do the smoothest of low passes of the hotel before setting sail. I can remember on more than one occasion sitting on the beach and watching the Lufthansa 707 gently cruising by at about 300 ft about 500 yards off-shore and then sweeping to the East on its travels. In the evening when the 'flypast' crew arrived back in the hotel then a crew forum would be held over a few beers to discuss the merits of the flying skills earlier in the day.

Likewise when we departed for Blantyre we would cruise just offshore past the hotel with the added advantage of a deafening departure as we turned towards the sea. I have the feeling that the hotel foundations shook somewhat as we left. In the evening the usual debate took place at cocktail hour whilst sitting cross legged on the beach as the African sunset produced a wonderful backdrop.

It was on one of these trips in the August that I got acquainted with my first female of German origin. Her name was Inga and she came from Frankfurt. You see, in the evenings the hotel was the only place for entertainment since we were pretty much isolated and to venture out after dark was not recommended. There were, maybe, up to 30 of us airline crew in the hotel on any one night being a mix of Lufthansa and BA. When it came to dinner the hotel laid on one long table, large enough for all of us to sit, eat and drink together. Being totally sociable with our German friends we would make a point of intermixing the seating so that a 'true European Community' scene would prevail.

It was at one of these dinners that I got deep in conversation with

Inga and so the candle was lit between us well and truly. What was I to do! She was blonde, tall and very well put together and spoke excellent English and without any ties such as boyfriend or husband. She was one of the Pursers with Lufthansa and of course the option of a visit to Frankfurt was on the table. For the remainder of the stay in 'Dar' we enjoyed each other's company and it was agreed that I would come over to Frankfurt sometime soon.

As an aside to the romance of 'Dar' we also had a very good relationship with the hotel staff. The room boys were very dedicated in their role. I remember on a previous trip there my assigned room boy suffered from a lack of walkable footwear so I guessed his shoe size and when back home I bought him a pair of the 'Bata' shoes that were all the rage. On my next visit I presented the shoes to him on arrival at my room. You would have thought that I had given him the Crown Jewels and to see his face light up was a picture. From that moment on he was my shadow and I was looked after like a VIP. He seemed to sense when I would struggle out of bed in the morning and within minutes a tray complete with English tea and biscuits would be presented by my bedside. It even got to the point whereby, on subsequent visits, he would virtually threaten any other room boy who dared come within a yard of my suitcase on arrival. He then would proudly show me the latest state of his 'Bata' trainers. There is nothing like having your own personal valet on tap!

Back to Inga! I did go over to Frankfurt on a couple of occasions and stayed with her in her apartment. Fun was had by one and all and I would crawl back to the UK with my tail between my legs on each occasion. After a couple of months then the inevitable happened whereby the distance factor entered the equation and so my first foray into all things German ended. Little did I know that many, many years later it would raise its head once more.

The other passion that I rekindled was horse riding. Cairo was the place for that and, if you recall, I had a fleeting encounter with the four-legged beast way back on my 'Look See' trip in 1966. The experience then had not put me off and I persevered until I became quite competent again and would often arrive at 6 am at the stables by the Pyramids on my own to ride the stable stallion with the boss on a similar steed and we would tear across the desert neck and neck to arrive at the small eatery in the desert for a breakfast of fruit, toast and the strongest coffee put on this planet. By then, the crew stayed in the Swiss hotel that was right next door to the stables and the Pyramids.

On one occasion the complete crew were invited to join the boss for the celebrations to mark the end of the fasting month of Ramadan. I think maybe two or three of us went just before sunset and rode out into the desert to a huge Bedouin style tent and enjoyed a magical evening with all eyes cast on the New Moon rising in the East which marked the end of the Islamic fasting month. Obviously, there was no alcohol but the magic of the evening overshadowed the drink issue. It was really strange riding away from the tent back to the stables very late at night in virtual pitch darkness and putting all your faith in your horse to pick his way home unaided. It was one of those happenings that will be scratched on the brain forever.

In the October of that year there was nasty hijack of a Lufthansa 737 that ended up in Mogadishu, Somalia. The demands this time were for the release of members of the Red Army Faction terrorist group that were imprisoned in Germany. It was particularly brutal since the Palestinian hijackers murdered the aircraft Captain in front of the passengers. An assault by Somali, German and British commandos ended the siege. It was bitter irony that some members of the imprisoned group committed suicide soon after the events in Mogadishu.

It was also in the October that my helter-skelter life of failed relationships suddenly took a turn for the better. It was on an ordinary trip to Cairo and I can remember inviting all of the crew to my room for an arrival drink. The room opened up into the hotel garden so was ideal. Amongst the ladies that arrived was one who seemed to get my attention in more ways than one. She was a little shorter than me and it was her eyes and hair that attracted me. Her eyes were bright blue and sparkling and her hair was 'perm' style such that if she leaned forward and then threw her head back the hair would follow after a couple of seconds and just sit there as if she had spent a long time placing each strand by hand. Her name was Moya and I nicknamed her

'Dougal' after the Magic Roundabout TV cult series. Bloody lovely she was! I remember the evening was very relaxing with no shenanigans at all. In fact, the conversation was about our two lives. Moya was married to Dave though so it seemed that I had missed the boat yet again.

When we all returned to Heathrow we decided it would be really nice to stay in touch via the letter rack in the crew report centre. Now, therein lies a story about the famous letter rack in the crew report area. I would not like to know the things that went on between various crew members with the main point of contact being this letter rack. World decisions, marriage decisions, union decisions and affair updates all passed through this rack at some time. When crews arrived for a departure the first port of call was the letter rack and the second was the actual job in hand. This combined with the picking up and dropping off point downstairs on the ground level made the crew report centre the hub of the British Airways social scene.

In the November Moya and I bumped into each other again when I checked in to go to Tehran. It put a whole new slant on the trip. In Tehran we teamed up together and went off to explore the fleshpots of downtown Tehran. In those days the Shah still ruled with absolute authority and any chance of an Islamic revolution just did not seem to be apparent. Anyway, in 'Rays Pizza 2' it certainly didn't seem that way with Moya and me enjoying each other's company oblivious of our surroundings. We finished the trip more than just good friends.

In the news in November the visit of Anwar Sadat, President of Egypt, to Israel to address the Jewish parliament made headlines. Maybe there was a chance of peace in the Middle East. However, he was assassinated in October 1981. On a more cheerful note in November the Concorde was finally allowed to operate into JFK after a long and agonising wait. BA operated two services a day priced at about £9,000 one-way. The service was very popular amongst the elite business and well-to-do types. In New York, another table was allotted for the Concorde lot in Joe's bar.

As for Moya, we kept in touch via the letter rack and our relationship seemed to give me a new bounce in my step whereby I felt there was a future outside of my present disastrous marriage. Back in Southampton Pam and I decided to go down the 'quickie' divorce route and we started to get the paperwork organised to get it done. There was an incredible tension in the house as you can imagine with all that was going on around us, with claims and counterclaims being thrown about like confetti.

In the early December Moya and I linked up again on a trip where we ended up in Khartoum and for a couple of days the city became the party capital of the world. We seemed to have the right mix of people on the crew. The Co-pilot was Chris Challenger and the Flight Engineer was Garry Cowan. I cannot remember all of the Cabin Crew names but I remember the Chief Steward was Maxi Hall. In those days Sudan had not banned alcohol and the local beer flowed well plus some other concoctions. By the time we hit the trail back to Heathrow I think everybody was ready for a complete drying out session. I can always remember seeing the state of Garry Cowan's eyes and wondering what they were like from his side. Once we all got back to Heathrow Moya and I decided that come what may we would keep in touch despite both of us being married to other people.

1977 came to a close and can be summarised by a chaotic year for the first nine months and then a rather nice three months. Besides, Moya had outlasted all of the other relationships since either I had finished them or I was given the honourable boot.

1978 arrived with me back in Khartoum for the New Year and then onto Dar es Salaam. On our return Khartoum closed on us due to sandstorms and we ended up in the idyllic small airport of Kilimanjaro, Tanzania. It nestled in the foothills of Mount Kilimanjaro and with us on the ramp the airport was full. We elected to fly direct to Rome from there and I called BA to get a fresh crew out to Rome to take the aircraft onto Heathrow. I can remember sitting up in the small control tower drinking tea with the controller and watching the small refuelling bowser make what must have been its sixth or seventh trip to the fuel farm to get all the fuel on board. After take-off I did a low lazy turn to the north and caught some magnificent views of Mount Kilimanjaro as we climbed away. When we arrived at Rome sure enough there was a fresh crew to take the flight on to Heathrow. The system worked like clockwork! We all stayed in Rome and then travelled back home on the Trident the next day.

In the news in the January an Air India 747 crashed shortly after departure from Bombay due to an instrument failure. In the March the ex-Premier of Italy Aldo Morrow was kidnapped by a rebel group and his body was found two months later. The age of headline grabbing sensational kidnappings had arrived. Also in March the Israelis invaded Southern Lebanon in what was to become a disastrous campaign. An insignificant news item occurred in April whereby there was a coup in Afghanistan and a republic was declared. This seemed unworthy of note at the time but it started a chain reaction, the results of which are with us today.

In the April a nuclear explosion took place at home. I had just returned off a flight arriving in the late afternoon and by then I was back to the Mini. On the trip I had just done I had made arrangements through a contact to have the car sprayed courtesy of the BA paint shop. So there I was driving this car complete with a new coat of paint in red and a white roof. It looked really good but did nothing for the performance of the car. In the early evening Pam arrived home in the MG-BGT and the mother of all rows started. No idea what about but I think by then we were both at the end of our tethers. After maybe 30 minutes of this I decided that it was safer to leave rather than stay since we could well have killed each other.

By an amazing fluke my suitcase and briefcase were still in the Mini and so I announced that 'I was off'. I stomped out of the front door in the failing light to the awaiting Mini hotly pursued by Pam who was pretty mad. As I got into the car, that was maybe about 20 metres from the house, she stood defiantly screaming at me words that would make a sailor blush and then looked around the door area and picked up a small rock from the garden and lobbed it at the car. That act took me totally by surprise and as I fired up the 4-cylinder 800ccs 40 BHP monster engine. I managed to force open the famous Mini sliding window and shouted:

"Please don't hit the paintwork – I have only just had it sprayed."

Not a good thing to say in the circumstances and Pam's reaction was to grab a bigger rock and lob it at the car with more force than an Olympic Greek Discus thrower. Fortunately her aim was off and she missed the car again. I think if I had stayed any longer then she would have uprooted the whole house with her bare hands and plonked it on top of my head plus the car. She was pretty mad! At this point I was roaring backwards as fast as the car could carry me and burst onto the main road on the run. Fortunately the road was clear or that could have been the end of the tale and my life. The gearbox on the Mini in those days were not reputed to be the strongest but with controlled strength I managed to engage first gear without depositing the engine and gearbox on the road and with a mighty roar of clutch versus power me and my trusty steed roared off at a fast trot up the road. As I raced through the gears willing the car on I had to clear the mind and think straight.

Where do I go?

What will Pam do?

How much petrol do I have?

Missed my dinner and I am hungry.

Right, the best place to go was Pete Dyson's in Teddington and yes, I have just about a full tank of petrol since I had filled the tank just before getting home. Food can be bought on the way. That left the question of what Pam would do. So after a mile or two I pulled into a local estate and brought the seething mass of metal to a halt just out of sight of the road. My thoughts about Pam were answered within minutes when the familiar throb of the MG-BGT shot past my window like a blur.

Oh my God, she is out to kill us both, was my scared thought.

I had to get to Pete's somehow and I knew the roads and back lanes quite well so I felt that I would be quite safe waiting a few more minutes and then setting sail. Remember in those days we did not have mobile phones or Tom-Tom's to help me. It was all down to instinct as I gingerly started up and entered the road and started the run up to Pete's place. Little did I know but Pam had reasoned out as to where I was going and lay in wait further down the track. So there I was driving along on the road I had always taken when 'Zappo' the MG-BGT fired in from the left at a junction. I was now confirmed as the target and slammed the foot down to coax the extra HP that I needed. Remember the film 'Four Weddings and a Funeral' where the girl says.

"It only does forty mile an hour!"

That was me trying to get the extra mph out of the Mini. As I roared along at 41 mph I spotted a dusty lane off to the left and swung into it with maybe two wheels off the ground. By this time it was just about dark and I took a chance and drove on with just the sidelights until I was well clear of the road. I was really scared for my life since the Mini would be no match against the MG-BGT and Pam knew it. I pulled over and slipped into a farmer's field and swung round and stopped. I am not sure who was panting more – me or the car.

After some minutes and a packet of cigarettes later I gingerly ventured out of my hiding place and decided that the best way to go was to keep to the back roads all the way and so I turned left instead of right and drove steadily away. I got lost! Amazing! Suddenly I saw a sign for Southampton in five miles. So, not only had I got to avoid possible death by collision but I had to find my way out of this maze. The time was now approaching 10 pm and I needed to get to Pete's somehow before the night was over. I skirted around various lanes and eventually started heading in the right direction. After about an hour with no mad female in sight I started to relax a bit and even got to the point where I needed to stop for a call of nature. I pulled over into a lay-by and after my intended mission I sat leaning against the car smoking a cigarette as the clock passed midnight.

I am sure Pete will be fine whatever time I turn up, I thought.

I knew he was at home as we had passed each other at the crew reporting since we arrived home at about the same time that day. I casually looked up at the road and saw a set of headlights coming my way. The chances of it being Pam were very remote since my route was way outside the normal route. That was until the sound of the engine behind the headlights hit the ears.

"No way, it can't be – but it might just be!" I shouted to myself.

Well it was! I flew into the driver's seat like Flash Gordon and started the engine and without lights moved closer to the hedge and wished I had some of that vanishing powder that I wanted to use on my sister many years before. As the headlights passed suddenly I heard the screech of brakes from the other car as if driven by someone possessed. I fired out of my lair like a rocket, or was it a damp squid, and drove off in the other direction as fast as the car and my legs could carry me. I had to hand it to Pam – she was pretty persistent and just maybe still pretty mad. I took no chances and assumed the worst. I was driving as fast as I could and watching the rear view mirror for signs of life. There were none! Maybe there was another reason for the braking. Within a few miles I arrived at a large A-Road and saw the signs for London. I joined in with the small amount of traffic trying to hide in the nearside lane. Amazingly enough the road behind me kept clear so either she had missed me, given up or needed some petrol. As I passed Heathrow only then did I feel totally safe since I had never taken Pam beyond that point and certainly not into London. I eventually knocked on Pete's door at about 3 am totally burnt out and hungry. Pete finally answered the door and took one look at this wreck of a person and ushered me in. As it was he was wide awake and he cooked me a cracking meal of 'Cheese on Toast' which tasted like nectar. I felt safe at last and was no longer hungry.

I stayed with Pete for a couple of weeks while I gathered my thoughts. Eventually I swallowed deeply and rang Pam at our home and suggested a meeting to sort things out. That went down like a lead balloon but finally we did meet up and it was nice to feel that she was not in killing mode. In fact, she was very quiet and I did wonder what that was all about. We agreed to sell the house, split the profits and complete the paperwork for the quickie divorce. She also agreed to buy all of the furniture in the house out of her half. Little did I know that at the time she was pregnant by a Royal Marine, hence the haste for clearing out. I took the remainder of my stuff out of the house and went back to Pete's place. In the end I went home to Wokingham with Dad and Thirza. They let me stay for a while since I felt that I could not burden Pete any more.

By the June the 'Decree Nisi' paper landed on my plate and ten turbulent years of my life with Pam ended with this small scrap of paper. This event coincided with the sale of the house and at that point all dealings with Pam and my first marriage came to an end. That was, in fact, the last time I ever saw her and I do wonder sometimes what happened to her and her Marine. I can remember dropping Moya a note telling her I was now as free as a bird. Now, one would think that after such a dramatic time with marriage and finally getting the release I would go mad and date a female again. You know what, with all that had happened, and with Moya maybe being more than a passing phase I settled into what can only be described as a normal existence since I felt that Moya was too good to play silly sods with. I felt really good about it all because there was no more ducking and diving going on.

I moved back in with Pete Dyson on a more permanent basis whilst I licked my financial wounds and continued flying the VC-10 on the worldwide routes. The price of oil was creeping up all the time and a few low cost carriers hit the airways. Freddie Laker's Sky train flights from Gatwick to JFK had started in late 1977 and boasted extremely low fares across the Atlantic. BA decided to ignore the threat and continued its higher fare structure. I remember the slogan from Sky Train of '£99 one-way'. He used Douglas DC-10 aircraft and could cram in over 250 passengers at a time and was very transparent with his business model explaining how he could make a profit at that price.

The only aircraft in BA that could come anywhere near the same economics was the 747 with the poor old VC-10 down the bottom of the pile in terms of profitability. BA had also ordered the Lockheed Tri-Star to cover routes to the Gulf and other ones where the 747 was just too big. There was a feeling on the fleet that it was only a matter of time before our beloved VC-10 would be paid off and retired from service. In 1978 BA reluctantly matched the Sky Train fares and so an Atlantic fares war broke out. Panam and TWA also got in on the act. BA lost money that year on the Atlantic route and it was sad to think that even a jam-packed VC-10 to JFK lost money. Cargo-hold freight was beginning to emerge as a profit centre in its own right but again the VC-10 had small holds so lost out again.

We were, however, still the champions of Africa and the new route from South Africa to Hong Kong via the Seychelles and Colombo. It was on a departure from Colombo to the Seychelles that I met up with my favourite 'Man from the Ministry' who was exercising his right to look at my operation again. We were old friends by now having first met some two years before. It was one of those nights when the heavens were letting rip over the airport. The expression of 'Raining Stair Rods' springs to mind. We gingerly taxied out to the runway and since we were the only departure that night we sat on the runway staring into this mass of rainstorms beating six bells out of the windscreen wipers as they battled to keep the wind screen clear of the deluge. I suggested that we sit tight until the rain eased off and that was met by the usual nodding approval. After about ten minutes the rain suddenly stopped as if someone had just turned the tap off.

"Right folks, we will give it another minute to make sure it was not a fluke and then take-off," I announced.

More nods. After a minute or so all looked good and so we powered up to full power and held the aircraft on the brakes and with a mighty roar started our take-off run. Now, here is the twist: this storm that had suddenly stopped had in fact moved half way down the runway and we re-entered it doing about 120 mph. The noise was deafening as the rain pelted down on us as if there was retribution in hand for daring to mess with the rain gods. The runway was invisible from the cockpit and so I just put my head down and concentrated on keeping the aircraft on the runway heading using the compass. There was no point in trying to stop since we would have run off the end and that was a certainty. At last the Co-pilot shouted at the top of his voice: "Rotate."

I pulled the aircraft into the air with the Flight Engineer hanging onto his seatbelt and keeping the engines against the full power stop and there I was trying to fly the aircraft on instruments with the airspeed going up and down the scale like a yo-yo. The turbulence was pretty vicious but I just hung on with the Co-pilot calling the things out that were pretty important at the time. He was ex-RAF and had only just joined BA having flown the 'Shiny Ten' in the RAF. After what seemed like an eternity, but was maybe only two minutes or so, things calmed down and suddenly the clouds parted and there was the moon welcoming us to smoother skies.

"Thank God we are in a VC-10 coming through that lot back there," was the CAA inspector's only comment.

A rather shaky Chief Steward came onto the Flight Deck and enquired who had fired at us after take-off since the sounds outside reminded him of the fire fight he had encountered in the last war.

"No, it was the angry gods giving us hell for daring to invade their patch," was my non-committal reply.

"A bucket load of your finest tea would be lovely please," I added.

I wished it was something stronger but that would have to wait. When we arrived at the Seychelles we found that the paint on the nose and back about six to eight feet had all but been ripped off revealing the original factory undercoat of lime green. Looked really wild it did!

In June, Moya and I got together a few times at various venues and I have to say we were really getting on so well that we both felt that there could be a future for us both. We were extremely compatible in all senses. So there I was having just got out of one long relationship now contemplating another one. Strange but true! In July we managed a few days away together in New Forest and took the decision that we should set up shop together very soon. Moya, by this time, had decided that she wanted a divorce from Dave, her husband. I hasten to add that her relationship with Dave was quite amicable and that her divorce would go through smoothly.

It was at about this time that I was invited to go sailing off the south coast with my old friend John Penwill and Mark Hodgkins, who was another freshly promoted Captain. The small yacht involved was a Marcon 21ft 'Tomahawk' which was kept in a marina close to Hayling Island at Chichester. Now, this is a not a sport for the faint-hearted, since it involves hanging off a small slippery deck and mixing it with all sorts of ropes, or 'sheets' to be correct. It is to great advantage to the general performance of the yacht when there is a good strong breeze blowing but not so good for the poor souls on board since the formula of 'more wind = getting wetter' comes into play. Having said that when the sun was shining it was quite exhilarating to be charging across the Solent powered only the wind. The Solent was the stretch of water from Southampton to the Isle of Wight. The other problem was that the cost of keeping the various bits and pieces working properly was like 'standing under a shower ripping up five pound notes'.

I found that as a driver I was not that good so I generally settled down for the role of the foredeck crew and was content to do the sail changes as we went along. We did at one point enter ourselves in the local races and that added to the fun since as the chief of the foredeck I had to follow the instructions of John or Mark as to what sail to put up and when. The pressure was on when racing and the wetter I got. We entered the famous 'around the Isle of Wight' yacht race in the

July to coincide with the famous 'Cowes Week'. We sailed over the night before from Chichester on a lovely balmy evening and tied up at Cowes. I was tucked up for sleeping right at the front end or 'bow' and as the night progressed I got the impression that the weather was getting a bit vicious and the rain was thundering down. I was right under the foredeck hatch that had a small leak and in the early hours, when all three of us were awake, I swam out of my swamp and looked desperately at the sky hoping for even a small smidgen of cloud that was not black and horrible looking.

"Not a bloody chance!" I said as we settled down and started the engine to make our way to the start line for a 7 am blast off.

So there I was all tonked up in my waterproofs struggling to grab some sort of foot or hand hold. I also had a life jacket and harness on so I must have resembled some sort of 'yellow Yeti'. Our yacht was pretty small compared with a lot of the other ones but, in theory, we were entered in the race in our class of similar mounts so things would balance out OK. So there we were mixing it with the big boys with all the engines shut down and sails up ready to race around the island. The start line was from north to south with Cowes at the southern point. All we had to do was to head westwards towards the famous Needles, turn left around the island ending up where we had started from. The wind was from the east and so it was simply a case of hoisting the spinnaker and sitting back and relaxing for the first leg to the Needles.

A spinnaker was a very large flimsy colourful sail that would literally drag the yacht along at a good speed. The problem is that it was supported by sheets and booms that worked beautifully once the wind got behind it and it billowed into shape. It is a bit like a hot air balloon that seemed to have a mind of its own while being heated up but once done just sat there quietly awaiting orders. Likewise with the spinnaker that fought you all the way when it is pulled out of its storage below decks. The trick is to pull it up the mast as quickly as possible and at the same time with your other set of arms hold the boom and sheets so that when the wind catches it is tied down and not disappearing up the mast forever. Now, try all that with the rain sheeting down, hanging on for dear life, watching other yachts and hearing Mark or John shouting that one of the support booms is flying free as a bird. Eventually I got the spinnaker up the mast and all secured before the wind got there first. It was one heck of a way to wake up in the morning. I looked across to the other yachts and it was quite a sight with all these spinnakers billowing out and creating a kaleidoscope of colours across the Solent. I felt a bit chuffed that I had got ours up after a bit of a struggle since there were a few yachts with spinnakers wrapped around the top of the mast like flags. Obviously they had not had their Weetabix for breakfast.

The run down the Needles, on the extreme western tip of the island, was to prove to be the easiest part of the race. As we approached the famous landmark every yacht wanted to be as close to the shore as possible since there was a left turn onto the south-east heading looming. We were already placed close to the shore so had some advantage but as we got nearer the turn I could have walked across several decks since we were all crammed so close in.

There is a call 'fore' made when two boats look like they are on a collision course and one of them is designated to turn away. Out here on the water nobody seemed to care about how close to each other they were and were seemingly all hell bent on the left turn. Once the turn starts the spinnaker had to be hauled down and a replacement sail or 'jib' had to be raised since the wind was no longer coming from behind but from the left side. The net effect is that the yacht leans over to the right at a precarious angle with me trying to pull and shove the sails this way and that to make out to all around me that I am on top of the task. Either John or Mark came forward to help but with the limited deck space available all we did was to fall over each other.

We finally made it around the corner and headed south-east towards the most southern tip of the island known as St Catherine's Point. By this time the wind was beginning to pick up speed and become quite squally. There were three sorts of jib sails on board which were the Genoa designed for light winds, the main jib for normal winds and the storm jib exclusively for the stronger winds. The skill with racing was to match the jib with the wind to get the best speed and so when it is squally I might make three to four sail changes in 20 minutes. The rain then started and so life on deck became pretty miserable. At one point we were sailing quite well but the water was getting rougher and rougher and I was getting wetter and wetter.

"This I am not enjoying!" was one of my passing comments when I did struggle on the odd occasion to the rear or stern of the yacht to get a well-deserved cigarette break.

I remember sitting out on the deck at one point and a huge catamaran just roared passed us as if we were standing still. The chap at the helm, or steering wheel, was casually sipping a cup of coffee as if he was on a gentle Sunday afternoon stroll.

By the time we arrived at St Catherine's Point we had been racing for about three hours and in that time the sea had got rougher and the sky had got blacker. We then turned north-east towards the eastern end of the island and if I thought the last run was bad it was like a walk in the park compared with what we were starting to encounter now. There is a phenomenon in sailing where all the bad weather elements get together for the sheer purpose of upending even the most experienced sailor. It was known as 'wind across the tide'. So there we were right up to our necks in this cauldron of wind, rain and sea. Both Mark and John were really struggling with the helm and the main sail to adjust to the weather. The main sail was the large sail centred round the main mast and needed to be reduced in size or 'reefed' all the time when the wind blew up and then released when the wind dropped in strength. As for me I just hung on to one of the sheets and awaited orders. I was, by now, totally and utterly soaked through with a mix of sea water and rain.

"Wow – what I would give for a nice cosy log fire and a cup of tea?" I muttered to myself.

There was a point when the weather cleared for a short break and I grabbed one of my last remaining dry cigarettes and lit it with great defiance and sat strapped around the mast facing backwards puffing away. John and Mark were at the helm and suddenly their facial expressions changed and they shouted at me to hang on tight. I turned around to see what they were looking at and low and behold there was a wave, which seemed about five times the height of our small yacht, bearing down on us like a monster from the deep. I just grabbed the mast tighter and I must have asked for all my sins to be forgiven at that moment. When the towering inferno hit us I disappeared under it like a lamb to the slaughter. It must have been only a few seconds that I was submerged but it felt like an eternity when I suddenly bobbed up still clinging onto the mast and, amazingly enough, with a rather wet and dishevelled cigarette still between my lips. It had gone out by then!

We did a head check and discovered we were all still on board but even Mark and John were totally soaked through. We had taken on a lot of water and it was swilling about down below. The bilge pump, designed to get rid of this water, was thumping away trying to empty the excess water overboard. Suddenly the noise of the pump died and we knew that water had got into the battery compartment. We were now back to Nelson's day with no electrical power and so John, Mark and I abandoned the thought of racing and set about with buckets emptying the water out of the boat. I think if another wave like the last one had hit us we could well be swimming for it. After about 30 minutes of hard graft most of the water had been thrown overboard and the weather eased a bit to allow us to regain our composure and get back into the race. We saw the rescue boat and the local lifeboat out amongst the fleet so obviously a few of the yachts did get into trouble.

As we approached the eastern end of the island we had all been at it for about seven hours and apart from being totally drenched we were all pretty exhausted and hungry. The weather seemed to have settled down a bit so I disappeared down below for something to eat. I found my food amazingly dry still and settled down for a cheese sandwich. The storm gods must have spotted me and threw a final salvo at us. I was wedged in underneath the fore hatch when I heard the rumble of the impending arrival of something horrible. The leak that I had found the night before whilst trying to sleep sort of opened up and what seemed about fifty tonnes of sea water fell onto my head and what's more onto my lonely sandwich. By the time I managed to refocus my poor old sandwich had become a molten mass of sodden bread. By that time I didn't care anymore and simply ate it as if nothing had happened. It had become a cheese, pickle and seawater delicacy.

After another two hours of bailing out duties and sail changes we eventually approached the finishing line and triumphantly crossed it as if our life depended on it after some ten hours of hard sailing. At about that time there was the famous 'Whitbread round the world' yacht race where yachts were raced for days on end. The likes of Claire Francis and John Ridgeway spring to mind.

Bloody super heroes they all are, was my thought.

Having crossed the line we had decided the day before to motor across the Solent and to berth on the Hamble River for the night. With the battery now out of action we had no way of starting the motor so we were forced to turn northwards and sail for another two or so hours. The weather had abated by then and things had calmed down somewhat. As we entered the Hamble River we got a tow from another yacht which was called 'Morning Cloud' with a white haired gentleman at the helm. It was Ted Heath, who had been our Prime Minister up to about four years before. He must have looked at us and thought: "What a wretched bunch of sailors we have here."

We finally berthed and I believe John's wife Bridie came and picked us up and dropped Mark and me off at the train station for a rather wet and soggy ride home. Like golf, I felt at that point that I should become a 'fair weather' sailor and leave the hero stuff to others. We did learn later that we came about half way down the list of winners in our class with so many retirements. Quite an experience!

As an aside in the news in August a trivial but interesting item was that the Pope had died in Rome and a new Pope John Paul I was appointed. He was known as the laughing Pope but 33 days later he died to be succeeded by John Paul II who was the first ever Polish Pope. Was he pushed or did he fall?

Also in the August Moya and I moved into a rented house in Woking and started our life together. It was a matter of getting all our bits together of which I had very few. I just brought along myself and the ever faithful Globetrotter suitcase that had all my worldly possessions in. This was not very good for a 32-year-old who had been working for 12 years. I think Moya brought along the washing machine as her souvenir from her marriage. Having said all that it was all very cosy for Moya and me. For the first time in quite a while I actually had a home base to come back to after every trip. Moya was still flying so sometimes we were home together and sometimes not. The arrangement seemed to work out well. In fact, it did and life was good.

It was at about this time that Dad and Thirza had an invite to go to my godfather's, Bill McLaren, to stay for a few days and they organised the staff travel ticket to fly with me, as their Captain, to New York. The day arrived and there they were both tucked into First Class on 'my' VC-10 on their way to New York. Dad came for the take-off and stayed for quite a while. What a contrast it must have seemed to the both of us since the last time we flew together on an aeroplane was back when I was a youngster coming home from Sydney. Being an ex-navigator Dad was intrigued with the workings of the inertial navigation system.

"Nothing like having a real navigator on the flight deck," he remarked sarcastically.

"Perhaps you are right, Dad," was my diplomatic reply so as not to offend.

Dad came up for the arrival into New York as we flew the old fashioned 'Canarsie' approach and I think secretly he took great pride that his son was where he was. It was a long way from trying to find my bike! My godfather met us outside the terminal and I stayed for a coffee and then hitched a ride with the next arriving crew. I really felt proud to have flown my dad and Thirza to New York that day.

For the next couple of months my life became very settled and in the November Moya and I did another Khartoum flight together which was not as riotous as the last one we did but still great. The only drawback was a rather stroppy Chief Steward who linked up with one of the girls and made snide remarks about the two of us. Jealousy!

In November there was an uprising in Iran whereby the people turned on the Shah of Persia and they wanted to declare Iran an Islamic Republic. Up to that time BA were flying two services per day into Tehran which were always full. Little did we know that this small uprising would develop as it did.

I had flown many times into Tehran. One particular service was routed through Düsseldorf, Germany. It was a new transit stop for us on the route and I flew the second service through there. As we pulled up onto the gate I was met by a contingent of airport personnel who questioned the departure noise the VC-10 made. What had happened was that when the first service went through the day before it 'Blew all the bells' on the departure noise monitor and since the Germans were starting to get into the 'Green Scene' as far as airport noise was concerned I was put under the spotlight by this lot and was assured that we would be monitored very closely on our departure. As we lined up on the runway it was obvious to us that there was no way we could be quiet on our departure. The VC-10 engine, the mighty Conway, was one of the noisiest engines around and built in the days when no-one gave a thought to quiet engines. In fact, the air emerged out of the tailpipe at supersonic speed hence in addition to the roar there was this loud crackling sound which overlaid everything. So what we decided to do was to let these monitoring people really have something to write home about. We took off at full power and once airborne we very slowly reduced the power and a bit of the noise so that these people would get the full roar plus crackle. When we landed at Tehran there was a signal from Operations at Heathrow informing us that the German authorities had banned forever the VC-10 to go anywhere near Düsseldorf and that the 707 would replace us on the route. The world was moving into this ever protective scene of doing what the minority groups wanted and to hell with safety. In Tehran the revolution took hold and BA services were suspended, be it the 707 or VC-10.

Christmas came and I actually made a point of being at home for a change. I seem to remember Moya being delayed. I think it was a 707 Freighter where she was the only Cabin Crew member and her duties were to look after the crew and act as a fire-watch. They had a problem with the brakes on the ground in good old Prestwick but eventually made it back to Heathrow just in time for Christmas. Bloody 707s nearly ruining our Christmas! So, after years of nothing, it was wonderful to really get stuck into Christmas and enjoy it all. We both had about one week off including New Year's Eve. And so 1978 ended much better than it had started.

Jeddah, Saudi Arabia was one of our destinations and, as you know, the laws there are pretty strict with the main one being that no alcohol is allowed into the country. Aircrew devised many schemes to get the dreaded nectar into Jeddah. It is funny but a couple of days without the drink is not a disaster yet still we rose to the challenge of smuggling some in. The favourite one was based around the fact that in those days the catering section always loaded on board a Dundee Cake for the first class passengers. Amazingly enough it was often forgotten to be served and then the Chief Steward could be spotted in the galley with a syringe decanting the hard stuff into the heart of the cake which ended up 120% proof. It would then be put back in its box and popped into his carry-on bag. I never knew why the Cabin Crew had such large carry-on bags but there was always method in their madness. So, we would arrive in Jeddah and go through customs with an innocent looking cake amongst our bits and once in the hotel there would be a 'Dundee Cake Party' and I have to say a few mouthfuls were all that it took to relax the brain.

On a rather sad note I remember being with a group of us in the souk or marketplace one afternoon when there seemed to be an attraction in the main square. There were food stalls and lots of local entertainment around so naturally we took a look as to what was going on. After a while a van pulled up and a wretched chap was dragged out of the back of it and paraded for all to see. Another guy arrived brandishing a short evil-looking machete type of sword. We were about to witness a beheading and the shock of it all galvanised us into beating a hasty retreat. The amazing thing was that we got some quite quizzical looks from the locals. What a weird and vicious country! The main riches of the country lay below the surface in the form of oil and that attracted a lot of foreign workers to man the rigs. The Scottish people seemed to hold the monopoly on the oil scene and being without alcohol for some months on their contract made them pretty thirsty once they got on board to go back home. As far as BA was concerned the laws were adhered to up to the point that even if we were in Saudi airspace the aircraft was to serve no alcohol to the passengers. So, once we had departed we made an announcement on the cabin address as we left their airspace to the cheers of the passengers and the dismay of the Cabin Crew. The party then started!

The year started with the news that the Shah of Persia had fled Iran and sought refuge in Egypt as the Islamic revolution tightened its grip throughout Iran. In the February, Ayatollah Ruhollah Khomeini, who had been in exile in Paris for many years, returned to Iran and so the Islamic Republic of Iran was born. 1979 would become quite a year in the world of politics. On a lighter note in the March the first ever music CD was shown to the public.

My flying continued on the VC-10 without too many dramas. I had an interesting flight out of JFK where a first class passenger decided to die on me about two hours into the flight. We actually made a diversion into Halifax, Canada to try to save him and had to dump about 60 tons of fuel but he died before we landed. On the ground the airport authorities transferred the poor guy to the morgue and by law I was obliged to identify him. It was the first time I had seen a dead body and the experience was not pleasant. Then there came the paperwork. He was an American flying with a British Airline and flying over Canada at the time of his demise. Once we had refuelled and departed on our way it took me most of the Atlantic to complete the forms. Not a nice trip at all.

I did another rather amazing flight at about that time out of JFK to Prestwick and on to Manchester. This was one of the main routes ex-JFK and on this occasion when I checked in with operations at JFK the flight time shown on the plan was about five and a quarter hours which was pretty quick so I asked what the record was for the route and they ferreted around and said that it was held by a 707 at five hours and eight minutes. My tail was up and so I put a little bit of extra fuel on and told the people that we were out to beat that time. Little did I know that they had informed the control tower and so just after take-off we were told to route direct to Gander, Newfoundland and to ignore any speed restraints and they wished us good luck in our venture.

"Wow, we are off and running!" I said to the rest of the crew triumphantly.

After about two hours or so we were in the Gander area and we called for our 'Atlantic clearance' and would you believe it they were in the picture as well. They told us to route direct to Prestwick and not on the normal track system. As for the speed we were given a free hand as to how fast to go.

Super VC-10 G-ASGC, now preserved at Duxford Air Museum, hurtled across the North Atlantic at a speed that was just below the maximum the aircraft was allowed. The Flight Engineer was in his element and spent the night fine-tuning the engines to keep the speed spot on. After a short time the Chief Steward came onto the flight deck and announced that the dinner service was complete and that the passengers were now all bedded down for the night.

"I am sorry to spoil your rest break but we will be landing in just over two hours," I said.

"What are we flying? A bloody Concorde or something! I will have to wake them up for a full English breakfast in one hour," he replied.

"Scrub the breakfast and give them champagne for landing," was my reply.

We arrived off the Scottish west coast after about four and a half hours' flying and the Air Traffic Control fellow let us go direct to the downwind point for the landing. I woke the passengers with the news that we will be landing in about half an hour. That must have surprised them!

We finally landed just five hours and one minute after take-off from JFK. The scheduled time was six hours and 20 minutes so this was some achievement in my mind. Besides we had beaten the 707's record by a wide margin. The amazing thing is that my time has, to this day, never been beaten by a scheduled aircraft. Not bad for a Hamster! It was party time in Manchester that night.

As for Moya and me things were going very well and so we decided to buy a flat in the Binfield area together. It was only about five miles from Wokingham and so in the April we moved into No. 2, Avon Court. At last I was back on the property ladder. Moya's divorce came through soon afterwards so all our ducks were finally in a row. By chance we met a group of people from the Woodley area which was about five miles away and so a great social life started to develop.

Back in the flying world it was becoming obvious that the VC-10 would be prematurely retired from service maybe by the end of 1979 and we rapidly fell back to about eight aircraft doing the business. The routes by now were mainly to Africa and the Gulf area. As I said before we still had two aircraft based in the Gulf and on a couple of occasions I would fly to Doha and sit around for a week or so at the beck and call of the Sheik of Doha. We had our own specific BA Cabin crew to run the show. It all sounds very nice just sitting in the sun but it was fraught with problems. Quite often the Sheik's secretary would call us up and ask us to be ready at 9 am the following morning for a flight to Europe. We would get to the airport at about 8 am and get all prepared for the proposed departure time and then sit around all day in the heat until maybe 5 pm when it would all happen but to a different destination. No flight time limitations here!

I also did a stint in Abu Dhabi with the other VC-10 and had a few interesting flights out of there. The great sport of the Arabs was falconry and on one occasion we were asked to fly to Karachi to pick up a falcon that was not too well. Fuel was no worry for the flight so we departed and flew up the Gulf at about 500ft and rounded the United Arab Emirates peninsular and flew down the Strait of Hormuz and along the Iranian and Pakistani borders just off-shore all the way at low level. We had the call sign of 'Emiri 1' and were entitled to go anywhere in the Gulf at whatever height we fancied. I can remember coming back from Karachi and flying low over the Arab Dhows just off the coast of Dubai while they were taking part in the annual Dhow racing contest.

In the May there was a General Election in the UK and a woman became the new Prime Minister. Maggie Thatcher was her name. So there we were being ruled by a woman. Whatever next!

In BA a big problem was discovered in the Trident aircraft with fuel leaking out of the mid-section of the wings. This involved the grounding of each aircraft in turn for about ten days to repair the cracks found in the fuel leakage area. Enter the VC-10 to the rescue and suddenly we were doing fights to Amsterdam, Brussels, Paris and the like. This was alien territory to us since we were used to getting airborne for at least four hours minimum before landing and suddenly we were in the air for maybe 30 minutes before landing in Paris. Bloody shock to the system it was! I remember that on one occasion BA pressed into service an ex-Gulf Air aircraft complete with Arab writing all over it and flew it to Athens on a charter to fly back a party of Jewish people. It took a lot of persuasion to get them on board and that we were in fact kosher.

Our social life in Binfield was building all the time and we found it difficult to fit in all the parties and flying duties. Bloody hell, our life was good!

My flying in the European arena continued together with the usual African and Gulf trips. The situation in Iran was getting really nasty and plans were put into place to evacuate the British people as soon as possible. What BA did was to position two or three aircraft in Kuwait and fly to Tehran maybe twice a day and try to get our people out. There was, by this stage, no effective Air Traffic Control in Iran and so we relied on talking to other aircraft on a common frequency and juggling our own approach positions. We carried an extra pilot whose sole job was to maintain a lookout for other aircraft that could be getting too close for comfort. I flew a couple of flights into Tehran and the ironic thing was that as we departed we would have on board a large majority of Iranians who seemed to be part of the wealthy brigade and feared for their money so bribed their way out. Strange how people react!

In the June Southern Rhodesia, under the premiership of Ian Smith, ended 14 years of conflict and handed power to the black president Robert Mugabe and his henchmen. The handover was orchestrated by Lord Carrington at Lancaster House in London. There were two rivals for the presidency battling it out and Mugabe won much to the dismay of the British Government. Mugabe has ruled with an iron fist to this day. You can draw your own conclusions!

In the July one Saddam Hussein took control of Iraq and we all know where that led us. Funnily enough we would stay in Baghdad for a few days on trips and seemed to encounter no problems. Mind you don't get too many locals in the famous British Club.

The Trident gradually got better and out of the blue we started going back over the Atlantic to the States and Canada. It made a nice change to get away from the heat of the Gulf and Africa.

It was a busy year for world events and August was no exception when Lord Louis Mountbatten, cousin of the Queen, was killed by an IRA bomb whilst holidaying in Ireland. Not good!

Also by the end of August there was a master plan that the VC-10 fleet would run down and finish by the end of the year. There were various options available to us since it would create an excess of Captains within BA. One option was to take three months' paid leave and I opted for that and so on September 14th 1979 I flew my last flight on the VC-10 from Cairo to Heathrow on G-ASGM – which, incidentally, was its final flight in BA. All of the aircraft were gone by the end of the year. What they did, in fact, was to store the aircraft at various locations around the UK and eventually the RAF converted some of them into airborne tankers. G-ASGM soldiered on with the RAF and finally retired in April 2013 after 45 years of faithful service. This fact emphasises to me the excellence in British aviation engineering capabilities in bygone years which, alas, has been lost. So after three and a half wonderful years as Captain on the 'Queen of the Skies' we parted company.

Now, here is a piece of history for you. In 1982 the Falklands were invaded and the RAF decided to mount a long range bombing operation to hit the runway at Stanley on East Falkland. The delta-winged Vulcan bomber was chosen to do the raid but lacked the precision navigation equipment to do the round trip. Then somebody remembered the VC-10s that had been parked up for some three years. Each had an INS unit in its electronics bay so off the boys went and ripped them out, started them up and bolted them to the floor of the Vulcan Cockpit and off they went to war. They worked after all that time off to within a square mile. The good old VC-10 was still useful even after it retired.

So there I was on a paid holiday for three months and I took full advantage of the free time with Moya since she had stopped flying as well. We could attend every social function around. Life was very good. In the November a bunch of students invaded the American embassy in Tehran and totally overwhelmed the staff and took them all hostage. It was the start of a tense time in the world with the might of the USA seemingly powerless to act against a small band of hooligans. It becomes more dramatic as time went by. In the December the Russians invaded Afghanistan which created their own Vietnam style noose around their neck. As I said, for me 1979 was a lively year on the world stage.

Dad went into hospital in the December for a prostate operation and Moya and I got together with Thirza a few times. On one occasion when socializing with her it transpired that Thirza had a leaning towards cherry brandy and at one point after a few of these she seemed to gently slide under the table. Bit of a revelation it was at the time. The relationship between Thirza and Dad was as good as could be expected but seemed on occasions to be rocky. I think that Dad tended to rule the roost when my Mum was around and then suddenly he found that Thirza hit back on many an occasion and that did not go down too well. Bit like me I suppose! I suspect 1979 would surely have ended with Moya and me at some wild party somewhere.

1970 B747-100 G-AWNB in BOAC Colours

1972 B747-100 G-AWNP in British Airways Colours

1974 Me as Co-pilot 747-100

1976 VC-10 'VM' Trainer

1977 Super VC-10 G-ASGB in British Airways Colours

1977 Me in the Left hand seat (I had more hair then)

And so we come to the end of 1979 with me being laid off from my magnificent VC-10. I have one failed marriage behind me. I am fast approaching 34 years of age. I have achieved the ultimate in the flying world by being qualified as a Captain within British Airways after a hard and interesting upbringing starting with the rigours of BOAC following in my father's footsteps.

So where do I go from here?

In part two of my story I continue from the start of 1980 and finish in January 2001 when I finally retired from British Airways. My adventures continue both in my flying world and my private one.

Here is a taster of what's in store in Part two:

"It was in the March that I nearly met my maker. I was operating BA941 from Heathrow to Düsseldorf in the late afternoon on a Friday. The Co-pilot was Chris Challenger who, ironically, had come from the VC-10, having crossed the great divide like me some years before. I was in the descent and there was a small amount of turbulence so I had the passengers strapped in. As we passed 10,000 ft I brought the speed down to the required 250 knots. We had just cleared the cloud cover and into clear skies and I was just changing a radio frequency when I suddenly looked up and saw a light aircraft about half a mile ahead coming straight at me descending at the same rate as I was. At our closing speeds we would have collided within a few seconds so there was no time for the standard recommended avoidance procedure of each aircraft turning to the right. I remember grabbing the control column and shoving it fully forward to go underneath the guy but at that instant he did the same. The force that I used disconnected the autopilot accompanied by the loud wailing sound. It was similar to walking along the road when someone comes the other way and you both try to avoid each other and end up meeting noses.

So there I was heading steeply down with the opposition doing the same. I instinctively pulled the controls fully backwards to try to go over the top of him. So what did he do? You've guessed it! He did the same. So I just kept pulling back harder and harder until the control column was fully wedged in my stomach. This all happened over a timespan of about three seconds and he was looming larger and larger in my windscreen and there was nothing I could do about it. My aircraft reacted well to my demands and with the other aircraft about 200 metres away a small escape gap was forming and he passed under the nose with about three metres to spare. He was so close that, if asked, I could recognize the pilot in a line-up. Seeing him up so close and passing just under me I fully expected him to hit us somewhere in the central section of our belly but suddenly we were in the clear with our aircraft now climbing skywards at an alarming rate. It took a couple of minutes to restore the aircraft to what could be considered a normal flight path.

The time taken for my gyrations in the sky covered a timespan of just under three seconds and that included going from pushing the controls all the way to pulling them all the way back – such was my desperation to avoid ending up scattered all over the German countryside as a statistic. Once we got the aircraft under control it was then a matter of assessing what had happened behind the flight deck door during our escapade. It was a blessing that I had strapped the passengers in since all they would do is to bounce up and down within the confines of their seat. The Cabin Crew were all female and it was established that the two at the front had got through OK by just hanging onto the door handle although they did do an airborne ballet routine during the episode. The girls 'down the back' were not so fortunate and they ended up careering upwards and literally bounced off the roof of the cabin and then were thrown the other way as I reversed the controls. Clearly these girls were in need of some medical attention."

I hope you have enjoyed my story so far and maybe you would like to read the rest of my tale in:

'With my head in the clouds Part 2'

Footnote

It is worthy of note to expand on the legacy of the VC-10 since it played such an important role in my life.

In historic terms it all began in the early 50s when Vickers initiated a project intended as a strategic transport for the Royal Air Force with the possible attraction towards an embryonic civil world dominated at the time by the Americans. The prototype was being assembled along the lines of the Vickers Valiant V-bomber and powered by Rolls-Royce Conway engines buried in the wing roots. The design was designated as the V.1000 and with the first flight only months away in 1955 the order for the RAF was cancelled and BOAC showed no interest in buying the aircraft so the project was cancelled and the partly built aircraft was scrapped in front of the very employees that had slaved away constructing it.

BOAC, in the meantime, settled for the Bristol Britannia and the De Havilland Comet 4. The Britannia suffered from a host of development delays and, being a turboprop, suffered in the new world of the pure jet engine which had brought new standards of comfort for the ever demanding passengers. The Comet 4 was more of a success but lacked the seating capacity that Mr Boeing was now offering on the all-new shiny 707. In 1957 BOAC ordered the 707 and incidentally cost the UK Government lots of precious dollars which it could ill afford.

It was about this time that BOAC also put out a request for an aircraft capable of performing in the Middle East and Africa (frequently known as the 'hot and high' scene) with little restrictions since these areas were not suitable for the 707. So along come Vickers reviving the old V.1000 plans and moving the engines aft in pairs either side, refining a clean wing with very capable slats on the leading edge and massive 'Fowler' flaps on the trailing edge. The VC-10 was born. BOAC was very pleased with the VC-10 on paper and ordered 12 of the Standard VC-10 version which had exceptional performance but a passenger capacity of 12 first class and 99 economy seats only. The Super VC-10 offered more seats at the expense of performance and seemed suitable for the emerging North Atlantic routes. BOAC ordered 30 of this version making an order of 42 aircraft which was a good starter for Vickers or British Aircraft Corporation (BAC) as it was now known. Some international airlines started to take an interest in the VC-10. Notably, Panam actually sent a team of pilots and engineers to Weybridge and were suitably impressed.

The first deliveries were due in 1964 with the Standards being delivered initially and the Supers following one year later. BOAC chopped and changed the order many times up to that point and it all finally came to a head when the new chairman, Sir Giles Guthrie, arrived and decided that he didn't want the VC-10 anyway since it was far more expensive to run than the 707. The government of the day and BAC went into overdrive trying to sort out the mess. Yes, the VC-10 was more expensive to run since its impressive performance was at the expense of its high cruising fuel consumption for say 90% of the flight. In the end the good old English compromise, over tea and muffins no doubt, was reached and the order was reduced to 12 Standards and 17 Supers with the RAF being persuaded to take a few more on. The one factor that was overlooked was that the VC-10 had tremendous passenger appeal and on quite a few occasions the aircraft would be full to the gunwales whilst the 707 alongside would be half full even though it left a bit earlier to the same destination. The VC-10 was particularly popular on the North Atlantic routes with the American passengers clamouring to get on board and enjoy the 'silent and serene' experience.

I joined BOAC in August 1966 with eight Supers left to be delivered and so initially my flying was generally split between the two types. In 1969 a Standard was sold to Nigerian Airways which unfortunately crashed a few months later. There is a mention of this crash in my book since I got a bit involved with the aftermath of it. The remaining Standards soldiered on until 1975 when five were sold to Gulf Air, one was sold to the United Arab Emirates government and one was leased to the Qatar Government. The last Standard to be delivered became simply known as 'VM' and was the ever-faithful trainer which I abused regularly on my command course at Prestwick. While we were doing the technical course prior to going to Prestwick we were invited by the Engineering department to have a look over three Standards that had been stored in the Engineering base at Heathrow for some two years. They were in pretty bad shape having been neglected for some time. On one of the Flight Decks I rescued the famous 'Compass Log Book', which was synonymous with the days when we actually navigated the aircraft and sure enough, there was my signature in the log when I navigated that particular aircraft from Los Angeles to Honolulu.

"Is that a fly in my eye that is making it water?" I remarked to myself as I surveyed the remains of what was the cabin.

A few days later we once again made our way over to the Engineering base and watched while the three Standards that we had looked over were unceremoniously chopped up in front of our very eyes. What had happened is that these three Standards had been put up to Mr Boeing as part-payment for a 747. Boeing had decided that the best solution was to eradicate any possible competition by scrapping any aircraft put up as part-payment. To actually do the deed in front of the Engineers who had religiously maintained the VC-10 fleet was, in my mind, a crime and a very insensitive act.

Why don't they do the work in the middle of the night at least? was my lingering thought as the contractors hacked away for all to see.

The ironic thing was that the machine used was incapable of breaking the 'wing centre box' section and a heavyweight machine had to be brought in to finish the job. Perhaps they were used to breaking up old 707s which had a weaker structure. The basic weight of the VC-10 was about seven tonnes heavier than the 707.

The Supers flew on until 1980 and remained the passenger's favourite aircraft. Two were destroyed by terrorist action, one was preserved at Duxford Air Museum and the remaining 14 were sold to the RAF for conversion into airborne refuelling tankers or as a spares source for their existing fleet. It was in 2013 when the final aircraft was retired from active service after some 50 years. Could you imagine keeping your car going for that time? The fact that the VC-10 was 'drilled out of the solid' was the main reason that it survived as long as it did and shows, in my mind, the excellence of British engineering in its day to produce such a wonderful aircraft. Where has it all gone?

Lightning Source UK Ltd.
Milton Keynes UK
UKOW06f2104060616

275723UK00003B/14/P